THE
MAAMTRASNA
MURDERS

To Michael Kelleher and Kieran Cooney

THE
MAAMTRASNA MURDERS

LANGUAGE, LIFE and DEATH
in NINETEENTH-CENTURY IRELAND

MARGARET KELLEHER

UNIVERSITY COLLEGE DUBLIN PRESS
PREAS CHOLÁISTE OLLSCOILE BHAILE ÁTHA CLIATH
2018

First published 2018
by University College Dublin Press
UCD Humanities Institute, Room H103
Belfield
Dublin 4
Ireland
www.ucdpress.ie

ISBN 978-1-910820-42-1

10 9 8 7 6 5 4

CIP data available from the British Library
The right of Margaret Kelleher to be identified as the
author of this work has been asserted by her

Typeset in 11pt on 14pt Caslon by Marsha Swan

Printed in Spain on acid-free paper by GraphyCems

CONTENTS

List of Illustrations   vi
Map of Maamtrasna region   vii
Acknowledgements   ix
Preface   xv

Part I
Language Crossings

1 MURDERS: 'ALL QUITE DEAD'   3
2 LANGUAGE SHIFT: 'HAVE YOU IRISH?'   28

Part II
The Maamtrasna Case

3 ARRESTS: 'THEY WOULD PUT PEOPLE IN FOR THE MURDER'   61
4 LAW AND THE STATE: 'THE LANGUAGE WHICH HE KNEW BEST'   79
5 TRIALS: 'THE SHAMBLES OF MAAMTRASNA ARE AVENGED'   100
6 EXECUTIONS: 'FOCLA DÉIGHEANACHA MHAOLMHUIRE SEOIGHIGHE'   134

Part III
Last Words

7 AFTERMATH: 'JUDICIAL MURDER'   151
8 AFTERLIVES: 'THESE WRETCHED HEARTBROKEN MEN'   175
9 JAMES JOYCE: 'IRELAND AT THE BAR'   195

CONCLUSION: MAITHIÚNAS   215

Appendix I: Key Personages in the Maamtrasna Case   223
Appendix II: Pardon   227
Notes   229
Bibliography   301
Index   319

Illustrations between pages 136 and 137, and between pages 168 and 169

LIST OF ILLUSTRATIONS

Inside cover

Front: Detail from *Weekly Freeman*, Saturday, November 25 1882. Image courtesy of the National Library of Ireland.

Back: Map of Maamtrasna area by engineer Ryan, commissioned by the Crown Prosecution, August 1882. Image courtesy of the National Archives.

Plates Section I

1–10 Photos of the 10 Maamtrasna accused, November 1882, from the 'Invincibles' Album compiled by John Joseph Dunne. Images courtesy of the National Library of Ireland.

11 'Let Justice be "Done"', *Weekly Freeman*, 29 November 1884. Image courtesy of the National Library of Ireland.

12–13 Extract from 1936 account by Seán Seoighe (Tomáis) on the Maamtrasna murders. Reproduced by permission of the National Folklore Collection, University College Dublin.

14 Joyce house, Maamtrasna, today. Image courtesy of Brian Dolan.

15 Joyce house exterior, *Weekly Irish Times*, Saturday, 18 November 1882. Image courtesy of the National Library of Ireland.

16 Plan of Joyce house interior by engineer Ryan, August 1882. Image courtesy of the National Archives of Ireland.

17 Line drawing of the Maamtrasna area by engineer Ryan, August 1882. Image courtesy of the National Archives of Ireland.

Plates Section II

18 'The Murder of the Joyce Family in Ireland', *Illustrated Police News*, cover page, Saturday, 25 November 1882. Image courtesy of the National Library of Ireland.

19 'Examination of the Boy Joyce', *The Graphic* (London), 2 December 1882. Image courtesy of the National Library of Ireland.

20–25 Prison photos of Tom (Thomas) Joyce, Paudeen (Pat) Joyce and Martin Joyce at commencement of imprisonment (1882) and on release (1902). Images courtesy of the National Archives.

26 Sample pattern table, *Census of 1851, General Report, Part VI*. Image courtesy of the National Library of Ireland.

27 'Lamentable lines on the execution of the Maamtrasna murderers' ballad. Image courtesy of the National Folklore Collection, University College Dublin.

28 Note by Anthony Philbin to Prison Governor, Kilmainham, 8 November 1882. Image courtesy of the National Archives.

29 Extract from confession by Patrick Joyce on eve of execution, 14 December 1882. Image courtesy of the National Archives.

30 Petition written by priest or neighbour on behalf of Bridget Joyce, wife of Myles, 11 December 1882. Image courtesy of the National Archives.

31 '*Focla déigheanacha Mhaolmhuire Seoighighe air an g-croich*. Myles Joyce's dying words on the scaffold', facsimile image included in Frederick Higginbottom's *A Vivid Life* (1934). Image courtesy of the National Library of Ireland.

32 List of names including 'The Actual Murderers (alleged)', from Timothy Harrington, *The Maamtrasna Massacres* (1884). Image courtesy of the National Library of Ireland.

MAP OF MAAMTRASNA REGION

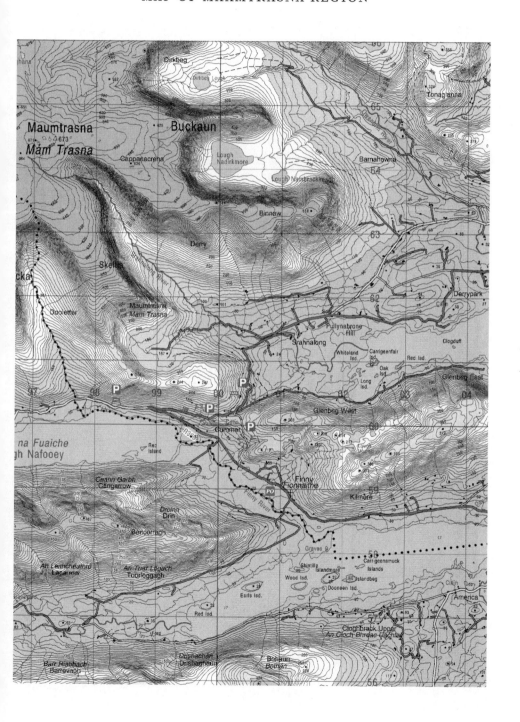

ACKNOWLEDGEMENTS

My interest in the history of language change in Ireland is inspired in part by my own family history. The 1911 census schedule for the Kelleher family of Dromahane, Dromore, County Cork (located four miles from my home town of Mallow), is revealing. The census records the language-use of the six listed family members: Michael, a 73-year-old Catholic general labourer, spoke Irish and English and was illiterate; Mary, his 61-year-old Catholic wife (occupation unstated), also spoke Irish and English but could read. Their four unmarried children could read and write and all are described as English-only speakers; the youngest, Michael, then a 17-year-old general labourer, is my paternal grandfather. What the census showed me is that, in my family, as in countless others, an older generation's bilingual practice gave way to monolingual use of English, but this occurred much later than I would have expected. It also underlined the preciousness of educational opportunities newly open to my generation.

The 1911 census schedule for the Catholic Ahern family in Kilshannig, some five miles away, provides very different linguistic and social detail. Maurice Ahern, a 51-year-old railway gateman, could read and write, as could his 48-year-old wife, Norah, whose recorded occupation (bravely different from the blanks listed for many of her married female peers) was 'head of family'. Four of their children are recorded, including Margaret Ahern (the future wife of Michael Kelleher, and my paternal grandmother), who appears as a 13-year-old 'scholar', and her brother, Maurice, aged 6-and-a-half, also listed as 'scholar'. Strikingly, Maurice and Margaret are listed as speaking 'Irish and English', but their parents as English only. The children's acquisition of Irish at school was clearly a source of particular pride to their parents, to be emphasised in this official return.

As I read further on the subject of language in late nineteenth-century Ireland, the case of the Maamtrasna murders and trials came quickly into view as a salutary example of an Irish-speaking man wrongly convicted of murder in an English-speaking court. As I examined the surviving archival materials, its significance deepened with respect to the co-existence of monolingualism and bilingualism in 1880s Ireland. Who spoke what language mattered greatly in the Maamtrasna trials, as this book will show. My hope is that this study will not only further an appreciation of the deep injustice that the trials produced and how that occurred, but also generate more recognition of the intricate linguistic character of late nineteenth-century Ireland when Irish was still, for very many, a family language known and used.

*

In 1992, Jarlath Waldron published *Maamtrasna: The Murders and the Mystery* and this has been a key resource for my work; I am also greatly indebted to his brother Canon Kieran Waldron for encouragement from the outset and for providing me with access to Fr Waldron's papers. My warm thanks to Seán Ó Cuirreáin for generously sharing with me his research and findings, published in *Éagóir: Maolra Seoighe agus Dúnmharaithe Mhám Trasna* (2016), and I salute his central advocacy role in the campaign for Myles Joyce's pardon. The knowledge and insights of Johnny Joyce, great-grandson of the murdered John Joyce, have been of great value; his determination that the events of 1882 be remembered in a spirit of inclusivity is a powerful reminder of the personal and private dimensions of this historical story.

My work on this book began in earnest during a semester as Visiting Fellow at St John's College, Cambridge, in autumn 2012 and my thanks to Professor John Kerrigan and his colleagues for their hospitality. The opportunities to give talks on the subject have been vital to its germination and I am very grateful to the following institutions and hosts: Boston College Adele Dalsimer Memorial Lecture (Marjorie Howes and Oliver Rafferty); Cambridge Group for Irish Studies (Eamon Duffy, John Kerrigan and

Máire Ní Mhaonaigh); Dublin James Joyce Summer School (Anne Fogarty and Luca Crispi); IASIL Japan and Kyoto University (Naoko Toraiwa and Hiroko Ikeda); Mahindra Humanities Centre (Paige Reynolds and John Paul Riquelme); Oxford Irish Seminars, Hertford College (Roy Foster); Trinity College Postgraduate Seminar Series (James Little); Trieste Joyce School (John McCourt and Laura Pelaschiar), University College Dublin School of Law (Imelda Maher), and University of Virginia Institute of the Humanities (Debjani Ganguly and Victor Luftig).

So many people have provided generous help through suggestions, insights and observations drawn from their own expertise: my warm thanks to Sam Alexander, Beatriz Kopschitz Bastos, Rosemarie Bodenheimer, Angela Bourke, Ciara Breathnach, Cara Brophy-Browne, Eamonn Ceannt, Jim Chandler, Danielle Clarke, Brigid Clesham, Maurice Coakley, Vincent Comerford, Karen Corrigan, Catriona Crowe, Tony Crowley, Brian Dolan, James Donnelly, Damian Downes, Martin Doyle, Myles Dungan, Anne Fogarty, Roy Foster, Joseph Hassett, Brian Griffin, Anna Heussaff, Niamh Howlin, Mina Karavanta, Ross Keane, Mr Justice Peter Kelly, Liam Kennedy, Terence Killeen, Vera Kreilkamp, Felix Larkin, Joep Leerssen, Clíona Lewis, Suzanne Lopez, Críostóir Mac Cárthaigh, Margaret MacCurtain, Martin Maguire, Barry McCrea, Lucy McDiarmid, Joanne McEntee, Frank McGuinness, Henrietta McKervey, Richard McMahon, Katherine McSharry, Gerardine Meaney, Lia Mills, Carolina Amador Moreno, Maureen Murphy, Caitríona Ní Chathail, Éilís Ní Dhuibhne, Clíona Ní Riordáin, Grace Neville, Niall Ó Ciosáin, Prionsias Ó Drisceoil, Cormac Ó Gráda, Gearóid Ó Tuathaigh, Íde O'Carroll, Micheál P. O'Cearúil, Ian O'Donnell, Bernard O'Donoghue, Eilís O'Donoghue, Philip O'Leary, Patricia Palmer, Mary Phelan, Rachel Pierce, John Paul Riquelme, Simon O'Connor, Ciarán O'Neill, Ann Rigney, Noel Rubotham, James Shapiro, Gordon Snell, Gwen Walker, Nicholas Wolf, and the late Mr Justice Adrian Hardiman.

Sometimes it can be difficult to identify when and how a vague idea (or many vague ideas) turns into a 'doable' book project, but for me its inception is clearly remembered as a book-writing conversation in summer 2012 for which I offer deep thanks to Claire Connolly, Pat Coughlan and Moynagh Sullivan. For her crucial perspicacity along the book's way, I thank Paige Reynolds; Máire Ní Mhaonaigh has given wise and ever-stalwart counsel; and Breandán Mac Suibhne's incisive and constructive comments have been invaluable. Maeve Lewis has provided a second home in Dublin and my thanks also for the precious friendship given by Susan Brennan,

Harry Browne, the Cooney family, Catherine Ann Cullen, Marion Curtin, Maurice Devlin, Kathleen Edwards, Rita Foley, Marie Kearney, Celia Keenan, the O'Donovan family, Kathy O'Malley, Teresa Roche, Kathleen Rush, Petra Schurenhofer, fellow book-clubbers Therese Caherty, Clare Farrell, Deirdre Ní Dhuillearga, Siobhán Ní Laoire, Máirín Nic Eoin, *agus ár gcairde ionúine* Caelinn Largey and Mary Mulvihill. And for transatlantic connections continuing over the decades, my gratitude to Eleanor Byrne, Mohsen Marefat, Tamara Pitts, Mary Ann Smith, Leslie Swanson, Terri Trafas, Maura Twomey and Unn Villius.

Colleagues at the School of English, Film and Drama, University College Dublin, have provided much-appreciated support for this project. I also wish to acknowledge the inspiration I've received from seminars with Masters students in Anglo-Irish Literature and Drama (2012–18), doctoral students Eve Kearney, David McKinney, Katie Mishler and Jennifer Preston, and postdoctoral fellows Lindsay Janssen, Ken Keating, Dathalinn O'Dea, Catherine Smith and Karen Wade. The book's early germination was inspired by working with colleagues at *An Foras Feasa* Humanities Institute, Maynooth University, and by my time as O'Brien Visiting Scholar at Concordia University in the uniquely multilingual Montreal.

It has been a pleasure throughout to work with UCD Press and I am most grateful for the assistance of Acting Executive Editor, Ruth Hallinan, Executive Editor, Noelle Moran, and Editorial Assistant, Conor Graham; my thanks also to the Committee of UCD Press and to my two manuscript reviewers.

A section of chapter 2 was published as 'Census, history and language in Ireland and Canada: The origins of the language question', in *Ireland and Quebec: Multidisciplinary Perspectives on History, Culture and Society* (Dublin: Four Courts Press, 2016), and I warmly thank my co-editor, Michael Kenneally, and fellow contributors including Rhona R. Kenneally, Vera Regan and Patricia Lamarre for their comments on that chapter. An earlier version of chapter 6 appeared in *The Body in Pain: Irish Literature and Culture* (Basingstoke: Palgrave Macmillan, 2016) edited by my colleagues Fionnuala Dillane, Naomi McAreavey and Emilie Pine, and their input was immensely helpful for this project.

I acknowledge with gratitude the assistance of staff in the following libraries: the National Archives Dublin, including Gregory O'Connor, Zoe Reid and Brian Donnelly; the National Library Dublin reading room and manuscript collections; the British Library Manuscripts Collections

(Althorp Papers); Trinity College Libraries; Queen's University Special Collections; the Royal Irish Academy; Special Collections and the National Folklore Collection at University College Dublin; the Valuation Office, Dublin; and the Royal Archives in Windsor Castle. Quotation from texts held at the Royal Archives at Windsor has been granted by the permission of Her Majesty Queen Elizabeth II and the reproduction of images is by kind permission of the National Archives Dublin and National Library of Ireland.

Finally, I acknowledge with deep gratitude the financial support provided by the NUI Publication Fund.

And to come full circle back to Mallow, my final thanks are to my sister, Gemma, whose great skill in genealogical searches is just one of her gifts to this book, to my late mother, Jo, whose love of history was infectious, and to my recently deceased father, Michael, who would have loved the book launch. I dedicate this book to him and to my much-missed Mallow friend, Kieran Cooney.

PREFACE

Late in the night of 17 August 1882, in the rural townland of Maamtrasna, County Galway,[1] a group of seven men, some carrying sticks and others revolvers, burst into the home of the Joyce family. The house was a two-room cabin, comprising a kitchen which was 22 feet long and 10 feet wide, part of which functioned as a cow house, and a second room which was 9.5 feet long and 6 feet wide.[2] The men wore white flannel vests, or *báiníns*, and their faces were blackened and disguised using burnt oak. At least one of the men carried a bogdeal light, made from a long sliver of pine timber taken from the local bog – 'the poor man's candle' – which was lit on entering the house. The only family member to survive the attack declared that the men 'did not speak a word to me or to any one in the house'.[3] Later, three local men testified that, while the murders took place, they had watched from the potato field behind the Joyce house, some seven yards away, from where they heard 'shouting, and crying, and screeching'.[4] The Joyces' home was part of a cluster of cabins along a narrow road: yet none of those who lived in the neighbouring houses reported to the authorities as having heard any sounds of violence.

Early the next morning, a Friday, the bodies of the family were discovered by John Collins, a local neighbour. John Joyce, the head of the family, was lying naked on the kitchen floor; his wife Bridget (Breege) lay dead in their bed, located in a recess off the kitchen, and her dying stepson Michael lay nearby. In the room adjoining was one bed on which lay the bodies of John's mother, Margaret, and his daughter, also called Margaret (Peggy); the young girl 'lying with her head towards the old woman's feet'.[5] Also on the bed lay John's youngest son, Patsy,[6] who was severely injured but who would recover from his injuries. The other surviving member of the family of seven was Patsy's brother Martin, who was absent from the house that night since he lived in service in Clonbur some ten miles distant.

Collins quickly relayed the news of the murders to other neighbours: then he and ten other men from the village reported the deaths to the local Royal Irish Constabulary (RIC) officers stationed in the nearby police hut in Finny.[7] The next day, Saturday, 19 August, the three men who testified to having heard the sounds coming from the Joyce home – Anthony Joyce, his brother John, and John's son Pat – identified ten local men as belonging to the murder party: Anthony Philbin of Cappaduff; Martin Joyce of Cappanacreha; his brothers Myles Joyce and Paudeen Joyce (also from Cappanacreha); Tom Joyce (son of Paudeen); Thomas Casey of Glensaul; Patrick Casey of Derry; his brother John Casey; their uncle Michael Casey (all of Derry), and Patrick Joyce of Shanvalleycahill.[8] Myles Joyce and his brothers were first cousins of the Joyce informants and also first cousins of the murdered man, John Joyce – that such close family ties existed between Joyce victims, accused and witnesses would generate much public comment during the ensuing murder trials, but outsiders would also struggle to understand the full density of relationships between those implicated for the murders. For example, Martin Joyce was married to Judy Casey, who was the sister of John and Patrick Casey and the niece of Michael Casey; Thomas Casey of Glensaul was married to Mary Philbin, sister of Anthony Philbin. Only Patrick Joyce of Shanvalleycahill was unrelated to any of the other accused.

Contemporary media reports drew particular attention to the violence of the attack on the Joyce household and the brutal nature of the injuries to the dead. These injuries included a number of bullet wounds on the bodies of John (aged about 50 years old) and Michael (about 17). Extensive head fractures were found on the bodies of the young Margaret (about 14), her stepmother Bridget (about 45), and her grandmother Margaret (about 80), who had been beaten to death. Speculation as to the motive for the murders was also immediately rampant, with the most prevalent theory being that a member of the Joyce family had recently acted as an informer in relation to the notorious murder of bailiff Joseph Huddy and his grandson John in nearby Clonbur earlier that year.[9]

In the days following the murders, the ten suspects identified by Anthony Joyce and his relatives were arrested and were brought before an inquiry in Galway city on 26 August; soon afterward they were transferred to Dublin, where they stood trial in November at the Special Commission Court in Green Street. Immediately prior to the trial, Anthony Philbin and Thomas Casey 'turned Queen's evidence' and became approvers. Less than four months after the Joyce killings, on 15 December, three men were executed in Galway Jail: Patrick Joyce of Shanvalleycahill, Patrick Casey, and Myles Joyce, each of whom had pled innocent. The five others tried were sentenced to life imprisonment after changing their plea to guilty under the advice of their local clergyman. Of these five, Michael Casey died in Maryborough (now Portlaoise) Prison in August 1895; John Casey died in Mountjoy Jail in Dublin in February 1900; and Tom Joyce, Martin Joyce, and Paudeen Joyce were released from prison in October 1902.

Immediately prior to the executions in December 1882, Patrick Joyce and Patrick Casey made statements attesting to their involvement in the murder party and declaring the innocence of the condemned man Myles Joyce as well as the innocence of Martin Joyce, Paudeen Joyce, Tom Joyce, and John Casey. Despite a number of appeals to the Lord Lieutenant's office, Myles Joyce was executed; witnesses to the hanging reported that his impassioned protests of innocence led to the rope's slipping and to his death by strangulation. Over their 20 years of imprisonment, frequent memorials and petitions for early release by the five prisoners and by their public supporters were unsuccessful. In 2015, the Irish government commissioned an expert review of the case of Myles Joyce from Dr Niamh Howlin of the Sutherland School of Law, UCD. Her examination concluded that his conviction was unsafe and on 4 April 2018 President Michael D. Higgins signed a posthumous pardon for Myles Joyce.

*

The Maamtrasna murders were one of many notorious murders of the era; how and why these events acquired and maintained their distinctive notoriety is one of the subjects of this study. At the time of the murders, their gruesome details were seen as offering evidence of rural lawlessness, or 'barbarity', in the midst of debates as to the efficacy of coercive or conciliatory political policies and, more fundamentally, as to the capacity of the Irish for self-government. These were long-standing subjects for the British administration in Ireland but were especially heightened by widespread rural protest, agitation for land reform in Ireland and an incipient movement for Home Rule in the early 1880s. The particular ferocity of the Joyce murders and the rapid attention that they garnered nationally led to intense pressure on local police and judiciary to identify the guilty parties quickly, while later the trials were monitored closely by a Castle administration heavily impacted by the Phoenix Park murders of British Chief Secretary of Ireland Lord Frederick Cavendish and Under-Secretary Thomas Henry Burke in May of that year.[10] The outcome of the trials and subsequent executions, and, more specifically, eyewitness accounts of the 'botched' execution of Myles Joyce, led to the Maamtrasna case quickly becoming a *cause célèbre* for Irish nationalists and a recurring subject for parliamentary comment in the later 1880s. Personal reflections on the political consequences of the Maamtrasna murders are to be found in key analyses of late nineteenth-century Irish political history, ranging from T. P. O'Connor's *The Parnell Movement* (1886) to Tim Healy's *Letters and Leaders of My Day* (1929) and to John Lawrence Hammond's 1938 biography *Gladstone and the Irish Nation*. Strikingly, the case of Maamtrasna returns as a 'troubling' force in recent, diverse accounts of British treatment of nineteenth-century Ireland, such as Patrick Joyce's social history *The State of Freedom* (2013) and James Murphy's *Ireland's Czar* (2014), a biography of Lord Lieutenant Earl Spencer.

In 1992, Jarlath Waldron, a parish priest in the area, published *Maamtrasna: The Murders and the Mystery,* and this extensive local history has done much to keep interest in the case alive. Waldron's history served as a key inspiration for Sean Ó Cuirreáin's 2016 Irish-language study *Éagóir* (meaning 'injustice'), which drew from additional newspaper sources and newly available official documents including photos of the accused.[11] Ó Cuirreáin places his narrative emphasis more squarely on the Maamtrasna case as a miscarriage of justice and has been a key campaigner for the granting of an official pardon to Myles Joyce; his work also underlay the 2018 Irish-language docudrama *Murdair Mhám Trasna.*

My interest in this topic grew from my earlier research on nineteenth-century Ireland and on the large cultural and linguistic shift that occurred during that century. I came gradually to recognise that language change in that period is a much more complex (and what socio-linguists might term a 'messier') phenomenon than had previously been recognised, with far reaching implications. The events that constitute the Maamtrasna case – the motivations, murders, trial, executions, and aftermath – make possible an especially illuminating case study of this language shift in action and its consequences. For the accused and witnesses, whether one spoke Irish only or had knowledge of English would prove to be of critical importance in interactions with police and with the legal and judicial systems, and for a number of men this would prove an issue of life or death.[12]

That Myles Joyce was a monoglot[13] Irish speaker who failed to receive the services of an interpreter and translator is one notorious feature of the legal case with reverberations that extend to the present day. In subsequent coverage of the Maamtrasna trials, and in particular following the journalistic writings of James Joyce on the topic, it became commonplace to describe all of the ten accused men as monoglot speakers of Irish. This is incorrect, and instead a closer examination of their life stories reveals a startling diversity of linguistic abilities. Patrick Joyce, the first man executed, spoke English well, as did Patrick Casey, the second man executed. His brother John and uncle Michael were Irish monoglots, as were Myles Joyce and his two brothers; Myles' nephew Tom, the youngest of the accused, may have had some competence in English. Most significantly for the outcome of the trial, the two men with the most advanced ability in English were Anthony Philbin and Thomas Casey, both men having returned to the area only recently after spending a considerable amount of time working in England. These were the two men who, days before the trial in early November 1882, would 'turn Queen's evidence' and become state informers against the eight other accused. The three main witnesses for the prosecution – Anthony, John, and Pat Joyce – were Irish monoglots whose evidence was tendered to the court through the use of an interpreter throughout the trial; the reliability of their testimony, and the credibility of their claimed status as monoglots, would prove especially contentious in the course of the judicial proceedings and subsequently.

That ten men of more or less the same social class, from the same community, and extending over just two generations in age, could range from Irish monoglots to speakers of Irish who possessed limited competence in English to well-functioning bilinguals illustrates in vivid detail the language shift that was still taking place in the Joyce Country in the early 1880s. Who spoke what language mattered greatly in the aftermath of the Maamtrasna murders. The diverse linguistic competencies of those involved, and the crossings between Irish and English that occurred in their interactions with each other, extended from the ten accused and their families to the witnesses against them, the constabulary who arrested them, the judicial system that tried them and executed three men, the prison system charged with incarcerating five other men, and the broader society – local, regional, and national – of late nineteenth-century Ireland in which these events took place. Within these domains, the social reality of individuals' monolingual (Irish) or bilingual practices came into collision with the monolingual (English) ideology of the state, with fateful consequences.

Strangers who crossed through the mountain-pass of Maamtrasna in 1882 (*mám* meaning 'col' or 'neck'; *trasna* the preposition 'across') entered a valley where Irish was the main language of local communication; local people who left the valley encountered a world in which commercial and legal transactions were to the advantage of those who knew English. These language crossings – in political, judicial, social and even familial spheres – provide a compelling insight into the dynamics of a larger cultural change from Irish-speaking to English-speaking, a process whose traces extend into the closing decades of nineteenth-century Ireland. Yet this shift in language use is more often treated as self-evident or inevitable by historians and cultural critics of the period, if acknowledged at all. A central objective of this work is to demonstrate that the significance of the Maamtrasna narrative is at once historical and contemporary and to provide a vivid snapshot of a place and time in which the complex social dynamics within processes of cultural change are starkly visible – and occasionally audible. To write this historical study in the early twenty-first century, in the context of large-scale migration and newly-enforced state barriers to movement and citizenship, is also to be cognisant of the extent to which these dynamics continue to influence the destinies of monolinguals and bilinguals today, and the fate of languages that they seek to retain.

*

The miscarriage of justice inherent in the conviction and execution of Myles Joyce has been central to the continuing notoriety of these cases, reinforced nationally through local histories, radio documentaries and theatrical treatments, and internationally, in large part owing to references to Maamtrasna in the work of James Joyce. In 1907, a then 25-year-old journalist based in Trieste, Joyce first included an account of the trial in his article 'Ireland at the bar', initially published in Italian in the Trieste newspaper *Il Piccolo della Sera*. Here, James Joyce gave new currency to the figure of Myles Joyce, whom he depicted as a 'bewildered old man, left over from a culture which is not ours, a deaf-mute before his judge', and a 'symbol of the Irish nation at the bar of public opinion.'[14] Joyce's father was a close friend of the nationalist politician Tim Harrington, MP, who had published influential articles in the 1884 *Freeman's Journal* and in a subsequent pamphlet *The Maamtrasna Massacre: Impeachment of the Trials*. In this pamphlet, published just two years after the events, Harrington went as far as naming those whom he believed to be guilty of the murders, including three men who remained at large (see Image 32, p. XVI). James Joyce's career is bookended by two invocations of his infamous namesake: the first by the newly diasporic writer in 1907 and the second in his last work *Finnegans Wake* (1939). His symbolic appropriation of the figure of Myles is frequently cited in studies of Joyce but usually just in passing reference. Why this cosmopolitan artist, famous for multilingual wordplay, was drawn to the fate of the monoglot rural man remains a challenging question, as is the uneasy interplay of affiliation and dissociation in his journalistic and novelistic retellings of the Maamtrasna narrative.

In 2012, two members of the House of Lords, David Alton (whose mother came from the Tuar Mhic Éadaigh area, near Maamtrasna) and Eric Lubbock (Baron Avebury) launched an as yet unsuccessful campaign in the British Houses of Parliament to declare Myles Joyce the victim of a miscarriage of justice. The granting of the Irish presidential pardon in April 2018 (on the government's recommendation that the right be exercised) was the fifth to be awarded since 1937 and only the second instance of a posthumous award, the first granted to Harry Gleeson in December 2015. Notably, it was the first pardon relating to a case prior to the foundation of the State and, in his accompanying comments, President Higgins underlined the important role played by Howlin's expert report and by the legal advice of the Attorney General.

Clearly the symbolic weight of the Maamtrasna murders from the 1880s to the present is considerable: over the decades, nationalist commentators and their opponents have invoked the events for very different political ends – an ideological process to which my study is inevitably itself a contribution. At the centre of the case is a series of brutal murders that took place in the most domestic of spaces. Fuelled by local grievances, the murders reveal shocking levels of hatred and conflict within a small community and the gross breakdown of familial and affective connections as well as their strength and endurance. Yet the Maamtrasna murders, along with what preceded and succeeded them, are also part of a much larger historical narrative, one that includes the violence of the state's response and tangled questions of retribution and judicial punishment.

I suggest that a hidden, and still overlooked, strand in the complex interrelations of violence and retribution, of justice and injustice in late nineteenth-century Ireland was the relationship between law and language. 1880s Ireland was a bilingual society in many regions[15] and western areas included significant numbers of Irish monoglots,[16] yet the English-language judicial system and its official policies and procedures largely ignored the social reality of linguistic difference. In practice, such difference could prove hard to avoid and the resulting clash between individuals' diverse monolingual or bilingual competencies and a state ideology, deeply committed to an English 'monolingual *habitus*' or norm, conferred an important role on those with the ability and social status to serve as interpreters, most especially the police or court interpreters deployed by the state.[17] Many of the key themes of this book resonate with continuing concerns in today's society, particularly those relating to the just operation of our legal systems: the role of state interpreters in a bilingual courtroom, the monolingual paradigms sponsored by state systems, and the challenges still experienced by those speaking in a language other than that of state authority.

The force of the language shift in eighteenth- and nineteenth-century Ireland, from a country predominantly Irish-speaking to one that was predominantly English speaking, also required periods of 'transitional bilingualism' within communities and families. A full comprehension of this linguistic process and of its social impact requires much more flexible understandings of linguistic competency, and of what 'bilingualism' means in individual practice, than have characterised studies of Irish culture to date. Here my work is indebted to recent analyses of multilingualism and sociolinguistics in a contemporary global context. In the words of Monica Heller, language is 'a set of resources which circulate in uneven ways in social networks and discursive spaces'; thus, studies of language practice must recognise 'the messiness of actual usage' and 'the situation of speakers in space and time'.[18] If we see language as a resource that is available differently and 'unevenly' to people, then we are also better positioned to recognise what Heller terms the 'relations of power which inform the material conditions of our lives'.[19]

In recent decades, large-scale movement and migration has led contemporary commentators on language contact to argue for new models that focus, in Jan Blommaert's words, on an individual speaker's 'mobile resources' rather than on abstract concepts of 'immobile languages'.[20] A term like 'bilingual' can suggest the fixity of two known languages but, as Blommaert rightly argues, the linguistic resources and repertoires of individuals who move across countries or even continents are much more likely to be 'truncated' or 'unfinished'[21] rather than static or complete. This is also true of those bilingual or multilingual speakers who are not especially geographically mobile, since, as Blommaert reminds us, 'no one knows *all* of a language'.[22] Actual language usage is very often 'messy' and an individual's competence, comprehension and knowledge of a second language can vary greatly in different social registers. Yet such diversity and specificity can find poor accommodation within monolingual judicial systems and legal processes. Writing of the infamous trial of Gaston Dominici in Provence in 1954, Roland Barthes discerned how the 'appearance of justice in the world of the accused' had been made possible by a pernicious 'intermediary myth, always made good use of by officialdom', namely 'the myth of the transparency and the universality of language.'[23] Barthes' comments still pertain to judicial experiences today wherein the 'myth of the transparency and the universality of language' conceals the reality of linguistic diversity and of state (mis)translation. These are processes that the judicial systems ensuing from the events of Maamtrasna bring starkly into view.

*

This book moves through three parts, from introductory chapters to the events of Maamtrasna to their continuing significance. The first chapter, beginning with the murders on 17 August, examines economic and social conditions in the Ross district and what can be known regarding the domestic lives of the Joyce families. Chapter 2 situates social patterns in Maamtrasna in the larger context of language shift and cultural change in nineteenth-century Ireland, for which the events of 1882 provide such an illuminating case study. Beginning with the 1851 census, in which a question regarding language-use was first posed, it investigates who spoke what languages in late nineteenth-century Ireland, uncovering not only the fate of Irish monolingualism but also the rich and much neglected history of bilingualism.

The second section begins with the arrests of the Maamtrasna suspects and examines the initial encounters of these poorly-educated men with the judicial system and the making of a case against them, drawing in detail from the crown brief for the prosecution that details the arrests and first depositions in August and September 1882. Moving from the arrests of the Maamtrasna accused to the wider subject of law and language in late nineteenth-century Ireland, Chapter 4 analyses the key role of the interpreter in bilingual courtrooms and the changing discourse, both local and national, concerning the rights of Irish-language speakers. The next chapter, on the Maamtrasna trials and executions, provides an in-depth analysis of the trial proceedings from 13–21 November 1882, illuminating what would prove to be crucial moments of linguistic misunderstanding and misapprehension. The execution of Myles Joyce, Patrick Joyce, and Patrick Casey in Galway City on 15 December 1882 is the subject of Chapter 6, which draws in detail from the state inquiry into the 'botched' execution of Myles Joyce in December 1882 and brings to light the potency rapidly acquired by *na focla déigheanacha* (the last or dying words) of Myles Joyce.

Throughout this book, contemporary newspaper accounts provide an invaluable textual source and, at times, a crucial mediating mode between the historical events and the judicial processes of investigation, trial, and execution. For this reason, a core methodology in this book is that of close reading of the surviving records and archives, seeking evidence, or hints of such, as to when and where languages crossed or collided and where a language was made audible or silenced. Given that these are English-language archival sources, they require reading between, or below, the lines to recover the traces of the Irish-speaking monoglots or bilingual informants and subjects. Since it is in the nature of the state record to suppress its own interpretative and mediating practices, and to preserve solely its translation rather than the other-language or dual-language original, this involves, at times, an exercise in reconstruction – informed by other contemporary sources – as well as in rereading.

Following the trials and executions, their political and cultural aftermath is the subject of the final section of this book, 'Last Words', commencing with the parliamentary inquiry prompted by the publication of Tim Harrington's highly influential pamphlet in 1884. Chapter 8 probes the afterlives of those involved in the Maamtrasna murders and investigates previously unexamined records for the five imprisoned men as well as what can be known of the lives of the many others affected by the murders. The most famous literary appropriation of the events of Maamtrasna by James Joyce is the subject of Chapter 9, and the concluding discussion explores how and why the subject of Maamtrasna continues to matter.

Part I

Language Crossings

MURDERS

'All Quite Dead'

Mám: a yoke; bond, duty, service, oppression; a mountain pass, a nek, a summit, a hollow; …

    fá mháim an chruadhtain, under the yoke of oppression;
    daimh ghacha máma, oxen of all work;
    fear máma, a serf;
    mám trasna, a mountain-pass, a breach, *al.* a place-name (Gal.)
                    Patrick S. Dinneen, *Irish-English Dictionary*[1]

Around half-past nine on the morning of Friday, 18 August, 11 men[2] arrived at the Royal Irish Constabulary (RIC) hut in Finny to report that a number of murders had taken place at the home of John Joyce in Maamtrasna. One of these men was John Collins, a neighbour of the Joyces, who had been the first person to arrive at the murder scene early that morning. Collins, accompanied by two local women, Mary O'Brien and Margaret O'Brien, had travelled there to borrow a pair of paddles to card wool. The following day Collins provided a sworn account to the coroner's inquest:

JOHN COLLINS, duly sworn, saith – I live in the townland of Maamtrasna. I am tenant farmer. On yesterday morning, about two hours after sunrise,[3] I was going to the house of the deceased, John Joyce, for the loan of a pair of wool cards. I had two women with me, who stood outside. The women had two spinning wheels on their shoulders. I went into the house of [the] deceased. The door was open and off its hinges. I saw John Joyce lying dead on the floor, naked. I at once went out to the two women on the road and told the women, Mary O'Brien and Margaret O'Brien, that John Joyce was killed. I went then and told the people of the village. I then returned to the house of the deceased, John Joyce, and we then found John Joyce, Margaret Joyce, senior, Margaret Joyce, junior, and Bridget Joyce, all quite dead. We then saw Pat Joyce and Michael Joyce. They were in bed; we spoke to them. We asked them what happened to them. Michael Joyce at first said he did not know. We asked again what happened [to] them. Michael Joyce then told us he thought he saw three men in the house. We then asked Michael Joyce if he knew the men. He said he did not know them, as they had their faces dirty. I did not speak to Pat Joyce.[4]

Once he received the men's report that murders had taken place, Constable John Johnston, along with his colleague Sub-Constable Lenihan, immediately travelled to Maamtrasna (a one-mile journey by track along *Bóithrín a tSléibhe*).[5] The following day, Johnston also provided a sworn deposition to the coroner's inquest. This is his account of what he had witnessed inside:

Constable JOHN JOHNSTON, duly sworn, saith – I am stationed at Finny. At about half-past nine on yesterday morning, the 18th instant, a number of men came to the barrack and reported to me, eleven men in all, that John Joyce, his wife, mother, and daughter were murdered in their own house at Maamtrasna. I proceeded at once to the scene along with Sub-Constable Lerhinary [*sic*].[6] I went to Joyce's house and found the door open. I went into the house. I saw John Joyce lying on the floor, with his head towards the fire – lying on his face, dead. I saw his wife Bridget in bed, dead; his mother Margaret and daughter Margaret, both dead, in bed, in the room, and the two sons Michael and Pat, badly wounded – both able to speak. I asked Michael, through Sub-Constable Lerhinan, who spoke Irish, what had happened to them last night. Michael Joyce said in reply that two or three men came into the room and shot him in bed, and that he saw one of the men take up something like a stick and strike his sister, and that he heard his grandmother screaming about the break of day. He said he got out of bed and came down to the kitchen for a drink, and said he saw his father lying on the kitchen floor; after getting the drink, he returned to the bed in the kitchen where his stepmother was lying. She was then living; before the men came into the room, he heard shots. I asked Michael Joyce how many men did he see, and if he knew them. He said no, that their faces were black, and that there were three or four men. I then asked Pat Joyce what happened to him last night but got no reply. I then asked him how many men did he see in the house, and he said two or three. I asked him did he know them, and he said no, that their faces were black. I asked him if they had a light; he said yes, a piece of bogdeal. I found a bullet, which I produce, on the floor near where John Joyce was lying.[7]

According to the police records, Johnston was the first to question the two injured boys, whom he described as 'badly wounded' but 'both able to speak', but *de facto* he required the translation services of his junior colleague Lenihan.

DYING DECLARATIONS

On Friday afternoon Resident Magistrate A. Newton Brady recorded the dying declarations of the two boys, also using the translation services of Lenihan. Michael was the more severely wounded of the two, having been shot in the head and in the stomach. The deposition taken and translated from him reads starkly since it was recorded just before he died of his injuries:

> Two or three men came in. They had black on their faces. I did see my father and my brother killed. I am very sick. I cannot raise myself up. I was a little while in bed when they came. I was asleep when they came in. I heard the dog bark – my own dog. They said something to my father; I do not know what. I have no pain at all. I was at Mass yesterday at Finney.[8] My name is Michael. John O'Brien told me not to tell, and Michael Malley. It was last night when they told me not to tell. They swore me on a book not to tell. It is John O'Brien of the Wood. I am sure of it.[9]

Patsy had two major head wounds, one over his left eye and one behind his left ear, and was considered also to be near death by first-comers to the scene (the boy later recovered from his injuries and would make a brief appearance in the subsequent murder trial in one of its most poignant and commented-upon scenes). The traces of Johnson's questioning are more overt here, but the declaration still conveys the eerie silence and disguised appearances of the murder party:

> I did not know any one who came in. I would tell if I knew. Three men came in. It was not near morning. I was long in bed. I think it was about one o'clock. I did not hear any shots. I was struck on the head. I don't know who struck me. They were 'married men.'[10] They had soot on their faces. They had whiskers. They had bog deal lights. They had a 'kippeen' each. They lit them inside in the house. I was asleep in the inside room when they came in. I got three strokes. They did not speak a word to me or to any one in the house. I think they had no coats but 'boneens.' They had three old hats. I believe I am dying. I might know them again.[11]

Dying declarations had (as now) a particular legal status. In late nineteenth-century Ireland, they were exceptions to the usual prohibitions on hearsay evidence, though admissible only in charges of murder or manslaughter and where the dying person identified the party or parties directly responsible. Their admissibility also required proof that the person making the declaration was doing so in apprehension that death was imminent; hence the translated phrase 'I believe I am dying' in Patsy's declaration and, more contentiously, 'I am very sick' in Michael's case.[12]

On Saturday, a large group of spectators gathered at Maamtrasna to observe the coroner's inquest which took place in the open ground outside the house of the Joyce victims. The inquest required the swearing-in of a jury whose role was to deliver a verdict as to cause of death. A neighbour, Andrew (Andy) Joyce, made the formal identification of all five victims, noting that he had not seen any of them 'living' since the Tuesday before.[13] These three inquest statements (by Andy Joyce, John Collins and Constable Johnston) and the boys' declarations are part of the evidentiary documentation gathered for the crown prosecution brief, which survives as part of the vast holdings of documents from the Chief Secretary's Office, held at the National Archives in Dublin.[14] The 49-page brief prepared by George Bolton, Crown Solicitor, on behalf of the crown, opens with the inquest records, but Patsy's declaration is inserted near the end, with the accompanying crown note, '*Patrick Joyce has recovered, but his evidence is worthless.*'[15]

According to the account of the coroner's inquest published in the *Freeman's Journal* on Monday, 'a jury of 18 of the people of the district were sworn, some of them in Irish.'[16] The need for a swearing-in in Irish suggests that at least some of the jury members were Irish monoglots, with limited or no understanding of Constable Johnston's testimony in English. Even at this early stage in police investigations of the murder, gathering evidentiary materials posed various linguistic challenges. For the purposes of a later prosecution case, any eyewitness statement that had been tendered in Irish had to be interpreted and transcribed into English before inclusion in the police records. Yet very rarely do the official sources acknowledge this act of translation and more often the existence of such an intermediary process is suppressed. One example relates to the 'dying declarations' of the two boys to magistrate Brady, which had been translated from Irish but were included in the prosecution brief without any reference to the boys being Irish-speakers only. And in his sworn account, Constable Johnston directly acknowledged his colleague

Lenihan's role in translating only in the case of Michael even though he was needed in the questioning of both boys.

The most striking instance of Irish-language testimony being concealed is that of John Collins, the neighbour who was first to arrive at the scene. Newspaper coverage of the inquest acknowledged that his evidence was translated from Irish but the crown brief failed to record this. The statement in English attributed to Collins bears obvious signs of the RIC interpreter, such as, 'I was going to the house of the deceased ... I went into the house of deceased,' but traces of the local man's Irish speech may also be heard in the idiomatic words, 'I am tenant farmer', and, most resonantly, in his account of his conversation with the dying Michael: 'He said he did not know them, as they had their faces dirty.' In his lengthy account of the events in Monday's *Freeman's Journal*, the reporter showed some linguistic understanding of this choice of word: 'Their faces according to the evidence were blackened. The Irish speaking persons used a word which, literally translated, means "dirty," but it was probably intended to convey the same meaning.'[17] (The Irish word used by Collins may have been *smúit* or *smúid*, meaning 'soot' or 'dirt' and also 'obscured.')

What is also captured in the newspaper account, and omitted from the police records, is that the simultaneous translation of Collins' evidence which took place at the Saturday inquest was not straightforward and led to a dispute between the coroner and interpreter. According to the newspaper account, Collins testified that he had seen John Joyce lying naked 'on his face at the left hand side of the fireplace' and that 'he was dead (moro)'. Coroner and interpreter disagreed on how the specific Irish word used by Collins should be translated (it was phonetically rendered by the journalist in brackets as 'moro' and was probably the Irish word *marbh*). The argument centred on whether *marbh* (dead) or *marú* (killing) was the term in question, a disagreement carefully transcribed by the newspaper reporter:

> The coroner asked, did the witness say 'dead' or 'killed'.
> The interpreter replied that it was 'dead'.
> The coroner and a gentleman who happened to be present said the meaning of the Irish word more, which the witness used, was 'killed,' not dead.[18]

Thus, once again, the contemporary press report acknowledges the instability of evidence first tendered in Irish and requiring translation, unlike the crown records from which any such ambiguous reference is removed.

Immediately following the conclusion of the coroner's inquest, a post-mortem examination was conducted on the five bodies, and the official findings underline the brutal nature of the injuries inflicted on the family. Various bullet wounds were identified on the body of John Joyce ('aged about fifty years') and on the body of Michael Joyce ('aged about seventeen years'). In the case of the three females, Margaret, or Peggy, Joyce ('aged about fourteen years'), Bridget Joyce ('aged about forty-five years'), and Margaret Joyce ('aged about eighty years'), extensive head fractures were noted; for example, in the case of Bridget Joyce, 'we found all the bones on the right side of head and face extensively fractured and driven in on the brain substance.' Of the body of the 80-year-old Margaret Joyce, the doctors reported that 'we also found the muscles of left forearm completely torn and lacerated.'[19]

More amplified accounts of the victims' injuries were circulated by newspaper correspondents, some of whom reported from the murder scene. For example, the *Freeman's Journal* correspondent speculated in gruesome detail that the blunt instrument by which the women had been beaten to death was 'the handle of a spade, to which was attached the iron holdfast which forms the upper part of the spade itself and binds it to the wooden handle.' And this reporter also surmised from the location of John Joyce's body on the floor that the intruders had found the door 'on the latch as is the custom in most remote rural districts' and had entered the house before John had heard them: 'He probably had just time to get out of bed, and had not time to face his assailants when he was struck down with a blow aimed at the back part of his skull. By this he was stunned and silenced, and no alarm was communicated to the rest of the inmates of the house.'[20]

Decades later, people from the Maamtrasna district still harboured troubling questions as to why such brutal murders had occurred, as oral sources preserved by the Irish Folklore Commission demonstrate. In particular, musings as to why such brutal physical violence had been visited on the Joyce women percolated in local retellings. In 1936, in Moyrus parish in Ballynahinch, Galway, 80-year-old Seán Seoighe (Tomáis) spoke to Brian MacLochlainn of the 'Maamtrasna Murder'. According to Seoighe, the murderers, having killed John Joyce, overheard his mother ask his wife if she recognised the men; following her reply that she did recognise them, the men returned and 'killed all in the house' (*mharuigheadar an méid abhí sa teach*). Seoighe concluded by stating that the origin or cause of the murders was unknown: '*Níl fhios cén t-údar abhí le é a mharú*[21] (see Image 13, p. V).

Similarly, in the 1944 account from 60-year-old Máirtín Ó Duithche from the parish of Ross in Mayo, the tale of such a conversation between the women is foregrounded: '*Well chuaidh siad amach taobh amach go'n doras*

annsin agus sheasadar taboh amuigh g'on doras. Agus d'fiafhruigh an t-sean-
bhean go'n bhean óg – dhá bhean seisean – d'fiafhruigh a mháthair dhá bhean
ar aithnigh sí na fir a rinnigh an marbhú. Agus dubhairt sí gur aithnigh sí 'ch
uile cheann acú. D'fill na fir isteach annsin agus mharbhuigh siad fré chéile iad
*cé's moite g'aon stócach amháin a chuaidh síos imbairrille ánn.'*²² Ó Duithche,
whose father was a neighbour of the murdered family, provides some
further details on the murders: that the night was *'chomh dubh le súighe'*
('as black as soot'), that there were seven men in total in the party, that the
men attacked John Joyce *'agus é ina chraiceann'* ('naked'). The reason for
the murder, according to Ó Duithche, was the local belief that Joyce was
a sheep-stealer: *'Well 'sé an t-úghdar a bhí lé na mharbhú mar bhí sé ráidhte*
*go rabh sé ina ghadaidhe caorach.'*²³

SPREADING THE NEWS

Maamtrasna is part of a district still known as 'Joyce Country' (*Dúiche*
Sheoighe) on the border of northwest Galway and south Mayo. The region
stretches from Maam Cross in the south to Tourmakeady in the north and
is surrounded by the Maamturk mountains to the west; upper Lough Corrib
lies to the southeast and lower Lough Mask to the northeast. It includes
the villages of Clonbur (*An Fhairche*), Finny (*Fionnaithe*) and Cong (*Conga*).
Maamtrasna townland is situated deep in the mountain valley, bounded
by *Loch na Fuaiche* (Loch Na Foofey) a little over a mile to the west and
Maamtrasna Bay, an inlet of Lough Mask, a mile to the east.²⁴

At that time, the easiest way for locals to travel from their townland
to neighbouring villages was by water: a walk along *Bóithrín a tSléibhe*
('mountain path') south to Finny village and then a boat trip across a half-
mile stretch of Lough Mask Upper to Cloughbrack. For those travelling
to Maamtrasna by land, approaching from Mayo required fording the
Owenbrin river on horseback, when the waters allowed; approaching from
the southeast (from Clonbur, or Cong, or far away Galway) involved a ferry
crossing at *Béal a tSnámha* (Ferry Bridge) five miles away, a crossing which
a horse might or might not follow. From Maam Cross, over ten miles to the
southwest, a long walk or rough horse-ride over boggy mountain terrain
was needed.

The winter before the murders occurred, a makeshift bridge across the Owenbrin river had been swept away by a flood, reinforcing the isolation of the valley among what Andrew Dunlop, reporter for the *Freeman's Journal*, termed 'the mountain fastnesses of Maamtrasna'.[25] Over and over again, the first reporters emphasised the valley's remoteness, blind to the obvious: that a place is not remote to those who live there. And for those who scrutinised the lives of the Maamtrasna protagonists more closely, proximity and intimacy would emerge as far more unsettling tropes, given the brutality of what took place on 17 August: how near the protagonists – victims, killers and witnesses – lived to one another and how closely they were related.

News of the events first reached Dublin Castle shortly before 2 p.m. on Friday via a telegram from Cong police station: 'Report received here that on last night John Joyce, his wife, mother & daughter were murdered & two boys wounded in their own house at Maamtrasna Finney, am starting for the scene.'[26] Telegraphs with more information arrived from Clifford Lloyd, Resident Magistrate at Loughrea, to Edward George Jenkinson in Dublin Castle. Jenkinson had recently, and in the aftermath of the Phoenix Park murders, been appointed Assistant Under-Secretary for Police and Crime. Lloyd reported that a magistrate had taken 'information of two sons, one since died of wounds'.[27]

Accounts appeared in regional papers on Saturday. The *Galway Vindicator*, which was published twice weekly, made a brief reference to events on Saturday, 19 August: 'The particulars have not yet reached us. The murders are no doubt agrarian, but [it] is said that Joyce was suspected of having given information to the police about the murder of the bailiffs in the neighbourhood.'[28] The weekly *Ballinrobe Chronicle* featured a story entitled 'Frightful Murder in Connemara', with brief accounts of the deaths and injuries and with closer attention to the beginning of police inquiries:

> Four or five arrests have been made, which, from circumstances that have transpired and led thereto, are considered important.
>
> On yesterday a number of the people of the locality, as in a representative body, reported the outrage to the constabulary. Mr Gibbons, SI, with a party of police, soon after left Cong for Maam Trasna;[29] and on the report reaching the town, Mr M'Ardle, SI, RIC, who has considerable knowledge of the mountain district, also left for the scene of the murder, and both are still engaged in making inquiry.
>
> There is some mystery as to the cause of the murder; a rumour in circulation is that the unfortunate family were suspected of having given some

information in some quarter touching the murder of Joe Huddy and his grandson in Cloughbrack village, and the immersion and finding of the bodies in the lake.[30]

In the weekly *Galway Express,* deeply conservative in its politics, the deaths were recounted in much more lurid detail:

> The unfortunate victims were first shot, then their heads were battered in with hammers and hatchets, and finally the most fiendish of loathsome act had yet to be perpetrated – that of setting dogs to worry them while they lay dying. One of the daughters had her breast and side completely torn open by the dogs, and the other persons were also disfigured. Oh! what inhumanity! It must cause the blush of shame to mantle on the cheek of every Irishman. The scene of the murder is an evicted farm at Finney in the Derrypark district, about five miles from Clonbur, and in the neighbourhood where the two Huddys, Lord Ardilaun's bailiffs, were murdered and thrown into the lake. Joyce was herd upon a farm from which a tenant had recently been evicted.[31]

In January 1882, Joe Huddy, bailiff to Lord Ardilaun of Ashford Castle, had been murdered along with his young grandson, and their bodies had been tied in sacks, weighted, and taken to Lough Mask. Later that month, the location was revealed to the police – reputedly by an old woman with the surname Joyce – and their bodies were recovered from the lake.[32] Initial press speculations linked the Maamtrasna murders with this act of informing, while later accounts would emphasise links between John Joyce and a local agrarian secret society.

As early as Friday afternoon, the first reports of the murders were dispatched by telegraph to Dublin and Galway from Cong by the Press Association and special correspondents directly employed by the national newspapers. One such correspondent, Andrew Dunlop, who worked at the time both for the pro-unionist *Daily Express* and nationalist-leaning *Freeman's Journal*, would subsequently feature the case of Maamtrasna in his memoir, *Fifty Years of Journalism in Ireland* (1911). Dunlop's reminiscences attest in vivid detail to the difficulties of travel from urban east to rural west.[33] He had received the news in Dublin on Friday afternoon and left for Galway on the night mail train, at half-past seven, along with two other Dublin journalists. Presented with a choice between the Mayo branch line from Claremorris via Ballinrobe to Cong or the Galway line from Dublin to Galway, and onwards by mail car and special car, the correspondents chose the Galway line and what proved to be the much more circuitous journey.

Reaching Galway at one in the morning, they took the Clifden mail car at two, left the mail car at Oughterard at four, and reached Maam Cross on a hired horse and car by seven (a total of 26 miles from Galway). Over ten miles of a difficult road journey remained to Maamtrasna; about three miles from their destination, they encountered a dilapidated wooden bridge, now impassable for their horse and car, and had to complete the journey on foot. They reached Maamtrasna at nearly one o'clock the following afternoon (a journey of some 18 hours), two hours ahead of the coroner's inquest.[34]

Following the inquest, the men left the Joyces' house for Maam Cross hotel at five o'clock on Saturday afternoon and proceeded to Cong later that night, arriving there at one in the morning. Cong was the location of the nearest telegraph station: as Dunlop noted, 'the Post Office [had] sent a Wheatstone instrument to that remote part of the country.'[35] Its use was far from easy, however, and the vagaries of the instrument meant that while the deadline for taking copy in Dublin was 3 a.m., the correspondents were 'still in the Post Office an hour later looking at the tape passing through the Wheatstone.' As a result, 'all despatches appeared in a more or less incomplete form in Monday morning's issue of the papers which we respectively represented.'[36] An additional challenge, as Dunlop's memoirs recorded, was that 'two of us represented more than one journal, and had to write, therefore, more than one account of the occurrence.'[37]

Monday's *Freeman's Journal* featured a composite of the first reports telegraphed from Cong under the headline 'The Massacre Near Cong: A Whole Family Butchered', and with the byline 'Special telegram from our special correspondent'.[38] Readers received a lengthy and dramatically entitled two-column account of the murder scene, 'one of the most extraordinary, take it for all in all, ever witnessed in this or any other country.' It is clear also from this account that visiting journalists had been allowed admittance to the Joyce home while the bodies of the murdered family still lay there. The *Freeman's* correspondent expanded on the intimacies of the household in deeply unsympathetic tones:

> The house, I should first mention, is a hovel of the worst Connemara description. The cattle have a separate shelter, but the entire family of six persons – the aged grandmother, the husband and wife, and three children – may be said to have lived and slept almost in one apartment. There is, no doubt, a partition, which serves as an open chimney as well, separating the kitchen from a small apartment opening off it. In this apartment, of about ten feet by five, there slept in one bed of the rudest description, lengthened out by a barrel turned on end,

the old woman (the mother of the deceased) and her three grandchildren – Margaret, Michael, and Patrick, aged 18, 16, and 11 years respectively.[39] Joyce and his wife slept in a small recess formed by an opening being made in the side wall of the house and outer walls, the shape of the bed being built outside. The house contained little furniture, and what there was was of the most primitive kind. When I arrived, the five dead bodies were with one exception lying where they had met their doom. The exception was Michael, who, having survived some time after the attack, had been removed from the bed in which he had been found to the floor of the kitchen, near the fire-place.[40]

The next day's reports filled in further aspects of the murder scene. One of their starkest details was the refusal by local women to give help to the young wounded boy, Patsy, in spite of appeals by Brady, the resident magistrate, for their assistance:

> Groups of peasantry sat on the hillside above the house, where the dead and wounded were lying. They had an ample supply of pipes and tobacco for the 'wake,' and the women cried bitterly. The police were moving about or sitting lazily on the wall, save those who were in attendance on the poor wounded boy Patrick. No one could be got to assist in attending him or nursing him, although Mr. Brady, on his arrival on Friday, appealed to the women, who were then, as on Saturday, gathered in large numbers on the hillside, to give their assistance in nursing the unfortunate lad. He offered any reasonable sum as remuneration, but no one would volunteer for the duty.[41]

This refusal was also given prominence in a long account published in the national *Daily Express*, which reported that the 'eminent Dublin physician' Robert McDonnell, who was staying with Richard McCausland, a local justice of the peace, in nearby Cappaduff, had come to treat the injured boy. The article concluded with a description of the 'child brought out, with its blood-marked and bandaged head, and laid on the improvised ambulance bed,' underlined by the author as 'one of the most distressing sights, I think, ever witnessed.'[42] Patsy was moved to Cong later on Saturday, and the *Freeman's Journal* reported on Tuesday that he was 'making considerable progress towards recovery'.[43] A short article in that day's *Daily Express* reported that the funeral of the five murdered people had taken place and had been attended by 'about 100 of the neighbours from the surrounding mountain district.' It also reported that the remains of Bridget Joyce had been buried with 'those of her first husband', and that the bodies of the four other victims were laid in another grave in the same burial ground.[44] On Wednesday the newspaper focused on Patsy's fate, reporting correctly that he 'is happily, gradually, though slowly recovering', but not enough 'to enable him to do more than articulate a single word or two at a time.' Patsy's status as an Irish monoglot was brought strongly to the fore here: 'Of course, he cannot speak one word of English, but he has been placed under the care of an old woman who speaks both tongues, and who appears kind and attentive.' The *Daily Express* also relayed the hope that his evidence would 'still further strengthen the hands of the crown', and that the boy could possibly identify one or more of the prisoners.[45]

On Saturday, 19 August, the day after Collins and his companions had visited the Finny police hut, two men, Anthony Joyce of Cappanacreha and his brother John Joyce of Derry, gave informations[46] to Resident Magistrate Gardiner through a sworn but unnamed interpreter.[47] Their translated statements are preserved in the court brief and comprise a short version of the events they claimed to have witnessed on Thursday night. The statement by Anthony Joyce described how he had been awakened 'sometime before twelve o'clock' by the sound of dogs barking, had looked out of the door, and 'saw people going up the old road':

> They were a distance away from me, and I went round the house and came out the other end of it. I saw them when I came round the house, and the dogs barking after them. I then went along an old wall, and then along another old wall, and got before them and stooped under the wall and saw them then. I knew them then.[48]

The six men identified first by Anthony Joyce were Martin Joyce, Myles Joyce, Patrick Joyce, and Thomas Joyce (Pat), all four from Cappanacreha; Anthony Philbin of Cappaduff; and Thomas Casey of Glensaul. Anthony's identification was unequivocal: 'I knew every one of them perfectly well for the last twenty years.'

Joyce then recounted following the men to the townland of Derry: 'After they passed, I went after them, until I went to my brother John's house at Derry. I called my brother and his son Pat and wakened them, and they came with me, and we followed them a good distance behind, to see what they would do. We saw them go into Michael Casey's house at Derry. They were not long in it.' According to Joyce, ten men in total came out of Michael Casey's house, the four others being Pat Casey, John Casey, Michael Casey (all three of Derry), and Patrick Joyce of Shanvalleycahill. Once again, Joyce's identifications were unwavering, his tone of certainty accentuated by traces, in translation, of his original idiom: 'I knew these four as well as I did the others. I know them since I got any recollection' (possibly *'ó tháinig mé i gcéill'*).[49]

Anthony Joyce's statement continued with the account of how, accompanied by his two relatives, he followed the men 'along the road for some distance', 'along then through the fields', 'still followed, to see where they would go to', until they reached 'John Joyce's street of Maamtrasna.'[50] His evidence as to what and whom he witnessed at the scene itself was more equivocal: 'They came to the door of Joyce's house, and we heard a noise, the same as if they were breaking it in. They did get in. I cannot say if they all went in. I heard murder and shouting inside, and I ran away. The three of us ran away. I ran away, I was so much frightened. I did not wait to see them afterwards. I went home straight.' Presumably in response to questioning (which is not recorded), his testimony ended with an explanation as to his reason for following the ten men: 'When I followed them first, I did so to see if they would go to my brother's house, as I was afraid. My brother has lost sheep, and so have I. When they were breaking the door in, we were in the field of potatoes under the house.'[51]

Anthony Joyce's 'information' was supported by that of his brother John, who described seeing 'six men going into the house of Michael Casey of Derry'.[52] He reported: 'Michael Casey's house is within two or three score of yards from my house. After a short time ten men came out of Casey's: I was nearer to them when they came out than when they went in, and I knew them then.' The ten men identified by John Joyce matched those names given by his brother, and he similarly attested: 'I knew them all since they grew up, and I knew them well.' As in his brother's testimony, their situation as witnesses to the murders was carefully detailed: 'When I heard the screeching and the shouting in John Joyce's house, I was in the tillage garden under the house with my brother and my son.' And John Joyce similarly testified to the existence of earlier acts of agrarian violence in the area: 'I was in dread until they passed my place that they would do something, as my sheep were killed before, and my mare and foal thrown into the lake, with stones about their necks. I followed them, as I thought they were going to do something to somebody else.'[53]

The following day, on Sunday, 20 August, Anthony and John provided formal depositions at the petty sessions district of Clonbur, repeating their testimony and now supported by a third witness, Patrick, John's son; this evidence was further substantiated by a deposition from John's daughter Mary, taken at Clonbur petty sessions on 28 August.[54] The significance of their evidence for the potential success of the murder investigation was immense: within two days of the murders having taken place, three local witnesses had testified under oath to the presence of ten men at the crime scene and had identified all ten men without reservation. The crucial significance of the Joyces' narrative of watching and 'recognition' in securing convictions against the accused is especially visible in a large graphic image, which appeared on the cover of the English *Illustrated Police News* on 25 November 1882 (see Image 18, p. IX). The very first panel was entitled 'The Recognition' and showed a man crouching behind a wall, on the other side of which was the murder party.[55] A series of scenes offered readers a dramatic narrative of the events, including 'The Murder of the Father', 'Shooting the Eldest Son' and 'Murdering the Grandmother and Children', and stark images highlighted the disparity between the numbers of armed killers and the defenceless victims.

'HEARTLESS OPPRESSION': SOCIAL CONDITIONS IN THE ROSS DISTRICT

In 1888, as part of his testimony to the Parnell Commission, Fr William Ganby, a Catholic curate in Clifden, provided an arresting description of the extent of poverty in the Clonbur district in the 1880s.[56] Ganby, who became curate in Clonbur parish in September 1879 and who had lived in Leenane from December 1879 to August 1881, was asked to comment on conditions in the parish of Ross. He began by outlining the parameters of this 'very wild and extensive' parish, which stretched 'from the borders of Lough Mask to Glanagimla near Leenane, at the mouth of Killary Bay, a distance of 25 Irish miles.' Regarding the living condition of the poor, he testified as follows:

> It was wretched in the extreme. There were some extensive graziers who were in possession of lands from which tenants had been evicted in the years 1847, 1848, and subsequently. With these exceptions the destitution of the people was almost incredible. I frequently went to attend sick persons in houses where there was absolutely nothing except the four bare walls.
>
> There is a village near Clonbur called Gorthnarupp, and in this village the houses are more like dog-kennels than human habitations. When administering the sacraments, I was frequently obliged to go out several times to breathe fresh air, so foul was the atmosphere in these miserable hovels.

The villages of Cremlin and Doughty are nearly in the same condition. The holdings consisted of small patches of land varying from two to six acres. It was of the worst possible description. The rents were in all cases far in excess of the valuation – sometimes double and treble the valuation. The people lived entirely on the potatoes grown on this land. They had no other means of substance.

When this crop failed, famine was inevitable.

Crime was almost unknown.[57]

Questioned as to the conduct of landlords toward tenants, Ganby expounded with some force: 'The heartless oppression practised towards the tenants by the landlords of this parish caused them to be looked upon as the worst enemies of the people, and the priests found it hard to keep the parishioners from wreaking vengeance on their oppressors.' One of his examples was Lord Leitrim, who had cleared whole townlands in the barony of Ross: 'The tenants were driven like vermin to the fringes of bogs or to the sides of mountains. The district between Leenane and Maam is a waste. A blackened gable is seen here and there.' Ganby also explicitly alluded to 'the district called Derrypark, near the scene of the Maamtrasna murders,' which he described as 'a huge grazing farm' under the governance of Lord Ardilaun and where prohibitions against taking heath or heather were strictly enforced:

> According to the game laws on this estate, the tenants are prevented from taking heath from their holdings. This regulation, whose infraction is severely punished, is a severe privation to the poor tenants. It is the only bedding they can procure for their cattle. During my residence in Clonbur some miserable looking creatures were fined heavily for this crime, and I am under the impression that some were sent to Galway for a similar offence.[58]

An unnamed witness from Clonbur, who also testified before the Parnell Commission, corroborated Ganby's evidence with respect to the dire results when tenants were unable to cut heath:

> It was in consequence of this prohibition that the people had no bedding for their cattle and subsequently no manure. A further consequence was that their little stock was poorer than it would otherwise be, and finally that the people were obliged to pay as much for artificial manure as they had to pay in rent, so that virtually their rents were 200 per cent above the valuation.
>
> I was in court at Clonbur petty sessions on one occasion when a number of tenants were summoned for cutting heather on the beds on which they paid

rent and taxes. The usual fee of half a crown or a fortnight's imprisonment was imposed on all, save one, who because he merely made the remark that it was too bad to be fined for cutting what grew on the land he paid rent for, had his fine doubled by memorable Scully of Oughterard.

On another occasion I saw over 20 persons, one of them a mother with a few weeks old baby on her arms, going to prison for the same offence. It was a few days before Christmas, so that they spent that festival in jail in order to satisfy their landlord's mania for game.[59]

In September 1892, a decade following the Maamtrasna murders, Major Ruttledge-Fair reported on conditions in the district of Partry, in his role as inspector for the Congested Districts Board. In the electoral division of Ballinchalla, home of Myles Joyce and his relatives, 157 of the 201 families held holdings of under £2 value. The total population of Partry was 6,703 people of whom, the inspector observed, 'more than 550 labourers in the district migrate annually to England and Scotland, leaving home in May and June and returning in October, November and December. They earn on an average £10 each, free of all expenses.'[60] Writing of the nearby 'Joyce country' (which included the electoral divisions of Clonbur, Cong and Ross), Ruttledge-Fair reported that 'The people of this district chiefly depend on the profits derived from grazing cattle and sheep, especially the latter, on the mountain commonages adjoining their holdings, and also by weaving and spinning coarse flannel and stockings.' The local domestic economy depended on a vital supply of credit for much of the year: 'So far as food supplies are concerned, the people generally pay cash for what they purchase between the latter end of August and the commencement of February, or in good years for six weeks later. They then run into debt for flour, meal, tea, sugar, etc., etc., till they are able to dispose of their stock. During this period a family in fairly good circumstances would probably incur debts to the amount of £8 or £10.'[61]

Ruttledge-Fair's recommendations for improvements to the area were primarily concerned with remedying what he considered to be its extraordinary isolation: 'The first step that should be taken to improve the condition of the people in the district is the construction of six roads leading to and opening up communication with the thickly populated mountain villages which are at present completely isolated and cut off from means of communication with their market towns.'[62] But what sharply distinguishes his report from most of his contemporaries is his commendation of local work and industry and his recognition of the immense labour required to make the land fit for cultivation:

The people of the district are industrious and thrifty, indeed the district generally is a lasting monument to their enterprise. From the Finny river, its southern boundary, to the northern portion of Tawnynagry Electoral Division near Castlebar, almost all the cultivated land has been reclaimed from barrenness and wildness.

This extensive reclamation was made possible by the proximity of limestone and the facilities for its transit afforded by Lough Mask. Only those, however, who have witnessed the conveyance of limestone from the shores of Lough Mask along the rugged sides of the Partry Mountains where no roads exist, sometimes in panniers, borne by mountain ponies, but more often carried for miles by men or women, can realise the difficulties which have been experienced in carrying out reclamation.[63]

Journalists who visited Maamtrasna in the period after the murders, often staying for a matter of hours, characterised the poverty of the district in much less sympathetic terms. The following account from the conservative daily *Belfast Newsletter*, which appeared on 16 December 1882, a day after the executions, is typical:

Maamtrasna has more than once in the newspapers been described as a village situated near Clonbur, in the county of Galway, but this description is calculated to mislead. It is not a village in the ordinary sense of that term … Mountains lie between, and even such civilising influences as the so-called town can exercise are utterly shut out from the growing generation in the district that has furnished the theatre of a crime which it is not too much to say has astonished the civilised world. It is no wonder that the people are ignorant. They live in what may, by a stretch of imagination, be called a collection of straw-thatched huts. The word collection, however, means a widely-scattered, straggling number of dwellings, little fitted for the accommodation of anything better than pigs and cows. The pigs and cows dwell with the people there, and the sanitary officers are seldom heard of and never seen.[64]

Less usually, the reporter went on to describe matters of language, education and religion. He depicts an Irish-speaking community largely unable to comprehend the languages of religious instruction (mostly Latin and English) and where many young women avidly seek to learn English:

The nearest school is miles away; the nearest place where God is worshipped is as far. Nominally, the religious persuasion of the people is Roman Catholic, but in sober truth their religious persuasion is nil. The schoolmaster has not taught them, and they speak a vulgar dialect of the Celtic tongue; the priest has not taught them, and their morals are regulated by a doubly vitiated creed. Many of the younger women reckon a knowledge of English an accomplishment, and in the same way that the town-bred girl seeks proficiency at the piano, they endeavour to gather up an oral knowledge of the English tongue. This they do weekly, standing or kneeling on the sanded floor of the distant country chapel. The teacher is really the priest. His sermons are mostly preached in English, and he is not always particular whether they are suited to the capacity of his hearers or not. Both the Latin and the English are generally misunderstood. They are both equally foreign to the benighted peasants of Maamtrasna, and little effort is made to bring even the more familiar home.[65]

The Ross district had, in the late nineteenth century, one of the highest levels of illiteracy in the country.[66] In 1881 the national figure for illiteracy was 25 per cent of the population (that is, the proportion of the population, five years old and upwards, who could neither read nor write). The figure for Connacht was 38 per cent, and Galway had the highest proportion of illiterate people of any county (45.8 per cent). The rate of illiteracy in Ballinchalla parish, home to Myles Joyce and his relatives, was significantly higher than even the county rate at 77.1 per cent (72.6 per cent for men and 81.1 per cent for women).[67] Putting this more directly, in the parish in which Myles Joyce and his family lived in 1881, only 32 people (18 men and 14 women) from a parish of 530 could read and write. An additional 74 people (42 men and 32 men) could read only.[68]

The contemporary testimony of Ganby and report from Ruttledge-Fair give some valuable insights into the grinding poverty experienced by many living in the Ross district in the 1880s and the cruelties of the land-lord-tenant system. But what also made the murders in Maamtrasna so notorious, and of such potency even today, is their origin in deep animosity between neighbours, fuelled by familial feuds, and ending in a series of brutal killings. A simple narrative of oppressive landlord and desperate tenant is not sufficient; the bringing to light of the true identities of the seven members of the murder party would ultimately reveal that the 'whys' of the Maamtrasna murders were more directly related to rivalries between small farmers who were growing more economically powerful, and also to acts of intimidation by newly emerging 'strong' farmers against those weaker than themselves.[69] Yet most of those men were just one generation away from desperate poverty, an intimacy with hunger that would have further strengthened both ambition and antagonism. To be poor and uneducated added to the vulnerability of those unjustly charged with murder, since innocence as known among one's near neighbours would not necessarily translate into innocence as determined by law.

'I SLEPT IN THE ROOM WITH MY TWO BROTHERS':
DOMESTIC CONDITIONS AND FAMILY LIVES

In his 1892 report to the Congested Districts Board from the Joyce Country, Major Ruttledge-Fair included a short description of people's homes:

> The dwellings of the people of this district are nearly all of the same description, the houses being built of rough stones; no mortar is used, and they are not plastered. In some houses, there are no chimneys, the only exit for the smoke being the doorway, or a small hole made in the roof directly over the fireplace. At least 90 per cent of the houses are thatched, either with straw or rough sedge, and they are very small, often consisting of only one apartment, and seldom more than two. Cattles &c, &c, are kept in the houses during the winter, generally occupying one end of the kitchen.[70]

Surveys of the Joyces' dwelling were solicited by the prosecution case, and these were further disseminated by a voyeuristic press who delighted in reproducing, for the titillation of their readers, descriptions of a home (more usually termed 'hovel' by them) in which six or seven people lived in two small rooms. In August 1882 the crown commissioned a map of the murder scene from a consulting civil engineer, named John Henry Ryan[71] (see inside back cover). Ryan included in the left lower corner of the map a rough sketch plan of the interior of the Joyces' home at Maamtrasna[72] (see Image 16, p. VII). On a scale of ten feet to one inch, it shows the small room where most of the family slept, the kitchen with its recessed bed area (where the married couple slept) and a cow house within the same structure along with an adjoining barn. An early *Freeman's Journal* account, published 21 August 1882, described the kitchen interior in some detail, noting that a partition which 'serves as an open chimney as well' separated the kitchen from the small recessed apartment and that the apartment, measuring about ten feet by five feet, contained a bed 'of the rudest description, lengthened out by a barrel turned on end.'[73]

Ironically, of the surviving contemporary records, one of the most vivid responses to the living conditions experienced by the Joyce family was that provided by Earl Spencer in a private letter to Queen Victoria. Spencer, the Lord Lieutenant of Ireland, visited the Maamtrasna murder scene in September 1882 and on his return to the Viceregal Lodge wrote to the Queen as follows: 'It is incredible to believe that human beings could live in such a hovel as that where the murder was committed, it resembles much more a rude cavern in a rock, so cramped for room and destitute of light and ventilation as the house is.'[74]

Some of the police evidence gathered in the days after the murders offers a glimpse into how these large households negotiated such cramped domestic spaces. For example, some of the alibi statements gathered from relatives of the Maamtrasna accused refer in some detail to families' sleeping arrangements. In a statement taken on 28 August, Honor Joyce of Cappanacreha (the niece of Myles Joyce, whose father Paudeen and brother Tom had been arrested a week earlier), testified as follows:

> I live with my father; my sister Mary sleeps in the loft over the kitchen, and when any strangers used to come the way, I used to sleep with my sister on the loft. I recollect the night the Joyces were murdered. My brother came home the day before the murder ... I slept in the room with my two brothers, Tom and little John. We all slept with our heads the same way. I heard him, Tom, getting up to tie the cow.[75]

Another instance is the deposition of Constable John Johnston, one of the eyewitness accounts of the murder scene with which this chapter began. Johnston recounted finding three bodies in the kitchen: John Joyce who lay naked on the floor, Michael Joyce, lying badly wounded, and 'lying behind him in the same bed his stepmother, Bridget Joyce [who] was quite dead.' In the other room and in its one bed lay the old woman Margaret Joyce and her granddaughter Margaret 'lying with her head towards the old woman's feet', the girl's head 'partly raised up' and 'resting on a piece of timber or board at the foot of the bed'. Beside her, 'lying about the centre of the bed' and 'in the same direction as his grandmother' was her brother Patsy.[76] The minuteness of detail comes from a trained police constable doing his job and, read at this historical distance, it can offer valuable social insights; yet it also marks a gross intrusion into the intimacies of a family's life by observers accustomed, then as well as now, to different domestic norms.

LOCH NA FUAITHE: FAMILY RELATIONS AND FAMILY HATREDS

Both at the time and subsequently, one of the most compelling aspects of the Maamtrasna case is the consanguinity of its main protagonists: Anthony and John Joyce, the chief prosecution witnesses, were first cousins of the murdered man, John Joyce, and also first cousins of the accused men Myles, Martin and Paudeen Joyce. The names of the main protagonists in the Maamtrasna events can be difficult to distinguish when given in English, but their Irish-language names convey much more precisely both the relations between individuals and the three distinct family lines. Named after their father 'Maolra' or 'Myles', Anthony (Antoine Mhaolra Seoighe) and John (Seánín Mhaolra Seoighe) were 'Maolra Seoighe', or 'the Maolras of Cappanacreha and Derry', as was John's son Patrick (Páidín Mhaolra Seoighe). The victim John Joyce, or Seán Mháirtín Antoine Seoighe to give his full name in Irish, was one of 'the Máirtíns', called after his father Máirtín or Martin.[77]

Another line of Joyce cousins consisted of 'the Shauns of Cappana-creha,' named from their father 'Seán' or John Joyce, and first cousins of 'the Maolras' and 'the Máirtíns.' This branch included four of the men accused: Myles (Maolra Sheáin Seoighe), Martin (Máirtín Sheáin Seoighe), Paudeen or Patt (Páidín Sheáin Seoighe), and his son Thomas (Tomás Pháidín Sheáin Seoighe). Three of the other men accused were from the Casey family of Derry: Michael (Mícheál Ó Cathasaigh), his nephew Pat (Pádraig Shéamais Ó Cathasaigh), and Pat's brother 'Little John Casey' (Seáinín Beag Ó Cathasaigh). Among the other accused, Patrick Joyce (Pádraig Seoighe) was not related to the other Joyces, nor was Tom Casey (Tomás Ó Cathasaigh) related to the other Caseys; but the tenth man Anthony Philbin (Antoine Mac Philibín) was a brother-in-law of Tom Casey.

Based on the information provided by Crown witnesses and on his own physical survey of the region, engineer Ryan produced a drawing that outlined the respective routes taken by murderers and witnesses on the night of 17 August (see inside back cover). His map also illustrates well the geographical proximity of the key Maamtrasna protagonists. On a scale of 12 inches to a mile, the map delineates the respective locations of the town-lands of Maamtrasna, Derry, Cappanacreha, Shanvalleycahill, and Derry Park, bounded on the south by Lough Mask and with the road to Maam leading from the west. At the most westerly point of the map, the scene of the murder is highlighted. Along the road east, the townland of Derry stretches to the homes of the accused John, Patrick, and Michael Casey and to the nearby home of witness John Joyce. What is especially evident from the map is how close the homes of the accused were to those of the chief prosecution witnesses: Michael Casey's home, according to John Joyce, was only 'two or three score of yards from my house'.[78]

Set apart from the others, in the northwest of the townland, is the house of 'Big' John Casey, a local strongman who is reputed to have played a large part in orchestrating the murders but was never arrested.[79] North and east of Derry lie the townlands of Cappanacreha and Shanvallycahill. Shanvally-cahill was the home of Patrick Joyce, the first man to be tried for the Joyce murders. Cappanacreha, just over two miles from the murder scene, was where four of the Maamtrasna accused men lived: Myles, Martin, Paudeen and Tom Joyce. It was also the home of witness Anthony Joyce, whose house, as the map shows, was situated between those of Myles and Paudeen.[80]

Ryan's map indicates, at its western corner, the murder scene and also the nearby home of John Collins. In fact, the home of the Joyce victims was one of a row of some ten houses along a narrow road, and many of the neighbouring families, named O'Brien or Joyce, were related either to John or to his wife Bridget.[81] In his 1884 pamphlet, Tim Harrington drew attention to the 'strange' fact that so many relatives 'lived within a hundred yards or so of the house' in order to question why the witness Anthony Joyce had not sought their help 'to stay the hands of the assassins'; the disturbing fact that such close neighbours, and relatives, did not themselves intervene during the violent events was left unquestioned.[82]

For governmental records, the Maamtrasna home of the murdered John Joyce and his family was located in the civil parish of Ross and barony of Ross.[83] In 1882 the townland of Maamtrasna was situated in County Galway (in 1898 it was transferred to County Mayo under official adjust-ments to county boundaries). According to the census of 1881, the townland of Maamtrasna had 21 houses with a population of 108 people (50 men and 58 women).[84] The nearby townlands of Cappanacreha, Derry, Derrypark, and Shanvalleycahill (along with Dirkbeg and two inhabited islands in Lough Mask) belonged to the parish of Ballinchalla, also in Ross barony.[85] Cappanacreha, home of Myles Joyce and his relatives, had 24 houses inhab-ited by 122 people; Shanvalleycahill, home of the newly-married Patrick Joyce, consisted of 20 houses occupied by 107 people; and Derry, home of the Casey family, was the most populous of the townlands with 44 houses and 241 people.[86]

Griffith's Valuation for the area was compiled in 1855.[87] For the townland of 'Maumtrasna', 15 occupiers are listed with a total value of 39 pounds and five shillings.[88] The rateable annual valuations in the townland were comparatively high: the highest was held by Daniel O'Brien at £5 while one of the lowest was held by a man called Patrick Joyce (at £1 10s. for land and 5s. for buildings). From the cancelled valuation books held at the public Valuation Office in Dublin, more information can be gleaned as to what size of holding was owned by some of the main protagonists in the Maamtrasna events and how these compared.[89] The fullest record exists for the murdered John Joyce who, in 1870, acquired the lease for a holding of 24 acres in the townland of Maamtrasna, previously held by a 'Catherine Joyce'; John Joyce would appear to have leased land in nearby Derrypark prior to this point.[90] A holding of 24 acres was the biggest in the townland in 1870 (many others were only from five to nine acres), but its rateable valuation (at £1 15s.) was significantly lower than those of his neighbours, suggesting a poor quality of land.[91]

According to the civil marriage records, on 13 February 1879, John Joyce of Maamtrasna, a widower and landholder, married Bridget or Breege O'Brien (née Casey), also of Maamtrasna, who was listed as a landholder in her own right as well as a widow.[92] John Joyce was then the father of four children, and their mother's death seems to have taken place five years before, just months after the birth of Patsy.[93] Bridget's first husband, Daniel O'Brien, was a significant landholder, according to *Griffith's Valuation*, and was much older than she: when he died in 1874, at the age of 75, Bridget was in her late thirties.[94] According to some newspapers at the time who drew on local informants, John Joyce had been evicted from a previous holding and all of his property came from his wife;[95] this would appear an exaggeration since Joyce had held a lease in Maamtrasna for some time before this but his marriage to the landholding Bridget O'Brien in 1879 certainly consolidated his economic position significantly.[96]

The huge contemporary impact of the Maamtrasna deaths is visible even in these formulaic state registers. In one of the ledgers, the observation column alongside the listing for the 24-acre Joyce holding includes a pencilled comment dated 1882: 'whole family murdered', and a year later, a comment in pen noted that the farm had been made 'vacant by the murder of the family in August 1882.'[97] Subsequently, the land remained vacant for many years.[98] Traces of the murders' lingering effect can still be seen in 1895 when the record for the holding was adjusted and a line struck through the valuation for any buildings; in all the subsequent records only a land valuation is recorded and the holding was never again inhabited.[99]

In nearby Cappanacreha (parish of Ballinchalla), home of Myles Joyce and his relatives, 18 occupiers are listed in 1855, with lands leased from the Earls of Leitrim and Charlemont. The total valuation for the townland was £31 19s., and individual occupiers held much poorer properties than their Maamtrasna neighbours. The cancelled valuation books are less informative

here, but they suggest that, in the early 1880s, Myles Joyce, recorded officially as 'Patrick Joyce (Myles)', held a lease for land valued at £1 2s. and for
buildings valued at 5s.[100] A common practice was for holdings to be leased
jointly but this could also become the source of bitter contention, as could
the custom of grazing sheep and cattle on the surviving commonage lands.

Drawing on local stories that were still circulating a century later, Jarlath
Waldron suggested that deep animosities had developed in the mid-1860s
between the families of Anthony and John 'Maolra' Joyce and their neighbours over land newly allocated from the sons of Shaun Joyce to the Maolra
Joyces.[101] Disputes over the trespassing of animals and allegations of sheep-
stealing further strengthened family conflicts, leading Waldron to suggest
that the valley could easily have been called 'the Valley of Vendettas'.[102]
In September 1879, Anthony Joyce was accused of sheep-stealing at the
Clonbur petty sessions but he was acquitted of the charge at the Galway
quarter sessions of the following year. In September 1880 his wife Margaret
levelled a charge of assault against Anthony's first cousin Myles Joyce
and his wife Bridget, and against Myles' brother Paudeen and Paudeen's
son Thomas. The charge arose out of a quarrel about boundaries between
holdings and about the trespassing of Anthony's and Margaret's animals
onto their cousin's adjoining lands. Although Myles Joyce issued a counter
charge of assault, this was dismissed and the primary charge brought by
Margaret Joyce was found to be proven. Myles Joyce, Paudeen Joyce and
Thomas Joyce were each fined 20s., with 2s. 6d. in costs, or one month's
imprisonment (with one-third of the fine to go to the complainant); Myles'
wife Bridget was fined 10s., with 2s. 6d. in costs, or a default term of two
weeks in prison. Myles did not pay the fine, due most likely to financial
hardship, and the Galway prison register shows that he spent a month there
from early December 1880 to early January 1881.[103] Crucially, in August 1882,
as evidence was gathered and alibis checked, members of the local constabulary such as Constable Johnston, who had arrested Myles Joyce two years
earlier and who was familiar with the longstanding conflicts between the
families, would deploy these past incidents, erroneously, as evidence of
Myles' guilt in murder rather than as solid grounds for scepticism regarding
the testimony of the Joyce crown witnesses.

While this past history might account for the false incrimination of
Myles Joyce, the motive for the brutal murders that lie at the heart of the
case is more elusive. Harrington, writing just two years after the events and
drawing from his visits to the area and conversations with many local people,

strongly emphasised the leading role of 'Big' John Casey in the murders, arising out of a fierce animosity between him and John Joyce.[104] According to the court brief, 'Big' John was briefly questioned by the local police in late August 1882. In his information, he acknowledged that there had been a history of bad relations between him and the murdered man and that he had accused John Joyce 'about four years ago of stealing sheep from me'.[105] Supporting evidence for Harrington's theory appeared in the *Freeman's Journal* in September 1884 from a high-profile source: the Archbishop of Tuam, Dr MacEvilly. MacEvilly's informant was a local magistrate who described a long-standing conflict between John Joyce (with others) and members of the Casey family, including a violent assault on John Joyce over ten years before and 'a perpetual feud among the parties ever since, each injuring the cattle of the others, suing them for trespass, etc.'[106] One startling detail from this source is that John Joyce's second wife (born Bridget Casey), who was one of the five murder victims, was related to the Casey faction and, according to the magistrate, was 'said to be implicated in the quarrel'.[107] Antagonisms would appear to have been fuelled further by John and Bridget's marriage and the resulting consolidation of Joyce's local status versus that of Casey.

These are tantalizing insights into a community's hidden history, and yet they, too, fall short of accounting for why almost an entire family lay shot and battered, 'all quite dead', in their home on the morning of 18 August 1882.

— 2 —

LANGUAGE SHIFT

'Have you Irish?'

'What is the matter with her?' The man hesitated a reply, either from want of
English or of power to express himself; at last he said—
    'Have you Irish?'
    'Enough to understand you,' replied O'Brien, in the same language.
Lady Morgan, The O'Briens and the O'Flahertys (1827) [1]

The fate of the Irish language in the nineteenth century is most often
characterised in sweeping terms as a tale of loss and of inexorable decline.
Nationalist versions of that cultural narrative have inflected some of its
details differently, by emphasising the role of an oppressive state educational system or by illustrating instances of the language's heroic survival or
by foregrounding the still more heroic tale of the language's (partial) resurgence. Yet all of these tellings and retellings of the story of language change
share certain 'predestinarian assumptions' – to borrow Vincent Comerford's
useful phrase – namely, assumptions of cultural loss and inevitable language
change. Thus, the figure of 38,121 monoglot Irish speakers in the 1891 census
(or the more graphic statistic of under one per cent of the population) is
commonly cited to indicate the near death of the language. In the more
nuanced analyses of language shift offered by Garret FitzGerald and
Brian Ó Cuív in the 1980s and 1990s, the survival of the language in a few
monolingual areas in 1891 points to the continuance of Gaeltacht (Irish-
speaking) regions in the late twentieth century. [2] But even their influential
and insightful studies largely ignore the figure for bilingual speakers of Irish

and English in 1891: 642,053 in 1891, or almost 14 per cent of the population.[3] In 1881, when the census recorded 64,167 people as speaking Irish only, the figure for bilingual speakers was 885,765: 17 per cent of the population.[4] The barony of Ross at the time in which the Maamtrasna murders took place had an especially high proportion of Irish-language speakers: in 1881 7,350 of its 8,260 population were listed as Irish speakers, approximately half of whom (3,714) were monolingual.[5] Consequently, a full investigation of what occurred in Maamtrasna in 1882 also requires re-examining the larger history of language shift in late nineteenth-century Ireland.

The social reality that extensive bilingualism, as well as degrees of Irish monolingualism, continued in some areas of the country into the late nineteenth century is rarely explored by historians and cultural critics, many of whom prefer a simple model of language change.[6] A shift in language usage from Irish to English was widespread from the mid-eighteenth to the late nineteenth centuries, yet for such a large-scale alteration to take place, then equally large-scale, if sometimes brief, periods of transitional bilingualism must also have occurred. Travellers in rural Ireland, from the late eighteenth to the late nineteenth centuries, encountered families whose children spoke little Irish while their grandparents or parents spoke little English, a familiar and continuing experience today for many different migrant groups. One such account, which details the operation of the infamous 'tally stick,' appears in William Wilde's *Irish Popular Superstitions*, first published in 1852.[7] In the opening chapter, entitled 'the way to learn English' William Wilde recalled a visit, 'some years' previously, to a Connemara village:

> the children gathered around to have a look at the stranger, and one of them, a little boy about eight years of age, addressed a short sentence in Irish to his sister, but meeting the father's eye, he immediately cowered back, having to all appearance, committed some heinous fault. The man called the child to him, said nothing, but drawing forth from its dress a little stick, commonly called a scoreen or tally, which was suspended by a string around the neck, put an additional notch in it with his penknife. Upon our inquiring into the cause of this proceeding, we were told that it was done to prevent the child speaking Irish; for every time he attempted to do so a new nick was put in his tally, and when these amounted to a certain number, summary punishment was inflicted upon him by the schoolmaster.[8]

Wilde's challenge to the child's father makes for compelling reading, as does the parent's responding self-justification. Not surprisingly, this is a passage quite frequently cited by subsequent writers on Irish folklore and culture:[9]

> We asked the father if he did not love the Irish language indeed the man
> scarcely spoke any other; 'I do,' said he, his eye kindling with enthusiasm;
> 'sure it is the talk of the ould country, and the ould times, the language of my
> father and all that's gone before me the speech of these mountains, and lakes,
> and these glens, where I was bred and born; but you know,' he continued, 'the
> children must have larnin', and, as they tache no Irish in the National School,
> we must have recourse to this to instigate them to talk English.'[10]

If the British-sponsored national schools are the institution most maligned
in folk tradition for sponsoring an abandonment of Irish, the most infamous individual is Daniel O'Connell; yet O'Connell was an accomplished
bilingual speaker who not only used Irish extensively in his private life but
also deployed it to strategic effect in various public addresses.[11]

Language competence among the families of the Maamtrasna accused
varied greatly: based on the official records of the arrests, Patrick Casey
could understand English but his monolingual brother John and uncle
Michael required the services of an English-speaking interpreter. Details
from the arrests and subsequent trials confirm that the brothers Martin,
Paudeen and Myles Joyce were monoglot Irish speakers; Myles' nephew
Tom may have some limited competence in English and the two 'approvers'
Anthony Philbin and Thomas Casey were bilingual speakers as was Patrick
Joyce from Shanvalleycahill, the first man to be tried. Even these few examples point to a complex social history of language change and generational
difference as late as the 1880s in rural Ireland: what socio-linguists term 'the
messiness of actual usage'[12] within and across individual families, in people's
day-to-day interactions among rural communities, and by extension within
the baronies and counties recorded by official census statistics.

If 'Ireland was at all points between 1750 and 1850, an intensely bilingual and diglossic society,' as Niall Ó Ciosáin observes,[13] what traces exist
of the continuance of bilingualism in many regions in later nineteenth-
century Ireland, and when and how did being a monolingual or bilingual
matter? The events at Maamtrasna starkly illuminate the different fates
of those who could speak English and those who were monoglot Irish
speakers, when they were compelled to interact with the judicial system.
Consequently, a closer examination of this case suggests that our prevailing
narrative for language change in post-famine Ireland (Irish to English)
needs to accommodate the many instances of linguistic interconnectedness
and gradual transition: the baronies, towns, parishes, villages, and townlands in which English and Irish co-existed, and the forces and influences

which led families and individuals to replace their use of Irish with the use of English.

To repeat, a society cannot undergo a large-scale language shift without there being many instances of 'language crossings' and periods of transitional bilingualism, yet this remains a much under-researched topic in studies of eighteenth- and nineteenth-century Ireland. One factor is the bluntness of our existing conceptual models. The basic terms 'bilingual' and 'monoglot' fail to capture the wide spectrum of individuals' actual competence in language(s), which can range from full fluency in two (or more) languages to partial knowledge of one or more language to limited comprehension of a language other than one's mother tongue, to a monoglot speaking and comprehension of one language only. This spectrum is hard to identify and to verify, challenges compounded by the reality that such competences can vary hugely over an individual's lifetime. For instance, those who are 'retentive bilinguals', that is, people who have sufficient exposure to a language to comprehend it but not speak it, may lose or expand that ability in later years. And when one seeks to extrapolate from individuals to social groups, the conceptual vocabulary is also limited: what constitutes 'transitional bilingualism' can be difficult to pinpoint with precision, and similarly how this may be differentiated from instances of 'stable bilingualism' where families and individuals continued to use both English and Irish for different social functions over a number of generations.

LANGUAGE AND SOCIETY IN PRE-1851 IRELAND

The national figures for Irish speakers, whether bilingual or monoglot, cannot be firmly established for the pre-famine period. According to the *General Report* to the 1851 census, of a total population of 6,552,386 people, Irish-only speakers comprised 319,602 people and Irish and English speakers 1,204,684 people; to put this in percentage terms, in 1851 23.3 per cent of the population were speakers of Irish of which 4.88 per cent of the population were monoglot Irish speakers and 18.38 per cent bilingual.[14] The language situation prior to 1851 has been variously estimated: writing in 1851, John Windele offered a retrospective estimate for 1731 that two-thirds of the whole community used Irish as their ordinary language, giving a total of about 1,340,000 out of estimated population of about 2,011,000.[15] In 1799, Whitley Stokes asserted of his contemporary situation that 'at least 800,000 of our countrymen speak Irish only and there are at least twice as many more who speak it in preference.'[16] The implication of his assertion is that Irish speakers at the turn of the century constituted almost 2.5 million of a population of about 4.75 million, i.e. slightly over half the population. In his 1812 *Observations*, Daniel Dewar argued that there were two million people 'incapable of understanding a continued discourse in English,' noting that 'even if an exaggeration to the extent of half a million be admitted, there remains a number to be provided with instruction, in Irish, five times greater than the whole population of the Highlands of Scotland.'[17] In his recent study, *An Irish-Speaking Island*, Nicholas Wolf starts with the following observation: 'By the third decade of the nineteenth century, it is estimated that Ireland was home to between three or four million speakers of Irish language, more than any other time in the history of this language community,' i.e. Irish speakers in the 1820s represented the largest ever number in real terms though a declining proportion of the overall population.[18]

Garret FitzGerald's 1984 publication 'Estimates for baronies of minimum level of Irish-speaking amongst successive decennial cohorts, 1771–1781 to 1861–1871' continues to rank as one of the most innovative and revealing analyses of Irish usage in pre-famine Ireland.[19] Projecting backwards into the earlier nineteenth century, on the basis of information for older cohorts from the 1851 and subsequent censuses, FitzGerald estimated that 'something approaching half – perhaps even half or more – of the children in Ireland at the start of the nineteenth century spoke Irish.'[20] A sharp decline in these numbers is visible in the 30 years between the first and fourth decades of the century, and accelerated further between the 1830s and 1860s, especially in areas where the decline had previously been slow. The following statistical summary by FitzGerald is now generally accepted and suggests an acclerating pace of change in language use well before the Great Famine:

> 41 per cent of the cohort born between 1801–11 were Irish-speaking in 1881;
> 28 per cent of the cohort born between 1831–41 were Irish-speaking in 1881;
> 13 per cent of the cohort born between 1861–71 were Irish-speaking in 1881.[21]

The subsequent circulation of FitzGerald's figures has, however, involved a regrettable simplification; thus, for example, a recent historical study features the confident statement that 'only 28 per cent of children born in the 1830s grew up with a knowledge of Irish' whereas FitzGerald's finding is a much more cautious estimate of those born in the 1830s and who, still living in 1881, describe themselves as Irish-speaking.[22] Moreover, FitzGerald is at pains to emphasise that his are minimum figures since some of the older group documented in the 1881 census 'may have forgotten the Irish they had spoken as children,' especially in areas where 'Irish had been dying out during their life-time.'[23] This would suggest that the numbers of monoglot Irish speakers and of bilinguals were higher than recorded, and the existence of this occluded population further points to bilingual practice having, within the cultural life of nineteenth-century Ireland, a much longer and more influential duration. The continuance of macaronic Irish-English verse through the early decades of the nineteenth century, as examined by Liam Mac Mathúna, is another indication of widespread public bilingualism though, as Mac Mathúna also observes, it remains unclear as to whether such bilingualism was rapidly transitional, lasting for as few as two generations in a family, or a stable social feature in early nineteenth-century Ireland.[24] This is a key question in seeking to understand social interactions in the Maamtrasna area in the 1880s where significant numbers of people were bilingual, some were monoglot Irish speakers and a handful were monoglot English speakers, and where linguistic competence differed significantly within families, even among those of the same generation.

The lives of bilingual Maamtrasna men such as Anthony Philbin and Thomas Casey, who had lived in England for significant periods of time, remain for the most part in shadow beyond fleeting references in the crown brief and judicial interrogations. However, two quite detailed biographical trajectories, relevant to the 1830s period, may be established for two other men. These are the emigrant Edmund Ronayne, born in 1832, and schoolmaster Amhlaoibh Ó Súilleabháin. Ó Súilleabháin compiled a now-famous diary between the years 1828 and 1835.

Ronayne's *Ronayne's Reminiscences*, published in Chicago in 1900, provides vivid insights into his early life in an Irish-speaking family and also records his later occasional use of Irish as an emigrant to North America.[25] Ronayne was raised in Gurtrue, near Youghal, County Cork, where he attests, the 'language of the people was Irish, especially in the country places, and even in the inland towns that language was most generally spoken.'[26] All of his immediate family and neighbours in 1830s rural east Cork were monoglot Irish speakers: 'Neither of my parents nor any of their families on either side could speak a word of English, and until I was old enough to go to school, I never heard any other than the Irish language spoken. It was Irish at home, at church, at play: Irish always and everywhere …'.[27] Following his family's move to the town of Killeagh in 1841, he began schooling in English though religious instruction, given after last Mass every Sunday, was 'entirely in the Irish language':

> After last mass every Sunday the boys and girls used to sit on the bare floor, the boys in one part of the chapel and the girls in another, and then some man who could read Irish or had the catechism well by heart used to walk up and down in front of each group, proposing the question and also giving the answer, which the whole class repeated after him. That was how I learned my Catholic catechism, and that was how every boy in the parish of Killeagh learned his.[28]

Ronayne's later career included many adventurous episodes, as detailed in his memoir, including his experiences as teacher for the Irish Society in East Cork, emigrant to Canada, member of the Orange Society in Quebec, member of the Masonic Lodge in Montreal (later a celebrated repudiator of Freemasonry), and pedlar of Fenian paraphernalia, specifically lithographs of John O'Mahoney, in Chicago. Around 1866, he rented rooms on Ontario Street in Chicago, 'only a few days west of Market street, almost the very center of an Irish and Catholic settlement', where his ability to both speak and read Irish became a talking point: 'It soon became generally known that I too had come from "the ould sod", and could speak and read the language, but why didn't I go to mass as all "good Irishmen" do?'[29] Later in his reminiscences he relays a local Chicago account – which he claims has 'never before been published' – that the cause of the 1871 Great Fire was 'some frolic' by a young couple in the O'Leary barn, on the night of a party 'in honor of a relative recently arrived from Ireland'. Here, shared language with an emigrant community makes Ronayne privy to special confidences in spite of his official role: 'I learned these facts some weeks later, when, as an employee of the General Relief Committee, I visited De Koven street, and conversing with the people in the Irish language received the above information in which, as might be expected, I was deeply interested.'[30]

The years 1827–35, roughly contemporaneous with the birth and early years of Ronayne, are the subject of the Irish-language diary of Kilkenny schoolmaster Amhlaoibh Ó Súilleabháin (Humphrey O'Sullivan, c. 1783–1838). Ó Súilleabháin was born in the Glenfesk/Loch Léin area of Kerry near Killarney, son of a schoolteacher; in 1789 the family moved to Waterford and then to Kilkenny.[31] The form of the diary, or *cín lae*, a term coined by its author, is itself noteworthy, marking – in Proinseas Ó Drisceoil's words – a convergence of the traditionally 'public but handwritten form of the manuscript with the private and handwritten form of the diary,' but with a self-conscious awareness of its *léitheoir* or reader who is directly addressed from time to time.[32] And as Siobhán Kilfeather highlighted, the diary also illustrates a particularly interesting dynamic between its contents and 'the material space' of their inscription:

> The ledger is specifically a 'desk' diary printed in English, with columns set out to collect and process information on excise duties … Ó Súilleabháin writes both across the columns of the ledger and in the margins. He replaces the English calendar with entries that recognise a different system of ordering the year – saints' days, pattern days, local market days, days mentioned in Gaelic poetry, anniversaries of private events – and his own way of tracking the years through bird migrations and the blooming of wild flowers.[33]

Ó Súilleabháin's acquisition of English (and Latin) is an example of the increasing prevalence of bilingualism (or in his case the rarer instance of multilingualism), in late eighteenth- and early nineteenth-century Ireland. At a social level, he belonged to a class termed by Lesa Ní Mhungaile as the 'Catholic middling sort,' a group defined by Vincent Morley as 'a middle stratum of comfortable tenant farmers, craftsmen, schoolteachers, publicans, shopkeepers and priests, a stratum which was increasingly literate in English and which maintained a vigorous oral and manuscript-based literature in Irish.'[34]

The text of *Cín Lae,* almost entirely in Irish, comprises an account of quotidian meteorological information along with many references to local, national and international events; this amalgam offers what Ó Drisceoil has rightly summarised as 'a fascinating insight into how the process of modernization was both celebrated and resisted by native speakers.'[35] The more specific subject of language change is occasionally addressed with direct comments but its traces also appear in the diary's form. On 14 May 1827, the author conveys his deep fears as to the influence of the new schools that are teaching *an teanga nua*:

> *An fada go n-imeoidh an teanga Ghaelach so ina bhfuilimse ag scríobh? Atáid tithe scoile breátha móra dá dtógáil go laethúil chum an teanga nua so .i. an Béarla Sasanach, do mhúineadh iontu. Ach faraor! Níl aon suim dá cur sa teanga bhreá mhín Ghaelach ach ag suaidléirí beaga, ag féachain an bhfaighidís clanna Gael do mhealladh leo chun a gcreidimh nua mhallaithe.*

Translation: Will it be long till this Irish language in which I am writing goes too? Fine big houses are daily being built, to teach in them this new language, the Saxon tongue. But alas! no attention is being paid to the fine smooth Irish language, except by wretched swaddlers, who are trying to see whether they can wheedle away the children of the Gael to their accursed new religion.[36]

Some days previously, at the end of the entry for 11 May, he includes a phonetic rendering of spoken English in the Callan area: 'Vuisen fare var yea now?' 'I was sooin praties pon Ned a Grah's ground.' 'Vuel Ime gooen to Caln to sell milk. Vuill you take a dhrink?'[37]

The diarist's interest in global affairs, in Europe and beyond, is notable throughout, as in the references, via the *Kilkenny Independent*, to the 1828 Russo-Turkish War and the 1830 revolutions in France and Belgium, and to his empathetic commentary on the plight of the Irish in Montserrat (1 April 1831): '*Is clos dom gurb í an teanga Ghaelach is teanga mháthartha i Montserrat san India Thiar ó aimsir Oilibher Cromaill, noch do dhíbir cuid de chlanna Gael ó Éirinn gusan Oileán sin Montserrat. Labharthar an Ghaeilge ann go coiteann le daoine dubha agus bána.*' A translation of this passage is: 'I hear that Irish is the mother tongue in Montserrat in the West Indies, since the days of Oliver Cromwell, who transported numbers of the Children of the Gael to that island, Montserrat. And now Irish is spoken there by people, black and white.'[38]

Within Ó Súilleabháin's life, Irish clearly functions as the language of commerce and politics as well as the domestic realm; thus, his diary entry for 8 July 1832 records his attending a large assembly at Ballyhale or *comh-thionól Bhaile Héil* at which he himself spoke in Irish:

Bhí céad míle fear ann, an chuid is lú de. Bhí fiche míle marcach ann. Bhí fir Chontae Loch Garman agus Chontae Thiobraid Árann ag cur in aghaidh deachú agus sraith teampaill agus ag iarraidh an pharliament do thabhairt thar ais go Baile Átha Cliath. Labhras i nGaeilge ann.

Translation: I was at the meeting of Ballyhale, near Knocktopher and Carrickshock. There were a hundred thousand men there at the very least, of whom twenty thousand were on horseback. We had there the men of Kilkenny County, Waterford County, Wexford County and Tipperary County opposing tithes and Church cess, and demanding the restoration of the parliament in Dublin. I spoke Irish there.[39]

However, later in the diary, a number of brief entries in English attest to the growing power of the language, a wider social development which was directly to the detriment to his own career. Thus, the entry for 8 September 1831, recording the close of his school, is rendered bilingually: '*Lá breá gréine néaltana ciúin. D'fhág Clann Shealbhaigh agus Chéitinn mo scoil. Bhriseas suas. Níl aon scoil agam anois.* Ceased teaching on the 8th Sept. when my school consisted of 3 Shellys, 2 Keatings, Townsend, Going, Walker and Grainger and Loughlan.'[40] And on 3 March 1833 an entry commencing in Irish ends in English: '*Tháinig Maor Mór na bpíléirí* (Major Brown) *ag scrúdú daoine in aghaidh an phíléir noch do mharaigh an capall inné* ... Commenced at T. Corr's, teaching at 10s. pr. mt.'[41]

For the second half of the nineteenth century, and in particular after 1881, census data exist with regard to language usage in Ireland: the language question was asked in Irish census schedules from the very early date of 1851 (as part of a question on education) and as a stand-alone question from 1881. As is well known, very few of the original returns from 1851 survive, the majority of these papers having burnt in the 1922 Four Courts fire.[42] That fire infamously destroyed all of the census returns for 1821, 1831, 1841, and 1851 (apart from a handful of records); a less well-known fact is that most of the census records for 1861–91 were pulped for waste paper in 1918. Consequently, most historians have tended to view the question of language-use as largely 'unanswerable' from census data, given the absence of individual schedules that could chart the dynamics of language-use and the trajectories of language change within specific families. Yet, as the following section will explore, surviving documentation does enable a fuller understanding of why and how the language question was first asked in Ireland, and shows the significance of the 1851 census within the longer narrative of language change in nineteenth-century Ireland. In addition, some fragmentary archival evidence and surviving individual returns can illuminate both the nature and limitations of the census results through specific family examples.

'THE PEOPLE WILL HUMBUG US': LANGUAGE AND CENSUS IN 1851

In early 1851 the census schedules distributed in Ireland, unlike their counterparts in England, Scotland and Wales, featured for the first time a question about the use of languages (English and Irish). Such an inclusion was remarkably early when compared to census practice internationally: the first country to introduce a language census question was Belgium in 1846 with Prussia and Switzerland following in the 1850s,[43] and the Irish initiative preceded by two years the first International Statistical Congress (1853) which inaugurated a European debate as to whether a question on the 'spoken language' should be included in censuses.[44] When compared with its Celtic relatives in the United Kingdom, Ireland was also a pioneer: the enumeration of Gaelic speakers in Scotland was introduced in 1881 while the first census to collect data relating to the prevalence of the Welsh language was in 1891.[45] To situate this in a wider international context, the languages of India were enumerated for the first time in 1891, and in 1890 the Census Bureau in the United States introduced a question about languages into its family schedule, with the 'inquiry' phrased as follows: 'able to speak English. If not the language or dialect spoken'.[46] Canada introduced a language question in 1901 with three components asked of persons five years of age and over: 'Can speak English,' 'Can speak French' and 'Mother tongue (If spoken)'.[47]

Since census entries on language are usually self-declarations by individuals as to their language competence, their reliability can be open to question. The stated fear by one Irish census official in 1851 that 'the people will humbug us'[48] was most likely a concern that respondents, eager to appear 'modern', would overstate their knowledge of English to the RIC members who distributed and collected the census forms. On the other hand, the 1891 Welsh census, the first to include a question of language in Wales, was the subject of national controversy when the author of the *General Report* accompanying the published census alleged that a large-scale 'fixing' of census returns had occurred to inflate the numbers of monoglot Welsh speakers.[49] His comment, included in a section entitled 'Untrustworthiness of the returns', reads like an early progenitor of Myles na gCopaleen's *An Béal Bocht*: 'Indeed, so desirous do many householders appear to have been to add to the number of monoglot Welshmen, that they not only returned themselves as speaking Welsh, that is, Welsh only, but made similar returns as to infants who were only a few months or even only a few days old.'[50]

Elsewhere in Europe in the late nineteenth century, census questions on language also served as a flashpoint for debates concerning the codification of the nationality of individuals, with the interpretation of terms such as 'spoken language', 'native language', 'mother tongue' or 'language of use' being highly factious.[51] For example, the definition of 'spoken language' as 'language of use' (*Umganssprache*) rather than 'mother tongue' was an especially contentious issue for Czech nationalists on the language border with

Germany between 1880 and 1910.[52] In Belgium, the 1910 inclusion of a census question regarding language 'most frequently used' led to much controversy, with charges that many Belgian parents of Flemish descent had chosen French as the 'language they *wished* their children would use in public'; subsequent controversies, culminating in 1947, would lead to the elimination of the question from the Belgian census.[53] In nineteenth-century Prussia, Hungary, and Imperial Russia, the use of the term 'mother tongue' included the implicit assumption that the individual's response could change over his or her lifetime, a point made explicit in this instruction within the 1910 Hungary census schedule: 'it may happen that the mother tongue of the child differs from that of the mother.'[54]

From the outset, the phrasing of the Irish language question emphasised language speaking as the key criterion, and for the censuses of 1851, 1861 and 1871 it formed a footnote to a question on Education. The instruction to enumerators read as follows: 'The word "Irish" to be added in the Education Column to the name of each person *who speaks Irish, but who cannot speak English*; and the words "Irish and English" to the names of those *who can speak both the Irish and English Languages*' (emphases in original).[55] The speaking of 'English only' was thus the official default or standard position which did not require an explicit denotation. Yet the wording of the Irish census, in acknowledging and recording bilingual usage (those '*who can speak both the Irish and English Language*'), was in marked contrast to the prevalent tendency in other countries to assign a single primary language and actively resist double or hybrid responses.[56] Such hybrid responses to the Irish census, as will be examined later, would in turn challenge official pronouncements on the direction of language change.

On 25 March 1851, five days before national census day, the *Freeman's Journal* devoted a substantial opening article to the topic of 'The Census' and reproduced a copy of the main schedule. The importance of a newly-introduced question on language was discussed in some detail, and welcome was expressed for an initiative relating to 'the *Irish* language', one that would 'ascertain the localities where, and the number of persons by whom, that tongue is now spoken.'[57] However, from the Freeman's editorial perspective, the language question was also unquestionably a cultural post mortem:

> This, in a national point of view, is a most useful investigation; and we are glad to find that the subject of the ancient language of Erin has occupied the attention of those engaged in drawing up this table. From causes too numerous here to specify, the Irish, the last remnant of the purest and most original language

of the British Isles, and probably of North Western Europe also, is fast fading from amongst us, and we look upon it as a matter of the greatest importance to have some authorised document left to the historian to say hereafter when, to what extent, and where it existed as a spoken tongue.[58]

The process through which the language question came to be added is quite intriguing, and the surviving papers of Cork antiquarian John Windele and senior government official Thomas Larcom allow it to be reconstructed at least in part. The Dublin-based census commission was under instruction by London's General Register Office, yet vulnerable to influence by a powerful local cultural elite. Windele's papers show that quite intensive lobbying took place in Ireland in early 1851 among Celtic scholars and antiquarians, who argued for the language question to be entered in the census schedules. Robert MacAdam, the Belfast industrialist who was said to have had knowledge of 13 languages, wrote to scholar John O'Donovan on 29 January to ask his support in 'suggesting to the proper quarter the desirableness of using the approaching Census to ascertain the extent of our <u>Irish-speaking</u> population.'[59] O'Donovan in turn sought the help of Windele, William Reeves (the Church of Ireland bishop of Down, Connor and Dromore), and antiquarian Thomas Swanton, urging 'as many of our intelligent scholars' as possible to write to the Registrar-General and Census Commissioners on the question.[60]

The value of featuring a question on language was not agreed among census officials, as Larcom documented. In October 1850 he himself conveyed an interest in tracing the numbers of 'Irishspeaking' to his colleague Farr in London's General Register Office.[61] The issue also appears to have been one of many causes of tension within the Dublin office between William Wilde as Assistant Commissioner and William Donnelly as Registrar-General. On 11 November 1850, Edward Singleton, the Commission Secretary, wrote to Larcom:

> Wilde is pushing hard for his own way on the Census and Mr Donnelly is not inclined to give way to him … On the question of knowledge of the Irish language – Mr Donnelly is very doubtful. He thinks the people will humbug us; the utmost length he will yet go is to add a foot note to the A form requiring that the terms 'Irish language' be written opposite the name of each adult native of the country who cannot speak English.[62]

The grounds for Donnelly's concern are not made explicit here but it seems likely that what he feared was that 'the people' would claim a greater knowledge of English than they possessed, on the grounds that it was the prestige language, and that the numbers of Irish speakers would be understated as a result.[63]

MacAdam's attitude to the issue of 'incorrect returns' was much more sympathetic to the perspectives of those being counted; writing on 14 March 1851, he noted 'there are many people who, when asked by the Police, will be afraid to acknowledge that they know Irish: lest some harm might come of it afterwards.'[64] This is an especially resonant comment (the underlining is by MacAdam) and suggests not only that Irish was associated with subalternity and opposition from an official viewpoint, but also that Irish speakers were aware of this and adjusted their public speaking practices accordingly. MacAdam then made an alternative suggestion, namely to send a circular simultaneously with the census but specifically directed to clergy 'requesting them to ascertain the numbers who speak Irish in their several localities ...'.[65] His plan did not succeed, however, and provoked angry dissent from John O'Donovan. O'Donovan considered the force of religious antagonisms to be an indomitable obstacle and trenchantly attributed blame for the decline in Irish jointly to the Catholic clergy and 'the English':

> I am obliged to you for complying with my request about the Census. We shall obtain some results but I expect that the most of our Irish speakers are in the poor houses ... I know that the Catholic clergy who are the real anti-Irish party at present, are moving heaven and earth to put out the Irish language. I would not, therefore, advise my northern friend to have recourse to them, or any other other denomination of the Irish Clergy. We must take chance! If the Police returns be incorrect we cannot help it, as the jealousy of the antagonistic religions at this moment precludes the possibility of making any efficient use of any denomination of them in the manner suggested by Mr MacAdam. The Gaelic language will be put out by the English in despite of all exertions.[66]

Read in the context of contemporary correspondence, this letter from O'Donovan also stands out for its rare, direct acknowledgement of the grim contemporary reality of post-famine Ireland and its widespread continuing poverty. His fierce condemnation of the role of the Catholic Church as a force for anglicisation would be vindicated, at least in part, by later historians. However, O'Donovan's deep pessimism regarding the language's future was not idiosyncratic and was shared by all his contemporaries. Perusing the correspondence of the time, what is especially striking to a twenty-first century reader is the unanimity among these mid-nineteenth-century commentators, themselves powerful cultural lobbyists, that the census would provide a valuable historical record for an inexorably dying language.

In a lengthy submission to the Registrar General on 27 February 1851, for example, Windele, writing as Secretary of the South Munster Antiquarian Society, employed a discourse of linguistic endangerment and inevitable loss similar in terms to those used by the *Freeman's Journal*, quoted earlier, and richly revelatory of mid-nineteenth-century language ideology. The census, Windele argued, provided 'a highly favourable', even urgent, opportunity for 'the ascertainment of the the number of persons now wholly or in part speaking the Irish language' before its final disappearance:[67]

> We are aware that that it is now impossible to arrest its final decay and disappearance and that a few generations more will doubtless witness its total extinction. We are therefore anxious in observing its final phase that its existing statistics should be satisfactorily ascertained whilst yet the opportunity is afforded.[68]

RESPONSES TO THE 1851 CENSUS

Census night for 1851 took place on Sunday, 30 March. Forms were distributed and collected by the constabulary or metropolitan force, and in some cases verified by them.[69] As part of the instructions for superintendents, a special clause applied to 'those Districts where the Irish language prevails, or that many persons are to be found who do not speak English'; here it was recommended that 'Enumerators should be chosen from persons well acquainted with the Irish language, in order to avoid the necessity and expense of employing interpreters.'[70]

To aid heads of families in completing the form, the census materials included 'pattern tables', providing sample entries for each of the three census tables. Ironically, the sample 'pattern' for the education column only served to make visible the many confusions that could arise from the manner in which the language question was posed (see Image 26, p. XII).[71] The '1st table' lists sample entries for a Moran family of County Kildare, whose head of family, John Moran, is given the entry 'Read [Irish]'; under the Education column, entries for the other family members, including John's wife Eliza, do not contain any indication of language. A strict interpretation of the form would suggest that Moran was partly literate (able to read though not write) *and* a monoglot Irish speaker, unlike his English-speaking family. Much more likely is that the sample was intended to convey that John could speak Irish as well as speak and read English.

A few fragments of the 1851 census survive, largely as a result of requests for copies of census returns made by applicants for the Old Age Pension in the early twentieth century, as evidence of age.[72] The sample is very small and obviously skewed, but it does enable some glimpses into the diversity of linguistic ability within households. One example is that of the Ashe house-hold from Ballinvoher parish in the barony of 'Corkaguiny' in Kerry, all of whose ten members are bilingual with the exception of John Cahallane, a 'farmers labourer', who is a monoglot Irish speaker and illiterate.[73] In the case of families such as the Fitzmorris family in Moybella South, Kerry, both parents are bilingual speakers while their son aged three speaks English only; conversely, in the case of the Downing family of Templemichael parish in the barony of Coshmore and Coshbride, Waterford, the widowed mother, head of family, is listed as speaking Irish and English, while her five children aged between 5 and 15 speak Irish only.[74]

The return for the Cregg family of Tibohine parish, Frenchpark barony, in Roscommon, provides another illustration of the confusion caused by the education and language questions. The table lists the information provided for each of the five family members: the mother and head of household is recorded as bilingual and illiterate; two of her sons are recorded as mono-glot Irish speakers and literate; one son is bilingual and illiterate; and the youngest son can read and appears to be a monoglot speaker of Irish.[75] The related tables which list 'members, visitors and servants of the family' who had died since the last census, make for especially poignant reading; in the case of the Cregg family, three family members had died: the father, Patt Cregg, whose cause of death in summer 1847 was listed as 'swelling in his foot,' a daughter Bridget, aged 17, whose death in autumn 1847 is attributed to 'decay'; and an infant son who died of colic in spring 1843. The relationships of language and literacy as recorded for this family, however, seem unlikely for the period, i.e. monoglot speakers of Irish who were literate. The ages of the older sons might suggest that they received some education in Irish prior to the gradual introduction of the official national school system in the 1830s, where their youngest brother is more likely to have learned to read.[76]

The evidence of this and other returns, along with the sample pattern table, suggests that, in some cases at least, the 1851 findings for monoglot speakers of Irish were overstated and the accompanying figure for bilingual speakers underestimated. Yet more significantly, almost all of the surviving returns attest to significant differences in language usage between generations, testifying to the social disruption within families that rapid language shift inevitably entails but which can remain hidden from nation or region-focused scales of enquiry.

The content of other census schedules in 1851 one may only imagine. The Cappanacreha return for the family of Myles Joyce (then aged around 10–12 years) and his brothers would have contained details of a family none of whose members could read and write and, depending on the constabulary member's adhering to the footnote instruction, may have also recorded their being Irish speakers only. A very different case is the family of another key player in the Maamtrasna trials, prosecutor Peter O'Brien. Born in Clare in 1842, he had – according to the later memoir published by his daughter – some childhood knowledge of Irish, picked up 'from the peasants in Clare', and was raised by a bilingual nurse.[77] The child's ability to speak at least some Irish is unlikely to have featured in the family return, yet its traces would appear in O'Brien's later legal career. In one of his cases as Lord Chief Justice (a post he held from 1889 to 1913), as recounted by his daughter, the case issue depended on 'the exact meaning of a word in the Irish language':

> The services of a professor of Irish, who had written several books in the Irish language, were enlisted, yet he did not speak or understand what the Irish peasant so aptly calls 'cradle' Irish – that is to say, he had not heard it spoken from the cradle, but had acquired it late in life. The professor, according to himself, was a very efficient Irish scholar ...
>
> My father, who, when a boy, had picked up a little Irish from the peasants in Clare, said: 'Now, Professor, can you tell me how to say this simple sentence in Irish – Have you seen a hare pass by here?'
>
> The expert admitted defeat. 'Well,' continued the Chief Justice, 'can you say, Are the hounds in sight?' The Professor had again to acknowledge himself defeated. 'And yet,' said his interrogator, 'you call yourself an Irish scholar. I fear your Irish is not of any practical use.' Turning to one of the Irish-speaking witnesses, my father said a few words to him in Irish. The man, who was overjoyed at being addressed in his own tongue, left the court probably under the impression that the Judge spoke Irish fluently.[78]

This anecdote is part of a long-established tradition of bilingual courtroom humour, to be discussed in more detail in Chapter 4 in which the linguistic competence (or lack therein) of accused, or witness, or judge is made the target of humour. But the case of the 'professor of Irish' – able to read and write but not speak Irish in practical terms – was far from unique among nineteenth-century scholars and antiquarians.

A vexing example is that of William Wilde regarding whom the seemingly simple question – did he speak Irish? – is tantalisingly difficult to answer. Wilde, as Assistant Commissioner, was one of the 1851 census' chief architects and, as discussed earlier, clashed strongly with his colleague Donnelly on the structure of the census forms. As a young boy in Roscommon, he had accompanied his doctor father on local rounds, experiences credited with fostering his interest in the legends and folklore of rural Ireland.[79] At the time of the census-taking, he was still single (he married Jane Francesca 'Speranza' Elgee in November 1851). A year later, he published *Irish Popular Superstitions*; its contents, first published in the *Dublin University Magazine*, were drawn both from childhood recollections and from his experiences while a young medical student working in the west of Ireland in the 1830s, of which it is said he 'often bargained with his country patients for stories, instead of fowl or eggs, as payment for his services.'[80]

Rather than remaining separate spheres of informal and formal activity, the influence of Wilde's folkloric collections can be seen in his census work, not only in his determination that the language question be included but also in his subsequent analysis of the causes of famine mortality in his influential 1856 *Table of Deaths*. As Angela Bourke remarks, 'Wilde's note on marasmus – emaciation and wasting in children – places scientific and vernacular taxonomies of illness side by side. It reflects his understanding of Irish fairy-narratives in both languages and how they were sometimes tragically implemented.'[81]

In his 1965 article on the demographic work of Wilde, Peter Froggatt credits William unhesitatingly with 'fluency in Irish'.[82] However in his biography of the parents of Oscar Wilde, Terence de Vere White relays a lengthy account by 'the late Dr Conor Maguire of Castlemorris' who recalled as a teenager meeting Wilde in Cong. According to Maguire, Wilde was unable to understand any of an Irish-language conversation which took place between the teenager and an elderly local man: 'After that Sir William would always take me with him as interpreter with Irish speaking farmers when he was investigating old forts or any archaeological remains.'[83] An accompanying footnote from De Vere White notes: 'It is surprising to hear that Wilde could not speak Irish.'[84] It is salutary to note the judicious middle ground – between the attribution of full fluency or lack of any competence – which was taken by a contemporary of Wilde, the author of his biographical portrait in the May 1875 issue of the *Dublin University Magazine* who described William as 'understanding somewhat of the language of the people.'[85]

'NACH LABHRANN TU GAEDHEILG?': BILINGUALISM IN POST-FAMINE IRELAND

The actual census findings from 1851, circulated in the *General Report* of 1856, ran against the expectations of many and prompted greater confidence among some commentators as to the language's future. Writing in the *Ulster Journal of Archaeology* in 1858, Robert MacAdam forcefully argued that the published figures on language were an underestimation; here he reiterated his arguments made some seven years earlier as to the popular fear of disclosing one's ability to speak Irish:

> but even this large figure by no means indicates with accuracy the entire number of persons who understand it, or who have learned it in their infancy. It is well known that in various districts where the two languages co-exist, but where English now largely predominates, numbers of individuals returned themselves as ignorant of the Irish language, either from a sort of false shame, or from a secret dread that the Government, in making this inquiry (for the first time) had some concealed motive, which could not be for their good. Their native shrewdness, therefore, dicated to them that their safest policy was to appear ignorant of the unfashionable language. For this reason, we may add very considerably to the number given by the Census.[86]

Over a century later, research on the validity of language census figures in Ulster by G. B. Adams supported MacAdam's thesis. Adams estimated that the census had recorded only about two-thirds of the total number of Irish speakers then surviving, and proposed an alternate figure of 2.25 million speakers of Irish in 1851, based on an estimate of some 4 million on the eve of the Great Famine six years before.[87] And in an argument that would greatly influence the later work of Garret FitzGerald, and which powerfully recognises the hidden realities of transitional bilingualism, Adams demonstrated how the shortfall in numbers of Irish speakers was likely to have increased for older cohorts: 'people who had lived long enough to become effectively bilingual, and for their knowledge of Irish to be overlooked, were more likely to be omitted from the number of Irish-speakers recorded than younger people who could not speak English effectively.'[88]

Similarly by 1857, John Windele had sharply diverged from his pre-census prognostications regarding the inevitable death of Irish to adopt a more confident tone. In an article published in the *Ulster Journal of Archaeology*, he used the census numbers to substantiate his argument that 'as a spoken and written tongue, the Irish is actually more widely disseminated, more generally spoken, and at least as efficiently cultivated by scholars as at any fomer period of its existence.'[89] The 1851 figure for an Irish-speaking population when viewed in absolute terms, he argued, was 'more than double that of the reign of Charles II, when Irish was the tongue of the majority of the nation.'[90] Windele did acknowledge the strategic selectiveness of his statistical evidence but remained determinedly positive regarding the living status of Irish: 'We are therefore within the strict limits of truth in asserting that a *larger* number of human beings use, at the present day, the time-honoured Celtic dialect of Ireland than at any former period – certainly within the last three hundred years.'[91] MacAdam supported a similar argument with a contemporary European analogy, arguing that even the conservative figure of Irish speakers, 'between a million-and-a-half and two millions of persons living amongst us now,' is 'a greater number, for instance, than the entire population of Norway.'[92]

Over the following decades, much debate continued as to the accuracy and completeness of census returns on language. In 1879, E. G. Ravenstein, in his influential article 'On the Celtic languages in the British Isles', cited an address by the Society for the Preservation of the Irish Language which argued that the 'figures shown by the last census returns are by no means to be received as the total, as the council are aware that the returns do not include the entire number of people who speak Irish, since it is well known that many persons, for want of education in the vernacular, and of due appreciation of its value, do not admit their knowledge of the language, and that many more who know it were never questioned on the subject at the census taking.'[93] Two years before, 'Hibernicus', in a letter to the *Nation* newspaper, had argued that the question itself had an ill motive: 'the desire of the government for the extirpation of the Irish language is shown by the inquiry made in each decennial census as to the number of persons in this kingdom who still speak it.'[94] While Ravenstein conceded that the figures might not be 'absolutely correct, more especially as regards persons able to speak a little Irish in addition to English', he held that the census was overall a fair reflection of 'the linguistic condition of Ireland': 'If persons able to speak a little Irish have been omitted, the omissions of those able to speak a little English are in all likelihood more numerous.'[95]

The Society's belief was however vindicated a year later with the publication of a remarkable upward swing in numbers of bilingual speakers recorded in the 1881 census, conducted nationally a little more than a year before the Maamtrasna murders took place. This increase was markedly different to the results forecast by William Wilde who had observed in 1871 with regard to the figure of total Irish-speakers: 'I think I may prophesy that that is the largest number that in future we will ever have to record.'[96] As can be seen in the following table, the census returns showed a downward movement in monoglot Irish and bilingual speakers in 1861 and 1871,[97] but a striking increase in 1881.

	1851	1861	1871	1881	1891
Irish only	319,602	163,275	103,562	64,167	38,121
Irish & Eng.	1,204,684	942,261	714,313	885,765	642,053
Total Irish-sp.	1,524,286	1,105,536	817,875	949,932	680,174
Total pop.	6,552,386	5,798,967	5,412,377	5,174,836	4,704,750

Table 1: *Numbers of monoglot Irish speakers and bilingual speakers, 1851–91 censuses*

What Adams terms the 'upward kink' in bilingual speakers in the 1881 census cannot be explained by an equivalent decrease in monoglot Irish speakers, being of a much larger order than this decrease – over 171,000 people in comparison with some 39,000. Instead, it is generally agreed that it was largely a consequence of a change in the layout of the census schedule. In the 1881 census the question of Irish-speaking ceased to be a footnote and was incorporated into the body of the form, with a specific column dedicated to the use of the Irish language: enumerators were instructed to enter 'Irish' opposite the name of the person who spoke Irish only, and 'Irish and English' for those who could speak both languages; again for those who spoke English only, no entry was to be made. While some contemporary commentators sought to accredit the increase to the success of the newly launched language revival,[98] the change in status given to the language question would seem the more plausible explanation. In turn this supports the arguments by MacAdam and others that the figures for Irish speakers, particularly for bilinguals, were significantly underestimated in the earlier censuses. The 1881 increase also occurred despite a system of double-checking; in areas where Irish was not considered to be widely spoken, and where family forms were returned as speaking Irish, a further check was often requested.[99]

By 1891, the recorded figure for monoglot speakers of Irish had declined to 38,000 or under one per cent of the population. As noted earlier, some historians instance this figure as evidence of the language's near death at the end of the nineteenth century, while language advocates can cite it to underline the revival's subsequent success. All downplay the equally, and arguably more, revealing evidence regarding bilingualism and its continuing significance in late nineteenth-century Ireland. To repeat the figures cited earlier, bilingual speakers constituted 18.4 per cent of the population in 1851 and 13.6 per cent in 1891. To put this differently, in 1891 while just over 4 million of the 4.7 million population were recorded as monoglot speakers of English, 642,053 people were recorded as bilingual and 38,121 as monoglot. Viewed nationally, 136 out of every 1,000 people were bilingual and 8 out of every 1,000 people were monoglot speakers of Irish, though this figure reveals none of the huge differences between regions.

The recorded census figures for the barony of Ross in 1881 and 1891, home to the Maamtrasna victims and accused, are remarkable for a few reasons. In 1881, of a total population of 8,260 people, 7,350 people were recorded as Irish speakers, and just over half of these (3,714 people) as Irish monoglots. Put in percentage terms, 89 per cent of the population of the barony of Ross in 1881 identified themselves for official record as Irish speakers and 45 per cent of the population as monoglot speakers of Irish. Just 11 per cent or 910 people in the barony were English monoglots, who must have lived in privileged isolation from much contemporary local interaction. Of the monoglot Irish speakers, 44 per cent were male and 56 per cent female; of bilingual speakers, just over 50 per cent were male and just under 50 per cent female.[100] The age breakdown by decade, as repro-duced here shows that monoglot speakers of Irish exceeded the number of bilingual speakers in the younger and older age groups, while among those aged between 10 and 30 (male and female) and among males aged 30 to 60, bilingual competence was more common.

Barony		Under 10	10 and under 20	20 and under 30	30 and under 40	40 and under 50	50 and under 60	60 and under 70	70 and under 80	80 and under 90	90 and under 100	100 and upwards	Ages not specified	Total
Moycullen: Irish only	M	1347	1019	542	311	389	322	357	141	74	6	1	0	4,509
	F	1381	1197	607	434	526	398	511	187	100	12	4	0	5,357
														9,866
Moycullen: Irish and English	M	864	1873	970	511	578	448	427	176	65	8	1	0	5,921
	F	861	1612	724	524	545	338	358	107	49	10	0	0	5,128
														11,049
Ross: Irish only	M	478	401	171	98	121	108	163	75	28	4	2	0	1,649
	F	459	422	223	189	232	181	245	72	34	7	1	0	2,065
														3,714
Ross: Irish and English	M	357	594	233	174	183	135	98	45	17	2	2	0	1,842
	F	378	572	286	183	153	93	86	23	15	4	1	0	1,794
														3,636

Table 2: *Number and Ages of Persons who spoke Irish only, and of Persons who spoke Irish and English in Baronies of Moycullen and Ross, 1881*

Barony	Under 10		10 and under 20		20 and under 30		30 and under 40		40 and under 50		50 and under 60		60 and under 70		70 and under 80		80 and under 90		90 and under 100		100 and upwards		Ages not specified		Total
	M	F	M	F	M	F	M	F	M	F	M	F	M	F	M	F	M	F	M	F	M	F	M	F	
Moycullen: Irish only	648	706	597	552	461	430	270	353	316	402	356	360	263	294	133	142	69	95	17	23	1	3	0	0	3,131 / 3,360 / 6,491
Moycullen: Irish and English	1069	990	2260	2072	1114	766	540	526	532	461	460	440	365	273	182	170	104	69	12	2	1	0	0	0	6,639 / 5,769 / 12,408
Ross: Irish only	553	606	875	907	372	338	241	246	203	202	197	142	97	107	72	34	29	28	2	5	0	0	0	0	2,641 / 2,615 / 5,256
Ross: Irish and English	285	296	443	481	207	184	106	118	115	113	102	71	49	56	30	17	16	17	0	3	0	0	0	0	1,353 / 1,356 / 2,709

Table 3: *Number and Ages of Persons who spoke Irish only, and of Persons who spoke Irish and English in Baronies of Moycullen and Ross, 1891*

The census figures for Ross in 1891 are startling. In other local baronies such as Moycullen and Ballynahinch, as one might expect, the figures for monoglot speakers of Irish fell from 1881 to 1891, with changes also in the number of bilingual speakers. In Ballynahinch, 3,664 people were registered as monoglots in 1881 and 2,070 in 1891; bilingual speakers decreased from 15,056 people to 13,149.[101] In Moycullen, the fall in monoglots was from 9,866 people to 6,491 though bilingual speakers increased from 11,049 people to 12,408. In the barony of Ross, however, the total figures for self-declared monoglots rose sharply between 1881 and 1891: from 3,714 people in 1881 to 5,256 in 1881.[102] The number of bilingual speakers decreased from 3,636 to 2,709 people.

This change, which sharply diverges from the trend of neighbouring areas and is counter to any expectation of the nature of language shift at the time, is very difficult to comprehend, and even more so when one looks at divergences between cohorts. For example, the cohort of those between the ages of 10 and 20 in the barony of Ross in 1881 comprised 401 male monoglots and 422 females; in 1891 that cohort, aged between 20 and 30, comprised 372 and 338 monoglots respectively, a decrease in Irish monolingualism in line with changes elsewhere. However, an older cohort, aged 30 and under 40, showed a significant increase in monolingualism: from 98 males and 189 females in 1881 to 203 men and 202 women (aged 40–50); this represents an increase of over 100 per cent in male monoglots.[103] Some surprising divergences in the size of cohorts suggest that at least some of the figures in 1891 may have been inaccurately tabled,[104] but the trend does demonstrate a marked determination among many who lived in this barony to self-declare as an Irish-only speaker. Given that this increase in monoglot Irish speakers is at odds with its neighbouring areas, it further suggests a determined 'closing of ranks' within the Maamtrasna community in the years following the massacres. Similarly, the 1901 census, for which individual schedules exist, shows a strong monoglot character for the area: for example, of the 13 Maamtrasna residents aged between 60 and 70, all were Irish speakers and 11 (7 men and 4 women) were Irish monoglots.[105]

Of course, such statistical overviews fail to capture the myriad linguistic encounters and misencounters that occur in a society undergoing language change. Some contemporary records help to fill this gap and to give human life to the term 'transitional bilingualism'. One of the most eloquent accounts of what Liam Mac Mathúna has aptly termed the 'practical working out of the language shift from Irish to English' is that included by Douglas Hyde in the published text of his famous 1892 address 'The necessity for de-Anglicising Ireland'.[106] The now much-cited passage first featured as a footnote to Hyde's published address. With some similarities to William Wilde's 1852 account, it was intended by Hyde to serve as an admonitory instance of 'the shameful state of feeling – a thousand-tongued reproach to our leaders and statesmen – which makes young men and women blush and hang their heads when overheard speaking their own language.'[107] However, in its ethnographic detail it now reads as a more powerful record of the mobility and dynamism of bilingualism 'in action':

> As an instance of this, I mention the case of a young man I met on the road coming from the fair of Tuam, some ten miles away. I saluted him in Irish, and he answered me in English.[108] 'Don't you speak Irish,' said I. 'Well, I declare to God, sir,' he said, 'my father and mother hasn't a word of English, but still, I don't speak Irish.' This was absolutely true for him. There are thousands upon thousands of houses all over Ireland to-day where the old people invariably use Irish in addressing the children, and the children as invariably answer in English, the children understanding Irish but not speaking it, the parents understanding their children's English but unable to use it themselves. In a great many cases, I should almost say most, the children are not conscious of the existence of two languages. I remember asking a gossoon a couple of miles west of Ballaghaderreen in the Co. Mayo, some questions in Irish and he answered them in English. At last I said to him, '*Nach labhrann tu Gaedheilg?*' (i.e. 'Don't you speak Irish?') and his answer was, 'And isn't it Irish I'm spaking?' 'No *a-chuisle*,' said I, 'it's not Irish you're speaking, but English.' 'Well then,' said he, 'that's how I spoke it ever'! He was quite unconscious that I was addressing him in one language and he answering in another.[109]

In his reading of the Hyde passage, Mac Mathúna rightly underlines the 'truly remarkable' guilelessness of the second account, that of the 'gossoon', which vividly conveys 'the vagueness of the individual's appreciation of the mechanics of the language shift'.[110] Though one might also see another – if unintended – context for the scene, as part of a long-established comic lore in which the seemingly guileless native informant exposes the narrow presumptions of her or his interlocutor.

Hyde's phrase 'I saluted him in Irish, and he answered me in English' in turn provides the title for Grace Neville's insightful study of language shift as evidenced by the holdings in the Irish folklore archives. Here Neville instances a number of examples of 'passive bilinguals', those 'whose active language is English but who understand Irish though they cannot speak it'[111]

– a language group less frequently invoked in studies of language change in Ireland. She also highlights other accounts of native speakers of Irish 'refusing to speak their mother tongue and even denying that they could despite evidence to the contrary.'[112] Many such traces of language crossings, of individuals' comprehension of English and Irish and their flexible use or denial of such knowledge, are recoverable from nineteenth-century sources: travel accounts, fiction, ethnographic sketches, courtroom depictions, etc. Their coming to light requires, however, a conscious movement of perspective away from a view of language shift as inevitable and inexorable towards an appreciation of a culture and society in flux. Such a conceptual shift also poses important challenges to revivalist narratives that champion the heroic status of a restored Irish language or the creative achievement of Hiberno-English and neglect the subtle, even 'messy', dynamics of language change and continuance.

A fuller appreciation of the messiness of actual language usage in nineteenth-century Ireland also requires much more flexible conceptual vocabulary. The term 'bilingual' is a case in point. Introducing her 2014 study *The Bilingual Mind*, Anita Pavlenko writes:

> Who is a 'bilingual speaker'? Laypeople commonly view bilinguals as people with similar levels of proficiency in two languages learned from birth. In contrast, bilingualism researchers define *bilinguals* as speakers who use two or more languages in their everyday lives, be it simultaneously (e.g. in bilingual families) or sequentially (e.g. in the context of immigration or study abroad).[113]

When individuals possessed more than one language in late nineteenth-century Ireland, almost all were more likely to belong to the category of 'dominant bilinguals' i.e. those with greater ease in one language, rather than 'balanced bilinguals', those with 'relatively similar skills in their respective languages'.[114] As Pavlenko remarks, bilingualism is never 'perfect' and in the context of language contact 'it is this "imperfect" bilingualism that leads to language change.'[115] Cultural representations of nineteenth-century Ireland, including the essays of Hyde, include many instances of so-called 'imperfect' bilingualism. The more perceptive of these, however, also acknowledge that bilingual individuals possess positive linguistic capital, what Doris Sommer has termed 'the everyday arts of maneuvering and self-irony'.[116]

In foregrounding the interaction and crossings between languages, the more relevant and useful linguistic term may be that of 'multicompetence' which, as Pavlenko reminds us, 'is not equivalent to two monolingual states.'[117]

The competences of an individual bilingual speaker are crucially shaped by the demands and possibilities offered by her or his wider social relations and the relationship of a specific bilingual speaker to the surrounding community is inevitably a complex one. As Suzanne Romaine usefully observes, 'bilingual individuals may belong to communities of various sizes and types, and they interact in many kinds of networks within communities, not all of which may function bilingually.'[118] Thus long-standing members of a bilingual community may have an excellent 'receptive competence' of one language, including ability to understand, but with 'weak productive skills' in speaking that language.[119]

Such issues return us to the problematics of nineteenth-century census information on Irish and English speakers as discussed earlier. Language, argues Dominique Arel, is best understood as a 'fluctuating marker', that is, 'People often add languages to their linguistic repertoire, and might experience a shift in their "private" language (the language they feel most comfortable with) during their lifetime or, more commonly, might have children whose private language differs from their own.'[120] These forms of linguistic assimilation, she notes, can be portrayed from nationalist perspectives as 'forced, unnatural, and fundamentally illegitimate' – many instances of which can be provided by nationalist Irish historiography. Consequently, in the context of nineteenth-century Ireland, the widespread, albeit often temporary, prevalence of transitional bilingualism in regions, social groups and families remains under-researched and grossly undervalued as a significant cultural phenomenon.

'IRISH DOESN'T SELL THE COW': REASONS FOR LANGUAGE CHANGE

None of this is to gainsay the central importance of language shift in nineteenth-century Ireland. The fundamental question as to why Irish ceased to be used by hundreds of thousands of families who, often in a very short period of time, turned from speaking only Irish to speaking only English remains remarkably difficult to answer, as does the related question as to why – unlike some other European countries – bilingualism was not seen as a practice worthy of retention. Irish historiography to date offers few substantial explanations. With respect to language change in nineteenth-century

Ireland, Joe Lee provides one of the most succinct yet in-depth analyses (somewhat ironically, within the conclusion of his history of twentieth-century Ireland):

> It is instructive to ponder the reasons advanced for the loss of the language in the eighteenth and nineteenth century. The most frequent argument is that the language had to abandoned to ensure Irish participation in the economic progress of the modern world, because 'Irish doesn't sell the cow.' Only a knowledge of English could bring Ireland into the mainstream of material progress by faciliating intercourse with the most advanced British economy, and thus enabling the proverbial cow to be sold at a remunerative price. Strictly speaking, this argument would explain the acquisition of English, but not the loss of Irish, unless it be assumed that Irish brains were too small to accommodate two languages, or that the Irish were simply too lazy, or too utilitarian, to be bothered with the less materially useful one.[121]

Decisions to champion English rather than Irish by prominent political and church leaders in nineteenth-century Ireland (most infamously Daniel O'Connell) had much wider cultural consequences, as Tony Crowley notes: 'not simply that English was correctly perceived as the language of economic necessity – both within Ireland for purposes of emigration – it was also constructed as the language of social and cultural distinction. The hierarchy was set in place: the cultural hegemony of English entailed the cultural inferiority of Irish.'[122]

The fortunes of the Irish language are inextricably related with the history of the state or, as Joe Lee has pithily observed, with the damaging initiatives undertaken by two states, firstly the nineteenth-century British and secondly the post-independence Irish state.[123] Lee's history also provides readers with a welcome comparative European perspective to challenge some enduring economic and linguistic shibboleths. For example, he shrewdly observes that 'the assumption that industrialization was, through some mysterious mechanism, incompatible with minor languages, derives little support from the European record' and underlines that, in relation to a numbers of speakers, 'Irish was not a particularly minor language by European criteria in the early nineteenth century.'[124] Taking as comparator the case of Finland, he writes:

> Fewer people spoke Finnish in 1870 than spoke Irish in 1850. Finnish living standards lagged well below Irish living standards in 1880, yet Finland achieved an exceptionally high rate of economic growth in the following century. Far

from being associated with the abandonment of her language, her economic performance seems, if anything to have derived a certain impetus from a highly self-conscious national revival, including considerable emphasis on the language as a bearer of national culture in defiance of imperial power.[125]

The case of Czech might offer another suggestive comparison and point of contrast for Ireland given its instance of a widely successful language revival. A steep decline in the use of Czech vernacular was halted by the codification of modern literary Czech, led by Josef Dobrovský in the 1810s and 1820s, which in turn was succeeded by the gradual extension of the literary language into various social domains (against the expectations of its leaders).[126] Following the unsuccessful 1848 revolutionary demand for equality of Czech and German in schools, the late nineteenth century saw a growing recognition of Czech as an 'official public language' for use in courts and administrative offices.[127] The language decrees of 1880 enjoined officials in Bohemia and Moravia to reply to cases in the language (Czech or Germany) in which they originated while in 1881 the division of Prague's Charles-Ferdinand University and creation of separate Czech and German faculties marked a landmark in 'the book and the school' campaign.[128] In 1897, Premier Badeni's (short-lived) language decrees established both Czech and German as administrative languages in Bohemia and Moravia, effectively requiring all employees in ethnically diverse areas to be bilingual by 1 July 1901.[129]

What were the factors in Ireland that 'not only made acquisition of English attractive, but left Irish redundant for material purposes'?[130] The answer, according to Lee, is a combination of two factors: the social and political force of emigration (particularly parents' assumptions 'that their children would enjoy advantages as English-speaking rather than Irish-speaking emigrants') and the nature of the nineteenth-century state as the primary 'agency of anglicisation'.[131]

Subsequent to Lee's observations, our understanding of the relations between the modern state and Irish-language speakers in the eighteenth and nineteenth centuries has been advanced greatly by the work of Nicholas Wolf. As a result of painstaking archival research in English and Irish-language sources, Wolf decisively challenges earlier assumptions regarding the absence of Irish from the public sphere in the nineteenth century, tracing the interaction between Irish speakers and church and state authorities. He shows that a direct consequence of the nineteenth-century expansion of the modern state was that 'the language question arose again' as 'Irish speakers,

much more numerous and vocal than expected by authorities, made it difficult to enforce an all-English administrative regime.'[132]

While Wolf's work convincingly demonstrates a much longer history
of interaction between Irish speakers and church and state authorities than
previously recognised, Lee's narrative of the increasing redundancy of Irish
for material purposes is also persuasive. Their combined findings point to a
much more nuanced view of the linguistic scene in late nineteenth-century
Ireland, which my study of 1880s Maamtrasna supports: usage of Irish in
some communities was still widespread yet the social status of the language
was also increasingly weakened. Language shift in Ireland was not simply
a transition from Irish to English; particularly in its later stages, it involved
the change from widespread bilingual usage to a prevalent English monoglot culture. For this to take place, many speakers must, in their encounters or crossings with those charged with political or economic power, have
experienced the usage of Irish as an impossibility, or an irrelevance, or even,
as in the Maamtrasna trials, a liability. In other words, a language becomes
redundant in practice, and the cultural hegemony of another consolidated,
not only through 'attraction' and 'advantage'[133] but also – as later chapters
will demonstrate – through processes of attempted usage, prohibition and
the failure to be heard.[134]

Part II

The Maamtrasna Case

— 3 —

ARRESTS

'They would put people in for the murder'

I did not go to bed at all on the night of the murders, nor did my sister Mary Conaboy ... My husband and Peter Lydon went to bed the very minute they ate their supper. Myles went to bed first, and Peter Lydon went in after him without delay. They slept in the *callagh*, and Peter slept on the outside; no other person came in or left my house on that night.

Statement (translated) from Bridget Joyce of Cappanacreha,
wife of Myles Joyce, 9 October 1882[1]

The funerals of the five murdered Joyce family members took place on Sunday, 20 August. That same morning, following the evidence given by Anthony, John, and Patrick Joyce, police arrested the ten identified men: Patrick Joyce; the three Casey relatives, John, Michael, and Patrick; the four Joyce relatives, Martin, Myles, Paudeen, and Tom Joyce; Thomas Casey; and Anthony Philbin.[2] The men were taken to local police huts at Killitiane and Finny and then via Clonbur to Cong police barracks from where they travelled by steamer to Galway Jail on Monday. The following Saturday they were again remanded in custody pending a formal inquiry, which, following a series of delays, finally took place in the prison on 5 and 6 September. At this inquiry, 13 witnesses offered evidence, including the three Joyces, and detailed statements regarding the arrests and search for evidence were tendered by RIC members; at its conclusion, Dr Hegarty, who had conducted the post-mortems of the family, reported that Patsy Joyce was now out of danger.[3]

The evidence heard at the inquiry once again brought the horror of the murders to the fore. But other surviving documents point to a much murkier agenda: the determination by the constabulary to 'put people in for the murder'. Ironically this damning phrase is to be found in the pages of the crown's prosecution brief itself and attributed to Mary Joyce, young daughter of Paudeen and Tom.[4] Reading between – and, in some cases, against – the lines of these official records reveals how the local police force and magistrates treated those with limited or no English. What also emerges is that competency in English could crucially determine an accused's ability not only to comprehend but also to negotiate with the judicial system in which the ten men were now deeply mired.

CAUTIONS AND ARRESTS

One of the first depositions in the brief is that of RIC Constable Matthew Rudden of Cloughbrack, who testified under oath as follows:

> That I was present on the morning of the 20th of August, 1882, at the arrest of *John Casey* of Derry. Sub-Inspector Smyth arrested him. I heard him cautioned. I heard Mr. Smyth giving the caution in English, and I heard it then explained in Irish by an Irish-speaking man, Sub-Constable Kelly. I searched his house then, and I found a pair of moleskin trowsers [*sic*], which I now produce. When I took them down off the stick on which they were hanging, I asked *John Casey* were they his, and he said 'yes'.[5]

Another deposition came from RIC Constable Thomas Finn of Clonbur relating to the arrest of Patrick Joyce, aged in his early twenties, of Shanvalleycahill:

> That I was present on the 20th of August when Patrick Joyce of Shanvalleycahill was arrested by Constable Brien, who cautioned him in my presence and hearing. After being cautioned, I searched his house and found a pair of trowsers, which I now produce. I asked Patrick Joyce were these his trowsers, and he said they were.[6]

John Casey had clearly needed the services of an interpreter, and Kelly, Smyth, and Rudden had followed RIC guidelines in this regard; this was not needed for Patrick Joyce.

Details of the arrest of the other Casey family members show that markedly different linguistic competencies existed within the same family and even between siblings. Patrick Casey, who would be the second person tried for murder and who was in his mid-twenties, could speak English, but his 60-year-old uncle Michael and brother John, in his mid-thirties, could not. Sub-Inspector Smyth of Dunmore deposed that he had arrested the three men in their Derry homes:

> That on the morning of 20th August I arrested Michael Casey of Derry in his own house. I cautioned him in the usual manner. The caution was translated to him in my presence by Sub-Constable Kelly. I then arrested John Casey of Derry in his own house. The caution was given and translated in like manner. I then arrested Patrick Casey of Derry and cautioned him myself. He speaks English.[7]

Other constabulary members were less careful in recording the details of the arrests, or perhaps in ascertaining the linguistic abilities of the accused. Tom Joyce and his uncle Martin were arrested by Sub-Inspector Gibbons of Cong, who swore: 'On the morning of the 20th August I arrested *Thomas Joyce* of Cappanacreha in his own house and cautioned him in the usual manner. I then arrested *Martin Joyce* of Cappanacreha and cautioned him.'[8] Interestingly, the circumstances of Paudeen Joyce's arrest are not specified. Gibbons' deposition does not mention if he arranged for the 'usual' caution to be translated into Irish but later records show that Martin, in his late thirties, and Paudeen, in his mid-forties, were Irish-speaking monoglots. Tom Joyce, about 20 years of age and the youngest of the arrested men, may have had a working knowledge of English.[9]

The arrest of Myles Joyce (who was around 40 years of age) also took place on the morning of 20 August and was made by Constable Johnston, who stated as follows: 'I arrested Myles Joyce of Cappanacreha on the morning of the 20th August. I cautioned him duly. He spoke then to his wife in Irish, and I did not know what he said, but I heard the word "sheep" at the end.'[10] As with the cases of Myles's brother and nephew, Johnston did not clarify if the caution to Myles Joyce was translated into Irish, as was legally required. Johnston was at pains, however, to emphasise that he could not comprehend the conversation between husband and wife with the exception of one, especially damning word – 'sheep' – rendered only in English in the official record.

Johnston was the constable to whom the local men had first reported the crime on Friday morning, and he and his colleague Sub-Constable

Lenihan were the first police to arrive at the murder scene. According to the RIC List and Directory, Johnston was, at that time, in charge of the temporary RIC station at Derrypark. Yet Johnston also had an earlier judicial relationship with Myles Joyce: he had testified for the prosecution at the assault case taken two years earlier in October 1880 by Anthony Joyce's wife, Margaret, and which had resulted in the conviction of Myles and his brothers. According to the *Ballinrobe Chronicle* account of the petty sessions proceedings at that time, Johnston testified to having 'heard there is a bad feeling between the parties and before that; they are related.' He also warned: 'If the magistrates do not do something to prevent a recurrence, he could not say how the dispute may end.'[11] Thus, for Johnston to state in his arrest deposition that Myles had referred to 'sheep' in conversation with his wife was potentially highly incriminating.

The surviving RIC depositions do not detail the arrest information for the two remaining accused, Anthony Philbin and Thomas Casey. These two men – as would become obvious in the murder trials – had the most advanced ability in English among the accused, other than Patrick Joyce of Shanvalleycahill. Both men had spent a considerable time working in England. Anthony Philbin, then aged around 40, had only returned to County Galway in the previous November having spent four or more years in England. Casey, in his late thirties and married to Philbin's sister, Mary, had also travelled regularly between England and Ireland for seasonal work and had returned to the area three months before the night of the murders, unusually early for a seasonal migrant labourer.

On the day of the men's arrest an official inquiry was conducted at Cong police barracks under presiding magistrate Newton Brady. Here the Joyce witnesses presented their evidence formally and the accused received the opportunity to cross-examine. Anthony Joyce received a number of questions from Tom Joyce, briefly from his uncle Martin, and from Patrick Joyce, Thomas Casey, and Anthony Philbin. Myles Joyce and Tom's father declined to cross-examine. An interpreter was employed to translate the evidence from the prosecution witnesses into English and also during their cross-examination by the accused. The men's questions centred largely on issues of recognition and also on interrogating why the Joyces had not proceeded to the police directly – a matter raised by the young Tom in his cross-examination of his cousin Anthony Joyce: 'Cross-examined by *Thomas Joyce* (Pat)—If you saw us going to kill him that time of night, why did you not go to the police about it. *Answer*—Why would I go, as if I did, these people might be before us to kill us.'[12]

Exchanges in the second cross-examination, that of Anthony's brother John, illustrate how John sought to differentiate degrees of guilt among those to be charged with the murders. His testimony with respect to Philbin and Casey, for example, differed significantly from his deep animosity to Patrick Joyce of Shanvalleycahill, with whom a history of grievance clearly existed:

Cross-examined by Anthony Philbin. I never saw you doing anything, except that you were with them that night, and to best of my belief if you were left where you were, you would do nothing.

Cross-examined by Thomas Casey. I know you during your time in Glensaul. You were away in England and Scotland for some time. I never had anything against you myself. Your house is about four miles from the house where the thing occurred.

Cross-examined by Patrick Joyce. Had you any spite towards me? *Answer*—I believe there was nothing going on in the country that you were not at the head of; hanged you should be when the others are sent to gaol.

Question—Did you and your son and your brother Michael strike me in Michael's house for killing the horses? *Answer*—I struck little on you, I cannot say what time. It was in consequence of every badness that you were doing that I struck you.[13]

On Saturday, 26 August, the men were remanded to Galway for a further inquiry. Here the identities of ten men were entered in the formal prison register with a detailed inventory of each man's age, height, hair and eye colour, and complexion, as well as their trade or occupation, religion and degree of education (though not their ability to speak English or Irish).[14] For example, Myles Joyce is described as a 40-year-old farm laborer, 5 feet 5 ½ inches in height, with brown hair, blue eyes, and a sallow complexion.[15] All ten men are listed as Catholics and nine of them as 'labourer', the exception being Philbin who is described as the higher class of 'farmer'. All four of the Joyces and all four Caseys are recorded as having 'nil' degrees of education, but the 23-year-old Patrick Joyce of Shanvalleycahill is listed as able to read and write and Philbin as able to read.[16]

After a series of adjournments, the inquiry took place in Galway Jail on 5 and 6 September under Resident Magistrate J. C. Gardiner. These proceedings show some subtle shifts in the prosecution case, most significantly in the deposition by Constable Johnston. In this lengthy piece of evidence, the constable's conversations with the two injured boys are referred to only in the briefest of terms: regarding Patsy, 'I spoke to him', and regarding his dying brother, 'I spoke to Michael secondly after coming out of the room. He answered me.'[17] This constituted a significant editing of the initial evidence gathered at the murder scene. The substance of what the Joyce boys had said to Johnston concerning the number of men and their 'black' faces, and the presence of Sub-Constable Lenihan as the necessary trans-lator, are missing from this judicial record.

The inquiry took place in the intimidating space of the city prison and events were largely hidden from public view, receiving only a perfunctory reference in local media. By now the prisoners had been given a Tuam solic-itor, Henry J. Concannon, who appeared on their behalf. Concannon's father Edmund (or 'Mun') had established the (still surviving) legal practice in Tuam in 1838[18] and also served as a town commissioner and a member of the Tuam Board of Guardians; he was a renowned advocate and lived to the age of 86 (d. 1902).[19] According to Waldron, the hiring of Henry Concannon was surprising because cases from the Joyce Country were generally managed by solicitor P. J. B. Daly of Ballinrobe. Since Daly was already working on the Huddy murder trial and was in ill health, Waldron suggests, '[he] may well have refused the Maamtrasna case.'[20] Daly's unavailability was to the serious detriment of the prisoners, since Henry, unlike his popular father, did not have competency in Irish.[21] This particular instance of generational difference, while a common feature among local upper classes, was to have a wide social impact in reducing the provision of legal professional services in Irish, most significantly for the Maamtrasna accused.

The solicitor for the prosecution was George Bolton, Crown Solicitor for Tipperary, who was appointed in late August and was an especially high-profile and feared figure.[22] According to Waldron, Bolton was noto-rious for a 'special' technique: 'Always accompanied by eight or more of the tallest, beefiest RIC men he could select, he would stalk into the cabin of a suspect, eject everybody, commandeer a chair (if there were such), on which he would sit in majestic state, the representative of the Queen arrived in a remote village.'[23] Bolton was already well-known for his prosecution of agrarian crimes and, at the time of the Maamtrasna murders, his name appeared daily in the *Freeman's Journal* as prosecutor in the case of the infamous Letterfrack murders. On 17 August in the Commission Court in Green Street, Dublin, he had begun the crown case against Patrick Walsh, charged with the murders of Martin and John Lydon.[24] In his later memoir, he claimed with some considerable exaggeration, that he had taken informations or statements from some 643 witnesses in the Maamtrasna case; only 20 or so alibi witnesses are cited in the crown brief.

TESTING ALIBIS

In August 1882, five RIC stations were located in the Clonbur district: the headquarters at Clonbur, three temporary stations at Cloughbrack, Cornamona, and Derrypark, and a fifth station at Killitiane.[25] These posts were far from the county headquarters in Galway: Killitiane, the most isolated station, was almost 40 miles from Galway and over 13 miles from Clonbur.[26] Official fears regarding the instability of local political conditions can be construed from the number of extra police huts and protection posts specifically allocated to the Clonbur district at this period: four police huts (at Bohawn, Cloughbrack, Cornamona, and most relevant to the Maamtrasna case, Finny, which had been established three months before the murders) and eight protection posts.[27]

From the RIC statements preserved in the crown prosecution brief, we can trace the detailed activities undertaken by local constables in the weeks following the murders as they interviewed family members of the accused men and investigated alibi evidence. These interviews, unwittingly perhaps, cast some light on social relations in the area and provide some rare glimpses into the family lives of the accused, though the lens of official scrutiny is at times uncomfortably voyeuristic. Julia (Judy) Casey was the mother of Patrick Casey and her evidence, along with that of a young relative called Mary Casey, was of particular interest to the local police, who seemed to have quickly targeted Patrick as a chief suspect. Both women testified that Patrick had been present in the house all evening on the night of the murder and both women would later travel to Dublin as witnesses for the defence. Julia stated that she had heard of the murder from her daughter, the wife of Martin Joyce, 'who told me outside the door, on her way to the corpse-house, at about two o'clock in the day.' Mary Casey, she explained, was a local girl whose father 'was in the asylum in Ballinasloe, out of his mind'.[28] As recorded in a rough statement taken days after her son's arrest, signed by District Inspector Phillips, with Sub-Constable Collins as interpreter, the Irish-speaking Julia initially co-operated with the investigating police but then refused to give any more information:

> Pat was here on the night of the murder. Mary Casey was here also. She can prove that he was at home. Mary Casey was spinning, and it was for that purpose she was in the house. Pat was in before night fell. She (Mrs Casey) slept in bed with her son. Mary Casey did not go to bed at all because Pat was sick. He had a pain in his belly. (She then contradicted herself and said they both sat up at night with Pat.) Mary Casey is no relation; she is a young girl; [Julia] would not tell where she lived. Widow [Julia] Casey here ceased to give any more information and gave only surly talk to the constable.[29]

The constabulary records of these local interviews are increasingly careless in recording whether an interpreter had been used but, usually from occasional awkwardness in phrasing, traces of statements originally given in Irish can be detected along with familial details not easily rendered in English. For example, Jude Joyce, wife of Martin Joyce, testified under oath on 28 August that her husband had 'slept at home that night', and that 'Malachy Casey of Shraughanalung and my husband slept together that night.'[30] Casey was described by Jude as 'five or six akin of mine' – an awkward translation of the Irish term for cousin *col cúigear* (meaning 'first cousin once removed') or *col seisear* ('second cousin'). Her evidence was challenged by the testimony of Malachy Casey, recorded the same day, who denied ever sleeping overnight in Martin Joyce's house and stated that he had slept in his own home that night.[31]

Some of the most robust statements and informations related to Anthony Philbin's whereabouts that evening; it is clear that the nature of his alibi troubled the constabulary and their records noted that the witness statements were 'likely to be produced for the defence'.[32] Alibis were provided by Mary Philbin, his daughter, his mother-in-law, Mary Quinn, and his neighbor Katherine Derrig, all of whom testified to Philbin's having been at home that evening.[33] On the other hand, the alibis provided for Thomas Casey of Glensaul were broken rapidly by the local constabulary. These came from his wife, Mary, and his mother-in-law, Sarah Philbin (mother of Anthony). Mary's statement included a reference to a cousin of her husband – a man called Tom Boyle – having stayed the night,[34] but the information sworn by Boyle on the same day refuted this strongly and Boyle testified to having been asked by Mary Casey to swear falsely: 'I saw Mrs Casey last on Sunday last. She was in my house. She was coming home from Galway. She told me that there was no trial, but that she expected it would be next Saturday, and that she did not know whether or not the witnesses would be wanted then. I told her I would swear I was in Tom Casey's that night. I am Tom Casey's first cousin.'[35]

Many of the alibis or informations came from female relatives of the accused: these offer an uncommon instance of women's voices being recorded, albeit in a highly mediated way. In the immediate aftermath of the murders, women relayed key pieces of information to each other. Mary Ann Joyce, wife of Patrick Joyce of Shanvalleycahill, recalled in her statement how she had first heard of the murders: 'My husband was drawing stones next morning; he began a while after breakfast time. Everyone in the house was shocked to hear of the murder. I heard of the murder from Honor Joyce, daughter of Catherine Joyce (widow). I went into the house and sat down until my husband came in.'[36] The evidence from Mary Joyce of Cappanacreha, whose father Paudeen and brother Tom were among the accused, illuminates how information was passed on: at first stories circulated among the women working 'in the turf', including that the murdered man John Joyce had stolen a gun and that he had owed Anthony Joyce, the crown prosecution witness, £6. Then rumours spread regarding who would be found guilty: 'The day after the murder my uncle Martin came in and said that Anthony told him that they would put people in for the murder, but did not think they would put him, Martin, in, as they were great friends.'[37] This shows that as early as the day following the murder, the man who would prove to be the key crown prosecution witness was actively taking part in local speculation as to who would be 'put in'.[38]

Mary and her sister Honor both testified that their father and brother had been in the house on the night of the murders, evidence that, following all of the twists and false turns in the ensuing legal process, would prove to be a true alibi. Of her brother Tom, she stated: 'My brother was at service at James Gavin's, at Gawlaun, in the County of Mayo. He will soon be half a year there. He came home the Wednesday before the murder, it was near night; he went back on Friday morning … He remained here all the evening. He did not go out to any neighbour's house, he slept here.'[39] The nature of the young women's evidence meant that references to the sleeping arrangements of the family were central to proving alibis: such details were subject to particular scrutiny by the police in their efforts to undermine their testimonies. Honor described how she 'slept in the room' with her two brothers: 'We all slept with our heads the same way.' Mary's evidence also included intimate family aspects:

I slept in the loft over the end of the kitchen. It was a good time in the night when I went to bed. I had to milk the cows. They were all gone to bed except my mother. My brother slept in the room. My brother was in bed an hour after night-fall. I went back in it with that girl Kate Joyce and my father; it was a horrid place …[40]

While the gross intrusion into private details of family lives is disturbing, the insertion of the phrase 'it was a horrid place' within Mary Joyce's statement is quite bizarre and reads more like a comment from a prurient external observer.[41]

Alibis and statements concerning Myles Joyce are conspicuously absent from the body of the crown prosecution brief. A short statement toward the end of the document acknowledges this absence:

No information can be obtained as to the alleged movements of *Myles Joyce* on the night of the murders. Various attempts were made to see members of his family, but his house was invariably found locked up and the family absent, except on one occasion when some children were found in it, who, although tolerably grown up, would not answer a single question, having evidently been instructed not to do so.[42]

Subsequent to the completion and indexing of the brief, four supplementary pages were appended and titled 'as to Myles Joyce' in what appears to be an official determination to tie up 'loose ends'. The statements were credited to Bridget Joyce (Myles' wife), her brother Peter Lydon, her brother-in-law Patrick Conaboy, and her sister Mary Conaboy. Bridget's statement was dated 9 October, surprisingly late in the gathering of legal evidence, and witnessed by Constable J. McPartland; no reference is made to the use of an interpreter and Bridget's mark is not present on the document. Her testimony began: 'I am wife to Myles Joyce. He is in prison charged with the murders. I have five children, the eldest is near ten years old. I remember the night of the murders at Maamtrasna. I was at home spinning wool on the day before, and also minding two of my children that were sick.'[43] Her evidence detailed the events of the evening, including the arrival of her sister Mary and niece Kitty Conaboy. Here again the formal style of the woman's statement betrays some evidence of a mediating interpreter (for example, the precise phrasing of 'eldest' and the Anglicised *callagh*):

Kitty Conaboy and three children went to bed just before it was dark … The three children that lay with Kitty on that night were not in bed when their father came home; they came out of the room when he came in and asked him about the sheep. I did not go to bed at all on the night of the murders, nor did my sister Mary Conaboy. Neither of us slept any on that night on account of two children of mine that were sick – my eldest and youngest children. My husband and Peter Lydon went to bed the very minute they ate their supper. Myles went to bed first, and Peter Lydon went in after him without delay. They slept in the *callagh*, and Peter slept on the outside; no other person came in or left my house on that night ... I know all of the men that are arrested for the murders. I did not see any of them on the night of the murders except my husband.[44]

Peter Lydon's testimony, taken on the same day, firmly supported his sister's statement that Myles was at home that evening:

it was dark and Myles Joyce asked me in to eat potatoes, and asked me also to stop for the night as the night was dark and the way home ugly. I stopped in Myles Joyce's house on the night of the murder. I slept in the *callagh*[45] in the kitchen; Myles Joyce slept with me. I slept sound all night. I slept on the outside of the bed. Myles Joyce did not leave the house all that night.[46]

Bridget's testimony was further supported by her sister Mary Conaboy – 'No person but I, my daughter Kitty, and Peter Lydon were at Myles Joyce's house on the night of the murder, except his own family'[47] – but here the formal idiom of the testimony has the effect of occluding an alibi for Myles Joyce. Adding to this, an earlier statement from Patrick Conaboy, Mary's husband, taken two weeks before, directly contradicted his wife's claim to have spent the night in the home of Myles Joyce: 'I remember the night of the murder at Maamtrasna. I was at home all the night. *All my own family* were at home that night. No person came in or left my house that night. I know all the men who are arrested for the murder. I did not see any of them on that night.'[48] Conaboy's testimony, unsurprisingly, was given prominence as a key document in the crown brief, while the defence alibis by Myles' wife, brother-in-law and sister-in-law were listed as supplementary materials; none of these witnesses would be called upon to give evidence in the later court trial.

HEADLINE NEWS

Journalistic coverage of the events of Thursday night, 17 August, had been lurid in tenor throughout. As the scale of coverage increased, and with news of the arrest of suspects, reporters characterised the murders to national audiences as dramatically exceptional in the level of violence used but also as symptomatic of larger, implacable forces encompassing and indicting those agitating for land reform. The editorial from Dublin's unionist and pro-land-lord *Evening Mail* on 21 August provides a good example of this rhetoric:

> In the hideous annals of savagery and crime, in the history of Irish agrarianism, with its deadly guerilla warfare and its infernal cruelties, the massacre of the Joyces in Galway will stand out as an imperishable monument to the diabolical genius which called the Land League into existence. In unmitigated barbarity the crime of last week is unparalleled. There is not in the whole history of brutality an act to be compared with it. It is at once the most coldblooded and inhuman act of devilish ferocity that the world has ever been called upon to contemplate. Barbarous nations have before now butchered in cold blood whole families and whole garrisons. Revenge has mounted her victims by the score, and greed and lust have claimed their hundreds, but where will you find an example of undiluted savagery to equal this slaying of an innocent and helpless family in a time of peace at the hands of their neighbours and by the instigation of their own countrymen?

The *Weekly Irish Times* drew its analogy from sensational stories of the American west: 'This massacre, even in the bloodstained region where it occurred, stands unequalled in all that can excite emotions of horror and indignation, and probably has never been paralleled, save when in past ages on the border states of America a mid-night Indian raid converted a peaceful homestead into a shambles reeking with blood.'[49]

Nationalist papers were more concerned with whether the motivation for the crime could be adequately explained. A week after the murders occurred, the weekly *Ballinrobe Chronicle,* in text drawn from *Freeman's Journal* reports, provided its readers with the following summary of local speculations:

> As observed last week, the prevailing opinion still is that the family were suspected of having peached in the matter of the Huddy double murder and in regard to the finding of the bodies of the old man and his grandson in the lake. Again, that John Joyce, who had some time since got an addition of a few acres of bottom land to his holding, partly covered with water in winter,

and not being fully stocked in summer by him, many of his neighbours had persistently put their cattle in there, and that latterly he had shown signs of resistance and threatened legal proceedings against the trespassers. It is to be hoped that such is not true, for it would be a deplorable state of society if for such a trivial affair neighbours would destroy so many human lives. It has also been given as a motive and cause – that lately John Joyce had refused to continue his subscription to a certain society, and in refusing, the applicant had made use of some objectionable comment.[50]

Just two days after the murder, the *Galway Express* had published an account which seemed to corroborate directly the 'Huddy' theory and which castigated local police for not providing adequate protection to the Joyces:

> It seems that Mr Henderson, crown prosecutor, was engaged for three hours with the Joyce family on Thursday, taking their depositions relative to the murder of the Huddys, and shortly after Mr Henderson's departure the Joyces were murdered. It seems rather strange that, knowing the importance of getting evidence regarding the murder of the Huddys, and the danger to which any person giving the crown information on the matter is exposed, that some proper protection was not afforded to the Joyce family.[51]

But in the following edition, which appeared a week later, this account of a supposed visit by Henderson to the Joyce family was retracted and an apology supplied: 'We now find that we were misinformed on this point, and that no such examination took place. We regret that we were led into this mistake, and take the earliest opportunity of removing any impression it may have made on the public mind.[52]

Weeks after the arrests of the accused, the American newspaper, the *Irish World*, noted for its radical Irish nationalist editorials, returned to the topic of the murders and offered quite invidious further speculations as to relations between the Joyce family, including the young girl, Peggy, and the local police:

> The men who put the bodies there knew that only one person in the whole country *could* have given the information to the police, and this person was the mother of the Joyce family, who was murdered with all belonging to her, save one boy, in their wretched hut the other night. Policemen were seen to visit Joyce's cabin. The daughter was comely and an object of interest to the policemen. And so it was bruited about that some evidence was being gathered that would hang some men who were seen carrying out the sacks in a boat in Lough Mask.[53]

The rendition of shocking and gruesome detail notwithstanding, the contemporary press coverage of the Maamtrasna crimes exemplifies Janet Malcolm's argument that the core function of journalistic reporting of murder is to provide social reassurance and certainty. 'Murder,' she writes, 'violates the social contract and makes a mockery of privacy.' Amid-the social crisis emanating from such 'violation', journalism functions as 'an enterprise of reassurance': 'We do not wring our hands and rend our clothes over the senseless crimes and disasters that give us our subject. We explain and blame. We are connoisseurs of certainty.'[54] The 'certainties' established by the local and national press in August 1882 were quickly fixed on the guilt of the arrested men and on the veracity of the Joyce witnesses. According to the *Freeman's Journal*, 'the ten men who have been arrested are tersely described by the people of the district as "the biggest devils in the city."'[55]

Reinforcing its characterisation of the accused men as local outliers, the *Freeman's* report was at pains to relay the 'cordial' feeling displayed by local people toward the witnesses, which it described in the most emphatic of fashions:

> The witnesses are staying at the hotel in Cong under police protection, but if the feeling of the people is to be gathered from what occurred yesterday, they have [as] their bodyguard the people of the entire district ... They shook hands with the witnesses – said 'God bless you,' and in the strongest terms expressed their gratitude and rejoicing that this murderous gang, which had so long been the terror of the district, had at last been run to earth. They said it was God's doing. I understand that in the course of the investigation the prisoners frequently put questions in a form which only tended to make the evidence tell more dangerously against them.[56]

This and other press reports imply that journalists received regular and substantial updates from local RIC men, and the confident tone of articles regarding the imminent success of inquiries often resembled that of police statements. In his memoir, Andrew Dunlop recalled that even before the journalists' return to the murder scene on Wednesday, 23 August, they had received 'from the constabulary officers the details of the mid-night journey of the intending murderers across the wild country from Derrypark to Maamtrasna, and had forwarded an account of it to our respective newspapers.'[57]

Notwithstanding their primary function as instruments for the prosecution, the police depositions betray a complexity of alibi and denial, little of which makes its way into the press accounts. Relatedly, reporters rarely acknowledged that much of the relevant evidence was first rendered in Irish and made only sweeping references to their having to work in an area that was predominantly Irish-speaking. For example, the *Weekly Irish Times* account, published on 26 August, observed that 'Irish is the generally spoken language in the Joyce country, and scarcely any of the natives of the peasant class dwelling amid-these hills understand any other language' but then disregarded the topic of language almost entirely. The *Daily Express* reporter, clearly a monoglot English-speaker (and possibly Dunlop), alluded briefly in his first detailed report to his 'pantomimic endeavours to find out the straight course [to Maamtrasna] from a boy who knew not English and a man who at first feigned not' – once again a seeming monoglot was to be suspected of dissimulation and dishonesty.[58]

On 24 August, the *Irish Times* reporter recounted to his readers how he had witnessed a scene of appeal by one of the men's relatives to the local priest: this was probably Siobhán (Judy) O'Brien, the wife of Paudeen Joyce and mother of Tom Joyce. The reporter did not specify whether (as is likely) he required Fr McHugh's aid in translating: 'While here, an old woman whose husband and son are among the ten identified prisoners addressed Father McHugh in Irish, complaining bitterly of the arrests and arguing that the evidence of the witnesses could not be true, because as she said, if they knew that the murders were about to be committed, why did they not prevent them.' This brief reference was very unusual for the time in communicating doubt as to the reliability of the Joyce witnesses. Another instance came from the *Daily Express* reporter who, on 23 August, referred to his initial reservations as to the evidence tendered by the 'eyewitnesses', a scepticism that would come to be widely shared some years hence. However, the article then moved quickly to banish doubt and to endorse the witnesses' veracity unequivocally:

> When first informed of the fact, I confess I hesitated to believe it. My knowledge of the locality, its lonely solitude, the hour of the night, the darkest before the dawn, at which the tragedy was perpetrated, joined with the evil reputation of the neighbourhood and the consequently supposed connivance, or at least the sympathy, of the inhabitants with the criminals, rather resisted a full credence of the circumstance ... The event proves otherwise ... The crown will, in all probability, be able to weave together a sufficient narrative of the occurrence from its inception to its completion, which will, as I have said, prove as satisfactory to the public at large as it was absolutely astounding to the prisoners when confronted with it ... The story will, when the proper time comes, show a jury how justice may be vindicated and outraged society appeased.[59]

Knowing what later transpired in the Maamtrasna case, these observations on the 'weaving' ability of some crown officials become loaded with implication, but in their original context their purpose was to reassure a reading public as to an imminent and 'satisfactory' conviction.

One much-reported occurrence during these otherwise 'quiet' weeks was the Lord Lieutenant's three-day tour of Connemara in mid-September, during which the viceregal party visited Maamtrasna.[60] Spencer, accompanied by the solicitor Bolton, received a personal tour of the murder scene from Resident Magistrate Brady and Sub-Inspector Gibbons, who identified the route that the alleged murderers were said to have taken and 'the route by which the witnesses against them state that they tracked them to the very scene of the massacre.'[61] The visit was given much prominence in the press: the *Freeman's Journal* entitled its report of 15 September 'Earl Spencer and the Cong Tragedy' and described the group's entering what its reporter termed 'the hovel which had served as a home for John Joyce and his family', which had remained largely untouched since the events of a month earlier.[62] Remarkably, the Lord Lieutenant also seems to have embarked on his own form of detective work, including visiting the house next to the murder scene and questioning its owner as to what he had heard:

> The man, whose name is also Joyce, knew little or no English, and the services had to be procured of an Irish speaking constable as interpreter ... His Excellency made inquiries as to whether the noise and the probable barking of dogs – there was one in the house – would not necessarily be heard by the man or by some of the members of his family. Joyce replied to the effect that the dog did not stay in the house at night, and that even if the animal did bark, the circumstance would not necessarily have made any very strong impression on his mind. His Excellency, on leaving, remarked that it was a terrible affair.[63]

TURNING 'QUEEN'S EVIDENCE'

Under the Prevention of Crime (Ireland) Act of 1882, the location of the trial was moved from the County Galway Assizes to Dublin to be tried in the Special Commission Court: a move motivated in part by the fear of influence on local juries. On 2 October the ten accused men were transferred to Dublin's Kilmainham Jail. In the lead-up to their trials, their solicitor,

Concannon, requested permission from Dublin Castle to meet with his clients but was refused. The men were held in separate cells and not allowed to meet at exercise time; early in November, an exception was made for Casey and Philbin who were allowed time to converse.[64] Why their conversations were permitted, and to what consequence, became quickly evident. On Wednesday, 8 November, the prison governor received a short blotted note which he then forwarded to Bolton (see Image 28, p. XIV).[65] It read, 'Sir, I have a few words of important matter concerning the maamtrasna murder crown solicitor tell him only'; this cryptic note was signed 'Anthony Philbin'. The note appears to be in Philbin's own handwriting, though the possibility of assistance from a prison official cannot be discounted. Philbin's facility in English, as a result of four or more years working in England, thus offered him the opportunity for private, unmediated conversation and negotiation with the crown prosecution team, and ultimately enabled him to turn 'Queen's evidence'; in other words, to testify, as an approver, against the other accused in order to secure his own discharge.

Bolton met with Philbin on 9 and 10 November and recorded two statements from him. In these Philbin asserted that he had been part of the group of men drawn together on that fateful evening of 17 August and had accompanied Thomas Casey to Derry, where he met the other accused. He attested to having accompanied the men to Maamtrasna and to having observed three of the men enter the house:

> I asked Martin Joyce where were they going. He told me there was a boy there beyond that was taking all the good sheep in the village and fattening them to his own use, and they were going to pay him a visit. We went away towards the place they were going to (I did not know the place). When we came on the street at the house, three men of them threw the door open and went in – that's Patrick Casey of Derry, Patrick Joyce of Shanvallycahill, and Myles Joyce of Cappanacreha; noise started in the house, and I heard a screech, and in an instant I heard a shot. I then heard more screeches and noise. I got frightened and am frightened yet. I ran as hard as I could until I got home, and I was afraid they would kill myself the next night for leaving them.[66]

On Saturday, 11 November, news reached the prisoners' counsel that Anthony Philbin was now an 'approver' or informer. That same day a note was addressed to George Bolton from Thomas Casey: 'Mr. Bolton, I want to see you in Kilmainham Jail a mediately [*sic*]. I have a little important statement to make to you. I am your obedient servant, Thomas Casey. I want to see you soon here.'[67] Casey, too, had travelled regularly between England

and Ireland for seasonal work, and, like his brother-in-law, his competency in English (and what would appear to be his limited literacy)[68] facilitated his becoming to an approver.[69] The objective of his note, conveyed with both deference and urgency, was successful. Bolton met with Casey over that weekend and the substance of his testimony was agreed.

On Monday, 13 November, following the first day of Patrick Joyce's trial, Resident Magistrate Newton Brady officially recorded a statement from Thomas Casey, in the presence of Bolton at Green Street, which Casey signed. In it, he testified that he had been told by Patrick Casey to go to Patrick's uncle's house in Derry on the night of 17 August and to bring Anthony Philbin with him. His testimony continued as follows, fully supporting the identifications by Anthony and John Joyce of the remaining eight accused:

> Between Martin Joyce's and Myles Joyce's house, we met Myles Joyce, Pat Joyce of Cappanacreeagh, and his son Tom. We walked on towards Michael Casey's house and on the way met Martin Joyce, who came with us. In the house I saw Patrick Joyce of Shanballycahill, Michael Casey, John Casey, and Pat Casey, all of Derry … About a quarter of a mile from Michael Casey's house we were joined by two men, Pat Kelly and Michael Nee; the latter is a pedlar.[70]

Casey went on to assert that he saw Patrick Joyce, Pat Casey, and Myles Joyce 'go up to the door and push it in.' However his statement also majorly implicated two men not previously mentioned by Philbin or by the Joyces: 'I saw Pat Joyce of Shanballycahill go into the house, and also Kelly and Nee, and then I heard shots and screeches. I stopped at the gable-end of the barn on the street. After about 10 minutes in the house, they came out, and we all went away towards home, the way we had gone.'[71] On Tuesday, 14 November, his statement was shared with the court. The number of men on trial was now eight (no efforts were made to identify 'Kelly' and 'Nee'), and Philbin and Casey joined the ranks of crown witnesses for the course of the November 1882 trials.

— 4 —

LAW AND THE STATE

'The language which he knew best'

> The interpreter is a necessarily hybrid figure, straddling, linguistically at any
> rate, two cultures.
>
> Patricia Palmer, *Language and Conquest in Early Modern Ireland*[1]

On 1 November the men first appeared in Green Street courthouse for
the trial arraignment. An account published in the *Freeman's Journal* the
following day was somewhat sympathetic, describing them as 'decent-
looking countrymen' who appeared 'very much bewildered at finding themselves in the crowded court'.[2] Almost immediately after the arraignment
began, John Stritch, one of the counsel allocated for the men's defence, interrupted to point out that some of the men did not understand the language
of the charge and an interpreter was deployed to translate. Unusually for
such reports, the *Freeman's Journal* article named him:

> Each prisoner was called on to plead separately to the separate murder. Mr.
> Stritch said some of the prisoners did not know English. An interpreter
> named Kelly was sworn, and he interpreted the charge.
>
> Each of the prisoners pleaded not guilty, some saying in English 'they had
> nothing to do with it,' and others replying in Irish. Nearly ten minutes was
> occupied with formal pleading. One of the prisoners, being asked was he ready
> for his trial, said he was not ready.[3]

'Kelly' was Sub-Constable Patrick Kelly; however, when the trials opened on
13 November, the interpreter was one Constable Evans,[4] who would provide

79

all of the interpreting services throughout the eight-day trials. The reasons for Kelly's substitution are somewhat mysterious. Sub-Constable Kelly had worked as an interpreter during the arrests of the men in August and was employed by resident magistrate Gardiner during the gathering of prosecution evidence from Anthony, John and Patrick Joyce. He had travelled from Galway to Dublin by train in early September with the crown witnesses and stayed with them in lodgings near the crown-witness depot on Ballybough Road, located near Clontarf barracks.

Writing from Cong to Dublin on 18 September, Head-Constable Richard Cooke attested to Kelly's suitability for the post, remarking that Kelly was 'specially chosen for the duty' of looking after the crown witnesses, having been 'the medium' through which information on the murders was communicated from the beginning. Cooke also reported that Kelly 'speaks Irish well', that he 'enjoys the entire confidence of the magistrates and officers who were investigating the case', and that he had 'no hesitation in saying that no better man could be chosen for this duty.' Similarly Head Constable Heard at Clontarf barracks testified to Kelly's having been 'most attentive to the witnesses' and to his appearing 'in every way to be a most suitable man for the duty.'[5]

Cooke and Heard's references were sought by the RIC Inspector General in response to a letter of complaint received on 15 September from an official named Duffy, stationed in the crown-witness depot in Dublin. Duffy's letter appears to have been a deliberately provocative attempt to undermine credibility in Kelly's abilities as interpreter and, more significantly, his value to the crown prosecution. The letter also inadvertently points to some of the less salient aspects of the trial preparation, including the 'sounding' of crown witnesses by the constabulary. Duffy wrote as follows: 'I wish to inform [you] that there is witnesses here from Cong and is going to give evidence in the Maamtrasna murder case. The witnesses would be valuable in a good many ways only if they were properly sounded, but they can speak nothing but Irish language, which I cannot understand.' Duffy then proceeded to recommend that a sub-constable named Collins be moved to Dublin from Cong. According to Duffy, the 'man named Kelly', who was 'sent in his place', was 'not fit to grabble [with] what is to be got' and 'if Collins was here, he would be valuable to the government for the information of the inspector general.'[6]

Duffy's allegations against a key crown resource were clearly of sufficient importance to be brought to the attention of the Inspector General's office. Dublin Castle then requested the opinion of Kelly's superiors in Galway and the resulting correspondence threw light on Duffy's motivation. Writing from the police depot in Clontarf to Dublin Castle, Heard reported that from 'enquiries I have made, I believe Duffy wrote the annexed letter because the S. C. [Sub-Constable] refused to drink with him.'[7] Collins was not moved to Dublin and Kelly continued in his role, for a time.

In addition to supporting the Joyce witnesses, Kelly had an important role as translator for the young Joyce boy Patsy who was expected to give evidence also. In that capacity, and prior to the commencement of the trials, he accompanied Patsy and his brother Martin on a visit to George Lyster, the Dublin solicitor who was acting for them in their case for compensation. The state correspondence with Lyster refers to the boys being under the care of Constable Patrick Kelly in early October 1882 and specifically to Kelly's having acted as a sworn interpreter for Patsy when the boy testified under oath about the contents of his 'information'[8] at the Dawson Street solicitor's premises on 12 October 1882:

> Sworn at 16 Dawson St. through the interpretation of Patrick Kelly of Fairview, Clontarf, Sub-Constable of Royal Irish Constabulary, the said Patrick Kelly having been first sworn that he would truly and faithfully interpret the contents of this information to the deponent Patrick Joyce, and that he would truly and faithfully interpret the oath about to be administered to him, the said Patrick Joyce, who seemed perfectly to understand same, and that he saw him make his mark thereto this 12th day of October 1882.[9]

This apparently routine event is highly significant within the Maamtrasna judicial narrative: it provides verified evidence of the child Patsy's ability to understand a legal oath (a competency that, as we shall see, would be denied during the trial itself and his crucial evidence dismissed). Kelly could attest that an oath had been administered to the young boy at the solicitor's office through his translation, carefully implemented in accordance with legal protocol. His closeness to the boys as their interpreter and companion, and his knowledge of what had occurred in Lyster's office, may explain his removal from the case early in November (after he had survived the charges made against him in September).[10]

Constable Thomas Evans, Kelly's replacement, was not appearing for the first time in Green Street as a court interpreter.[11] Earlier in August 1882, he translated the evidence of Irish-speaking witness James Faherty during the Letterfrack murder trials of brothers Patrick and John Walsh, accused of the murder of Martin Lydon, his father John, and prosecution witness

Constable Kavanagh.[12] Evans appears to have been brought to Dublin in August from the west in order to testify regarding the gathering of evidence in Letterfrack in the aftermath of Kavanagh's murder; he was then was put into *ad hoc* service as court interpreter.[13] Evans would remain in Dublin when the Maamtrasna trials ended and served also as interpreter during the Lough Mask murder trials, which took place in Green Street courthouse a month later in December 1882.

In his history of the Maamtrasna murders, Jarlath Waldron attributed a Donegal origin to Evans, and argued that the replacement of a Connemara man (Kelly) with a Donegal man marked a further level of linguistic alienation for the accused since a Donegal Irish-speaker would not have been readily comprehensible to Connemara Irish speakers at this time.[14] Local newspapers, however, show that Constable Evans, a native of the area, had worked in the Mayo region for over a decade prior to the murders and had regularly testified at local petty sessions. An article in the *Ballinrobe Chronicle* in November 1877, detailing cases at the Ballinrobe Petty Sessions, referred to Evans having taken the deposition of the injured party in Irish and acting as interpreter on the occasion.[15] He appeared regularly in Green Street during the November Maamtrasna trials, and translated the Irish-language evidence proffered by the Joyce witnesses and also the evidence from some Irish-speaking defence witnesses. He briefly served as interpreter for the accused man Michael Casey but his role would prove most notorious when not deployed, since the court failed to make available his services to the Irish monoglot Myles Joyce.[16]

IRISH IN THE COURTS: REG. V. BURKE (1858)

A landmark legal judgement concerning the Irish language in the courts, made in 1858, resonated through the Maamtrasna trials almost 25 years later. In May of that year, the Irish Court for Crown Cases Reserved (the court of appeal for point-of-law cases) heard the reserved case of *Reg. v. Burke*, central to which was the status and credibility of an Irish-speaking witness. The year before, Burke had been convicted of rape at the Mayo assizes in Castlebar and his trial had featured a number of witnesses sworn and examined in Irish, including the victim, Margaret Sheridan, and a witness for the defence Martin Thornton. At the beginning of the trial Thornton stated that he could not speak English and was then examined through an interpreter. During the cross-examination the prosecution counsel produced two female witnesses to contradict Thornton's claim and thus to undermine his reliability as an alibi witness for the accused. The women testified to having heard Thornton sing an English song ('The Heights of Alma') and speak English in their presence – allegations denied by him but upheld in the judge's charge to the jury. Following the conviction, the prisoner's counsel George Orme Malley (who, 24 years later, would serve as defence counsel in the Maamtrasna trials) applied for judgment as to the admissibility of the women's evidence, in order to undermine the conviction against his client.[17]

In the verdict delivered on 22 May the ten appeal judges differed in opinion, three finding that the evidence by the women was admissible and seven finding that it was not properly received since the issue was a collateral or unconnected matter. The individual judgments make very clear that the judges considered this to be a significant case in relation to court treatment of Irish-speaking witnesses and a strong future precedent. James O'Brien (lead judge for the minority opinions) argued as follows:

> I may observe that the question involved in the case is one of considerable importance as affects the administration of justice in those parts of the country where many persons profess not to speak or understand the English language and are examined in Irish; and it is especially important with reference to cross-examination, the great value of which arises from the demeanour of the witness and the hesitation or fairness with which he answers questions unexpected by him and put suddenly to him, and his demeanour while being so cross-examined is powerful with the jury to judge of the credit which they ought to give to his testimony; and it is plain that the value of this test is very much lessened in the case of a witness having a sufficient knowledge of the English language to understand the questions put by counsel, pretending ignorance of it, and gaining time to consider his answers while the interpreter is going through the useless task of interpreting the question which the witness already perfectly understands.[18]

Uniting these judicial opinions, whether for or against, was a deep fear as to the undue advantage acquired in court by those who 'profess not to speak or understand the English language'. The judges also expressed concern that undue legal time would be spent on ascertaining from witnesses whether denial of knowledge of English arose from 'want of knowledge', 'fraud' or 'bias.'[19] A notable exception to this prevailing scepticism was the opinion

expressed by Chief Justice Lefroy, who began by emphasising his considerable experience with Irish-speaking witnesses, 'upon one occasion I remember sixteen Irish witnesses produced to prove *alibis*.' Lefroy continued:

> Upon all these occasions we have had examination, and the judge has always
> endeavoured to ascertain whether it was fit and proper to allow the witness to
> give his testimony in the Irish language, on the ground that it was not justice
> to him to oblige him to give his evidence on oath in a language he was not
> certain of; and whilst we are so very anxious for the cause of justice, are we to
> have no regard to what is due to the conscience of the witness? Why are we to
> presume that when the witness tells us he cannot give his testimony in English,
> … he does so from a bias?[20]

The opinion by Judge Jonathan Christian similarly allowed for the existence
of 'honest' motivation on the witness's part, a view that he supported by
drawing a rare analogy with other multilingual legal contexts:

> I apprehend it is perfectly possible that the witness was actuated by an honest
> motive in wishing to be examined in Irish. He may have wished to express
> himself in the language which he knew best, in which he could most clearly
> express his thoughts; and is it not easy to imagine that one of us, a person of
> a rank of life above that of this witness, if giving evidence in an Italian or a
> French court of justice, would prefer to do so in the English language?[21]

Yet, as was the case with Lefroy, Christian's more liberal judgment still rested
on the assumption that all witnesses in Irish courts possessed a knowledge
of English to some degree, albeit a lesser or 'uncertain' one. For their fellow
judges, bilingual competency was to be feared as a means of baffling judicial
practice or of concealing truths, and most especially as a threatening legal
advantage; the immense disadvantage experienced by those who were still
'Irish-only' speakers in the 1850s was not even countenanced. Yet, many such
people existed in the region: the 1861 census for Mayo, taken three years
after the Burke case, records 156,376 speakers of Irish (61.4 per cent of its
population), of whom 32,228 (one in eight of the county's population) are
recorded as speaking Irish only.[22]

INTERPRETERS AND THE LAW IN NINETEENTH-CENTURY IRELAND

While the majority view in 1858 had supported the 'honest motive' of witnesses wishing to be questioned in Irish, whether or not such a wish could be achieved in practice depended on the existence of translation services, poorly supported by government infrastructure. As the arrests of the Maamtrasna men showed, the local administration of law in some parts of Ireland into the late nineteenth century still required the deployment of police constables as interpreters. RIC handbooks and manuals from the period contain detailed guidelines for methods of arrest and charging of suspects but are generally silent on matters of linguistic difference. Two contemporary sources, relating to the powers and duties of magistrates in Irish, do provide brief guidelines on how oaths were to be sworn by monoglot speakers. In Edward Parkyns Levinge's *The Justice of the Peace for Ireland* – subtitled 'A treatise on summary jurisdiction and proceedings as to indictable offences' – instructions for the examination of those who did not speak English are tellingly included in a section beginning with 'deaf and dumb witnesses', and the example given is that of French rather than Irish! The following passage comes from the third edition of 1872, published in Dublin by Hodges, Foster, and Company, booksellers to 'the Honourable Society of King's Inns':

> *Deaf and dumb* witnesses, as well as all others who do not speak the English language, should be sworn through the medium of another person duly qualified to interpret them, the interpreter being first sworn faithfully to interpret the witness. Also, where the defendant, or the party charged, does not understand the English language, the evidence should be interpreted to him. The interpreter's oath may be in the following form:

> [*Interpreter's Oath.*] 'You shall truly and faithfully interpret the evidence about to be given, and all other matters and things touching the present charge, and the French [*or as the case may be*] language into the English language, and the English language into the French [*or as the case may be*] language, according to the best of your skill and ability; so help you God.'[23]

The case of Irish was explicitly mentioned in one instance only in Richard Nun and John Edward Walsh's *The Powers and Duties of the Justices of the Peace in Ireland and of Constables as Connected Therewith*, first published in 1841, and the second edition of which appeared with additions in 1844. Its copious appendices in volume 2 include the form of oath and *jurat* (or affidavit) for occasions where an interpreter was employed. This was the form of words widely used in the depositions and information taken in the immediate aftermath of the Maamtrasna murders:

> *If an interpreter be employed, add*: Sworn at, &c., by the above mentioned *A. B.*, the same having been first read over and explained to him in the [Irish] language, by *M. N.* of _____, who was first duly sworn to interpret the same to the said *A. B.* before me *J. P.*, &c.[24]

A notebook of words and phrases collected in Connaught in 1886 by 'an Irish student' includes the formal Irish wording to be used on swearing a trial witness. The witness is instructed to swear by the book (*beir ar an leabhar*), to raise his right hand and to swear: 'that you will tell the truth, the whole truth (*iomlán na fírinne*), and nothing but the truth if you want to save your soul', and then to kiss the book (*tabhair póg don leabhar*).[25]

Wolf's *An Irish-Speaking Island* provides the most thorough study of the status afforded or denied to Irish in the 'courtroom and polling booth' for the century ending 1870.[26] As he convincingly argues, wider access to the legal system from the mid-eighteenth century onwards led to language issues becoming 'more salient' rather than less relevant in these two domains. In his words, 'the expansion of the legal system vertically into the lives of middling- and even lower-class litigants through the expansion and formalization of new venues such as the petty sessions courts made the issue of language in the courts more visible than any time in the preceding hundred years.'[27] Irish manor courts in County Galway in the pre-famine period were 'predominantly Irish speaking', Richard McMahon suggests, and most of the other manor courts in the west of Ireland, prior to their abolition in 1859, were bilingual.[28] Statutes authorising the payment of costs to interpreters at formal quarter sessions courts in Ireland were passed as late as 1837 and 1851, building on earlier legal provisions. These included the stipulation that 'each county's assistant barrister was to certify whether an interpreter was necessary and determine if one individual might suffice for the whole county or if interpreting should be divided among several sessions' districts.'[29] Interpreting services at the local petty sessions courts were more *ad hoc*, and volunteers could be sworn from the local attendees, including in some cases the sessions-clerk.[30] A late instance of this is recorded in the *Ballinrobe Chronicle* regarding a July 1898 hearing when an objection was levelled against a man named Thomas Mellett, who was about to be sworn in as interpreter for an Irish-speaking witness, on the basis that he was a relative of the accused.[31] The needs of Irish-speakers in legal courts outside of Ireland can also be glimpsed on occasion: for example, in April 1852 the Proceedings of the Old Bailey, London's Central Criminal Court, recorded the use of an Irish interpreter for a female witness named Nance Nelligan 'who could only speak Irish, and was examined through an interpreter.'[32]

Court interpreters had, in theory, the dual function of translating the testimony of Irish-speaking witnesses into English and of rendering the English-language proceedings of the court into Irish, as needed, but the proceedings of courts cases, in particular at petty sessions level, show that in most cases the translation of Irish-speaking evidence into English was the only service provided. Lesa Ní Mhungaile's valuable research on Irish-speaking courts from 1700–1843 has uncovered a number of contemporary complaints about the poor standard of interpreters.[33] In reminiscences of his days as court reporter, published in the *Limerick Reporter* in the 1860s, Maurice Lenihan recalled: 'The "interpreter," indeed, was not always master of the tongue with which he professed to be thoroughly acquainted. I have seen an intelligent juror more than once trip up an "interpreter," and telling the court that the question was not properly put to the witness.'[34] Earlier in the nineteenth century, Gaelic scholar Pádraig Ó Néill (1765–1832) had written eloquently on the plight of Irish-speaking accused in an English-language court. His comments, penned in 1816, resonate powerfully over two centuries later: 'In this country how alarming, nay oft times how dangerously circumstanced is that person arraigned at the Bar of Justice who beholds any interpreter whom chance may throw in the way of the learned Judge, compelled to answer to interrogatories, on which his interests, and oft times his very existence depends.'[35] Ó Néill also pinpointed, with considerable prescience, the difficulties of adequate translation from one language's figurative idiom to the formal legalese of another:

> The Irish converse much in idioms which should not, and oft times could not be literally translated … their stile [*sic*] abounds with figurative expressions which amid the bustle of a court of justice and a crowded audience were difficult indeed to render into another language in their own proper colours; … besides the Irish abounds with words which have no corresponding terms in the English language to be known by; and therefore make the business of an hasty interpreter in an office of vast danger to the parties concerned.[36]

While Ní Mhungaile's research extends to 1843, and Wolf's book covers the century to 1870, considerable evidence exists, as will be discussed further on, that interpreting services for Irish-speaking monoglots were needed, and sometimes provided, into the closing decades of the nineteenth century. In 1894, a national registrar of petty sessions reported to the Chief Secretary John Morley that 109 of 606 national petty sessions districts continued to make provisions for interpreters.[37]

Court officials often treated the appearance of Irish monoglots in legal courts with suspicion or derision. A recurring concern, similar to that voiced by the 1850s appeal judges, was that such witnesses assumed the guise of being unable to comprehend English in order to gain additional legal advantage or to subvert the trial process. Lenihan's memoirs vividly describe a number of instances of such 'feigned incomprehension' or strategic incomprehensibility, which he himself had witnessed:

> I have seen some of them resist all the attempts of the 'interpreter' to give a reply at certain times, and sent off the table with a strong caution from the learned judge, an indignant shout from the Crown Counsel, which very well comprehended the cause: and on other occasions, when it was not perfectly safe or easy to assume deafness, the 'Irish' witness would adopt an incomprehensibility which would put the 'interpreter' to the blush, and force him to declare that he was not so complete a master of the language of the Gaedhil as to convey himself intelligibly to the witness.[38]

Yet, as Ní Mhungaile usefully notes, 'subterfuge should not be assumed in all instances of the services of interpreters being requested because even in cases where the witness may have spoken English, they may not have felt sufficiently comfortable to give evidence in that language.'[39] This spectrum of competence comes into particular relief when those with limited ability in English are faced with a highly intimidating legal setting and specialised vocabulary. As a result, the legal system conceded the need to accommodate Irish in the courts, per the 1858 judgement, but huge local variations in the actual practice of accommodation led to legal justice being dispersed very differently among Irish speakers.[40]

Interpreters were also employed on nineteenth-century census taking and the census instructions contained a provision for payment in this regard, though they urged that they be employed as rarely as possible: 'Where interpreters are indispensable an allowance of one shilling six pence a day will be made for them, but in those districts where the Irish language prevails the Superintendents are, if possible, to appoint Enumerators acquainted with that language, in order to avoid the necessity of employing interpreters.'[41] According to the 1871 census, a total of 10 people held the occupation of interpreter in the country, with intriguing references to three female interpreters and four foreign-born male interpreters.[42] In 1891 the former occupation of one workhouse inmate was also that of interpreter.[43] One male occupier of land who had the additional employment of being 'an Irish Interpreter at Assizes and Quarter sessions' is identified in Donegal in 1871[44] and a similar entry exists for Donegal in the 1901 census.[45] These tallies are not exhaustive, however, and do not include many interpreters who worked on a part-time basis or within the judicial system. For example, the individual 1901 census return for Pádraig Stúndún (or Patrick Stanton) lists him as an Irish interpreter and head of a bilingual household in Cork city, and a 1908 obituary describes him as having acted 'as official interpreter in the courts in Cork for a great number of years.'[46]

An in-depth study of the role of interpreters in nineteenth-century legal practice is greatly hampered by their inherent invisibility in most surviving records. To borrow Patricia Palmer's description of the professional interpreter in Elizabethan Ireland: 'The individual who crosses the lines – linguistically at least – often enters the text only *between* the lines. Unnoticed or erased, he usually exists only by implication, a medium who leaves no message to posterity.'[47] But local newspaper reports of petty session courts provide some of the most valuable evidence for the continuing use of interpreters in western regions through to the last decades of the nineteenth century.[48] In March, 1879, the *Connaught Telegraph*, reporting on a case brought before the Galway Spring Assizes that week, referred to all the witnesses having 'to be examined through an Irish interpreter.'[49] Similar reports are provided in the *Ballinrobe Chronicle* for proceedings at the Clonbur Petty Sessions in March 1882 and continue into the late 1890s in *Ballinrobe Chronicle* and *Connaught Telegraph* reports of the Castlebar Petty Sessions in August 1895, the Ballinrobe Quarter Sessions in 1896 and the Mayo Assizes in 1898, to name just some examples.[50] On a few occasions, these press reports note witnesses' resistance to or questioning of the role and impartiality of the interpreter, who was a person known to them from the locality. The *Ballinrobe Chronicle* of 1872 provides one example, in a case taken at Clonbur Petty Sessions by a plaintiff called Edward Kearney who had charged two neighbours with assault and who was questioned at length by the defence solicitor:

> He being an Irish witness, and the questions put through an interpreter, there was a regular passage of arms, or words, between them; the witness considered

it was highly impertinent for the man who acted as interpreter to be 'putting him such questions, as he had no right to be enquiring into his family affairs so inquisitively, it was no affair of his, that he was trying to make game of him, and putting cross-questions to make him slip a word for the attorney and damn himself, so he would not answer him anymore, but he would answer the gentleman himself.'[51]

Once again, Irish-speaking witnesses were the subjects of ridicule in many of these newspaper accounts, and their lack of knowledge of English explicitly questioned. In the Bandon Quarter Sessions in early October 1882, Daniel Donovan of Burgatia brought an action to recover a sum of twenty pounds, an 'alleged loss and damage' owing to trespass and destruction of his fences. The *Skibbereen Eagle* of 10 October records the following narrative of events:

> When the plaintiff was called, some amusement arose out of his denying his ability to speak English, while Mr Wright [counsel for the defendant] stated that he had examined him in English before now, and that he had spoken the language as fluently as any man. The witness, however, on being questioned on the subject persisted in replying in Irish, and could not be got to break ground in English. He intimated, through the interpreter, that he would be d____d if he spoke English, the grounds for this opinion that he had already sworn that he could not do so. This quaint way of putting the matter occasioned some merriment in court. The witness was then examined through the interpreter ... On examination by Mr. Wright, the witness swore he had no English, except such English as he did not half understand himself, and which he was sure none in court would understand. His cross-examination had, therefore, to be proceeded with through the interpreter.[52]

Surviving Crown Office papers for 1893, held in the National Archives, include a series of 'interpreters' papers' for County Mayo. Twelve men applied for the position of interpreter in Mayo County Court and this small but revealing archive includes both their letters of application and accompanying references. Quite a range of competence in Irish existed among those who considered themselves suitable candidates for the role, and also varying standards of literacy in English.[53] Patrick Deasy attested to having been 'over 18 years acting in continuation as assistant interpreter on one side of the court of Assize here and for several years past at the Castlebar October sessions without ever a fault having been found with me by any judge any member of the Bar or any of the professional gentlemen.'[54] The 60-year-old Patrick Hughes emphasised the trustworthiness of his credentials: 'I have a thorough knowledge of the Irish language and can write it down with facility as well as knowing it conversationally. Having been examined by the Board of National Education, I hold a certificate showing that I have a competent knowledge of Irish.'[55] Another applicant, Luke Loftus, high-lighted his ability to speak Irish since a teenager: 'I can speak Irish since I was fourteen years of age I can also read Irish and stand an examination if required' while Patrick Burke presented himself as 'a practical farmer. I can read and write Irish. I am 38 years of age and I am willing to stand before any examination.'[56] Writing of another applicant, the 25-year-old John Kane, a butler's son, his referee, J. F. Rutledge of Rossmally, Westport, noted that it was 'very unusual to get a man of his age so thoroughly well up in Irish.'[57]

How to evaluate an applicant's competence in Irish, and their facility to act within the judicial sphere, was clearly a huge challenge in this hiring process. The authors of testimonials ranged from land agents and landowners to certified teachers, rectors and parish priests; while some disavowed their ability to judge the applicant's qualifications as an Irish speaker, others attested to their own knowledge of the language. Thus in the case of Edward (Ned) Maguire, one reference was provided by his father, a medical officer, who described his son as an 'excellent Irish speaker and interpreter' while the other referee, Charles Lynch of 'Ballycurrin Castle, Headford', observed that he had 'personal experience of his qualities as an Irish speaker and can therefore bear testimony to his proficiency.'[58] But, most importantly, the very move to reemploy a court interpreter in Mayo in the early 1890s indicates that at least some influential parties recognised the need to provide legal services for Irish-speakers with limited or no compe-tence in English.

Under local government legislation, when interpreters were employed by courts, the court could pay such compensation as was considered reason-able, but only in cases where such interpreters were not already salaried officers.[59] The exact fees for interpreters are difficult to establish; although ledger entries for the Chief Secretary's papers for the years 1880 to 1900 contain references to extensive contemporary correspondence relating to fees and payments, only a handful of these documents survive.[60] In 1896, ledger references in the Chief Secretary papers record the payment of 2 shillings 6 pence a day to a man called Devaney who was employed as inter-preter in Oughterard petty sessions.[61]

By the turn of the century, officially employed interpreters were becoming more and more rare, and fewer such positions were sanctioned by the courts though Irish-speaking monoglots continued to appear before them.[62] In October 1899, a case in which the Ballinrobe quarter sessions judge refused to provide an interpreter to a witness (despite the presence of a salaried interpreter in court) received national notoriety. In numerous press reports, Judge Dane was described as having refused a hearing to a 'litigant who was ignorant of the English language, and dismissed his case because he was unable to give his evidence in English.'[63] Dane's defence, reported at length in the *Connaught Telegraph*, was that the interpreter 'a paid official of the court, a paid, sworn official', had demonstrated to his satisfaction that the man 'roughly spoke English, and that he spoke it and had been speaking it to him on that very day, and the day before.' The judge also reiterated the long-standing charge that those who spoke Irish and could comprehend English who sought the services of the interpreter did so to 'try to frustrate the ends of justice, because they think that by being sworn in Irish they will have time to hear the questions put, and to consider what kind of answer they will give.'[64]

Some days later, the case was the subject of an acrimonious debate at a meeting of the Ballinrobe District Council in which the translation services provided by the official interpreter, named here as 'Keane', were strongly criticised as 'very poor' and other instances of mistranslation by him were cited.[65] According to one of the councillors who had been present in the courtroom, and who knew Irish, the only English possessed by the Irish-speaking litigant was, in a heavy irony, the phrase 'fair play'.[66] Another councillor similarly attested that 'he knew the man and was aware that he was unable to buy as much as a ha'penny worth in English' and a published letter from Dr Edward Maguire, a Ballinrobe physician and court witness, was read to the meeting in which Maguire vouched 'his personal knowledge that the man knew no English'.[67] The council debate culminated in the passing, by a large majority, of a lengthy resolution. What is striking here is the degree to which the wording of this resolution, in 1899, drew upon an emerging revivalist discourse of language rights and also emphasised international precedents: 'We maintain that an Irish-speaking peasant has as much right to give his evidence in the Irish language as the Welsh people have to give theirs in a Welsh court; and we further believe that it should be compulsory for judges administering the law in Irish speaking courts to have a knowledge of the Irish language.'[68]

THE BILINGUAL COURTROOM

'Legal-linguistic' flashpoints comparable to the Maamtrasna trial can be identified in other European contexts; for example, the notorious French-language murder trial of Flemish speakers Coucke and Goethals in 1863, in which the innocent monoglot defendants were condemned and later executed, 'did much' as Joep Leerssen has noted, 'to fan the vehemence of the Flemish movement.'[69] A more recent example is the trial and conviction of Gaston Dominici in Provence in 1954, subject of a chapter in Roland Barthes' influential *Mythologies*.[70] Dominici was accused and convicted of the murder of three members of the Drummond family who were British tourists in the area; his death sentence was soon after commuted to hard labour and in 1960 he was freed. A key argument for mistrial was that no real proof of guilt existed and that Dominic, a Provencal speaker with only a rough knowledge of French, had not understood the formal court proceedings. Extrapolating from the case, Barthes delivers a both resonant and disturbing observation as to how injustice can be hidden from view: 'This appearance of Justice in the world of the accused is possible thanks to an intermediary myth, always made good use of by officialdom, whether the Court of Assizes or literary tribunals: the myth of the transparency and the universality of language.'[71]

What Barthes' translators term, somewhat ponderously, as the 'intermediary myth' of official justice, namely that language is transparent (not in need of interpretation) and universal (lacking difference), can also become the target for satire and resistance when a culture experiences language shift and social change. Early nineteenth-century Irish fiction, for example, provides lots of examples of comic scenes set in courtrooms, where linguistic miscomprehension abounds and often where the character's bilingual prowess enables him or her (usually him) to short-change judicial process. The most famous instance is a scene in Gerard Griffin's 1829 novel *Collegians*, 'How the danger to the secret of Hardress was averted by the ingenuity of Irish witnesses.'[72] Here, Hardress Cregan's servants, Poll (sister of Danny Mann) and her husband Philip Naughten are interrogated with respect to accusations against their master and their responses involve a number of comic strategies of evasion:

> The man returned an answer in Irish, which the magistrate cut short in the middle.
>
> 'Answer me in English, friend. We speak no Irish here. Is your name Philip Naughten?'

'Tha wisha, vourneen—'

'Come—come—English—Swear him to know whether he does not understand English. Can you speak English, fellow?'

'Not a word, plase your honour.'

A roar of laughter succeeded this escapade, to which the prisoner listened with a wondering and stupid look. Addressing himself in Irish to Mr. Cregan, he appeared to make an explanatory speech which was accompanied by a slight expression of indignation.

'What does the fellow say?' asked Mr Warner.

'Why,' said Cregan, with a smile, 'he says that he will admit that he couldn't be *hung in English before his face*—but he does not know enough of the language to enable him to *tell his story* in English.'

'Well, then, I suppose we must have it in Irish. Mr Houlahan, will you act as interpreter?'

The clerk, who thought it *genteel* not to know Irish, bowed and declared himself unqualified.

'Wisha, then,' said a gruff voice at a little distance, in a dark corner of the room, 'it isn't but what you had opportunities enough of learning it. If you went in foreign parts, what would they say to you, do you think, when you'd tell 'em you didn't know the language o' the counthry where you born? You ought to be ashamed o' yourself, so you ought.'[73]

In Griffin's treatment of the bilingual courtroom, failure to know 'the language o' the counthry' renders one a direct target for critique and satire. The scene vividly portrays the gaps in linguistic comprehension by which the legal system is itself indicted (the magistrate and clerk are the least qualified persons to follow the witness's evidence) and also the subversive actions of a bilingual witness who manoevres skillfully between what language is known and what is acknowledged to be known. A caustic footnote by Griffin explains '*hung in English before his face*' as follows: 'a common phrase, meaning that the individual understood enough of the language to refute any calamny spoken in his presence, which if uncontradicted, might leave him in danger of the halter. The acute reader may detect in the pithy idiom a meaning characteristic of the country in which it is used.'[74] Although convoluted in phrasing, the footnote is a telling reminder that a range of competence may exist, that a witness may have enough English to under-stand generally the events in court but not enough to relay his evidence fully. So Griffin's invoked 'acute reader' might further recognise that such gaps in comprehension are not simply the mark of 'non-elite' vulnerability before the law but can, as some of the 1850s appeal judges expressly feared, be strategically deployed as linguistic weapons against the judicial formalism and inflexibility of the legal sphere.

Humour, as Nicholas Wolf has well argued, is an 'unexpectedly dominant form used to express the experience of language contact in modern Ireland':

> Of at least 450 documented allusions to the Irish language that can be identified among the oral interviews collected by the Irish Folklore Commission in the 1930s and 1940s, more than half consisted of jokes and humorous short stories centering on a foolish character whose mishaps in negotiating a world of two languages provided occasion for laughter.[75]

And, as he goes on to demonstrate, jokes, 'this seemingly incongruous and lighthearted popular response to language contact' can also be viewed 'as a formal site for renegotiation and reinvention of the status of the Irish language.'[76] A number of the jokes examined by Wolf feature the Irish speaker in the courtroom. While the effects of such jokes might be expected to underline the difference between 'Irish-speaking and English-speaking worlds', the more telling division produced by such language humour is in fact between monoglot and bilingual: 'between the monoglot characters in the jokes (both English and Irish) and the bilingual audience and joke tellers.'[77] In other words, to be bilingual is to 'get the joke' at the monolingual's expense.

As late as 1903, a lively example of the interrelations of language, humour and the courtroom can be found in Somerville and Ross's essay 'An Irish Problem.' Like Griffin's scene, over 70 years before, their account of the operations of a bilingual courtroom yields lots of comic material though the particular target of satire in this case is the hapless interpreter. As a portrait of legal interpretation in practice – or at least in attempted practice – in early twentieth-century Ireland, the essay possesses much ethnographic interest (as well as being very funny), pointing to the continuing use of interpreters in western Ireland much later than one might have expected and also to widespread comprehension of Irish in the local area. In August 1901, Edith Somerville and Violet Martin attended a Petty Sessions court in Carna, County Galway, by invitation from the Resident Magistrate, W. McDermot, and fellow magistrate, local hotelier J. O'Loghlen.[78] According to Martin Ross's diary for 15 August, 'Johnny O'Loghlen drove Edith and me, with three other female visitors, over to Carna, for the Petty Sessions there. There was only one case, of the drowning of a sheep, but J. O'Loghlen and W. McDermot worked it for an hour and a half for all it was worth.'[79]

In the ensuing story, first published in the *National Review* periodical, the court participants include two magistrates, a clerk, an interpreter and a District Inspector of Police. Darcy, the plaintiff, is an Irish monoglot: 'One could have believed him a soldier, a German, anything but what he was, a peasant from the farthest shores of Western Ireland, cut off from what we call civilization by his ignorance of any language save his own ancient speech, wherein the ideas of to-day stand out in English words like telegraph-posts in a Connemara moorland.'[80] The less sympathetically-rendered defendant, Sweeny, with 'a sisther [*sic*] married to a stationmaster and a brother in the Connaught Rangers' is keen to emphasise his lack of need for an interpreter: having 'as good English as anny man in this coort.'[81]

It quickly emerges that both magistrates, 'Dochtor' Lyden and the shop-owner Heraty, are also highly competent in Irish. According to the testimony of Mr Byrne the local schoolteacher, 'the Bench has as good Irish as I have myself, and better.'[82] In this company, therefore, the only mono-glots present, other than the Irish-speaking plaintiff Darcy, are the English-speaking narrators, a fact wryly observed by the narrators:

> 'The law requires that the thransactions of this coort shall take place in English,' the Chairman responded, 'and we have also the public to consider.'
>
> As it was pretty certain that we were the only persons in the court who did not understand Irish, it was borne upon us that we were the public, and we appreciated the consideration.[83]

As the questioning proceeds, the 'unctuous' court interpreter – 'small, old, froglike in profile, full of the dignity of the Government official'[84] – becomes the object of general ire because he delivers a series of imprecise translations. His final mistranslation of Darcy's account of his mother's injury – 'a stone fell on her and hurted her finger, and the boot preyed on it, and it has her desthroyed' – marks the comic demise of the translator's reliability:

> William's skinny hand covered his frog-mouth with all a deserving schoolboy's embarrassment at being caught out in a bad translation.
>
> 'I beg yer worships' pardon,' he said, in deep confusion, 'but sure your worships know as well as meself that in Irish we have the one word for your finger or your toe.'[85]

In Somerville and Ross's fictional depiction of a bilingual courtroom, unlike most other such representations, the monoglot plaintiff retains a rare dignity, in marked contrast to the officious government interpreter. The other culpable character is the bilingual defendant who has attempted to manipulate the law in his favour, 'in a tissue of sworn lies before his fellows for the sake of half a sovereign and a family feud.'[86]

The bilingual courtroom is a space in which the consequences of rapid cultural and linguistic shift can appear in especially vivid human detail, as individuals struggle to find ways to express themselves in the language and legal processes belonging to the dominant culture. A recent example is the legal system of Hong Kong, subject of Kwai Hang Ng's pioneering ethno-graphic study *The Common Law in Two Voices* (2009) in which courtroom examples resonate strikingly with the treatment of the Maamtrasna Irish-speaking defendants in late nineteenth-century Ireland. Since 1997, Hong Kong possesses a bilingual common law system with trials officially classi-fied as English or Chinese, but very often mixed-language in practice, and featuring the extensive use of interpreters to translate witnesses' utterances in Cantonese to English-language evidence. Ng's opening description of the 'lively exchanges' that are 'not uncommon' in early twenty-first century Cantonese courtrooms evokes details similar to Somerville and Ross's depiction above:

> The exchange is fluid, jaunty, and, above all, carnivalesque, in the subversive Bakhtinian sense of the term. Witnesses are let loose; they talk more and are often more pugnacious. Freestyle storytelling, intense sparring matches, peppery sarcasm, and slaphappy remarks prevail in this environment, and the trials are louder, noisier, and often edgier. They are also less predictable.[87]

However, rather than mere evidence of 'local colour', such exchanges illus-trate for Ng how Cantonese has become 'a language of resistance in court-room interactions':

> The use of Cantonese opens up a space, albeit highly contested, that allows litigants to articulate, debate, and even manipulate local senses of justice in a formalist legal institution in ways unseen during the colonial era. Legal bilin-gualism does not simply cause less order and more arguments in the courts of Hong Kong. It has also begun to change the social character of the legal system in Hong Kong.[88]

Through a series of linguistic case studies, Ng shows how the challenge of Cantonese in Hong Kong courtrooms 'pushes into the fabric of juridicial formalism'.[89] For legal outcomes to be accepted as legitimate, 'usual social moorings' must be superseded by – and be seen to be superseded by – 'the putative objectivity of the story once told in the apparently dispassionate language of the law', to use legal scholar Elizabeth Mertz's widely-cited terms.[90] Yet the very presence of the interpreter in the courtroom and her or his interactions with other legal parties are constant reminders of a linguistic otherness not readily assimilated within a 'universal', 'transparent' or 'dispassionate' language. What Ng and Somerville and Ross recognise, albeit in very different narrative styles, is the potency of the court interpreter as a force of stabilisation or destabilisation: at stake are some of the most fundamental assumptions about the impartiality of legal process.

Given these high stakes, it's not surprising that the role of the legal interpreter has received more focused attention in contemporary translation studies, but with some significant divergences in how that function is to be understood.[91] In an article provocatively entitled 'The gum syndrome', Ruth Morris usefully summarises the different metaphors that have been used over time to convey the function of an court interpreter, which include phonograph, transmission wire or telephone, translating machine, conduit, etc.[92] Some understandings of the role are in potential conflict with each other, most obviously in the difference between the historical model of interpreter as 'conduit' – which assumes a verbatim and unproblematic transfer from one language to another – and a more contemporary view of the interpreter as a key participant in the linguistic transfer rather than neutral agent. As Morris writes, 'These two contrasting situations have been liked by interpreters to being a piece of gum on the bottom of a shoe – ignored for all practical purposes, but impossible to remove.'[93] From the early 1990s onwards, the dialogic aspects of the interpreter's role have been emphasised by Cynthia Wadensjö and subsequent commentators; in other words the interpreter does not simply relay but also coordinates conversations, the consequence of which is that the interpreter may also serve as a 'gatekeeper' in legal interactions.[94] Consequently, the extent to which the interpreter may intensify rather than neutralise cultural conflict has become an urgent subject in legal studies today.

Writing of the work of court interpreters in contemporary United States, Sandra Hale notes that 'the bilingual courtroom presents us with a process of cooperation, negotiation and even power struggle between the lawyers, the witness and the interpreter.'[95] And a substantial legal literature now exists which attests to the continuing challenges experienced by Australian Aboriginals in Australian courts and by linguistic minorities in the American courtroom.[96] Their analyses of the styles and practices of court translators support the view that the interpreter can often function as linguistic gatekeepers (what Ng terms 'linguistic marshals')[97] policing a boundary which separates legal, translated evidence in English from the language of the original utterance, and further enforcing what Angermeyer terms the 'societal subordination of minority-language speakers'.[98]

In 1882, the Dublin Special Commission Court was a central instrument in the government's response to agrarian crime and the large crowds who attended the November Maamtrasna trials were a further indication of their perceived public importance. But what was also 'at the bar' was the ability of the judicial system to provide a fair trial to a group of accused men, many of whom were unable to comprehend proceedings in English and for all of whom the Dublin court environment was deeply alien. From the surviving transcript of the Maamtrasna trials, supplemented by newspaper evidence, we can recreate where in the week-long legal proceedings the court interpreter appeared, and crucially failed to appear, and whose interests were served.

— 5 —

TRIALS

'The shambles of Maamtrasna are avenged'

We are all potential Dominics, not murderers but as the accused deprived of language or, worse, dressed up, humiliated, condemned in that of our accusers. To steal his language from a man in the very name of language: every legal murder begins here.

Roland Barthes, Mythologies[1]

Dublin's historic Green Street courthouse – now an administrative building for the Courts Service – was the location for the Maamtrasna trials. The courthouse is located in the Smithfield area on a site believed to be part of the burial ground of the medieval Cistercian St Mary's Abbey and next to the old Newgate Prison. It opened for sessions on 10 January 1797 and many high-profile trials in the nineteenth century took place there, including that of the Sheares brothers in 1798, Robert Emmet in 1803, John Mitchel and others in 1848, Fenian leaders in the late 1860s and the 'Invincibles' in 1883. In 1918 part of the election count was held at Green Street, including the announcement of Constance Markievicz's success; after independence it was the location of the Special Criminal Court and continued in this role until 2010. A young James Joyce is said to have observed trials at Green Street from the public gallery, and the 'Cyclops' chapter of *Ulysses* is set in Barney Kiernan's 'Court of Appeal' pub, adjacent to the Green Street court.[2]

A contemporary illustration from the London *Graphic* captures one moment from the second day of trial proceedings, during the brief examination of young Patsy Joyce[3] (see Image 19, p. X). In the upper left-hand

corner is the 12-person jury, seated in the petty-jury box, with the witness
table situated underneath; central to the picture, under the crown insignia,
sits the presiding judge Charles Barry, and in front of him the various
crown and defence counsel and solicitors, as well as various members of
the constabulary. In the dock is the first accused, Patrick Joyce (with the
pugnacious features common to late nineteenth-century illustrations of
the Irish). It is unclear from the image where the court interpreter stood,
but contemporary references suggest that he stood at a distance from the
accused, nearer to the counsel,[4] and he is possibly the constabulary figure
facing the judge near the centre of the *Graphic* illustration.

Public interest in the Maamtrasna events led to a packed court on
the morning of 13 November and tickets of admission were required. The
resulting uncomfortable conditions were criticised by the *Belfast Newsletter*
in its early accounts of the trial: the 'dingy and uncomfortable little courthouse crowded to excess' was filled, the newspaper observed, 'with the better
class of persons, none being admitted (besides the bar and the press) save
those who were fortunate enough to obtain tickets of admission from the
sheriff.' In the course of the trial Judge Barry complained that the court was
'positively stifling' owing to the 'disgraceful manner in which the windows
are allowed by the police to be closed, notwithstanding repeated remon-
strances from him.'[5]

The trials would last eight days. Proceedings began with the trial of
Patrick Joyce of Shanvallycahill, which ran from Monday, 13 November,
to Wednesday of that week; the trial of Patrick Casey followed from
Wednesday to Friday; the trial of Myles Joyce took place over Friday and
Saturday; the trial of Michael Casey lasted from the following Monday to
Tuesday morning; and the trial of the remaining four prisoners (John Casey,
Patrick Joyce, Tom Joyce, and Martin Joyce) ran briefly on the concluding
day, Tuesday, 21 November. Each of the accused men was charged with the
wilful murder of one of the specific victims: Patrick Joyce with the murder
of John Joyce, Patrick Casey with that of Bridget Joyce, Myles Joyce with
the murder of Margaret Joyce the younger, and Michael Casey with that of
the elder Margaret Joyce.

The Dublin papers covered the proceedings extensively: the *Freeman's
Journal, Daily Express,* and *Irish Times* all featured full-page spreads of the
preceding day's events, while the *Dublin Evening Mail* and the *Freeman's*
sister paper, the Dublin *Evening Telegraph*, provided same-day coverage
of the morning proceedings, and long accounts also appeared in the daily

Belfast Newsletter. The weekly journals, the *Irishman*, *United Ireland*, *Weekly Freeman*, and *Weekly Irish Times*, also furnished detailed coverage, the latter two papers including some illustrations in comparison to the relatively scant coverage by the weekly and then struggling *Nation*. Local western newspapers such as the *Ballinrobe Chronicle* reproduced the *Freeman's Journal* coverage, as did sister nationalist newspapers such as *United Ireland*.

The key primary source for the trial, and for the discussion that follows, is the 243 folio-page typescript account of the proceedings of what was entitled 'The Dublin October Commission', commencing on 13 November 1882. This transcript of the proceedings, recorded utterance by utterance, carries substantial official authority; contemporaneously published in typescript, still a rare occurrence in legal documents of the time: it is a further marker of the trial's immediate political significance.[6] As a legal document in English, it again testifies to what Roland Barthes has termed the 'intermediary myth' that makes possible the 'appearance of justice in the world of the accused', namely, 'the myth of the transparency and the universality of language.'[7] The Irish-language statements of accused and witnesses are recorded only in their English translation, indicated in supporting comment or in parentheses as 'through interpreter'.[8] Yet when one reads the transcript carefully in conjunction with accompanying contemporary newspaper coverage, it becomes possible to reconstruct at least some of the courtroom moments that fall 'between' or 'under' the formal lines of a court record, and some telling elisions and evasions with respect to the speaking of Irish during the November proceedings come back to view.

In her influential study of the 'language of the law school', Elizabeth Mertz has observed that a key factor in the legitimisation of a legal world is the translation of participants from their usual 'social moorings'. She elaborates, 'As the people in the cases become parties (i.e. strategic actors on either side of a legal argument), they are stripped of social position and specific context, [and] located in a geography of legal discourse and authority'[9] – a geography which would have been frighteningly unfamiliar for the Maamtrasna accused and for most witnesses. While the court proceedings, as captured in the November court transcript, sought to enact this process of legitimisation and denaturalisation, contemporary newspaper coverage of the Maamtrasna trials showed a continuing fascination with the signs of social and geographical difference displayed by the accused men. Repeatedly, the apparently impassive demeanour of the men was interpreted as a mark of their guilt, with little or no sympathy expressed for their situation in a culturally alien environment. Both the *Daily Express* and *Irish Times* of 16 November described Patrick Casey as 'of rather repulsive aspect' and asserted that he 'manifested no sense of anxiety at his position.'[10] Patrick Joyce was described by the *Freeman's Journal* as maintaining throughout the long sitting 'a calm and unexcited demeanour.'[11] A number of newspapers also carried descriptions of Joyce's wife, Mary Ann, who made a brief appearance in the courtroom. In the words of the *Irish Times* reporter, 'a rather fine-looking, fair-haired, young peasant woman was in the court when the accused, looking pale and anxious, appeared in the dock. She was then desired to leave.'[12]

For the accused men, the most alienating and inhospitable feature of the courtroom pertained to language. The vast majority of the evidence presented in the course of the trials was in English. This included the testimony of witnesses such as Ryan the civil engineer, the medical personnel who had performed the inquest and examination of bodies, the RIC constables and sub-inspectors, the 'approvers' Philbin and Casey, and one of Patrick Joyce's defence witnesses. Evidence presented to the court in Irish and requiring translation by Evans included that of Anthony, John, and Patrick Joyce, the statements of John Collins, and the alibis presented by various defence witnesses. As key witnesses for the prosecution, the Joyces were the prime targets for the defence counsel, who attempted to undermine their testimony in various ways. Conversely it was important for the prosecution to discredit the Irish-speaking defence witnesses drawn from the families and neighbours of the accused. Perhaps the most eagerly awaited evidence of all was that of the young Patsy Joyce, also a monoglot Irish speaker.[13] What is especially surprising today is that the accused men were not examined or cross-examined: until 1898, a prisoner in a criminal case was deemed 'incompetent' and excluded from testifying on her or his own behalf.[14]

Henry J. Concannon, the solicitor for the prisoners, had first appeared on their behalf at the preliminary inquiry held in Galway Jail in early September. Concannon's efforts to hire senior counsel for the defence were plagued with difficulties: the first counsel withdrew from the case citing health reasons; the second, having agreed to work on the case on 22 September, withdrew on 25 October.[15] As a result, the case was adjourned for a week in early November. Ultimately, the counsel for the defence consisted of George Orme Malley, Q. C., and John R. Stritch, instructed by Concannon. Malley, whose family was from Mayo, had a long legal career as a barrister and Queen's Counsel: in 1858 he had acted as counsel for the prisoner in the *Reg. v. Burke* case and his appeal had resulted in landmark judgments on the right to offer evidence in Irish.[16]

Acting for the crown were Attorney General William Moore Johnson (MP for Mallow), whose direct involvement in the case was a further signal of its status; James Murphy, Q. C., a highly experienced prosecutor; and another crown counsel Peter O'Brien, Q. C. (instructed by Crown Solicitor George Bolton). Born in County Clare, O'Brien (1842–1914) had built up a large practice on the Munster circuit. In 1881 he was appointed Junior Crown Counsel at Green Street and earlier in 1882 he was one of the principal prosecutors of the men accused of and convicted for the Phoenix Park murders. O'Brien later became Solicitor-General for Ireland, Attorney-General, and finally Lord Chief Justice of Ireland in 1889. His tendency, in his role as Attorney-General, to pack juries with members likely to convict led to his later being nicknamed 'Peter the Packer'.[17]

Presiding over the trials was Justice Charles Robert Barry. Born in Limerick, Barry (1823–97) served as Solicitor-General for Ireland from 1868–70, during which time he prosecuted many Fenian prisoners. He served as Attorney General from 1870–2 and then was appointed a justice of the Queen's Bench. In the year following the Maamtrasna trials, he was appointed Lord Justice of the Irish Court of Appeal and served in this role until his death in 1897.

Bolton's witnesses for the prosecution included two resident magistrates, three medical doctors, and several members of the RIC, all of whom were brought to Dublin at public expense to testify. On 13 November the *Irish Times* carried a short pre-trial article describing the departure from Claremorris of a small group of witnesses for the prisoners: 'Twenty-three witnesses, mostly women, left Claremorris for Dublin on Saturday to give evidence on behalf of the prisoners charged with the Maamtrasna murders, whose trial begins on Monday. None of the witnesses can speak English.'[18] It would appear from the trial evidence that this was a slightly exaggerated number; most, though not all, of the witnesses were Irish monoglots. However, few of those brought to Dublin would ultimately appear in court. The following day, the newspaper recorded that some of the witnesses 'occupied a house upon the opposite side of the street' from the Green Street courthouse, while others stood around its doors and 'attracted much attention by the peculiarity of their attire and their general appearance.'[19]

In all the trials the forming of a jury took a considerable time, becoming more contentious as the week progressed.[20] Writing of the first day of proceedings, the *Belfast Newsletter* journalist reported that 'some twenty jurors who were known to entertain strong opinions on the subject of agrarian crime were challenged, and thirty-five others, whose opinions were supposed to be of the advanced national type, were ordered to stand by.'[21] According to the *Freeman's Journal*, the occupations of the twelve men selected as the jury in the case of Patrick Joyce included a salesmaster, a shopkeeper, a jeweller, a lodging-house keeper, a saddler, a seed merchant, a wine merchant, a bank manager, a stockbroker, a landowner, and army major.[22]

DAY I: THE TRIAL OF PATRICK JOYCE

The crown case against Patrick Joyce was first stated by the imposing figure of Attorney General Johnson; then O'Brien called as the first prosecution witness the engineer Ryan and its second, John Collins. O'Brien's negotiation of styles of questioning for an Irish-language witness is worth noting: his questions to Collins were initially posed in the first person, as was the case with Ryan, and his answers were translated by Evans, also using the first person: 'Do you remember the morning of the 18th August going to the house of John Joyce of Maamtrasna?—I do.' Toward the end of Collins' testimony, when the topic moved to his conversations with the boys Michael and Patsy Joyce (which contained details awkward for the prosecution case), both O'Brien and the interpreter shifted to using the third person:

Did you see anyone else?—I did.

Who?—Two Peggy Joyces.

The grandmother and the grandchild, was it?—The grandmother and the daughter.

And where were they?—In the bed in the room.

Did you see anyone else in the kitchen?—Only Michael Joyce that was alive.

Michael Joyce who was alive—did he appear to be wounded?—He was able to speak, but bad speaking.

Did he see any one else in the room inside?—Pat Joyce was also alive—the son.

How old was the boy, does he know?—He had no judgment of the age.

Was he a little boy, ask him?—He was.

Did he then leave the house, ask him, having seen them dead?—He asked Michael Joyce what happened [to] him.

Well, never mind the conversation. I can't ask that. Had he a conversation with Michael Joyce—ask him did he go to the police at any time?—Yes, him and ten more went to the police.[23]

The sequence of question and answer contains a number of striking details: O'Brien's abrupt dismissal and swerve of topic away from the conversation between Collins and Michael, his (likely inadvertent) admission dutifully captured by the court reporter, 'I can't ask that,' and Collins' attempt, through the interpreter, to remain with the subject of his exchange with Michael.[24] Similarly in the case of Constable Johnston, who was the next prosecution witness to appear, the prosecution's questions focused only on the state of the dying boy Michael and on the Constable's search of the house.[25] The substance of his conversation with Michael and Patsy in which the boys had testified to the men having blackened faces, and which was recorded in detail in his August report, was now actively excluded from the court proceedings.

A further effect of this shift in style of questioning was to make the role of the interpreter more strongly audible and to distance further the voice of the testifying witness. As this sample extract illustrates, O'Brien's alteration to the third person in his questioning of Collins was accompanied by repeated exhortations to the interpreter of 'ask him'; at the same time the interpreter moved from first-person 'ventriloquised' replies ('I did') to a third-person style of summative reporting ('He was'). What might seem a slight shift in pronoun is a choice of some consequence and the significance of specific translation styles used by court interpreters, including the question of whether first or third person should be used, continues to be a topic of much debate within current sociolinguistics. For example, in a 2009 study of court interpreters in New York City, Philipp Sebastian Angermeyer studied variations in the use of first and third person, arguing that 'translation styles have profound consequences for limited English speakers, as the insistence on institutional norms in translating to them is viewed as a gatekeeping behavior that may impede their full participation in the proceedings.'[26] 'When translating in the first person,' Angermeyer observes, 'the interpreter behaves as *animator* of the translated utterance rather than as *author* or *principal*,'[27] and thus guidelines and protocols in many jurisdictions require court interpreters to use the first person when translating witnesses' words. Conversely, translations into the third person, where the source speaker is referred to as 'he' or 'she', and which emphasise 'non-involvement with a source-speaker's message', can function as a distancing tactic, making further evident the gap between the language of the original testimony and that of courtroom proceedings and amplifying the difference between jurors and witness.[28] The force of the first-person pronoun, reproduced by Interpreter Evans, may have been recognised by O'Brien and his choice to move to third person pronouns was a deliberate and effective distancing tactic.

THE JOYCE WITNESSES APPEAR

Evans' role was most to the fore when the prosecution witnesses, Anthony Joyce, John Joyce, and Patrick Joyce were summoned. Of the three, the lengthiest testimony was provided by Anthony, whom Murphy sought to establish as a key witness. In rebuttal, defence counsel Malley's cross-examination focused on the gaps in Anthony Joyce's testimony, most crucially his failure to identify who of the ten men had 'burst into' the Joyce home and who had stayed outside. The defence also underlined the Joyces' failure to travel immediately to the local police barracks at Finny to report what they had seen.

From the first moment that Anthony Joyce appeared on the witness stand, Malley sought to undermine his credibility by casting doubt on his self-description as a monoglot Irish-speaker:

Anthony Joyce, an Irish-speaking witness, sworn and examined through an interpreter.

Mr. Malley, Q. C. (to witness)—Don't you speak English?—(No answer).

You know very well what I am saying—can't you speak English?

The attorney-general—Ask him have you any English.

Mr. Malley, Q. C.—Oh, he understands both very well, can't you speak English?—(No answer).

Mr. Malley, Q. C. (through interpreter)—Ask him what is his name?—Anthony Joyce.

Ask him does he live at Cappanacreha near Maamtrasna?—He does.

At what hour did he go to bed on that Thursday night in August?—He isn't sure at what time, he had no clock.[29]

The examination and cross-examination of Joyce then proceeded, once again phrased by counsel in the third person with answers rendered in the third person by Evans as translator. The court transcript reads quite straightforwardly in this regard but those present at the November proceedings would have heard a much more elaborate, mediating process, one now lost from record. Evans had to translate counsel's questions into Irish and presumably into second-person pronouns, pose them to the witness, and then render his first-person answers from Irish back into third-person English.[30]

The only female member of the Joyce family to testify did so in English: John's daughter Mary (the niece of Anthony).[31] Mary's testimony was brief and was not subject to cross-examination in any of the four cases. Her evidence largely served to corroborate her relatives' accounts that Anthony had called to her father's house that evening and had said, as she recollected, 'to get up as quick as he could, that there were some parties going on the road.'[32] Yet in his closing statements Judge Barry commented repeatedly on the value of the testimony of the 'intelligent girl who spoke English'.[33]

The status accorded to the bilingual Mary Joyce was in marked contrast to the court's treatment of the two other female witnesses who appeared on the stand, both Irish monoglots. These two women, Mary Casey and Julia Casey, were the cousin and mother of Patrick Casey and were called as alibi witnesses by his defence counsel.[34] The prosecution's cross-examination of both women was conducted in deeply contemptuous tones. The Attorney General's cross-examination of Mary, in particular, sought to establish her obligation to the Casey family and therefore the partiality of her evidence. Armed with the RIC informations contained in the crown's brief, Johnston subjected the young woman to an increasingly hostile interrogation that drew out quite intimate facts concerning the young woman's life and livelihood. This level of scrutiny concerning the domestic lives of the accused was rare in the trial and demonstrates a strategy deliberately inflected by gender, accentuating the gap between upper-class English speaking male counsel and impoverished female Irish speakers:

Ask her has she any English at all?—No …

How many people are there in her own family at home?—No one but her mother and her brother.

Has she anything to do for her mother in the house at home?—She has nothing but her day's pay.

And was she getting her day's pay when she went to Patrick Casey's house?—She was not, but she was since on payment there.

Since on payment; but that is not what I was asking. Does she live by getting her day's pay? Is that how she gets her livelihood?—Yes …

Has she been living in the prisoner's house every day since?—She is half her time there …

Now, was there a bed in the place for her too?—There was.

Where was his bed?—In the kitchen.

And there is another room, I suppose?—There is.

Another room for her.[35]

Court reporters recognised the significance of the women's testimony by including them in the series of images featured in the *Weekly Freeman's* front-page coverage of Saturday, 25 November (see inside front cover), and later also in the header of the *Graphic's* image of 2 December (see Image 19, p. X). They were also the subject of a quite lengthy sceptical comment by Barry in his closing address to the jury. His skilfully phrased arguments confirm that the evidence by these monolingual women had been greeted in court by audible public derision:

There is many an honest, truth-telling witness that appears in a court of justice who would strain a point for a friend, and yet who would die on the scaffold rather than exaggerate against an enemy for the purpose of procuring his conviction. You must exercise your own judgment and discretion. It is to be considered with all calmness. It is not because they are *alibi* witnesses that they are to be disregarded. They are not to be laughed out of court or treated with contempt.[36]

THE APPROVERS' TESTIMONY

The two approvers, Anthony Philbin and Thomas Casey, provided the crown's other main fount of evidence against the accused. Both men were examined in English. The crucial significance of Philbin's evidence for the prosecution, and a key advance on that provided by the Joyces, was that he was willing to identify the three men whom he claimed to have seen breaking the door and entering the Joyces' Maamtrasna home, namely Patrick Casey of Derrypark, Myles Joyce of Cappanacreha, and Patrick Joyce.[37]

Philbin's answers were very brief, usually concluding with a deferential 'sir'; his carefully formulated replies ('I remained in the yard' or 'I don't know. I couldn't say') occasionally showed a more idiomatic style, as in his response to a question about whether he had previously known Tom Joyce, son of Paudeen Joyce: 'I hadn't known the son before I was taken back that journey'.[38]

During the August depositions, Philbin had exercised his right to counter the testimony of the Joyce witnesses, claiming that he had not been present at the Joyce house that evening – a statement retracted by him just prior to the opening of the trial. Malley's strategy was thus to argue that Philbin had exploited the numerous opportunities that he possessed to hear the Joyce witnesses' testimony, in order to change his own story, and that he had an added advantage in being able to understand both their original testimony and its translations.[39] The argument that Philbin's bilingual abilities conferred upon him an undue advantage in the judicial proceedings was, as we have seen, a familiar one in legal trials of the period and was made on a number of occasions by the Maamtrasna defence counsel. One of the implicit biases underlying this strategy was a view of the bilingual speaker as subversive of the legal process; in other words, the very linguistic abilities that had enabled Philbin and Casey's negotiations with the crown were now being deployed by opposing counsel to render them legally but also culturally suspect.[40]

Thomas Casey's replies under cross-examination were also brief, but his evidence, as noted earlier, introduced one complication to the prosecution case, namely, that the murder party consisted of twelve men in total, and that 'two men more', named as Pat Kelly and Michael Nee, had joined the group following their departure from Michael Casey's house. Casey further testified that Kelly had previously been unknown to him, but that he had seen Nee in the locality before, 'going about as a pedlar', and that he had previously 'minded' a revolver for Nee.[41] According to Casey, five men had broken into the Maamtrasna cabin: the first three accused, plus Kelly and

Nee. Oddly, Stritch's short cross-examination did not engage with this identification of two further men which might have supported the defence case.
Instead he focused on Casey's motive for testifying, which he suggested was
for the purpose of protecting his own life, an assertion with which Casey
ultimately agreed: 'Do you hear what I say? Have you given this information to save your life?—I have'.[42] Casey's replies to Stritch also referred to
'orders' he had received that evening[43] – a reference that the defence counsel
sought to suppress but that would later support crown arguments that the
crimes were part of an 'hellish organization'.[44]

THE APPEARANCE OF PATSY JOYCE

In legal trials there are sometimes moments that bring into view what Janet
Malcolm has aptly termed 'the artificial, and you might even say, inhuman
character of courtroom discourse.'[45] The appearance of the child Patsy on
the witness table, to testify for the prosecution in its case again Patrick Joyce,
was one such moment in the Maamtrasna proceedings. Aged eight or nine
according to official sources, he and his brother Martin had been lodged in
Dublin. His appearance, at the very end of the crown's case, was a brief one,
as the court transcript records:

> Patrick Joyce, a boy, one of the murdered family, was then put upon the table
> and questioned through the interpreter.
>
> Mr Murphy—Have you gone to chapel or do you know your catechism?—I
> do not know it.
>
> Have you said your prayers?—I have not said them.
>
> The attorney-general—Do you know what it is to tell a lie?—I do.
>
> Do you know what will happen to you if you tell a lie?—I do not.
>
> There is no use of asking him any other questions.[46]

Newspaper accounts of this moment further attested to its emotional power
and it featured as the central subject of the *Graphic*'s illustration of the trial
(see Image 19, p. X). The *Daily Express* recorded that 'a profound sensation
was caused in court' by 'the appearance on the witness table of little Patsy

Joyce, the sole survivor of the massacre, his head still marked by the terrible wounds he received on that occasion.'[47] The young boy, the reporter wrote, was 'an interesting, rather pleasing-looking lad but appeared very pale and somewhat weak. He seems to be between nine and ten years of age. His presence elicited general but hushed exclamations of surprise and sympathy as he was helped on to the table.'[48]

Children's giving of evidence was not uncommon in late nineteenth-century courts and a judge's determination as to whether or not this should be permitted usually stood on whether the child could understand what an oath meant and had received some religious instruction. The standing down of Patsy, and the refusal to return him to the courtroom, was a crucial moment in the trial and a huge boon for the crown case. The declaration he had given at the murder scene (evidence known to the prosecution) that the members of the murder party were disguised, and had 'soot on their faces',[49] was in sharp contradiction to the sworn testimony by Anthony, John and Pat Joyce that the guilty men were readily identifiable from afar.

The dismissal of Patsy was invoked later in the trial by the attorney general, who spelled out the court's reasons as follows:

> This little child will not be produced because it is not the duty of the crown to harrow the feelings of anyone in court. It was necessary to produce him once. It was found he was so young he had not learned his catechism nor his prayers, nor had he been taught any little hymn, and consequently did not know the nature of an oath.[50]

Archival records directly contract this claim: as discussed earlier, Patsy had successfully testified under oath at a solicitor's office a little over a month before in the company of his interpreter, Sub-Constable Patrick Kelly. Of Patsy's oath, Kelly had stated clearly to Lyster that 'he seemed perfectly to understand same'.[51] Yet all journalists accepted the characterisation of Patsy as unschooled without question, and this characterisation featured promi-nently in English newspaper coverage. As a result, a brief journalistic spat occurred between editorial writers in the *Spectator* and the Dublin *Evening Mail*. Responding to the London paper's depiction of 'the unhappy child … left so devoid of the most rudimentary training',[52] the *Evening Mail* angrily replied: 'The little child who did not know the nature of an oath and never said his prayers is paraded as though such a prodigy was unknown on the English side of the water.'[53]

MOVING TO A VERDICT

The interdependence of judge and interpreter, and the judge's determination to dismiss any criticisms of Evans' work, is a notable feature of the proceedings. Throughout the trials, and sometimes in a direct rebuff to defence counsel, Judge Barry was at pains to emphasise the excellence of the translation offered. Early on, he delivered a sharp retort to Stritch who had objected that a question of his remained unanswered: 'I must say I never saw a better interpreter in a court of justice. Now and then, he may not convey exactly what counsel wishes, but it appears to me he interprets extremely well.'[54] On one occasion, however, during the cross-examination of the young Mary Joyce, Barry intervened to disagree with Evans in his choice of the English idiom '[she] didn't know in the world' as a translation for Mary's words (possibly, in their original Irish, *ní fheadar 'en domhan*):

> Did she go to ask what Casey was taken for?—She didn't know in the world what he was taken for when she heard the news.
>
> Only knew he was taken by the police, that was on Sunday.
>
> Mr. Justice Barry—I don't think that is exactly what she means; I think what she intends to convey is that she was so astonished at his being taken.[55]

This (highly unusual) occurrence suggests that Barry – son of a Limerick solicitor – had some knowledge of Irish though the extent of this was never directly conveyed. His regular praise of Evans' translations showed that he was deeply invested in a view of the interpreter as a reliable judicial 'conduit' but also that he claimed the final authority to adjudicate on the interpreter's degree of competency and accuracy.[56]

By the end of Patrick Joyce's trial, efforts by the defence counsel to discredit the two bilingual approvers had been strongly countered by the prosecution. Changing targets in his closing statement, Malley focused instead on what he asserted was the undue advantage possessed by the Joyces as 'Irish-speaking' witnesses. The arguments he deployed here were also of long standing, and, as we have seen, had been rehearsed frequently in the appeal-court opinions on *Reg. v. Burke*. Malley had a specialist knowledge of that case, having instigated it himself as prisoner's counsel, but, 25 years later, he would align himself with the minority judges who had cast doubt on the very existence of a monoglot Irish speaker. Now Malley argued as follows:

An Irish speaking witness upon a table may as well be allowed to go down
when he gives his direct examination, as for endeavouring to make him
contradict himself when he has an opportunity of hearing that which every
Irish speaking witness understands – the English language, though he may
not speak it. When he has an opportunity of hearing the question, and then
having it interpreted by the interpreter, and listening to each word as it is
delivered, he has an easy opportunity of making up his mind, and we know
the mind of the Irish peasant is not so obtuse as not to be able to suggest the
safeguard to be adopted by a witness when giving his evidence. Gentlemen, I
might as well allow these witnesses to go down as to attempt to contradict
them out of their own mouths, or to shake their evidence by proving out of
their own lips that they are telling falsehood.[57]

The core of this argument was the assumption that any Irish-speaking
witness possessed the ability to understand English and thus the services
of the interpreter provided extra time to refine one's reply. Quite astonish-
ingly, in his anxiety to diminish the credibility of the Joyce witnesses for the
prosecution, Malley appears to have proceeded without contemplation of
the implications of this argument for his own clients, 'Irish-speaking' Myles
Joyce and his fellow accused whose trials were soon to follow.

The prosecution, in contrast, repeatedly stressed throughout the
proceedings the reliability of the three male Joyces. At the end of the crown's
case against Patrick Casey, when the evidence provided by the Joyces had
once again come under attack by defence counsel, Murphy forcefully
defended the authenticity of their being Irish monoglots: 'They were Irish
speaking witnesses. They had lived in that country all their lives; they never
appeared to be out of it any time where they found it necessary to acquire a
knowledge of even the English language.'[58] Murphy's argument was echoed,
and indeed bolstered, by Barry in his closing summary for the jury when
he delivered what now reads more as a lengthy encomium for the Joyce
witnesses and for what he termed 'their remarkable testimony':

I am sure you must have been struck with the uncommon intelligence, the
directness, and the graphic expressiveness of the mode in which they described
the whole route they took and all they saw; how they by their very gestures
endeavoured to make the non-Irish speaking people understand what they
were saying. It would be an omission of duty on my part to pass that without
observation. The question of what credit is to be given to their evidence is,
again I say, entirely for you. As far as I am concerned, I will give you no
opinion as to whether they were not the most accomplished liars and actors
that ever came into a witness box. But if they are telling what was untrue, or

wrongly fastening the guilt on men whom they did not see on that dreadful night at all, more accomplished actors never appeared on any stage.[59]

By endorsing the Joyces' evidence so explicitly, Barry had rendered it unassailable in the jury room: the 'appalling vista' that their identifications might not be in all cases correct, or that they were motivated by personal rivalries, could not be countenanced.

THE VERDICTS FOR PATRICK JOYCE AND PATRICK CASEY: 'I HAVE EXPECTATION OF HEAVEN'

All verdicts during the Maamtrasna trials were agreed in a matter of minutes. In the case of the trial of Patrick Joyce, the jury retired to consider its verdict at two minutes past noon on Wednesday, the third day of the trial, and returned after eight minutes. Joyce was then returned to the dock and the judge was summoned, arriving twenty minutes later. The absence of any visible emotional reaction on the sentenced man's part was made much of by the Dublin press. The *Irish Times* reporter, for example, contrasted the calm of the prisoner with the judge's emotion: 'he gazed straight into the eyes of the judge who, deeply moved, was pronouncing his doom. When the last scene was over, the culprit looked carefully about for his cap, saw it, picked it up, and stepped down the way to the cells as if nothing unusual had happened.'[60] This version of events continued to circulate in later accounts of the trial and its highly slanted account, in which apparent lack of feeling is equated with guilt, is the only record we possess for the response of the convicted Patrick Joyce. In his published reminiscences, prosecution counsel Peter O'Brien characterised the prisoner's and judge's reactions similarly: 'The prisoner heard the verdict unmoved, but Judge Barry, who had the kindest of hearts, wept when he sentenced him to death.'[61] This passage from O'Brien's memoir is in turn passed on without question by Vaughan in his 2009 study of nineteenth-century murder trials: 'Judges added to the drama. Barry wept when he sentenced Patrick Joyce for his part in the Maamtrasna murders. Joyce was unmoved.'[62]

Two days later, early Friday, 17 November, the jury retired to consider the case against Patrick Casey and returned twelve minutes later to deliver the verdict of guilty. The court transcript records that immediately following

the delivery of the verdict, Evans was asked to translate for Casey the standard invitation 'had he anything to say why judgment of death should not
be passed upon him'.[63] Newspaper accounts suggest that Casey had not
fully understood what one reporter termed 'the judge's forcible language of
condemnation'[64] and that Patrick Casey himself requested Evans to translate for him, the first time this had occurred in the case of the accused men.
The *Freeman's Journal* account reproduces this scene quite vividly:

> The clerk of the crown, in the language formally prescribed, informed him of
> the verdict of his country.
>
> The prisoner replied with a puzzled expression of face, 'I do not understand
> a word you are saying,' and looked around the court as if for the interpreter.
>
> The clerk of the crown (continuing the formal address) asked if he had anything
> to say why sentence of death and execution should not be awarded against him.
>
> The prisoner—I have to say that I had nothing at all to do with it.
>
> The court, thinking he was requesting the service of the interpreter, directed
> the interpreter to communicate to him the fact that the court now called upon
> him to say why sentence of death should not be passed upon him.
>
> The interpreter went to the dock and commenced to make the communica-
> tion in English, but the prisoner, being in an attitude of the greatest attention,
> requested him to speak in Irish.
>
> The interpreter did so, and the prisoner seemed dumbfounded by the commu-
> nication, but after a moment or two responded in Irish.
>
> The interpreter—He says, my lord, 'I have nothing to say: but I will say this,
> whatever happens to me, that I had no hand in it.'[65]

Although the sequence of Evans' actions is somewhat bewilderingly conveyed,
the newspaper record does illuminate some subtle aspects of the performance
of language in the courtroom: the interpreter seems to have thought initially
that Casey needed help in English in decoding the formal rhetoric employed
by the judge, but the emotional intensity of the events was such that their full
import could only be understood by Casey in Irish. His last words to the court
were also delivered in Irish, as also noted by the *Freeman's* reporter:

> The condemned man stood motionless in the dock for a little while, then took
> his cap from the seat beside him, and beckoned the interpreter to come near.
> He whispered to the interpreter, who informed the court that the prisoner

had asked, 'What day?' The unfortunate man was informed the 15th December, and he, looking upwards with a most reverent and touching aspect, exclaimed in the Irish language, 'I have expectation of heaven.' He then followed the warder to the cells beneath the court.[66]

DAY 5: THE TRIAL OF MYLES JOYCE

The trial of one man was very quickly succeeded by another. New juries were sworn in for each but without any concern as to potential bias among those who had been in court and audited earlier proceedings. Myles Joyce's trial began immediately after the delivery of the guilty verdict to Patrick Casey on Friday morning, and it ended on Saturday evening. In the account in Friday's *Evening Mail*, Myles was described as 'dressed in a suit of dark gray frieze, much worn' with 'neither a collar [n]or a kerchief about his neck.' His manner was viewed as both calm and passive: 'On entering the dock, he calmly looked round him and then took his seat with apparently the greatest composure and during the day watched the proceedings in the most listless manner.'[67] The *Freeman's Journal* reporter recognised not only that Myles was older than the previous accused and wore 'older garments' but also that 'unlike them, he did not appear to have the slightest knowledge of the language in which his trial is conducted.' The journalist also drew a startling and damning analogy between Myles, whose trial had just commenced, and the recently convicted felon 'Patrick Walsh': 'He sits in the dock like them, and like the young man Patrick Walsh, who was recently convicted of the murder of Constable Kavanagh, with his head leaning upon his arms, which he rests upon the bar of the dock.'[68] In a later *Weekly Freeman* pen-drawing, Myles was similarly differentiated from the other accused both in age and in his position in the dock, where in a relatively humanised portrait he was shown as gripping the bar in contrast to the seemingly nonchalant Patrick Casey and the austere Patrick Joyce (see inside front cover; also reproduced as the front cover image to this book).[69]

The fact that Myles Joyce did not understand English was brought to the direct attention of the court from the outset by his defence counsel Malley as part of a lengthy opening argument for postponement. Public knowledge about the verdict on Patrick Joyce, Malley argued, had already led to press comments that made an impartial trial impossible – a position compounded by Myles' illiteracy and linguistic disadvantage. Malley's statement to this effect and his appeal to constitutional sanctions guaranteeing an 'impartial trial', had a compelling power but were also predicated on the degradation of the accused man:

> Now, my lord, I need not mention to your lordship that it is the proud boast of this country in which we live that every subject of the realm, when called upon to stand his trial for his life at the bar of his country, is entitled as of right and by the sanction of the constitution under which we live, to the fullest and freest and the most impartial trial. My lord, that has been the proud boast of this country in its past history. But who could say, my lord, of this wretched Irish-speaking creature, who has never had the advantage of education, who is unable to understand the language in which his accusers will give their evidence, or the language in which the counsel will arraign him, or your lordship's address to the jury. My lord, illiterate as he is, and incapable of instructing us, I cannot but say I feel embarrassed to the extremest [*sic*] extent. And I feel also that if this case be brought on now, under the circumstances to which I refer in that affidavit, that proud boast of our constitution will not be maintained in this instance.[70]

These arguments, which included a powerful delineation of the various judicial functions inaccessible to the accused, were themselves a *volte-face* for a counsel who had, just three days earlier, refused to accept the existence of an Irish person unable to speak English. But a further effect of his rhetoric was to align all members of the court (defence and prosecution) against the 'embarrassment' posed to the legal system by what Malley had termed 'this wretched Irish-speaking creature'.

Malley's case for postponement was dismissed as 'vague and unsubstantial' by Barry, without explicit reference to the matter of language.[71] Yet, immediately after the judge's dismissal, the services of the interpreter were briefly employed in order to explain to Myles Joyce that a jury was about to be sworn and that he had the right to challenge individual jurors (this moment was recorded in newspaper accounts but not in the official court transcript).[72] In the *Freeman's Journal*, which, as usual, carried the most detailed coverage, the report was accompanied by the deliberate insinuation that Myles understood English: 'He professed to be able to speak only Irish, and the interpreter was again called to communicate to him that he had a right to challenge jurors. The prisoner looked at the interpreter as if he understood it, but said nothing.'[73]

The next morning, at the commencement of proceedings, the following
– and fateful – exchange took place, as recorded once again by the *Freeman's
Journal* reporter:

> At the sitting of the court, the attorney-general asked the learned counsel for
> the defence if the prisoner understood English.
>
> Mr. Concannon replied that he thought he did not, and that it might be
> better to have the evidence of the witnesses who speak English interpreted to
> the prisoner in Irish.
>
> The interpreter asked the prisoner in Irish if he understood the evidence
> that was being given in English, and informed the court that the prisoner
> replied in the affirmative.[74]

Although this set of exchanges was rendered verbatim in the *Daily Express*
of the same day, it tellingly does not appear in the trial transcript. What the
attending journalists recognised and recorded was a crucial moment of official misunderstanding: Myles Joyce's answering in the affirmative (that he
did understand the interpreter's speech in Irish) was taken to mean that he
understood evidence given in English; as a result, the services of the interpreter were not extended to him in the course of the trial and were restored
only at the delivery of the verdict of guilty.

The specific charge against Myles Joyce was the murder of Margaret
Joyce the younger, and the crown case against him featured graphic descriptions of her death, such as the following in the attorney general's opening
statement: 'Her skull was broken, and the brain protruding, and her young
life was then cut short in one instant.'[75] The prosecution's case again drew
heavily from the testimony of Philbin and Thomas Casey, and from the
Joyce witnesses. While the Joyce witnesses had named Myles as one of the
group of ten men whom they had observed that night, they also testified
that they had not been able to see who went into the Joyce house and who
stayed outside. In the course of O'Brien's questioning of Anthony Joyce,
the particular intimacy of the families' interrelationships began gradually to
emerge. Once again the court transcript edited down to a pithy exchange
what would have been, in the live courtroom, a much more involved series
of questions, requiring the interpreter to translate the counsel's questions
into Irish, presumably changing their third-person pronouns to second-
person, and then to translate the witness' Irish-language and first-person
reply to third-person standard English:

> Ask him does he see Myles Joyce there?—He does.

Ask him does he live at Cappanacreha?—He does.

How far from him?—Very short; a little above him.

Ask him does he know him all his life?—He knows him since he has memory to know him.[76]

Defence counsel Stritch's cross-examination of Anthony Joyce cast further light on Myles' domestic circumstances. Anthony testified that he thought Myles Joyce had five children and when asked if they were 'little children', he replied that 'They are small and they are weak'.[77] During the following cross-examination of John Joyce by Malley for the defence, a juror's remark[78] prompted the prosecution to interrupt to ask the following question: 'Tell me—ask him—is John Joyce the man who was murdered—was he any relation of his—was he any relation?—Yes, there is relation … Is Myles Joyce the prisoner any relation to him?—He is his first cousin too'.[79] These startling details, that the prosecution witness was a first cousin of both the deceased John Joyce *and* the accused Myles Joyce, appear to have come as a great surprise to all, including to Myles' defence counsel. The shocked reaction in court was captured succinctly in the *Belfast Newsletter*: 'Witness replied that he was first cousin to the murdered John Joyce, and the prisoner was witness' first cousin. (Great sensation in court).'[80]

The presentation of the Joyces' evidence again required the services of Constable Evans. On a number of occasions, in a much more oppositional stance than taken earlier in the trials, the defence counsel challenged the translations offered. A critical instance took place during the cross-examination of Anthony Joyce, in the course of which the defence counsel sought to undermine his testimony by drawing attention to his and his brother's failure to see the eleventh and twelfth men, Nee and Kelly. The significance of the evidence was such as to produce a request for clarification from a juror, and Stritch now objected forcefully to the qualification ('thinks') deployed by the interpreter in his translation of Joyce's responses:

Ask him could any men have left the party without his seeing them?—He could not think any men left them.

Or any men join them?—He can't believe there did.

A juror—What is the last answer he gave?

Mr. Murphy—He can't think any one joined them, and he can't think any one left them.

Mr. Stritch (to interpreter)—Don't mind what he thinks. Ask him will he swear that no men joined or that no men left them?—He swears that he thinks himself there did not. He did not see it.

I don't know what he thinks, but I want to know what he saw?—Well, judgment is the proper word for it, sir.[81]

Stritch's insistence suggests that he saw Evans' translations as introducing a problematic qualification, even alteration, of key witness testimony.

While the trial of Myles Joyce largely followed the format of the earlier two trials, other questions by the jurors prompted a number of significant interruptions. One led to the revelation of the protagonists' family relationships mentioned above; a second posed by juror William Pim, which occurred during Malley's cross-examination of witness John Collins, brought back to attention the testimony of the dying Michael Joyce:

A juror—He says he was speaking to Michael Joyce. May we ask him whether he said anything to him?

Mr. Justice Barry—No. The fact is that the boy was unconscious. He could not tell what he was saying. It could not be relied on at all.

Mr. Malley—I have no objection to the question being put.[82]

The juror's question about what Michael Joyce had said was not, however, 'put' to the court, and instead the proceedings moved immediately to the evidence of Dr John Hegarty, who testified that during his treatment of Michael for the last three or four hours of the boy's life, 'although he had lucid intervals when he was responsible – he was wandering'.[83] Thus a significant potential opportunity to discredit the Joyce witnesses by informing the court that members of the murder party had disguised their faces was quickly removed.

Surprisingly, and in contrast to their practice in the cases of Patrick Joyce and Patrick Casey, the defence counsel for Myles Joyce did not present any witnesses though it would appear that Peter Lydon, Myles' brother-in-law, and Mary Conaboy, his sister-in-law, were present in Dublin.[84] The derision extended to earlier defence witnesses may have been a factor in this decision. Instead, Malley's summary of the case for Myles rested on the argument that the case against him was different from those of the other accused and was weaker in character. In his rebuttal of the Joyce witnesses, rather than seeking to undermine their evidence in its totality, he now questioned their

ability to identify specific participants in the events of the evening, especially Myles. Malley then moved to deploy in Myles' favour the recently
revealed evidence as to his kinship with one of the victims, adding to this
the fact that Myles had attended the wake of his murdered cousins and
'looked upon those corpses as they lay out there'. By virtue of attending
the wake, Myles had, he argued, 'rushed into the arms of the law where the
police were on the Friday, the day after the day of the evening on which the
murders took place'.[85]

Here Malley's closing speech displayed a rhetorical power far greater
than the defence summaries that had closed the previous two trials. A quite
dramatic instance was his invocation of folkloric belief, to bolster his argument that Myles' attendance at the wake attested to his innocence:

> We have heard and read of the test which has been given, and I believe there
> is not a peasant in the land who is not familiar with it – that if you approach
> the corpse which your hand has violated, possibly blood may start from the
> re-opened wound. If it was possible with such a feeling as that he could rejoice
> in his impunity, or that he supposed it was not likely that a knowledge of the
> guilty would be discovered, he went there. That poor peasant, uneducated as
> he is, if he were guilty, he would have fled from the law. Instead of doing that,
> there were not alone two policemen in that house, but as one of the witnesses
> said, there were several others who were there.[86]

The speech ended with a potent – and what would prove a prophetic –
warning about the likelihood of a future confession that would exonerate
the accused Myles Joyce.

> Well, gentlemen of the jury, I bow, as I am bound to do, to the decision of his
> lordship, but I can say this, gentlemen, that if hereafter a confession could by
> possibly be obtained, if it should turn out, upon that confession, that things
> which are now mysterious disclosed the innocence of that man after he was
> condemned to death, I ask you, what would your feelings be if that confession
> or that elucidation of the mystery led to the conclusion that he was guiltless,
> what would be your feelings, what would be mine, what would be the feelings
> of us all?[87]

Malley's closing appeal was that the 'benefit of doubt' be given to 'this unfortunate prisoner' whose innocence might not be discovered 'until perhaps
months have passed away, and he has gone before his God'.[88]

Malley's stirring appeals were countered by a lengthy closing case for
the prosecution during which Murphy expressed repeated praise for the

Joyce witnesses: 'I can only say that the characters in accordance with the appearance they presented on the table there – that humble and though Irish speaking, I think you never saw three better representatives of the humble peasantry your land produced before you'.[89] Murphy painstakingly reversed a number of Malley's key arguments: the existence of a familial relationship between the Joyces was made to support the persuasiveness of Anthony Joyce's ability to recognise his cousin Myles, and the invocation of local folklore by the defence was turned into an object of deep ridicule for a modern judicial system: 'As to the starting up and attempts to approach the body, and so forth, tell that to distant ages, old gossips and so forth, but don't tell it to us who know the history of criminals and crime'.[90] The central tenet of the crown's closing statement was that all members of the party were equally culpable. This point was repeated in Barry's final and pointed comments to the jury: 'if on the evidence of the approvers you believe he was one of the party who entered the house, you could have no doubt about your verdict, but if you have any reasonable doubt in the case you are bound to give the prisoner the benefit of it.'[91]

In a direct echo of Murphy's closing statements, and repeating his own comments in the earlier trials, Barry took great pains to emphasise the credibility of the witnesses and their reliability under the 'disadvantages' of interpretation. Features of their evidence that might, in a less sympathetic reading, seem suspect were, in the judge's view, marks of its reliability:

> The most minute details they here agreed in, and had an answer to every question, no matter how complicated, or how apparently difficult, and recollect that they were examined through an interpreter, the questions being put by you in English, and by the interpreter in Irish under many disadvantages, and they stood the test of every question. Therefore, as regards their demeanour as witnesses, it will be certainly for you, and this is entirely a question for you; but there never were witnesses who appeared to give their testimony in a more satisfactory and faithworthy manner.[92]

DAY 6: THE VERDICT ON MYLES JOYCE, 'WHETHER HE BE HANGED OR CRUCIFIED'

The jury in the case of Myles Joyce retired at three o'clock on Saturday and returned to court at six minutes past three to deliver the verdict of guilty. The trial transcript records that at this point Evans was recalled in order to render to the court Myles' response to the guilty verdict.[93] This was the first court accommodation of Myles' identity as an Irish monoglot since the initial calling of the jury the day before:

> The clerk of the crown: What have you to say why judgment of death and execution should not be awarded against you according to law?
>
> [The prisoner spoke in Irish to the interpreter.][94]
>
> The interpreter – He says that by the God and Blessed Virgin above him that he had no dealings with it any more than the person who was never born; that against anyone for the past twenty years he never did any harm, and if he did, that he may never go to heaven; that he is as clear of it as the child not yet born; that on the night of the murder he slept in his bed with his wife that night, and that he has no knowledge about it whatever. He also says that he is quite content with whatever the gentlemen may do with him, and that whether he be hanged or crucified, he is as free and as clear of the crime as can be![95]

The expression of Myles Joyce's protests, that he was 'as clear of it as the child not yet born', deployed a long-established rhetorical trope, that of the innocence of the unborn child, whose usage ranges from earlier legal trials and scaffold speeches to fictional sketches.[96] Yet despite such stock phrases and the formalities of the court recording process, the cadences and syntactical structures of Myles Joyce's words in Irish emerge powerfully in the translation by Evans, including distinctive Hiberno-English linguistic features, such as the double negative 'no dealing with any more than the person who was never born'. A further indication of the strong auditory impact of his words on those listening was the court reporter's own (and exceptional) inclusion of a concluding exclamation mark in the written transcript: 'as free and as clear of the crime as can be!'

The emotional power of Myles Joyce's protest is captured even more powerfully in the *Freeman Journal's* account of the verdict. Here the punctuated short statements convey the manner and immediacy of his speech, translated sentence by sentence.

The clerk of the crown informed him in the usual language of the result. He listened with a quiet but melancholy expression of face, inclining his head to the right. When the clerk of the crown had concluded, he still kept his eyes fixed upon the Bench, made no attempt to respond, and seemed like a man who had only the vaguest notion of what was going on. The interpreter, Constable Evans, was called by direction of the learned judge, and he communicated to the prisoner in Irish the fact that he had been found guilty. A change then came upon the prisoner. He showed a little fear and clutched the bar of the dock, but, looking upwards with a fervent expression and attitude of invocation, spoke in Irish. The interpreter rendered it as follows – He leaves it to God and the Virgin above his head. He had no dealing with it, no more than the person who was never born, nor had he against any one [*sic*] else. For the last twenty years he had done no harm, and if he had, might he never go to heaven. He was as clear of this as the child yet to be born. He slept in his bed with his wife that night, and he had no knowledge about it whatever. He is quite content with whatever the gentlemen may do to him, but whether he is to be hung or crucified, he is as free as he can be.[97]

From the word choices made by the *Freeman's* correspondent, differing in a number of instances from the court transcript of Evans' translation, we can also infer that this reporter had some comprehension of Irish: 'He leaves it to God and the Virgin above his head' suggests the Irish prepositional phrase *os mo chionn* ('above me') and its fuller and more literal translation as 'above his head' (rather than Evans' translation as 'above'). Other phrases also heighten the idiomatic aspect of Myles' speech from the dock: the phrase 'no dealing with it, no more than the person who was never born' acquires a further negative; the phrase 'he had done no harm' departs from the more standard translation provided by Evans as court interpreter ('he never did any harm'), and similarly 'hung' is chosen rather than 'hanged'. The more colloquial and direct final phrase in the *Freeman's* report – 'he is as free as he can be' – omits the formal legalistic reference in Evans' translation of Myles Joyce's words ('as clear of the crime as can be').

Following his direct and detailed rendition of Myles' words to newspaper readers, the *Freeman's* reporter then proceeded to comment directly – and very unusually – on the limits of his and the court's translation. Here also he appeared to have sufficient knowledge of Irish to recognise the divine invocations employed by Myles, mostly omitted from the court interpreter's translation. This journalistic metacommentary also illuminates the reactions to the speech from the courtroom audience, including those of the counsel and judge:

The above statement was made and interpreted by sentences. It merely conveys the tenor, not the full words, of the condemned man, who, in making the protestation, frequently invoked the Son of God. Though exhibiting considerable emotion, the prisoner did not lose his self-control in the slightest degree. The scene was very painful, and it scarcely added to its solemnity to observe the many ladies who were amongst the audience, and the obtrusive manner in which the thronged courthouse gazed with the curiosity of interest, rather than of feeling, upon the condemned and sorrowful-looking man. The prisoner's counsel was much moved by the scene, and the learned judge showed considerable emotional feeling.[98]

The only newspaper to rival the nationalist *Freeman's Journal* in its detailed coverage and commentary was the conservative and pro-landlord *Daily Express*. On 20 November the paper provided a short editorial summary of these proceedings in which the writer referred to Myles' 'keen, cunning, and audacious expression' having forsaken him on the delivery of a guilty verdict.[99] However, as part of a page-long spread on the trial proceedings in the same issue, the newspaper furnished a much more nuanced and dramatic account. Its account included a vivid description of Myles Joyce's reaction to the guilty verdict but also a subtle evocation of the aural dimensions of the courtroom, wherein silence was a feature of the listening courtroom rather than of the 'voluble' Myles Joyce. Here the journalist's acknowledgment of his own distance in comprehension featured a rare recognition of the Irish language as a distinctive, even appealing, linguistic other:

> The prisoner received the dread announcement with visible trepidation. It was communicated to him through the interpreter, in reply to whose translated question if he had anything to say why judgement of death should not be passed upon him, he poured forth quite a torrent of words in his native tongue. His attitude was that of a man deeply, terribly excited. With head turned upwards, he stood rigidly erect, his outstretched arms accompanying in gesture the energetic, voluble language in which he protested 'before God and the Virgin' his utter innocence of the crime. The facility with which he spoke, the easy, rapidly changing, and not ungraceful motion of his hands as he accentuated his declaration, combined with the strange, unusual, but sonorous sounds of the mountain Gaelic in which he apostrophised, as it were, heaven to bear testimony to his freedom from guilt, made a remarkable impression on the court. There was a deep, intense silence, only broken now and again as the interpreter indicated or suggested the substance of his exclamations – for such, rather than speech, his utterance seemed to be. The doom of death he heard pronounced with a return to his former self-control, but there was still

apparent an undercurrent of agitated feelings which could not be concealed. The learned judge, having discharged his painful duty, the prisoner deliberately reached over for his hat and, ejaculating something in Irish, turned and left the dock.[100]

Perhaps the most evocative aspect of the *Daily Express* report is the Christ-like features deployed in its description of Myles, with 'head turned upwards' and 'outstretched arms'. Published two days after the events described (the following Monday), in a newspaper far removed from the accused in political sympathies, they suggest an underlying unease as to the fairness of the verdict. Read today, this passage further resonates not only because it signals the beginning of an iconographical tradition regarding Myles Joyce but also because it expresses our own distance from the condemned man's words of protests, heard and understood by very few even in their original moment of utterance.

Following Myles Joyce's reaction to the verdict of guilty, Barry delivered the sentence of execution. Addressing the prisoner, the judge began with his comments with the matter of language, reiterating his belief that an offer of translation services had been made and refused. His reported words in the court transcript were as follows: 'Although an opportunity has been afforded to you of addressing the court in that language which is more familiar to your [*sic*] than any other, yet you have informed us that you understand what I am saying.'[101] This was an extraordinary claim given that a graphic demonstration of Myles Joyce's need for an English-speaking interpreter in understanding the delivered verdict had just taken place. Barry's statement, which was reproduced in full by the *Freeman's Journal*, suggests that the judge was already on the defensive against an argument that proper legal support had not been extended, and that he was seeking to discredit the fact, evident to those present in the courtroom, that Myles Joyce had not understood much of the legal proceedings. In this sentencing address, Barry also constructed a damning alignment of personal filiation and political affiliation, remarking that the existence of 'ties of blood of the closest kind' between the victims and the accused was a source of 'peculiar horror' to him, as was 'the unknown authority' which had orchestrated the murders.[102]

The judge's delivery of the sentence of death concluded in a manner remarkably free of reservation or qualification:

> But if there was ever a case in which feelings of distress or pain or of hesitation at the performance of that duty should sink into abeyance, it is in a case

like yours, where the guilt has been so enormous, without a particle – even a shadow of any mitigating or even reasoning circumstances connected with it to justify – I cannot of course say to justify it – but even to palliate or excuse the committal of the dreadful act.'[103]

The court transcript for Saturday, 18 November, ended with the two lines: 'The prisoner was then removed. The court adjourned to Monday morning.'[104] Only the daily newspapers recorded Myles Joyce's final words – as 'mutterings' rather than decipherable words – as in this account from the *Irish Times* of 20 November: 'The prisoner hesitated as if about to add something more, but, recovering his self-possession, he reached over for his hat and slowly walked to the steps leading to the cells with his head bent on one side, and muttering some words in Irish, the meaning of which did not transpire, as he disappeared from view.'[105] The *Freeman's Journal* was somewhat more sympathetic: 'The condemned man, touched on the shoulder by the dock warder, then turned slowly away, and with a step lingering and sorrowful, and a heavy sigh, with which there was an indistinct exclamation in Irish audible only to a portion of the courthouse, he descended to the cells.'

DAYS 7 AND 8: THE TRIALS OF MICHAEL CASEY AND THE REMAINING 'MAAMTRASNA 4'

In the course of the break between the Saturday and Monday proceedings, rumours had begun to circulate that the remaining five prisoners might be tried together and that a plea change might occur. Writing of the courtroom on Monday morning, the *Freeman's Journal* noted: 'Public interest in the proceedings has not abated in the least judging from the crowded state of the court, and amongst the audience there were again some women.'[106] On that morning only Michael Casey, the fourth accused, appeared in the dock, charged with the murder of Margaret Joyce the elder. The physical appearance of the 60-year-old Casey was the subject of considerable news comment. The *Daily Express* described him as a 'much older and more careworn man' of 'stouter build' and, once again, the physical appearances of the men were seen to intimate guilt: 'He also possesses that feature which has been so remarkably conspicuous in the dock during the trials – a keen, quick, glancing eye which, in its haggy surroundings, rather suggests cunning, but which no doubt in more polished associations would be perhaps more suggestive of prompt perceptive qualities and a ready intelligence.'[107] The *Dublin Evening Mail* observed that Michael Casey's appearance was more affluent than that of his fellow prisoners; he was dressed in a suit of dark grey frieze like the other men, 'with this difference, that his clothes are quite new.'[108]

Unlike Myles Joyce, Michael Casey was unequivocally recognised by all court reporters as an Irish monoglot who was unable to understand the court proceedings. The *Irish Times* wrote that Casey looked 'ill, appearing to have suffered much from his confinement' and that 'his answers in Irish – for he neither speaks nor understands English – were given in a listless way and in a low tone of voice.'[109] A markedly different feature of Michael Casey's trial was the extension of the interpreter's services to the accused from the very beginning. The attorney general's offer of an interpreter was recorded in the transcript, with a result starkly different from the similar instance on the previous Friday. Unease about the treatment of Myles Joyce, and the failure to provide necessary translation services, would seem to have dictated a marked change in attitude here.

> The attorney-general—Has the prisoner any English?
>
> The interpreter (Constable Evans, RIC)—He says not, sir.
>
> The attorney-general—Then the interpreter will interpret all the evidence for him.[110]

Once Evans had been sworn in, Michael Casey was given a translation of the evidence of English-speaking witnesses, sentence by sentence – the first of the accused men to receive this benefit. The next day the *Freeman's Journal* commented upon this translation service as having been 'so satisfactorily accomplished by the interpreter' that 'the proceedings were in no way delayed.'[111] Casey was described as having 'nodded his head in acknowledgement of the interpreter's services each time that a sentence was translated.'[112] The court transcript, in contrast, recorded a more disjointed process that included, early in the trial, the interjection of a number of rebuttals by the accused man. During the opening evidence provided by the civil engineer Ryan, Murphy questioned him as to his meetings with Anthony and John Joyce. When Ryan responded to say that the murder party's route had been pointed out to him by both men, Michael Casey interrupted the interpreter as follows: 'The prisoner – They did not see me; if they said they did, they put a lie on it.'[113]

That simple line has a compelling force: in words translated from their original Irish into idiomatic English, the accused is heard to interrupt the case against him for the first time in the trial proceedings. For the accused to speak was itself a strong challenge to the judicial process, given that prisoners were largely excluded from examination or cross-examination as 'incompetent' witnesses.[114] In response to counsel's objections to the interruptions, Barry stated that he had no objection: 'It is not regular under other circumstances, but in this case it may be excused.'[115]

In order to prevent more interruptions, the judge recommended that the interpreter change his position in the court to stand nearer the prisoner and communicate his comments to his solicitor, a significant change in court proceedings.[116] Not only does this occurrence illuminate the physical layout of the courtroom, it also underlines the difficulties under which monoglot Irish-speaking Myles Joyce had previously laboured in not being able to confer directly with his own defence solicitor and it suggests a belated recognition by Barry of these difficulties. According to the *Belfast Newsletter*, 'the interpreter stood beside Mr. Concannon, but the prisoner made no further remark.'[117]

At 11 a.m. on Tuesday morning, the eighth and final day of the Maamtrasna trial began with the request by defence counsel Malley that the plea of not guilty by Michael Casey be withdrawn and that the rest of the prisoners appear in the dock. This was the first court appearance of the remaining four accused. The *Freeman's Journal* described Martin Joyce, John Casey and Michael Casey as standing in front of the dock, with Patrick (Paudeen) Joyce behind and the young Thomas Joyce almost hidden from view.[118] In turn each of the five men declared to the court, through the interpreter, an intention to withdraw the plea of not guilty and make a plea of guilty.[119]

Why all five men changed their pleas would become a matter of much debate in the aftermath of the trials. A local clergyman, Fr Michael McHugh, had travelled to Dublin for the trials and was called into Green Street to meet with them; he persuaded them to plead guilty on the promise of escaping capital punishment.[120] In a personal letter written to Tim Harrington two years later, Fr McHugh explained the reasons for his actions:

> The case was then laid before me, and in the interests of the prisoners I considered it the wiser course to plead guilty. I was by no means clear at the time that they were innocent. I was certainly inclined to the belief that they were, but I had no grounds for such a belief but their own declarations to me. I argued with myself thus – If the men were guilty, their plea of guilt can do them no

harm and will save their lives; and that if they were innocent, I felt that the truth would leak out, as from my knowledge of the locality and the people I believed such a huge wrong could not continue. In this way I saw a probability of these men coming back to their wives and families and homes without a stain on their character. This was the argument I made use of to the men themselves in the cell of Green-street Courthouse; and I dare say it was the argument which induced them to withdraw their plea of 'not guilty' and enter a plea of 'guilty.' From this you will see that in recommending the prisoners to adopt this course, I was by no means actuated by a belief in their guilt. On the contrary, I rather believed they were innocent.[121]

In national and international coverage of the trials the news of the guilty pleas served to reinforce the legitimacy of the earlier verdicts. The following editorial from the *Graphic* provides a good example of this tendency and vividly demonstrates the prevailing metropolitan view of the 'primitivism' of those convicted:

It has long been known to people concerned with ethnology rather than with modern politics that many of the natives of the West of Ireland are more on the level of New Zealanders than of Englishmen. The Joyce trial has made this evident even to politicians. Here we have a tribe, rather than a more civilised community, dwelling apart from modern life, speaking a dying language, ignorant of English, and owning no government but that of a bloody secret society worthy of the Admiralty Islands ... Ireland suffers as much as China from secret murderous societies, kept together by the oath and by fear of the knife.[122]

Notwithstanding the change of plea, sentences of death to take place on 15 December were delivered on all five men. Newspapers of the day carried extensive coverage of the accused's reactions to the verdicts. The response of Michael Casey, as depicted in the *Freeman's Journal*, was carried widely in other papers, including the *Connaught Telegraph*, the *Nation*, and the *United Irishman:* 'In a tone not much above a whisper, the prisoner responded in the Irish language, saying simply, "I am not guilty."'[123] With respect to the passing of the death sentence on the other prisoners, the *Freeman* noted that 'the prisoners, with the exception of John Casey, made no response; John Casey made an exclamation in Irish.'[124]

THE IMMEDIATE AFTERMATH: THE HUDDY TRIALS

The trial record ends with the closing words from Judge Charles Barry in which he singled out for praise the 'very difficult' work of interpreter Thomas Evans, along with that of engineer Ryan, who 'prepared those excellent maps which threw such light on the case'.[125] Evans returned to Green Street as interpreter early the following month when the Lough Mask murder trials began on 8 December. Three men were charged with the murder of Bailiff Joseph Huddy and his teenage grandson John in January of that year, and their trials lasted just under two weeks. These events, as we have seen, were much intertwined with the Maamtrasna case in that it was believed locally that a member of the murdered Joyce family had given evidence as to the location of the Huddys' bodies, but the trials differed greatly with respect to the interpreter's role.[126] Of the three accused, one man – Patrick Higgins (Long), aged about sixty[127] – did not speak English; the other two accused, Thomas (Tom) Higgins who was about 27 years of age, and Michael Flynn aged about 40, appeared to have some competence in English.[128] Evans, now Head Constable, was again the sworn interpreter but, unlike the case of Myles Joyce, his services were made available from the beginning to the accused Patrick Higgins, beginning with the communication of the indictment and continuing with the translation of English-language evidence into Irish so that it could be understood by Higgins.[129] It is certainly possible that the public injustice of Myles Joyce's treatment contributed to the provision of these services in Green Street to Higgins, a little over two weeks later. However these were not provided to all of the accused: when asked in court if he could speak English, Thomas Higgins replied 'a little'; Michael Flynn's reply was 'I understand a few words of it, but not very well' but in neither of their cases were the interpreter's services deployed.[130]

One other difference between the Maamtrasna and Lough Mask trials concerned the tendering of evidence by children. During the trial of Patrick Higgins, key evidence was provided by Martin Kerrigan, son of Matthias Kerrigan (the crown's key witness); the young boy testified in Irish to having seen Patrick Higgins 'strike the old man with a stone'.[131] Martin was then only eight years of age and defence counsel asked, prior to his testimony, that 'the lad should be tested in some way as to his knowledge of an oath.'[132] The judge's emphatic response was that the 'witness had already made a deposition, and he would therefore admit his testimony.'[133] Unlike the case of Patsy Joyce who was disqualified from testifying in court, having already made a number of sworn depositions prior to the trials, Martin Kerrigan was allowed to stand.

*

The verdicts passed in the Maamtrasna trials, finding all eight accused men guilty of murder, were warmly welcomed, without exception, in contemporary news reports. The *Freeman's* editorial declared in ringing Shakespearian tones: 'The shambles of Maamtrasna are avenged, and the bloodshed, hideous and appalling, calling louder than the surf upon the unnumbered pebbles of the shore, to Heaven for retribution, has been answered by the slow but sure decree.'[134] One-hundred-and-thirty-five years later, Dr Niamh Howlin of UCD Sutherland School of Law delivered a report on the trial of Myles Joyce to the Irish Department of Justice and Equality. The question posted to Howlin, for her expert review as a leading legal historian, was as follows: 'were the circumstances of the trial, conviction, or punishment of Myles Joyce so inconsistent with the legal standards of the period that they justify an act of public recognition?'[135] Following a study of the trial proceedings, analysed in the context of the contemporary criminal justice system, Howlin concluded that 'the evidence on which Myles Joyce was convicted was unreliable' and that 'the trial, conviction and execution of Myles Joyce were unfair by the standards of criminal justice at the time.'[136] Specifically, to quote the final lines of her report, 'The witness evidence against him was of doubtful reliability. Procedural irregularities, in particular in relation to language and translation and the refusal to admit the testimony of Patsy Joyce, rendered the trial process unfair.'[137]

— 6 —

EXECUTIONS

'Focla déigheanacha Mhaolmhuire Seoighighe'

By definition, in essence, by vocation, there will never have been any invisibility for a legal putting to death, for an application of the death penalty; there
never has been, on principle, a secret or invisible execution for this verdict.
The spectacle and the spectator are required. The state, the polis, the whole of
politics, the co-citizenry – itself or mediated through representation – must
attend and attest, it must testify publicly that death was dealt or inflicted, it
must *see die* the condemned one.

Jacques Derrida, *The Death Penalty*[1]

Late on Sunday evening, 26 November 1882, a train carrying the eight
Maamtrasna men arrived in Galway. Several hundred people filled the platform, along with military and police; the men, closely guarded, were then
transported in two open horse-drawn carriages to Galway Jail.[2] Each of the
eight men faced the same sentence: to be hung on the date of 15 December
at Galway Jail, for which task the services of the infamous English executioner William Marwood had been requested.[3] On 7 December, the *Irish
Times* reported that the erection of the gallows had commenced, and on the
same day referred briefly to prison visits by the mothers and relatives of the
condemned men: 'the interview was most affecting'.[4]

The case largely vanished from the press until news came of a reprieve
for the five men who had pled guilty. Their solicitor, Henry Concannon,
presented a memorial to the Lord Lieutenant requesting this reprieve in
early December and on 11 December a reply came that it was successful. The

sentences of death for Martin, Paudeen, and Tom Joyce and for John and Michael Casey were commuted to penal servitude for life; three days later, the five men were transferred to Mountjoy Jail. A report sent in late November by Judge Barry to Lord Lieutenant Spencer played a significant role in the ultimate decision to commute. In this affidavit, and to the dismay of Spencer, Barry supported the view that an offer had been made to the men that their lives would be spared: 'I could not help feeling that the pleas of guilty were given in the firm expectation, if not understanding, that the capital sentence would not be carried out.'[5] Still Spencer had been reluctant to agree.[6]

Public unease regarding the fate of Myles Joyce was expressed in a number of petitions sent to the Lord Lieutenant and editorial comment in the *Freeman's Journal* supported these. On 11 December, the newspaper office received a handwritten letter, composed in English, on behalf of Myles' wife Bridget (see Image 30, p. XV). The *Freeman's* owner Edmund Dwyer Gray directed that it be forwarded to the Lord Lieutenant's office.[7] Addressed from 'Derry High', the letter attested strongly to Myles' innocence, maintaining that he had 'never committed that crime nor left his house on that night.' It argued that the five men who had pleaded guilty would support this claim as would those facing the scaffold:

> The five prissioners [*sic*] that pleaded guilty will declare he is innocent, they will swear now and at their dying moment that he never was implicated in that fearful murder. Does not every one easily imagine a man going before his Almighty God will tell the thruth [*sic*], in telling the thruth they must confess that he never shared in it, will the evidence of two informers, the perpretrators [*sic*] of the deed, hang an innocent man whilst the whole party on the scaffold will declare his innocence.[8]

The letter concluded with an appeal to 'his Excellency the lord lieutenant to examine and consider this hard case of an innocent man, who leaves a widow and five orphans to be before long a dhrift [*sic*] on the world.' Its last plaintive line read: 'O I crave for mercy.' The *Freeman's Journal* published the letter but standardised its spelling; it also edited Bridget's allegation of guilt against Casey and Philbin to read, 'will the evidence of two hang an innocent man, whilst the whole party on the scaffold will declare his innocence.'[9]

Spencer directed that the letter be treated as a memorial or petition to be sent to Judge Barry for comment. Barry sent his terse response by telegram from Cork the next day: 'At the trial I entertained no doubt'.[10] A fuller letter sent by post reiterated his view that no doubt existed, on either his or the jury's part, as to the guilt of Myles Joyce. 'The only circumstance favourable to the prisoner,' Barry observed, was that 'he was, I think, the only one of the accused who attended at the wake of the murdered family, of whom John Joyce was also his first cousin.'[11]

Other key documents reached Spencer in the days before the executions. On 13 December, George Mason, the governor of Galway Jail, and his chief warder Richard Evans witnessed a one-page autographed statement, which appears to be in Mason's hand, and was signed by Patrick Casey. In it Casey acknowledged that he had played a role – he claimed a minor one – in the murder and stated unequivocally that Myles Joyce was innocent. He also expressly discredited the Joyce crown witnesses and implicated the approver Thomas Casey as member of the murder party:

> Statement of Patrick Casey, now a prisoner under sentence of death, makes the following statement at his own request and of his own free will: I say that prisoner Myles Joyce is innocent in that case, namely, the murder of the Joyces. There were present at the murder and in the house myself, Thomas Casey (approver), Pat Joyce (Michael), and Michael Casey. The other 3 are outside. I will not name them. Anthony Philbin was not there. Thomas Casey fired the first shot. John Joyce was the first man that was shot, and that by Thomas Casey. All I did in the matter was to put my hand upon John Joyce's shoulder. Neither Anthony Joyce, John Joyce, or John Joyce's son saw a light of any of the men that committed the murder that night.[12]

Mason and Evans also witnessed a short statement by Patrick Joyce on 13 December. In it Joyce similarly began by declaring, 'Myles Joyce is as innocent as the child unborn of the crime, of the murder of the Joyce family.'[13] Like Casey, he identified the murder party as consisting of seven men: he and Patrick Casey, the prisoner Michael Casey, the approver Thomas Casey, and 'three men now at liberty, and I don't like to mention their names.' He further alleged that Thomas Casey had done all of the shooting, and that 'two of the three men now outside had a hammer and used it to kill out those of the Joyces not dead.' Patrick Joyce's statement also directly addressed the issue of motivation: in it he asserted that the crime was 'not the work of a secret society' but was originated by a 'farmer' who 'is out-side' and who acted 'for spite'.[14] Joyce concluded by stating clearly that Paudeen Joyce, Thomas Joyce, Martin Joyce and John Casey were 'innocent of the crime', reiterating that they 'were not there at all.'

A fuller four-page statement was taken from Patrick Joyce on 14 December, the day before his execution; this document was also signed by

him but was now witnessed by magistrate Newton Brady. Brady's presence
was a further marker of the statement's significance since, as resident magistrate, he had been one of the first officials to arrive at the scene of the
murders in August.[15] In this longer testimony, Joyce provided additional and
gruesome details regarding how the murders were carried out, asserting that
Thomas Casey had brought three revolvers and a candle and matches with
him, that one of the three men still at large had lifted and held the candle
while Casey fired, and that shots had been aimed at John Joyce, who was
sleeping with his wife 'in the callagh'. His summary of the events makes for
grim reading: 'There was no screaming or shouting from beginning to end
that I could hear. We were not a quarter of an hour in John Joyce's house.'
The statement concluded with a ringing line 'Myles is no relation of mine in
the world – it is the greatest murder in Ireland that ever was if he is hanged.
Patrick Joyce' (see Image 29, p. XIV).[16]

The existence of the statements leaked into the national press but not
the texts of the confessions themselves. Writing from Galway on the eve
of the executions, the *Freeman's Journal* reporter relayed to readers that an
'inquiry, if inquiry I may call it, has been conducted by Mr. Brady, R. M.,'
and that 'it is said that the two men Patrick Joyce and Patrick Casey are
positive that Myles Joyce had neither 'hand, act, nor part' in the Maamtrasna
murders'.[17] Speculation as to what was said in these documents and how
they were handled would become highly contentious questions during the
later inquiries into the Maamtrasna verdicts. In the early morning of 15
December, execution day, a short telegraph was sent from the Viceregal
Lodge to Galway Jail. It read, 'Having considered statements, I am unable
to alter my decision. The law must take its course.'[18] Despite the supporting
authority of Brady, Spencer did not consider these declarations, given on
the eve of execution, and which unambiguously attested to the innocence
of Myles Joyce, sufficient to warrant further intervention.

THE 'SECRET' PRISON

Public executions in England and Ireland ended in 1868. The last fully public
hanging conducted in England was that of Fenian Michael Barrett, held at
Newgate in May 1868, and, under the Capital Punishment Amendment Act

of that year, executions were henceforth confined to behind prison walls.[19] This was part of a series of measures designed to improve the 'humane' quality of the manner of execution, but as historian V. A. C. Gatrell notes, even after the introduction of the long drop in the 1880s, which was designed to dislocate the cervical vertebrae and rupture the spinal cord, consciousness was thought to continue for two minutes and a heartbeat for several minutes longer.[20] In 1836, John Stuart Mill wrote with searing contempt on the processes by which the spectacle, and 'even the very idea, of pain,' was to be kept more and more out of the sight of 'those classes who enjoy in their fullness the benefits of civilization'. 'All those necessary portions of the business of society which oblige any person to be the immediate agent or ocular witness of the infliction of pain,' Mill remarked, 'are delegated by common consent to peculiar and narrow classes: to the judge, the soldier, the surgeon, the butcher, and the executioner.'[21] And, as Gattrell succinctly notes, 'Victorians' civility only veneered the state's violence over.'[22]

This consolidation of the 'secret prison' meant the elimination of public audiences and consequently a drastic reduction in the number of ocular and aural witnesses. However, in the words of Jacques Derrida (quoted as epigraph at the start of this chapter), the application or, more accurately, the infliction of the death penalty is never invisible: it requires both 'spectacle' and 'spectator': the state must and wants to '*see die* the condemned one.'[23] The hangings in December 1882 took place within the confines of Galway Jail and the number of eyewitnesses was limited to nine official representatives, including the prison chaplain and a medical doctor, and a group of some twelve journalists. These included Andrew Dunlop, special correspondent for the *Evening Telegraph* and the *Freeman's Journal*, who had visited Maamtrasna in August, and the young Englishman Frederick Higginbottom, later a journalist with the *Pall Mall Gazette*.[24]

Media reports, published in local newspapers such as the *Galway Express* and in several national newspapers including the *Freeman's Journal*, *Irish Times*, and *Belfast Newsletter*, allocated most attention to the circumstances of Myles' death and would play a key role in shaping wider unease as to his execution. The details of these accounts were and remain difficult to read and are disturbing to analyse closely. 'Squeamishness', however, as Gatrell demonstrates in his history, also enables a collective denial of the reality of capital punishment, and this remains a valuable caution. 'Empathy and sympathy', he writes, 'are democratic emotions, extending their generous warmth to all. Squeamishness by contrast refuses to accept the pain which sympathetic engagement threatens. It denies material reality or others' emotions and blocks the echoes of these within the self … defensively fastidious in the face of the rude and the unsightly.'[25]

DECLARATION OF INNOCENCE

Writing from Galway on Thursday evening, the eve of the executions, the correspondent for the *Irish Times* expressed the view that Myles Joyce, alone of the three condemned men, might 'yet be respited'. He also reported that the relatives of Patrick Joyce and Patrick Casey had visited the men in jail on the previous day, but that 'the friends of Myles Joyce had not seen him for two or three days previously.'[26] Also, according to the *Irish Times*, the men were 'quite resigned' to what awaited them though the reporter also acknowledged, with some understatement, their being 'rather despondent at times'.[27] Many newspaper reports referred to the men's religious practices: the Irish-speaking prison chaplain, Fr Greaven, attended them daily and local Sisters of Mercy nuns also visited them regularly. The three men were lodged in separate cells in the hospital section of the jail, close to the location of the gallows. On the morning of the execution, severe weather resulted in fewer than usual spectators gathered outside the jail and reporters commented on the streets of Galway being all but entirely deserted.[28]

The *Belfast Newsletter*, which had covered the trials in such substantial detail, also allocated considerable space to the executions, with a half-page spread on the day following. The article betrays the journalist's own fascination with what he termed the 'ghastly paraphernalia' of hanging, featuring a lengthy description of the gallows and only a passing reference to the three men:

> It was about twenty feet long and eight feet wide, while the uprights about the platform were about 10 feet high, which, with the height of the platform added, made the height of the whole structure about 20 feet. Leading up to the platform was a wide flight of steps, with a hand rail on each side, the whole being built of timber that was quite new. On the cross-beam were fixed three stout iron clamps, having rings on their nether sides, through which the halters were fastened with three half hitches. Below was the fatal drop, which was so arranged that by simply touching a lever at his side, the executioner

could secure the instantaneous and simultaneous precipitation of the three victims below the level of the platform, allowing for a fall of nine feet. All of this ghastly paraphernalia was ready for use when the three miserable culprits made their appearance in the yard.[29]

Eight o'clock on Friday morning was the scheduled execution time. The next day's report in the *Galway Vindicator* relayed some information from a prison informant: that the men had woken at five, made confessions in the prison chapel, attended Mass and received Communion; on their return to their cells, they were offered a substantial breakfast 'but they declined partaking of it.'[30] At eight o'clock, Marwood visited each man in his cell and pinioned them with arm restraints. The 'melancholy procession' to the gallows comprised the three men, each attended by a warder, along with Governor Mason and Chief Warder Evans (who had witnessed Casey and Joyce's statements), the prison chaplain Fr Greaven, Galway Sub-Sheriff John Redington, medical doctor Patrick M. Rice, followed by members of the press.[31] Myles Joyce walked first in the procession and was first to ascend the gallows, followed by Patrick Joyce and Patrick Casey. While Marwood was adjusting the ropes and caps on the men's heads, and the chaplain stood near reciting the Litany for the Dead, Myles Joyce turned his head to the group of reporters standing below the scaffold and spoke clearly, rapidly and with a memorable eloquence.

Every subsequent news report on the executions referred to Myles' speech from the gallows, some in summary form, some ostensibly 'word for word'. Of course, all such accounts were translated versions of his original words, and some of these differed slightly. The reporter for the *Galway Vindicator* acknowledged his reliance on two of the gentlemen present who 'understood Irish'.[32] The most compelling version of events is that provided by its nationalist rival the *Galway Express*, whose reporter appears to have understood Irish well and may have translated Myles' words himself. His article ran to almost three long columns and began with a gesture to his own reluctant witnessing: 'The spectacle is one which will be long remembered by those who in most instances were compelled, owing to their positions, to witness it.'[33] It included a brief description of the two other condemned prisoners, Patrick Casey of 'dogged aspect' and Patrick Joyce as displaying much 'earnestness', but as was the case throughout press accounts, mostly referred to the death of Myles Joyce. Extracts from this account are worth reproducing in detail.

On arriving at the foot of the scaffold Myles Joyce looked up, and repeating in Irish *Arrah thawmay glimmacht* ('I am going'),[34] darted from the hands of the two warders and rapidly ascended the steps leading to the platform, on mounting which he turned towards the reporters and prison officials and in a loud and firm voice declared he was going towards his God and had not been at the murder at all. He had neither hand, act, or part in it and was as innocent as the child in the cradle … Marwood then proceeded to adjust the nooses. The first he took in hands was Myles Joyce, who was very much agitated, and having placed him in position, after some slight difficulty succeeded in making him stand steady for a moment, when he slipped the noose over his head. No sooner did the condemned man feel the touch of the fatal cord then he again turned round, and speaking to Marwood said, 'Why should I die. I am not guilty.' This movement on his part displaced the rope, and the executioner had again to place it in the manner suitable for his purpose. He then put over the culprit's face the white cap. The next man was Patrick Casey who submitted to the operation without a murmur, as did also Patrick Joyce. Having done so much, Marwood moved back a pace or two for the purpose of ascertaining if all were right, but at the moment Myles Joyce turned in the direction of the reporters, the white cap still over his face, and judging from the working of his body, his mind must have been terribly excited. He said, 'I had neither hand or foot in the murder. I knew nothing about it, but God forgive them that swore my life away. It is a poor thing to die on a stage for what I never did.' This movement on his part again caused the knot to become displaced and necessitated Marwood to adjust it the third time, and it might be admitted on this occasion he used the poor fellow rather roughly. Having, as he believed, successfully completed his work for the third time, he proceeded to bind the man's legs, after which he moved toward the lever which regulated the fall of the trap, on which he placed his hand, Myles Joyce still continuing to attest his innocence. He was saying, 'I never did it, and it is a poor case to die. God help my wife and her five orphans. I had no hand, act, or part in it, but I have my priest with me.' At this moment the bolt was drawn and the three men were launched into eternity. Myles Joyce was actually protesting against his being executed at the moment the drop fell. The ropes from which Pat Joyce and Pat Casey were suspended did not even seem to quiver, but that which supported Myles Joyce was observed to oscillate greatly, which caused Marwood to go towards the body and take the rope in his hand which he shook, for what object could not then be ascertained. He then sat down on the trap and allowed his feet to fall into the pit into which the condemned men had already fallen, and was seen to push his right foot downwards as if pressing on some object below, at the same time sounds as if a struggle were taking place below were distinctly heard by those who were close to the scaffold.[35]

The sequential unfolding of this narrative is especially powerful, with each of Marwood's physical actions as executioner punctuated by Myles' strong verbal protests. The accumulating aural drama culminates in the stark simplicity of the line, 'Myles Joyce was actually protesting against his being executed at the moment the drop fell,' and the mediated aspect of his words – spoken in Irish, being rendered in English to newspaper readers – gradually fades from view. But most significantly this report starkly attests to the physical cruelty of the execution, and that Myles Joyce's death had not been instantaneous.

THE OFFICIAL INQUEST: 'DEATH FROM STRANGULATION'

As was standard judicial procedure, an official inquest immediately succeeded the executions, commencing at 12 noon; the first public disquiet was voiced about the manner in which the executions had been conducted. The inquest began with a formal viewing of the bodies which lay in cheap deal-wood coffins on the ground within a few yards of the scaffold. Here again the account from the unnamed *Galway Express* reporter is of value: Patrick Joyce's expression he describes as 'placid' but 'not so, however, was the case of Myles Joyce, for his features were much distorted, apparently with pain, swollen and blackened. His clothes were much blood-stained, and on his right forearm there was an extensive bruise, and the skin was torn.'[36] The presiding medical doctor Patrick Rice deposed that Myles Joyce had 'died from strangulation, no fracture of the neck bones having taken place at all. I consider death took place between one and two minutes after.'[37] And in reply to a query posed by one juror, Mr O'Mara, he responded with the gruesome detail that, in his view, Myles Joyce must have been alive from two to three minutes after the trap fell.[38]

When asked to account for the difference in cause of death between Patrick Joyce and Patrick Casey (fracture of the neck) and Myles Joyce (strangulation), Rice strongly implicated the actions of the executioner Marwood: 'Myles Joyce was addressing the reporters present and naturally turned to where they were standing, and Marwood fixed the rope around his neck first … My impression is that it was Marwood's fault, because seeing that Myles Joyce was not so passive as the other two, he should have fixed the noose around his neck last.'[39] Consequently, a number of jurors requested that Marwood be called to give evidence to the inquest, but the coroner declined to do so, deeming his evidence 'unnecessary'.[40] Another juror raised the issue of Myles Joyce's earlier protestations of innocence, observing that these had already generated significant public interest:

> Juror—It is remarked outside that Myles Joyce asserted his innocence, and the two other men also said he was innocent as well as the five others who have been respited. I want to know would the governor give us any information on the subject, and is it true he did not send forward a representation of it to the government?
>
> Captain Mason—That is a question I cannot answer.[41]

The recorded verdict of the coroner's jury, delivered in spite of the best efforts of the coroner to contain it, was that Patrick Joyce and Patrick Casey had 'died from fractures of the neck, the result of hanging, and that Myles Joyce died from strangulation.' It ended with a strongly worded criticism in which O'Mara expressed on behalf of the other jurors their 'disapprobation' of the failure by the corner to interview Marwood: 'Marwood had not done his duty properly', he stated, and 'great blame [was] attached to him in this matter.'[42]

In its leader article the next day, the *Freeman's Journal* drew particular attention to the cruel nature of Myles Joyce's death, and the horrific details that it included would greatly influence public opinion of the executions:

> The impression prevails that his innocence was formally affirmed by a number of the men sentenced for the awful crime at Maamtrasna. At all events he died with a declaration of innocence upon his lips. It has so happened that this man, Myles Joyce, met a crueller death than either of the other two executed. In the vehemence of his protestation on the scaffold he seems to have disarranged the awful preparations made by Marwood, who was obliged to strangle him by personal force in default of the ordinary vertebral dislocation. This incident adds a new element of horror to the tragic sequel to an awful massacre.[43]

That words spoken at the gallows are truthful words is a widely shared belief, and one difficult to dislodge. The *Freeman's* editorial contained a telling hesitation, torn between agreement with the guilty verdict against Myles Joyce and the moral force of his protests on the scaffold: 'It would of course be improper to lay down that because a man goes to the scaffold declaring his innocence, he is therefore innocent and ought to be reprieved. Yet it is hard to conceive how a man religiously prepared for a death, from which he is assured there is no escape, would elect to die with a lie upon his lips.'[44]

Press articles in the aftermath of the executions also display a deep fascination with the figure of Marwood as a quasi-inept – but all the more ruthless – executioner. Andrew Dunlop, as special correspondent for the *Evening Telegraph*, observed how 'Marwood got through the pinioning work as only Marwood can, adjusting the straps with an ease and alacrity that shows too plainly what a perfect artist he is in his horrible calling.'[45] Others relayed the executioner's response to the jury's criticisms, as in the following article published by Saturday's *Belfast Newsletter*:

> On being questioned afterwards as to the cause of the hitch which seemed to have occurred in the hanging of Myles Joyce, he replied that 'It was nothing. The rope had just caught the arm of the man as he fell, and he had had to disengage it with his foot.' The common hangman further remarked in reference to the vociferated statements of Myles Joyce that he 'would be bound he was abusing everybody,' although he admitted that he did not understand a word of what the wretched man had said.[46]

Witnesses to the hanging reported hearing Marwood exclaim 'Bother the fellow', lines cited as further proof of his heartlessness.[47] In a subsequent interview with the *Sheffield Telegraph* (which was reproduced by the *New Zealand Herald*, among others), Marwood deployed the gap of language between executioner and victim as exoneration: 'He was a wild, bad-looking fellow and kept jabbering and talking. I couldn't understand a word of his "lingo", and I don't think the priest knew much of it, for he seemed frightened. But there was enough force of the rope on his neck to finish him in a very little time.'[48] The story of Marwood's cruelty would be reinforced in later years by the writings of politician Tim Harrington and journalist James Joyce. Joyce's portrait was especially damning: 'The story was told that the executioner, unable to make the victim understand him, kicked at the miserable man's head in anger to shove it into the noose.'[49]

THE SECRET INQUIRY

An unprecedented further investigation into the Maamtrasna executions took place soon afterwards which was hidden from public view.[50] On 22 December, Spencer, the Lord Lieutenant, received a short, handwritten, anonymous letter, forwarded to his office by the editors of the London *Athenaeum.*[51] The full text of the letter reads:

> It was doubtless quite right to hang those three ruffians the other day, but it's a pity the hangman bungled. That gives occasion to the enemy to blaspheme.
>
> Then comes the question why should three men be all sentenced to be hung on the same day? And if sentenced for the same day, why should they all be hung at the same time? I assume that with more time and only one patient on his hands, Marwood would do his work without a hitch.[52]

Spencer's officials had already drawn his attention to the detailed reports in local and national newspapers about the 'bungling' of the execution of Myles Joyce. As a result, he and Under-Secretary William Kaye directed that a 'full enquiry' be held into 'all the circumstances' pertaining to that execution, 'with the view of ascertaining if any person was to blame with respect to the manner in which the sentence of the law was carried out on that occasion.'[53] The inquiry, held at Galway Jail on 29 and 30 December, was conducted by Charles J. Bourke, chairman of the General Prison Board, and Dr Charles Croker-King, a member of the Local Government Board. They examined ten witnesses, nine of whom had been present at the execution.[54] The tenth was Doctor Richard Kinkead, the prison's chief medical officer who had been unable to attend the execution and for whom Doctor Rice had substituted.[55]

Repeating the evidence that he had first tendered to the official inquest following the execution, Rice testified clearly as to the differing causes of death for the three men as follows:

> The cause of death in Patrick Joyce and Patrick Casey was dislocation of the second cervical vertebrae from the first and third, the spinal cord being pressed in consequence by the body of the vertebrae pressing them. The vertebrae was pressed forwards and consequently pressed on the cord. Exactly the same injury in both cases.
>
> Was standing on the ground when the execution took place at right side of platform, could not see into the pit.
>
> The cause of Myles Joyce's death was strangulation, no dislocation or pressure on the spinal cord.[56]

This evidence – with its direct diagnosis of 'strangulation' as the cause of death – would prove by far the most contentious within the overall inquiry.

On the question of when exactly Myles' death occurred, Rice was, however, more cautious and equivocal: 'I was separated from Myles Joyce [by] about sixteen feet. I formed my opinion from what I heard and the examination of the bodies afterwards. After the half minute I heard no more, but it does not follow that he was dead when I ceased to hear him breathe, but I could not say whether he was dead or alive at the expiration of that time – it is only a conjecture.'[57] And, in line with other witnesses, he firmly attributed blame for the 'disarrangement of the rope' during Myles' hanging to the prisoner being 'unsettled and talkative' rather than to Marwood's mishandling.[58]

What was actually said by the 'talkative' Myles Joyce was largely avoided in the inquiry, but two witnesses referred to his protests in their evidence. One was the prison chaplain Fr Greaven who was also careful to apportion blame for 'any mishap' to the prisoner:

> I understand Irish and distinctly heard and understood what Myles Joyce said. As far as I recollect, he stated in Irish that he was as innocent as the priest on the altar, and there was no greater injustice from the commencement to the end of the world.

> I consider everything in connection with the scaffold was in perfect order, and that every precaution was taken by the authorities here to make the execution as humane as possible. Any mishap that may have occurred I attribute entirely to the action of the prisoner.[59]

The evidence from the other witness, a 'warder in prison service' named Patrick Coen, was especially resonant: a bilingual speaker, Coen was one of the few witnesses to understand Myles Joyce's words. His recollections also illustrate how differing and contested versions of Joyce's last words had begun to circulate:

> I understand Irish.

> Myles Joyce declared his innocence to the last. He said he was glad he was dying innocent and said he was as innocent as the child unborn, and repeated it over and over again. Did not hear him say he was as innocent as the priest on the altar, but he might have said it in the hospital before I took charge of him.

> Heard Marwood, when he was taking the rope off the wrist, say 'Bother it,' I think.[60]

In their concluding report, Bourke and Croker-King as leaders of the inquiry were assiduous in distancing themselves from Rice's findings that

Myles Joyce had died of strangulation. Croker-King described the doctor's evidence as 'unsatisfactory and unreliable in every respect' and remarked that the injuries which he had reported 'even supposing that they [were] to have occurred, could only have been detected by a careful and minute post-mortem examination.' Terminating the formal inquiry, Spencer and Kaye together formulated a carefully worded statement as to the 'humane' character of the execution. This contained some striking prevarication as to what had occurred and what could occur:

> His Excellency [they spoke for the viceroy] is satisfied from the reports and the evidence as to the completeness of the arrangements in respect of the scaffold and to the precautions taken by the prison authorities to make the execution as humane as possible. It appears, however, that after the bolt was drawn and the bodies had fallen, the rope by which Myles Joyce was suspended became entangled in his arm and wrist, and that the executioner felt it necessary to exert himself to put it in the proper position. It was not proved that this prevented immediate death in this case, but it is clear that a similar accident might lead to a painful protraction of life.[61]

*

The 'last words' uttered by Myles Joyce would, in time, gather an iconic status and a highly incendiary political force; in tracing these words back to records of the original scene, one comes to recognise the crucial importance of their first auditors and translators. As mentioned earlier, one of the journalists present on 15 December was a 23-year-old Englishman named Frederick James Higginbottom, newly posted to Ireland on behalf of the English Press Association.[62] He seems the likely source for the lurid account of the executions published in the English press the very next day.[63] Writing over 50 years later, in his 1934 memoir *The Vivid Life: A Journalist's Memoir*, he recollected: 'I had only been in Ireland a fortnight when I was called upon in the course of my duties as a special correspondent to undergo a harrowing ordeal … This triple execution was my baptism of blood in Ireland, and its horror was accentuated by an incident so dreadful that its details have never faded from my memory.'[64]

To accompany Higginbottom's six-page recollection of the hanging, a special and quite remarkable plate was included in the 1934 volume entitled *Focla déigheanacha mhaolmhuire seoighighe air an g-croich,* translated as 'Myles Joyce's dying words on the scaffold.' The plate contains a number of striking features, including the reproduction of the Irish-language words in a Gaelic script and the inclusion of an accompanying autograph translation (see Image 31, p. XV). The image is thus presented as an 'original' textual source, though Higginbottom did not specify its provenance.

Whether Higginbottom had received a written Irish-language transcription from one of his fellow eyewitnesses at the execution scene and preserved it over some 50 years, or had the Irish-language text recreated in the 1930s from the surviving English-language account, is tantalisingly unclear. The latter seems more likely from a typographical perspective – in other words, the publisher is seeking to give the appearance of 'authenticity' by reproducing Irish-language words and script. Various amendments (such as the change from *cuid* to *páirt* for the English 'part') suggest hesitations or changes of mind by the translator from English to Irish. The language of the Irish text is highly rhetorical and literary in nature, but also at times carries more nuance than the accompanying English text.[65] How it is reproduced on the page is also highly accomplished, giving a flavour of oral speech by the use of apostrophes to indicate spoken elision ('s for *is*) or variants in speech such as *Cia'n fá* 'rather than the standard usage *Cén fáth*.

Writing in 1934, Higginbottom recollected that more than one of the 'shocked spectators' at the scene had 'conceived at the moment a dreadful doubt lest an innocent man had suffered the penalty of guilt.' He himself was at pains to convey his certainty as to Myles' guilt and the veracity of the judicial process that had convicted him: 'That Joyce was one of the three who entered the house of death at Maamtrasna was proved, and doubly proved. Whether he killed anyone or not, he was guilty in law.'[66] However, he was an exception in this regard and almost all of the other disseminations of *na focla déigheanacha*, and versions thereof, aimed to convey Myles Joyce's innocence and the duplicity and injustice of British law. The circulation of Myles Joyce's dying protests would, over time, help to produce a sea change in public attitudes to the Maamtrasna case, bringing to light the linguistic and cultural difference that official accounts of the trials had actively suppressed. And a central element of the 'memorial dynamics'[67] of the Maamtrasna murders was the brutal nature of Myles' execution.

Part III

Last Words

1. Thomas Casey (approver). Courtesy of the National Library of Ireland.

2. Michael Casey (imprisoned). Courtesy of the National Library of Ireland.

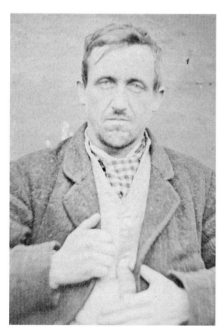

3. John Casey (imprisoned). Courtesy of the National Library of Ireland.

4. Patrick Casey (executed). Courtesy of the National Library of Ireland.

5. *Martin Joyce (imprisoned). Courtesy of the National Library of Ireland.*

6. *Myles Joyce (executed; pardoned in 2018). Courtesy of the National Library of Ireland.*

7. *Paudeen (Patrick) Joyce (imprisoned). Courtesy of the National Library of Ireland.*

8. *Tom (Thomas) Joyce (imprisoned). Courtesy of the National Library of Ireland.*

9. Anthony Philbin (approver). Courtesy of the National Library of Ireland.

10. Patrick Joyce (executed). Courtesy of the National Library of Ireland.

11. 'Let Justice be "Done"', Weekly Freeman, 29 November 1884. Image courtesy of the National Library of Ireland.

coimisiún béaloideasa éireann

conntae _na Zaillime_   barúntact _Baile na b-Jape_

paróiste _Muiz-Ruis_

Ainm an Sgríobnóra _Brian MacLoclainn_

Seolaд an Sgríobnóra _Baile Nua, An Closzeann_

Do rgríobar ríor an _ennaraí scéalta_ ro ar an _14/7/36_

ó béal-aicpir _Seán Seoize (Tomáis)_

Aor _80_ zairm-beata _feirméara_ atá in a comnui

i mbaile feapainn _Eorke Kiel a' Niama_

agur a raoluíoд agur a tózaд i _nDoike Kiel a' Niama, Skari Salaí._

Do cuala ré (rí) an _ennaraí_ ro _____ blian ó rin ó

_____(Aor an uair rin_____) a bí in a comnui an uair rin

i _____

[_Paitín Seiд , Paitín Zakú (?)_]

Well eapú la, le céili, Paitín ~~Seд~~ Seiд Paitín Zaku.
"Nac Zaku a la é "? adeir Paitín Zaku, le Paitín
Seiд. "Ó Séitir ré leir." adeir Paitín Seiд.

[_Tuztar "Paitín Zaku" ar la Zaka , Tuztar "Paitín Seiд" ar
la Zaoírar freirin_].

12. Extract from 1936 account by Seán Seoighe (Tomáis) on the Maamtrasna murders. Reproduced by permission of the National Folklore Collection, University College Dublin.

IV

amaċ. Aġus ḋ'iaṙṙuiḋ *an máċair* ~~bean~~ ~~Seán Seoiġe~~ go bean
Seán Seoiġe, :- "aṙ ainm uṙa" aḋeiṙ sí "na fiṙ
sin"? "ḋ'aiṫniġeas" aḋeiṙ bean Seán Seoiġe.
ḋ'fill na fiṙ ysteaċ aṙíṡ nuaiṙ a ċualaḋaṙ
an cainnt puḃ a' ṗiúl, eḋiṙ a beiṙt ban.
Aġus nuaiṙ a ḋ'filleaḋaṙ ysteaċ, ṁaṙuiġeaḋaṙ
an méiḋ aḃí sa teaċ. ṁaṙuiġeaḋaṙ an beiṙt
ban, Seán Seoiġe é héin 7 ní ḟeaḋaim aḃáḋ
ca méaḋ gaṙúṙ. Aċ nuaiṙ aḃí na fiṙ puḃ
a' maṙú na ngaṙúṙ - uṙa baḃaí - ṙuc gaṙúṙ
acú ríos ċeiḋ a ḃaḃaí. aġus fuaṙċeaṙ faoin
baḃaí aṙ maiḋin, é. Tuġċaṙ [tuġaḋ] a' ṗiúl
go dú ucín é, faiċíos go maṙṫóaí é.
Ansin cṙoċú feaṙ go Seoiġeaċ, ingeall aṙ a
"murder" puḃ, aġus ċuala mé Raiḃri é, náċṫe
aḃí cionnṫaċ gon oḃaiṙ ċoṙ a' biṫ - naċ
ṙo aon baint eiġe leis. Níl fios cén ṫ-úḋaṙ
aḃí le é amaṙú.

13. Extract from 1936 account by Seán Seoighe (Tomáis) on the Maamtrasna murders. Reproduced by permission of the National Folklore Collection, University College Dublin.

14. Joyce house, Maamtrasna, today. Image courtesy of Brian Dolan.

15. Joyce house exterior, Weekly Irish Times, *Saturday, 18 November 1882.*
Image courtesy of the National Library of Ireland.

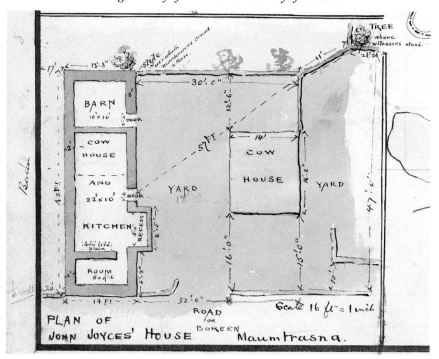

16. Plan of Joyce house interior by engineer Ryan, August 1882.
Image courtesy of the National Archives of Ireland.

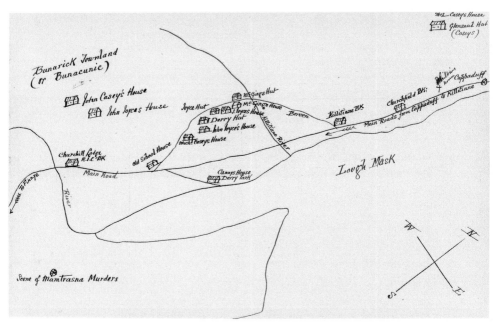

Image labels: Mrs Casey's House; Glensaul Hut (Caseys); Bunarick Townland (or Bunacunie); John Casey's House; John Joyce's House; Joyce Hut; McGings Hut; McGings House; J. Joyces House; Derry Hut; John Joyce's House; Killitiane River; Berven; Killitiane Bk; Churchfield Bk; Road to Cappaduff; Main Roads from Cappaduff to Killitiane; Muchl Casey's House; Old School House; Churchill Lodge R.I.C. Bk; Main Road; Road to Finnye; River; Cannys House Derry Park; Lough Mask; Scene of Mamtrasna Murders; N; W; S; E

17. Line drawing of the Maamtrasna area by engineer Ryan, August 1882.
Image courtesy of the National Archives of Ireland.

18. 'The Murder of the Joyce Family in Ireland', Illustrated Police News, *cover page,*
Saturday, 25 November 1882. Image courtesy of the National Library of Ireland.

1. Eye Witnesses.—2, 3, 4. Murderers Condemned.—5. Murderer Turned Approver.—6, 7. Female Witnesses.—8. The Boy Joyce.

MAAMTRASNA MASSACRE—THE TRIAL OF THE PRISONERS: EXAMINATION OF THE BOY JOYCE, AGED NINE YEARS
ONLY SURVIVOR OF THE MASSACRED FAMILY

19. 'Examination of the Boy Joyce', The Graphic (London), 2 December 1882. Image courtesy of the National Library of Ireland.

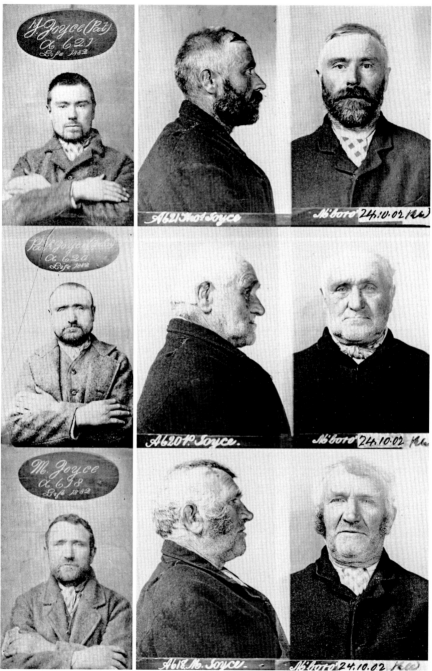

20–25. Prison photos at commencement of imprisonment (1882) and on release (1902). Top: Tom (Thomas) Joyce; Middle: Paudeen (Pat) Joyce; Bottom: Martin Joyce. Images courtesy of the National Archives.

THE CENSUS COMMISSIONERS beg leave most earnestly to entreat the Heads of Families to see that the several Queries contained in this sheet are distinctly and accurately filled up, since upon the accuracy of the answers given the value of the Census must mainly depend. As the information thus obtained will be published in General Abstracts only, and strict care that the Returns are not used for the gratification of curiosity, or any other object than perfecting the Census, the Commissioners feel that on National grounds,—apart from the requirements of the Act of Parliament,—they are warranted in making this appeal to the Heads and the various Members of Families to aid them in their important inquiries, as it is of the deepest interest to ascertain with all possible accuracy, the exact numbers and condition of the population of Ireland at the present time.

Census Office, Dublin, 1851.

PATTERN TABLES.

1ST TABLE.
Return of the Members, Visitors, and Servants of this Family, who Slept or Abode in this House on the night of, &c.

NAMES Of the Members, Visitors, and Servants, of this Family, who slept or abode in this House on the above night.		AGE.		SEX. Whether Male or Female?	RELATION Of each to the Head of Family, as whether Wife, Son, Daughter, or other relative, Visitor, Servant, &c.?	MARRIAGE. Whether "Married," "Not Married," "Widower," or "Widow?"	In what Year married? or in what Years if more than once?	RANK, PROFESSION, OR OCCUPATION. State the particular Rank, Profession, Trade, or other Employment; or if a child, whether attending school?	EDUCATION. Whether he or she can "Read," "Read and Write," or "Cannot Read?"	WHERE BORN. In what Country, County, or City?	Whether Deaf-and-Dumb or Blind?
Christian Names.	Surnames.	Years.	Months.								
John	Moran,	59	–	M.	Head of Family,	Married,	1818, 1842	Farmer,	Read [Irish],	Kildare.	–
Eliza	Moran,	55	–	F.	Wife,	Married,	1842		Cannot Read,	Do.	–
George	Moran,	26	–	M.	Son,	Not Married,	–	Woollen Weaver,	Read and Write,	Do.	–
Rose	Moran,	23	–	F.	Daughter,	Not Married,	–	Spinning Wool,	Do.	Do.	–
Peter	Moran,	14	–	M.	Son,	Not Married,	–	At Mr. Daly's school,	Do.	Do.	–
Mary	Murphy,	45	–	F.	Sister-in-Law,	Not Married,	–	None,	Do.	Do.	Deaf-&-Dumb.
Duncan	Macdonald	24	–	M.	Servant,	Married,	1846	Ploughman,	Do.	Scotland.	–
Ellen	Butler,	22	–	F.	Do.,	Not Married,	–	House Servant,	Cannot Read,	Dublin.	–
Jane	Whitmore,	23	–	F.	Visitor,	Not Married,	–	None,	Read and Write,	England	–

2ND TABLE.
Return of the Members of this Family whose Home is in this House, but who were Absent on the night of, &c.

NAMES.		AGE.		SEX. Whether Male or Female.	RELATION Of EACH to the HEAD of the Family, whether Wife, Son, Daughter, or other Relative, Servant, &c.	RANK, PROFESSION, OR OCCUPATION. State the particular Rank, Profession, Trade, or other Employment; or if a child, whether attending school.	In what Country, County, or City; at present residing.
Christian Names.	Surnames.	Years.	Months.				
Timothy	Moran,	31	–	Male,	Son,	Army,	America.
Bridget	Moran,	26	–	Female,	Daughter,	None,	Dublin.
William	Moran,	18	–	Male,	Son,	Haymaker,	England.
Thomas	Moran,	22	–	Male,	Son,	Constabulary,	County Down.

3RD TABLE.
Return of the Members, Visitors, and Servants of this Family, who have died while residing with this Family, since, &c.

NAMES.		AGE.		SEX. Whether Male or Female.	RELATION Of EACH to the HEAD of the Family, whether Wife, Son, Daughter, &c.	RANK, PROFESSION, OR OCCUPATION. State the particular Rank, Profession, Trade, or other Employment	Disease which caused death.	TIME OF DEATH.	
Christian Names.	Surnames.	Years.	Months.					Season.	Year.
Mary	Moran,	48	–	Female,	Wife,	None,	Fever,	Summer,	1841
Patrick	Moran,	12	–	Male,	Son,	None,	Small Pox,	Spring,	1846
Bryan	Byrne,	40	–	Male,	Visitor,	Pedlar,	Apoplexy,	Autumn,	1847

INSTRUCTIONS FOR FILLING THESE TABLES.

It is intended that the Enumerator shall call for this Return as soon as possible after the night of the 30th March, when he will assist such persons as may not be able to fill it themselves. But when competent, it is requested that the Head of the Family shall fill, or cause it to be filled, immediately after the said night, in order that the Enumerator may not be delayed when he calls for it.

This Return is divided into Three Tables.

THE 1ST TABLE is for those persons of each Family, the Visitors, and Servants, who slept or abode in the same house on the night of Sunday, the 30th March.

By a Family is meant either one person living on his or her own means of support, or several persons united under one head, and having a common means of support;—therefore when there are several Families in one house, a separate Form will be left for each.

OCCUPATIONS.—In order to arrive at a correct classification of the employment of the people, attention is requested to the following observations:—

One general principle which should be kept in mind is, that each person will be best described to whose name is annexed his or her principal means of support: thus, "Landed Proprietor,"—"House Owner,"—"Fund" or "Stock Holder,"—"Annuitant," &c., will best define the more independent classes, whose principal means are derived from any of these or similar sources.

PROFESSIONS.—A person deriving his income from a profession should state its particular nature; and professional men who are occupied with other avocations, should define their

P

26. Sample pattern table, Census of 1851, General Report, Part VI.
Image courtesy of the National Library of Ireland.

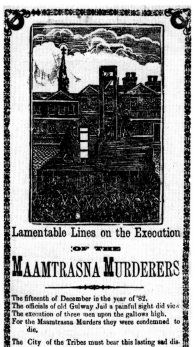

Lamentable Lines on the Execution

OF THE

MAAMTRASNA MURDERERS

The fifteenth of December in the year of '82,
The officials of old Galway Jail a painful sight did view
The execution of three men upon the gallows high,
For the Maamtrasna Murders they were condemned to
    die,

The City of the Tribes must bear this lasting sad dis-
    grace,
Which years of good behaviour from it will not erase,
The crime is more lamented than the hanging of the
    three,
And may we again such a tragedy in Ireland never see.

Their clergy have attended them with unremitting care
We hope their penitence and prayers to heaven has
    been sincere,
And that they may find favour before the throne on
    high,
Their sentence was a fearful one in manhood's prime to
    die.

The five who pleaded guilty each will have a troubled
    mind,
When to their dark and dismal cells in Spike they are
    consigned,
The ghastly scene that brought them there will be be-
    fore their eyes,
Whether day or night they'll have no peace these
    visions will arise.

The judge and jury have discharged their duty with
    much pain,
The verdict no one could dispute the evidence was
    plain,
Then let us pray that their poor souls on high may
    mercy find,
And to the five respited men give each a tranquil mind

Old Grania in deep sorrow weeps and calls on Irishmen
To abstain in from every kind of crime that would our
    men condemn,
And with our patriotic men in peace join hand-in-hand
And still repeat that holy prayer, God save old Ireland.

*27. 'Lamentable lines on the execution
of the Maamtrasna murderers' ballad.
Image courtesy of the National Folklore
Collection, University College Dublin.*

28. Note by Anthony Philbin to Prison
Governor, Kilmainham, 8 November 1882.
Image courtesy of the National Archives.

29. Extract from confession by Patrick
Joyce on eve of execution, 14 December 1882.
Image courtesy of the National Archives.

30. Petition written by a priest or neighbour on behalf of Bridget Joyce, wife of Myles, 11 December 1882. Image courtesy of the National Archives.

31. 'Focla déigheanacha Mhaolmhuire Seoighighe air an g-croich. Myles Joyce's dying words on the scaffold', facsimile image included in Frederick Higginbottom's A Vivid Life *(1934). Image courtesy of the National Library of Ireland.*

LIST OF NAMES.

ARRESTED FOR THE MURDER.

Patrick Joyce, Shanvallycahill,   executed, guilty
Patrick Casey,   executed, guilty
Myles Joyce,   executed, innocent
Michael Casey,   penal servitude, guilty
Martin Joyce (brother to Myles),   penal servitude, innocent
Patrick Joyce, Cappanacreha (another brother), penal servitude, innocent
Tom Joyce (son of Patrick),   penal servitude, innocent
John Casey (little), Cappanacreha,   penal servitude, innocent
Anthony Philbin,   approver
Thomas Casey,   approver

THE ACTUAL MURDERERS (NOW ALLEGED).

John Casey (big), Bun-na-cnic,   supposed leader, at large
John Casey, Junr. (his son), Bun-na-cnic,   at large
Pat Joyce, Shanvallycahill   executed
Pat Casey,   executed
Pat Leyden,   now in England
Michael Casey,   penal servitude
Thomas Casey,   approver

INDEPENDENT WITNESSES.

Anthony Joyce
John Joyce, Derry (his brother)
Patrick Joyce, Derry (John's son)

OTHERS.

John Joyce, Maamtrasna,   the murdered man
Michael Joyce (boy), do. (son),   who died of wounds
Patrick Joyce (boy), do. (son),   who recovered

John Joyce (young), Bun-na-cnic, the man whom the murderers
called out to join them

32. *List of names including 'The Actual Murderers (alleged)', from Timothy Harrington,*
The Maamtrasna Massacres *(1884). Image courtesy of the National Library of Ireland.*

— 7 —

AFTERMATH

'Judicial Murder'

> … the public are now in possession of the facts, and officials who would acquit
> themselves of the blood of the innocent will need to vindicate themselves.
> Inquiry was refused. It rests with those who demanded it to say whether the
> cry for inquiry should not now give way to one for prosecution.
>
> Conclusion to Tim Harrington's pamphlet, *The Maamtrasna Massacre* (1884)[1]

The events at Maamtrasna and the subsequent trials featured extensively in
British and American newspapers of the time. The *Spectator* magazine, on
18 November 1882, opened with the following comment, not untypical in its
anthro-political conclusions:

> The tragedy at Maamtrasna, investigated this week in Dublin, almost unique
> as it is in the annals of the United Kingdom, brings out in strong relief two
> facts which English-men are too apt to forget. One is the existence in partic-
> ular districts of Ireland of a class of peasants who are scarcely civilised beings,
> and approach far nearer to savages than any other white men; and the other
> is their extraordinary and exceptional gloominess of temper. In remote places
> of Ireland, especially in Connaught, on a few of the islands, and in one or two
> mountain districts, dwell cultivators who are in knowledge, in habits, and in
> the discipline of life no higher than Maories or other Polynesians.[2]

On occasion, the Irish-speaking character of the region was cited as a
further indicator of its primitiveness: for example in December 1882, the
North American *Globe*, in an article marking the launch of the bilingual

publication *Irisleabhar na Gaedhilge (Gaelic Journal),* commented that the Maamtrasna case had brought to light 'a state of deplorable ignorance mainly due to the fact that in certain parts of Ireland the Irish is the only language spoken.'[3]

For three years after the Maamtrasna trials and executions, the case reverberated loudly in British parliamentary affairs concerning Ireland. Its notoriety was such that it gave name to a parliamentary alliance: following the Liberal government's defeat in June, the fragile coalition that followed between the Irish Parliamentary Party at Westminster and the Tories was described by the outgoing Home Secretary William Harcourt as the 'Maamtrasna alliance'.[4] The individual most responsible for the political notoriety of the case during these years was the Parnellite MP Tim Harrington, whose campaigns and publications on behalf of the accused greatly influenced public awareness of the charges of a biased and unjust trial. Harrington's writings about the case have a compelling force, not only because of the miscarriages of judicial proceedings that he exposed, but also because of the immediacy of detail drawn from his interviews with relatives of the accused and with the two November approvers, Philbin and Casey. In August 1884, Casey's public recantation of his statement and the admission of his own complicity in the murder brought the case back to the public stage.

THE CASE MADE PUBLIC: RECANTATION AND RECRIMINATIONS

In February 1883, Timothy Harrington, then in his early thirties, was elected MP for Westmeath while serving a period of two months' imprisonment in Mullingar Jail. Harrington was a journalist and previously a correspondent for the *Freeman's Journal.* Following the dissolution of the Land League in 1882, he became principal secretary of the replacement National League. On 26 April, four months after the executions had taken place, Harrington rose in the House of Commons and posed a parliamentary question pertaining to the declarations of the executed men Patrick Joyce and Patrick Casey:

> Whether two of the three men executed in Galway Gaol on Dec. 15th, viz., Patrick Joyce and Patrick Casey, had made declarations admitting their own guilt and asserting the innocence of the third man Myles Joyce; whether these declarations were made in [the] presence of Mr. Brady, the resident magistrate

who first had charge of this case, and were deemed by him of such importance that he transmitted them by special messenger to the lord lieutenant with an expression of his own belief in the innocence of Myles Joyce, and caused the telegraph office in Galway to be kept open all night to receive the expected commutation of this man's sentence; if he will state whether he had been consulted and agreed to the reply transmitted at one o'clock on the morning of the execution that the law should take its course; and whether he will have any objection that copies of these declarations should be laid upon the table of the House?[5]

The parliamentary reply from George Trevelyan, Chief Secretary for Ireland, included a strong reiteration of the guilt of Myles Joyce as well as a highly erroneous reference to the final testimonies of Patrick Joyce and Patrick Casey: 'The statements did not say that Myles Joyce had no complicity in the murder. That complicity was distinctly proved, both by independent witnesses and by the approvers, and was not denied by the two other men who were executed. Mr. Brady gave no such opinion as is referred to in the question.'[6]

Some months later, on 13 August, Harrington returned to the topic of Myles Joyce's execution in detail during a debate on 'law and justice.' The case of Myles Joyce, he argued, explained why the 'working of the law in Ireland' failed to gain respect and had resulted in a deep political alienation. His fate had, he noted pointedly, failed to receive the notoriety of more 'exotic' contemporary cases such as the December 1882 trial of Egyptian nationalist Ahmed 'Urabi. Much of the rhetorical effect of his parliamentary address derived from Harrington's emphasis on the linguistic chasm that existed between the accused Myles Joyce and the court in which he was tried. In Harrington's imaginative reconstruction, the monoglot Irish speaker was pitted against the might of an exclusively English monoglot system, and any potential assistance from the interpreter was fatally undermined by his being a member of the RIC:

Hon. Members, who did not know much of the working of the law in Ireland, were often surprised that the law was not more respected in that country. All he could say was that if they would study the working of the law in Ireland, instead of being surprised that the law was not respected, they would be surprised that the law was even so much obeyed as it was. Let them take the case of this unfortunate man Myles Joyce. He was conveyed more than 200 miles from his home and put upon his trial in Dublin. Not a single word of English was he able to speak; not a single word of his own language were the jury who tried him able to comprehend. The judge who tried him

[Barry] was to him as much a foreigner as if he were a Turk trying the case in Constantinople. The very crier of the court, and the counsel who represented him, were foreigners to him; and the whole trial, as far as he was concerned, was an empty show and a farce. As if to make the farce still more ludicrous, the very interpreter employed by the crown to interpret the language of the court to this unfortunate man was a policeman. Hon. Members asked why was not the law respected in Ireland; why did not the people assist in upholding the law and the administration of justice in Ireland? He would ask in return, could any man of intelligence or common sense give his sanction to a system of law administered in such a manner as that in any country in the world? If this unfortunate man had had a foreign name, if he had been called Arabi or Suleiman,[7] his case would have drawn attention to it over and over again in the House of Commons. But unfortunately, he had not lived in a climate sufficiently foreign to excite the philanthropic sympathy of [the] hon. gentlemen on the opposite side of the House.[8]

The direct phrasing of Harrington's closing charge, 'that the man Joyce was foully done to death, and that perfect knowledge of his innocence was in the hands of the lord lieutenant', led to uproar in the House. He immediately rephrased the accusation to there having been 'perfect evidence of the innocence of Joyce' and materials for knowledge if the Lord Lieutenant had wished to make use of them.[9]

Capt. William O'Shea,[10] MP for Clare, reiterated Harrington's argument regarding the linguistically unjust nature of the trial proceedings in his supporting speech. O'Shea referred to having been present at the November trials (though he 'could not say that it was that of Myles Joyce'), and, in heightened terms, underlined the barrier between the interpreter-policeman, or in his terms 'natural enemy', and the accused:

He appealed to English Members whether it was right that a policeman should have occupied that capacity in such a case? He did not for a moment suppose that the arrangement was due to anything worse than want of reflection; but half the cruelty of the world was the outcome of want of reflection. It must have been a terrible thing for a man like Joyce to see that one whom he regarded as his natural enemy was the only person he could speak to.[11]

Yet just a few days later, on 17 August 1883, during a House debate on 'education, science, and art', and specifically on the subject of the National Board of Education's treatment of the Irish language, other MPs would firmly reject the assertion by Tim Healy (MP for County Monaghan) that 'there were in Ireland some hundreds and thousands of people who could not speak a word of English'.[12] The case of Maamtrasna was now cited by MP James Bulwer as evidence of prevalent bilingualism in Ireland:

> When the hon. member for Monaghan spoke of hundreds of thousands of people who spoke only Irish, he could only say that you might travel through the north and west of Ireland, where he had frequently been, and seldom – except, perhaps, in Donegal – would you come across a man who would not understand you if you spoke English. [An hon. MEMBER: Galway.] Yes; he included Galway, and the neighbourhood of Maamtrasna too, where those horrible murders were committed of which the hon. member might have heard.[13]

What's notable here is the strategic choice to deny the very existence of monoglot Irish speakers as the means through which the charge of injustice could be evaded. The counter-strategy of nationalist campaigners was to identify Maamtrasna as almost exclusively Irish-speaking, thus minimising the extent of bilingualism in the area.

In August of the following year, dramatic events instigated by the 'approver' Thomas Casey provided Harrington with substantial support for his charges regarding the 'misworking' of the law. On Thursday, 7 August 1884, during a Confirmation ceremony conducted by John McEvilly, archbishop of Tuam, Casey delivered a public recantation in his local church in Tourmakeady in which he confessed to having been a member of the Joyce murder party and to having sworn false evidence against the other accused. As the *Freeman's Journal* reported, 'in the presence of the archbishop of Tuam, and the parish priest, the Rev. John Corbet [*sic*], and the assembled congregation, he [Casey] stated that he had sworn falsely against Myles Joyce, one of the three men executed for participation in the Maamtrasna tragedy.' In the succinct terms of the editorial commentator, 'The gravity of this revelation cannot be exaggerated.'[14]

News of this extraordinary event had reached the *Freeman* on Saturday via telegram from Claremorris, and the journalist Andrew Dunlop (who had visited the murder scene and attended Myles Joyce's execution) was once again despatched to the west. Dunlop travelled to Glensaul on Sunday, where he interviewed both Casey and Philbin. He was accompanied by Corbett, who was parish priest of Partry and a well-known supporter of the Land League.[15] Casey stated unambiguously in the interview, published by the *Freeman's Journal* on Monday, that six of the original ten men (Myles Joyce, Paudeen Joyce, Martin Joyce, Tom Joyce, John Casey, and Anthony Philbin) were 'not in it'.[16] Casey also claimed that Bolton, the crown solicitor, had intimidated him into giving false evidence that would correspond with that of his brother-in-law, Anthony Philbin. Questioned about his motive in recanting and about why he had not made these revelations sooner, Casey replied that his objective in 'going before the bishop and before God' was 'to get pardon' and 'to make reparation as far as I could before I would die.'[17] Philbin, who, according to Dunlop, 'was not at all so inclined to be communicative,' admitted that he had not been 'in' the murder, 'though he had sworn that he was.'[18] He further stated that whatever knowledge he possessed had been gleaned from the evidence of Anthony Joyce, and under the influence of Bolton. Dunlop also observed that both Casey and Philbin were currently under police protection, with three constables almost within earshot while his conversation with Philbin had been taking place.[19]

The veracity of Casey's confession received a powerful imprimatur on the Monday following when Archbishop McEvilly reiterated its details at the Confirmation ceremony in the Clonbur parish, some five miles from Maamtrasna. McEvilly communicated them to Spencer by personal letter two days later. Over the next week, the *Freeman* continued its daily coverage of the case. Local priest Fr O'Malley immediately sent a *précis* of the Clonbur sermon by telegram to Dublin, and this was published by the newspaper on Tuesday. The archbishop's closing reference to the fate of Myles Joyce and the surviving prisoners produced, according to O'Malley, 'a profound sensation amongst the vast congregation':

> His Grace concluded by hoping the authorities, who could scarcely claim exemption from a share of the guilt of sending poor Joyce to an untimely grave and four others to penal servitude, would now at once do all that they could do by releasing these much injured men and by liberally compensating both them and the helpless family of Myles Joyce.[20]

The paper's editorial reminded readers of the 'universal attention' that the circumstances of Myles Joyce's execution had attracted, and then reproduced from the *Freeman* files the text of his declaration of innocence at the gallows. It read: 'I am going before my God. I was not there at all. The Lord forgive them who swore against me. I am as innocent as the child in the cradle. It is a poor thing to take this life away on a stage, but I have my priest with me.'[21] Locally, these surprising developments meant new hope for the families of the imprisoned men. Nationally, this meant a wide recirculation of Myles' dying declaration of innocence but with a new edge: one of the key people to swear against him had recanted his evidence publicly and in a holy place.

On 23 August 1884 Spencer's under-secretary, R. G. C. Hamilton, responded to McEvilly's letter of 13 August with an official memorandum. This detailed the conclusion from an internal inquiry into 'allegations as to the falsity of Thomas Casey's evidence and of intimidation of Casey to give such evidence.' The report rejected the allegations unequivocally and restated the Lord Lieutenant's confidence in 'the course of the law': 'Having satisfied himself after the fullest inquiry that the verdicts in the several cases were right, and that the statements of Casey and Philbin now made are wholly unreliable, his Excellency has come to the conclusion that no grounds exist for interfering with the course of the law in respect of the prisoners now undergoing penal servitude.'[22]

The press covered these developments avidly, most especially the *Freeman's Journal*, which during the months of September and October, also published eight lengthy letters by Harrington on the case. An interview with Philbin and Casey, much fuller than that provided by Dunlop in August and also facilitated by Fr Corbett, was published on 6 September.[23] The reporter, who was probably Harrington, described Philbin as 'obviously labouring under some influence or dread', and Casey as 'communicative, cheerful, and unrestrained' as well as 'penitent' and 'anxious to tell everything bearing on the affair.' He argued that Casey's literacy further bolstered the reliability of his information: 'Casey can read and write, and I have now in my possession the several statements made to me (a total stranger), each statement signed with his own name in a free and legible hand in the presence of witnesses.'[24]

Most startlingly, in the course of his interview Casey named 'without the slightest hesitation' the seven men he claimed were 'actually present at the scene of the murder.' Two of these men had been executed, one was in prison, one was Casey himself and three others were still at large. The reporter transcribed the names as follows, suppressing the identities of those untried: 'Michael Casey (undergoing penal servitude), Thomas Casey (himself), Pat Casey, and Pat Joyce (hanged), and three others whose names he gave me, which I have under his own signature; but those names I do not feel justified in giving to the public at this juncture through a newspaper, though they are known to many in the place and outside of it.'[25] According to Casey, two of these three men (a father and son, to whom he had referred in the trial as Kelly and Nee) were still living in the district, while the third had gone to England; the father, he attested, was 'the author of the massacre'. Casey's account of these men's role in the murders featured instances of stark and disturbing brutality, most especially with respect to the murder of the elderly Margaret Joyce:

> The party having come out without killing the old woman, whom they thought to be a stroller[26] and not connected with the family, this man, the author of the murder, compelled them to return and slay her also, which they did. This man (the author of the murder) used the expression – a common one in the Irish tongue – that not as big as the button on a great coat, or cotamore,[27] should be left alive in the house.[28]

One month after Casey's recantation, a further event would consolidate Harrington's campaign against the convictions. This was the discovery of the original crown brief, the prosecution's key document, which, since November 1882, was believed to have been missing. In his 1928 memoir *Letters and Leaders of My Day*, Tim Healy recalled that he had been approached in September 1884 by 'the late Edward Ennis, a barrister, who was a frequenter of Green Street Courthouse, Dublin', and who had come to him 'with a bundle of papers':

> He had gained access to a room where crown briefs were carelessly thrown after trial, and found the brief held in the Maamtrasna case by Peter O'Brien, Q. C. (afterwards Lord O'Brien, Chief Justice). Taking the printed 'informations' from it, he gave them to me. It was the right of the accused to be furnished with 'depositions'. Moreover, Lord Justice Barry declared from the Bench at Limerick in July 1891 that as attorney-general his practice was to hand a copy of the entire crown briefs to the prisoners' counsel. In the Maamtrasna case the accused had not been furnished even with the 'informations'.[29]

Healy, as he himself acknowledged, had not previously 'encouraged Harrington's protest' and had viewed it as largely based on an 'absurd' ghost story (described later). His view changed radically however when he read, within the brief, printed copies of Patsy's 'information', which had been taken by Lenihan and Johnston immediately after the murders. For Healy, the boy's words provided 'testimony straight from the scene of the assassination' that was 'in complete conflict with Casey's evidence' as presented at the trials[30] – and as the recovered brief showed, this testimony had, even before the trial took place, been deliberately deemed 'worthless' by the prosecution.

THE MAAMTRASNA MASSACRE: HARRINGTON'S *IMPEACHMENT*

While the extent of newspaper coverage pointed to continuing public interest in the Maamtrasna case, the most significant and contentious publication of the time was a one-shilling pamphlet printed by the *Nation* office.[31] Published in late 1884, its author was MP and journalist Tim Harrington who chose the ringing title *The Maamtrasna Massacre: Impeachment of the Trials*. The pamphlet comprised a short introduction and a 43-page text, which drew heavily from Harrington's previously published newspaper letters; it also featured a 46-page appendix reproducing much of the *Freeman*'s coverage of the original trials along with the August correspondence between Archbishop McEvilly and the Lord Lieutenant's office.[32] Incredibly to a modern reader accustomed to libel fears, it provided readers with a 'list of names', not only of those arrested for the murder, but also of those whom Harrington termed 'the actual murderers (now alleged)' (see Image 32, p. XVI). These included the three men still at large whom Thomas Casey had refused to identify: their three names – John Casey of Bunachrick, his son John Casey Junior, and Pat Leyden – were now in the public domain for the first time.[33]

THE ACTUAL MURDERERS (NOW ALLEGED)

John Casey (big), Bun-na-cnic	supposed leader, at large
John Casey, Junr. (his son), Bun-na-cnic	at large
Pat Joyce, Shanvallycahill	executed
Pat Casey	executed
Pat Leyden	now in England
Michael Casey	penal servitude
Thomas Casey	approver

Harrington's call for the overturning of the trials rested on a number of arguments: the falsity of evidence provided by the independent witnesses and approvers, the suppression of the depositions containing the dying declarations of Patrick Joyce and Patrick Casey, and an allegation that the accused had been convicted in trials featuring packed juries. 'This extraordinary history of this crime and its punishment,' he argued, formed 'a story that might well challenge the pen of the most sensational novelist of our time.'[34] Harrington was anxious to deny that his own interest in the case was sensationalist, or 'for the purpose of catering to the taste of the curious and sensational'; he defined his own motivation instead as that of part campaigner and part detective, seeking: 'to unravel to some extent the mystery in which this story is enveloped, and to strengthen the position of those who demand that justice shall be done.'[35]

In the autumn of 1884, Harrington paid a number of visits to the Maamtrasna area and held repeated interviews with the families of the imprisoned men, and also with the informers and their families. He even, in his words, 'conversed with the two men whom Thomas Casey states planned and paid for the murder.'[36] He vividly describes not only the physical challenges of a journey to Maamtrasna but also the difficulties of conversing with its inhabitants. In his telling, Maamtrasna was an area in which English was 'almost completely unknown':

> To those presented by the locality, and the almost impassible [*sic*] mountain track upon which the traveller has to trust himself to the instinct of his sure-footed pony, are to be added the extreme reluctance of the people to give any information in view of possible and very probable prosecutions against some of their near neighbours or relatives, and the fact that English is almost completely unknown among them, and any attempt at seeking information except through the medium of their mother tongue must end in failure.[37]

On his first visit, Harrington was accompanied by the parish priest, Fr James Corbett, and his curate Fr J. McDonnell. Corbett and McDonnell were both new to their positions (Corbett began as parish priest in 1883 and McDonnell in 1884) and, according to Harrington, neither had ever before been to the Maamtrasna district, some 18 miles away from their home base (along the western edge of Lough Mask). His opening chapter paid lavish tribute to the valuable presence of the clergymen as mediators and interpreters, given what he described as his own 'imperfect' Irish:

> But I could soon see that the fame of the rev. pastor of Partry had preceded him, that they were not unacquainted with the strong bond of sympathy between him and his people, while his skill in the use of their mother tongue made them quite at ease. Even my own very imperfect knowledge of it, which enabled me with some difficulty to hold converse with them, was, next to the introduction by the *soggart*, the surest passport which I could possess; and though my sins against syntactical law must have been manifold and grievous, and occasionally excited their laughter, I yet found that they had not the same dread of my open note book that they would have in the case of a more un-Irish 'special'.[38]

Harrington is likely here to be understating his own facility in Irish: his parents were Irish speakers from Castletownbere and he had used Irish in earlier Land League work in Kerry.[39] But, in his enthusiasm, Harrington certainly simplified the linguistic competencies of the various participants in the case. Patrick Joyce and Patrick Casey he described as 'purley [*sic*] Irish-speaking peasants', an error which would persist in later commentaries.[40] This characterisation of all of the executed men as Irish monoglots, to whom the services of interpreters had not been provided, enabled Harrington to indict further the 'disgraceful sham' by 'the Castle government' who had attempted to discredit their dying declarations 'upon the ground of vagueness'.[41] To support the innocence of four of the men in penal servitude, he reproduced three letters written from prison, two by John Casey from Mountjoy (dated 15 June 1883 and 27 June 1884) and one by Martin Joyce from Mountjoy on 5 September 1884. While Harrington drew his readers' attention to the 'simple, artless style' of the letters as evidence of their lack of guile, he proffered no explanation as to how these monoglot men had produced such English-language letters or how they were read by their Irish-speaking relatives.

Notwithstanding the role of Corbett and McDonnell, Harrington clearly won the confidence of many local people and his writings possess a vividness of social detail. His descriptions of widespread local belief in the innocence of Myles, Martin, Paudeen, and Tom Joyce and John Casey have an especially compelling authority. His informants were male and female and he had a keen understanding of the significance of intimate confidences shared between local women, knowledge that had been hinted at during the trials but not explored. As Harrington observed, the female relatives of the accused were those who knew best who had and had not been home that night. They were also able to exchange this knowledge among themselves during their visits to the men in Galway Jail and on trial in Dublin:

> Local gossip has long ago threshed out every feature of the case which presents itself to their untutored minds, and evidence of the very strongest character has come under my notice to convince me that long before the crown had proved its case, the women had got into one another's confidence during their visits to Cong and Galway and Dublin in connection with their husbands' defence, and no doubt remained with them, at least as to the men who were out of their beds on the fatal night, and the men who were not.[42]

Harrington targeted, in particular, the evidence provided by crown witnesses, Anthony and John Joyce, and here, too, his female sources were of value. He reported the local view that Anthony had learned of the murder of his cousin not as a terrified observer, as he had testified, but second-hand, 'from a little girl, his daughter, who came to the bog where he was working with several more of his neighbours.'[43] His local informants were especially damning with respect to the testimony of Mary Joyce, daughter of John and 'the only one of the women of the families that came forward to sustain the plot of the Joyces':

> 'How do you account for Mary Joyce coming forward to give evidence?' I said to a man living in the neighbourhood of the Joyces. 'She never came forward, sir,' he said, 'until some weeks after the father and uncle gave evidence, and only then because it was reported that her father and Anthony were to be taken themselves for the murder. Everyone said they would have been put on their trial, as no one believed their story.'[44]

Neither Mary nor her brother nor her father would consent to be interviewed by Harrington and Corbett: 'They were at work in a field close by, their police escort basking lazily in the warm sun near the fence, and though sent for by the other members of the family, they refused to come.'[45]

On the question of motive for the murder, a potentially explosive topic within the locality, Harrington was at pains to criticise the government for its determined insistence on the agrarian nature of the crime, in order to 'blacken the character of the Land League'. Yet he conceded that 'a sort of "Ribbon Society" existed in this district',[46] and argued that the society was under the control of Patrick Joyce (now executed), with members including the murdered man and at least six of the seven in the murder party. Harrington based this view in part on information given to him during his earlier interview with Thomas Casey:

> Was there not some Ribbon Society among you?
>
> Yes (hesitatingly).
>
> Is it true that John Joyce, the murdered man, belonged to it? He did; they said he was their treasurer, but I did not know much about it, as I was only three months home from England.[47]

Based on his conversations with local people, Harrington also asserted that 'big John Casey' (who remained at large) had given money freely 'to defend the guilty among the accused, but gave no assistance for the defence of those who knew nothing of his own criminality.'[48]

But the cornerstone of Harrington's argument was a fact uncovered by him in the course of his autumn investigations and which he delivered with some fanfare: 'Nice distinctions as to distances, minute examination of circumstances, contrasts and comparisons, may all be dismissed from consideration when I announce to my readers that beyond all question the men who murdered John Joyce and his family were disguised, had blackened faces, and wore white flannel vests, called among the peasantry of the west *bawneens*.'[49] This fact first emerged during Harrington's interview with Thomas Casey (who recounted how the son of 'Big' John Casey had blackened the men's faces with polish)[50] and his ensuing conversation with a local constable substantiated it. Here, the constable recounted the information which the injured Patsy, through the interpreter Lenihan, had given to Johnston: 'Indeed, they were disguised, sir. They all had blackened faces, for the little boy that was alive after the murder told Sergeant Johnson [*sic*] and the police when they went to the house in the morning. He said the people that killed his father and mother and beat himself had blackened faces.'[51] Harrington secured further corroboration locally from John Collins ('the first man who found the family at six o'clock in the morning') and by other villagers. But over and above such 'secondary evidence', Harrington dramatically proffered 'such primary evidence as my Lord Spencer cannot hide by any refusal of inquiry,' namely, the first-hand and post-trial evidence of Patsy Joyce:

> Patrick Joyce, the younger of the two boys, recovered from his wounds. I visited this young lad at Artane Industrial School, where, under the kind care of the Christian Brothers, he is being trained and educated, and in clear, intelligible language he fully corroborates this portion of Casey's confession.[52]

It is not possible to tell from Harrington's account what language was used in his conversation with Patsy, whether Harrington could communicate sufficiently in Irish, or (more likely) that by this time Patsy was able to converse in English; but once again the boy's evidence had become a central and potent moment in the Maamtrasna narrative.

The oral information gleaned by Harrington from his succession of interviews found textual corroboration with the rediscovery of the crown's 'lost' prosecution brief, and within it a record of the early depositions by Patsy and others. This led Harrington to what he termed the 'more startling and more damaging' revelation that the crown had deliberately suppressed key evidence. According to Harrington, 'no less than four depositions' referred to the assassins having blackened faces, but the prisoners' defence counsel had not received copies of these, and 'not a suggestion or hint was allowed to be thrown out during the trial as to the disguise and the black-ened faces.'[53] The prosecution argument that Patsy was unable to testify under oath received especially caustic comment:

> Mr. Brady, R. M., did not think this boy too ignorant to make a dying declara-tion, but three months later, he is found to have gone so far back in Christian knowledge while under George Bolton's moral care that he could not be sworn, 'as he did not know what would happen [to] him if he told a lie.' That evidently is a question of dispute among the saintly theologians of the Castle.[54]

An especially dramatic moment in Harrington's published pamphlet occurs towards its conclusion when he reproduces from the brief the crown solic-itor's italicised direction to prosecuting counsel: '*Patrick Joyce has recovered, but his evidence is worthless.*' This, he argued, was 'the key to the farce that was played before the judge and jury in placing this boy on the table.' And it was evidence of 'a terrible story', i.e. that the crown counsel had not acted in good faith in producing the child on the table to testify.[55] For Harrington, Patsy's case was the culmination of his indictment of the crown, and following this his pamphlet ends on a curiously muted note: 'I shall leave the public to make their comments. I freely confess I could not well trust myself to give expression to my feelings with regard to this feature of the case ... Inquiry was refused. It rests with those who demanded it to say whether the cry for inquiry should not now give way to one for prosecution.'[56]

THE CASE IN PARLIAMENT

The autumn 1884 session of parliament began on Thursday, 23 October, and in the course of its first day of business Tim Harrington moved an amend-ment to the opening address calling for a full and public inquiry into the Maamtrasna murders. A lengthy debate on the amendment ensued through that night and following nights before being adjourned at the end of the fourth night of debate. In the early hours of 29 October, the vote finally took place with 267 MPs present.[57] The debate featured a long opening contribu-tion by Harrington in the course of which he read into the parliamentary record extracts from letters by the imprisoned men and the testimony of their priest. Key to the trial's illegitimacy, he argued, was the men's failure to receive legal counsel in their own language. Once again, he stirringly portrayed the linguistic and cultural isolation experienced by the accused: 'Eight men were charged. They were taken 200 miles away from their home to be tried by a special jury who did not understand their language. Their own solicitor and counsel did not understand their language, nor did the court understand it. They were as absolute strangers in Green Street Court House in Dublin as if they had been translated from another sphere.'[58]

Later contributions to the House of Commons included speeches by Arthur O'Connor and John Redmond, along with an especially impactful contribution from John Eldon Gorst, MP for Chatham. Gorst, a former queen's counsel, had closely examined a record of the trial proceedings and observed the crown's occlusion of the statements of the Joyce boys. More rarely among his contemporaries, he noted how the declarations by the dying Michael Joyce had also been omitted:

> Well, again, he noticed on the second day of the trial a most remarkable thing. In the report of the proceedings which he held in his hand, it appeared that John Collins, who was first in the house after the murder, deposed to finding Michael Joyce still alive. That was on the morning of the 18th, and upon the witness making that statement, one of the jurors – a Mr. Pim – who appeared to be a most sagacious and intelligent man, inquired whether Michael Joyce had made any statement to him when he entered. The judge, however (Mr. Justice Barry), interposing, said – 'That question need not be answered. We have had already a statement of the doctors that Michael was raving and unable to make any statement.' Now, if Mr. Pim, instead of thus being interfered with and cut short by the judge, had been informed that Michael Joyce had made a statement to John Collins and to a police constable, and a dying declaration before a resident magistrate, in all of which he had given the blackened state of the men's faces as the reason why he could not identify them, he (Mr. Gorst) did not know but that that might have altered the verdict of the jury.[59]

Strong support was expressed by Randolph Churchill for Harrington's amendment and for his efforts to obtain a full inquiry. Churchill, along with Gorst, Henry Drummond-Wolff, and Arthur Balfour, comprised the so-called 'Fourth Party' for their vehement critiques of both Liberal and Conservative positions. Opposing them, firm rebuttals came from George Trevelyan as Chief Secretary and Samuel Walker, as Solicitor General for Ireland; both men quoted repeatedly from the contemporary and approving opinions expressed by the press at the outcome of the trials in November 1882, including those from the strongly nationalist *United Ireland*.[60]

Charles Stewart Parnell made a long contribution to the debate on its third evening, and began by expressing his conviction 'that some of the Irish Government officials have very good reasons why they consider that this inquiry should not be granted.'[61] Parnell went on to express his unequivocal view that the motive for the case was an internal agrarian feud:

> According to our case, a motive can easily be assigned for the crime. We can prove that the murdered man was the treasurer of a Ribbon Society, that he had been accused of making away with some of the funds – an accusation which is always sufficient to insure the murder of the person accused – and that, on more than one occasion, he had attempted to shoot the leader and paymaster of the gang who murdered him.[62]

The fourth and final night of debate featured pro-amendment speeches by Justin McCarthy, Charles Russell (later Chief Justice), and T. P. O'Connor, and rebuttals by Gladstone and the attorney general, Sir Henry James. The special potency of Patsy's testimony and of its dismissal by the court, arguments highlighted by Harrington, once again came to the fore in O'Connor's contribution:

> The home secretary had further said that one of the boys was placed in the witness-box in order that he might be examined by the prisoners' counsel, but that it was proved that the lad did not know the nature of an oath. But this boy had been for three months in the care of the police, and could not they in that long period have educated him sufficiently to let him know the consequences of giving false testimony? It must be remembered that the boy was nine years of age and was stated to be an intelligent lad who could easily have been taught such a simple matter as that. The police did not train the boy because they did not want his evidence. The note inserted in the crown brief by Mr. Bolton that the boy's evidence was unimportant was a deliberate lie, because his evidence would have been most important and pertinent. The inference was indisputable that the evidence was kept back wilfully and fraudulently.[63]

In the early hours of 29 October 1884, the House was divided on Harrington's proposed amendment with a strong majority against: 'Ayes 48; Noes 219: Majority 171.'[64]

A year later, a change of government offered the Irish party a strong opportunity to lobby once again for an inquiry into the Maamtrasna case. The support given by the Irish party to the Tories had ensured the Liberals' defeat and the creation of a caretaker government led by Salisbury in June 1885; in the new Conservative cabinet, Gorst was Solicitor General and

Churchill Secretary of State for India. Immediately following the formation of the new government, in July 1885, Parnell tabled the following motion: 'That in the opinion of this House it is the duty of the government to institute strict inquiry into the evidence and convictions in the Maamtrasna, Barbavilla, Crossmaglen, and Castleisland cases'.[65] Many contemporaries saw this as proof that a hidden 'Maamtrasna Alliance' existed between the new government and the Irish party, and Parnell's decision to withdraw his motion after a short debate appears to have been made in the expectation that 'a fair and impartial inquiry' by the new viceroy Lord Carnarvon would soon take place.[66] This proved to be a false hope and, a month later, it was evident that the government had backtracked. On 10 August, William Hart Dyke, the new Chief Secretary for Ireland, stated in the House of Commons that 'the lord lieutenant, in undertaking to consider any memorials presented on behalf of persons undergoing punishment for the Maamtrasna murder, only followed the usual course with regard to such memorial[s]'.[67]

Political interest in the case among the Irish party greatly declined after the summer of 1885. However, a decade later, in February 1895, Harrington sought to raise the question of the Maamtrasna prisoners still suffering 'penal servitude in Ireland'.[68] The reply to Harrington delivered by John Morley, then Irish Chief Secretary, detailed a long series of petitions received and considered by his office in the preceding ten years.

> Many years have elapsed since these events, and there have been a considerable number of inquiries in connection with memorials addressed to the several governments that succeeded the Irish administration of Lord Carnarvon. The cases were considered by Lord Carnarvon in 1885; after that, in December 1887, as I am informed, Lord Ashbourne, acting I presume as lord justice, had a memorial brought to his notice, and after considering it, directed that the law should take its course. The cases were next brought before Lord Londonderry, who took similar action. They again came before Lord Ashbourne in November 1888 with the same result – that the law should take its course. Lord Zetland considered the cases both in 1890 and 1892, and during the existence of the present administration they were also carefully considered in 1893. Therefore the hon. and learned member is asking us to institute an inquiry when as a matter of fact inquiries have been instituted by successive lord lieutenants and by more than one lord chancellor or lord justice.[69]

This list of petitions and memorials provides a different perspective on what occurred in the aftermath of the Maamtrasna trials, one that illuminates the experience of the five prisoners and their relatives. If one judges purely on the parliamentary record, then a decade-long neglect of the case ensued after 1885. However, as Chapter 8 will show, continuing agitation on their behalf by relatives and supporters continued unofficially behind the scenes.

POST-EXECUTION APOCRYPHA

Public interest in the Maamtrasna murders also led to their appearing as a lurid subject in popular ballads and chapbooks in the 1880s. These treatments usually took the form of apocrypha, i.e. of unknown origin and not officially sanctioned, but offering themselves as 'true' accounts of what had occurred. Historically, post-execution apocrypha have mostly taken the form of broadsheets or death songs, which functioned, as Michel Foucault has observed, as a kind of 'sequel to the trial' and as means through which its 'truth' could be copper-fastened and posthumously proven.[70]

A surviving broadsheet and accompanying ballad called 'Lamentable lines on the execution of the Maamtrasna murderers'[71] (see Image 27, p. XIII) is an especially good example; its exact provenance is unknown but it is believed to be a contemporary publication. The accompanying illustration presents a stereotypical public execution scene, very different from the gallows in the yard of Galway Jail. Its author would appear to have had only a general knowledge of the events: reference is made to the 'City of the Tribes' but erroneously to the surviving five prisoners being housed in Spike Prison. Reference is made to the 'unremitting care' of the clergy (a detail emphasised by many journalists at the time), but no allusion whatsoever is made to the protests of innocence by Myles Joyce or to the manner of his execution. Instead, the heinous nature of the murders is underlined: 'The crime is more lamented than the hanging of the three / And may we again such a tragedy in Ireland never see.' The verdicts of the Maamtrasna trials are firmly deemed to be incontestable: 'The judge and jury have discharged their duty with much pain / The verdict no one could dispute, the evidence was plain.' Notably, the ballad's closing lines refashion a cherished nationalist trope, invoking the Manchester Martyrs' cry of 'God save Ireland'[72] but as part of a call to refuse violent actions:

Old Grania in deep sorrow weeps and calls on Irishmen
To abstain from every kind of crime that would our men condemn.
And with our patriotic men in peace join hand-in-hand
And still repeat that holy prayer, God save old Ireland.[73]

A surviving chapbook provides a markedly different outlook to the ballad.[74] With the arresting title *Full Report of the Appearance of the Ghost of Myles Joyce in Galway Jail*, the text reproduces almost verbatim two *Freeman's Journal* articles: the first its account of Myles' execution in December and the second the following dramatic account published in the newspaper on 11 January 1883:

> The Freeman's Journal correspondent … sends a thrilling item of news from Galway; it is as follows – Myles Joyce, who declared his innocence of any participation in the Maamtrasna murders when about to expiate the offence on the scaffold in Galway jail upon the 15th ult [last month], has 'appeared' within the precincts of the prison. The apparition, it seems, was kept a secret at first by the officials, believing it to be some delusion or joke. But all doubts were set at rest when on last night two soldiers, who were on guard within the prison, were followed for some time by a tall mystic figure which at length approached them, actually touched the rifles, and vanished. They state that the figure is Myles Joyce in spirit. The correspondent further assures us that he had it on reliable authority that the matron and warders of the prison have applied for a transfer.[75]

That same month the *Illustrated Police News* of London alluded to the ghost story and ran a rejoinder which only served to extend the reach of the original tale: 'The sergeant of the guard on duty at Galway gaol on the night the "ghost" of Myles Joyce was reported to have appeared, flatly contradicts the story. There is no truth, he says, in the report that a man of the guard ran from his post on seeing the apparition.'[76]

Invocations of the ghost of Myles Joyce appear in many subsequent newspaper reports, and usually in a highly fraught political context. On 13 September 1884 the *Freeman* described an acrimonious meeting of Cork Corporation regarding an invitation to the Duke of Edinburgh, in the course of which the taunt to the mayor delivered by one member was: 'You have prostrated the character of the citizens of Cork. You have disgraced us and disgraced the city. I hope you will now go to Earl Spencer and take the ghost of Myles Joyce with you.'[77] In August of the following year, it ran a feature on 'the Arklow Bazaar', which described a table presided over by 'Miss Gerrards and Miss Morrissey': 'At this table a very telescopic arrangement entitled "The Mystery of Dublin Castle" came in for a good deal of attention. It showed when at proper focus the ghost of Myles Joyce as seen by Earl Spencer in a dream.'[78]

Writing in the 1970s, Joycean critic John Garvin confirmed that popular stories about Myles Joyce's ghost continued to circulate into the 1920s, at least. He surmised that James Joyce, in writing his 1907 'Ireland at the bar' article, 'must have obtained the bones of the material which he used in this account from Nora Barnacle'.[79] Garvin, then, intriguingly and in some considerable length, cited his own acquisition of the 'folk tale' as a student in Galway City as told by his landlady (a woman of 'naturally lively intelligence coloured by superstition and a penchant for the sensational'):

> The governor of the jail he was a Captain Mason and the night before the hanging didn't his wife wake up in a sweat and she woke the governor, and let you, says she, have nothing to do, says she, with the death of that innocent man. From the awful mixings I had in my sleep, says she, I warn you agin [*sic*] having any hand, act, or part in his execution, says she. But the governor wouldn't budge and Myles Joyce was hung. With that Myles Joyce's widow stripped her stockings down from her knees and she knelt on the bare ground and she keened her man and she cursed the captain, and she keened and she cursed so high and so hard that he met an idiot's death within in his quarters, shouting and roaring and bidding the dead man's ghost to keep away from him.[80]

Garvin acknowledges the strong parallel between his landlady's tale and the dream of Pilate's wife regarding John the Baptist (Matthew, 27:19) and then goes on to speculate as to the role of a more famous Galway woman in the story's wider circulation: 'It seems that the folk version of Myles Joyce's end, as told to me in Galway in 1924, was known to Nora Barnacle twenty years previously, that she related it to Joyce as her most memorable association with his name before she met him, and that he used the praying crowd scene and the hangman's allegedly brutal *coup de grace* for his 1907 journalism.'[81]

LAST WORDS: MEDIATIONS AND REMEDIATIONS

The case of Maamtrasna frequently appeared as a touchstone for Dublin Castle's judicial process (and its failures) within nationalist political writing of the late nineteenth and early twentieth centuries. Some took their tone from an early and quickly notorious article by journalist MP William O'Brien entitled 'Accusing spirits', which he published on 23 December 1882 in *United Ireland*, the journal of the Irish National Land League of which he was editor. In the article, O'Brien charged the government with mistrial in the case of a number of recent executions for capital murder (those of Patrick Higgins/Long, Francis Hynes, Michael and Patrick Walsh as well as Myles Joyce). Its publication led to O'Brien's arrest and prosecution for seditious libel; following the disagreement of the jury in February 1883, he was discharged.[82]

The influential study *The Parnell Movement*, a history of the Irish Parliamentary Party by journalist and parliamentarian T. P. O'Connor, was published in 1886. It featured a strong critique of agrarian violence but also of the legal processes employed in trials relating to such violence. Here, the execution of Myles Joyce (with details drawn from Harrington's writings and from O'Connor's own role in the parliamentary debates of 1884) functioned as forceful exemplar:

> The outbursts of bloody passion which had followed the arrest of Mr. Parnell had left behind feelings of profound horror, and these feelings were transformed into a sense of sickened loathing by the Maamtrasna massacre. But the effect of trials so conducted was to drive back public sympathy from the law to the criminals, and the conviction of each successive murderer was followed, not by a sense of relief but of anger and pity …
>
> The horrors at the execution of one of the persons convicted of the Maamtrasna murder tended to excite this feeling to one of supreme and angry horror. Myles Joyce, one of the men convicted, went to the scaffold still shouting out in the Gaelic – the only tongue he knew – asseverations of his innocence … That scene will live in Irish memory to the end of time.[83]

Nationalist invocations of Maamtrasna crossed the Parnellite divide, ranging from the pro-Parnellites Tim Harrington and T. P. O'Connor to Michael Davitt, who was a close ally of Harrington in the National League but opposed Parnell in 1890. In 1904, Davitt's *The Fall of Feudalism in Ireland* carried a short account of the Maamtrasna murders, in which he too denounced the brutality of the crime while condemning the wrongful execution of Myles Joyce. The terms chosen by Davitt to condemn the Joyce murders were deliberately forceful: 'a crime almost without a parallel for its atrocity in the annals of agrarian outrages'. So too was his invocation of O'Brien's 'Accusing spirits' editorial and its charge that the Crown was guilty of 'judicial murder':

The details of this revolting deed of blood inspired widespread horror, and the trial of the accused persons was an event of sensational importance. Both the culprits and the witnesses against them were Irish-speaking peasants, living under conditions of poverty and squalor, and one of the accused, named Myles Joyce, who protested his innocence insistently, in the only tongue he could speak, was found guilty with three others and hanged. Myles Joyce was undoubtedly innocent, but so eager was the Castle to obtain an adequate legal vengeance for the abominable double murders of the Huddys and the Joyces that this 'judicial murder,' as *United Ireland* rightly termed it, was carried out despite every effort that could be made to induce Lord Spencer to grant a reprieve.[84]

Neither O'Connor nor Davitt make any attempt to render the detail of Myles Joyce's protests, but instead briefly invoke his name and the symbolic potency of his fate. Higginbottom's 1934 memoir seems to have had an important role in recirculating the last words from the scaffold (he is likely to have been Garvin's source, for example, and is cited on a number of occasions by Waldron).[85] Myles' words reappear with much dramatic force in recent historical treatments of Maamtrasna. For example, on the back cover of Waldron's bestselling *Maamtrasna: The Murders and the Mystery*, Myles Joyce's 'cry from the scaffold' is reproduced in Irish and English though in a more simplified form than Higginbottom's text:

> *Níl mé ciontach. Ní raibh lámh ná cos agam sa marú.*
> *Ní feasach mé ní ar bith ina thimpeall.*
> *Go maithe Dia don mhuintir a mhionnaigh in mo aghaidh.*
> *Go bhfóire Dia ar mo bhean agus ar a cúigear dílleachtaí.*
> *Ach tá mo shagart liom.*
> *Táim chomh neamhchiontach leis an leanbh atá sa gcliabhán.*

> I am not guilty. I had neither hand nor foot in the killing.
> I never knew anything at all about it.
> May God forgive those people who swore against me.
> May God have mercy on my wife and her five orphans.
> But my priest is with me.
> I am as innocent as the child in the cradle.[86]

Waldron's evocative account of the execution and its aftermath includes the passing on of 'a local tradition' that Bridget Joyce 'had given birth to a baby girl the day her husband was executed, and that as soon as she was able to, she made her way to Galway.' According to this lore, 'she positioned herself at the western end of the "Salmon Weir" bridge, outside the main gate of the jail, and there, it is said, she spent nine days keening her husband.'[87] Waldron's influence is in turn to be seen on the work of Patrick Joyce, whose incisive social history of the British liberal state, *The State of Freedom* (2013), features some brief but charged references to Maamtrasna near the end of his work – Joyce had family connections with the area: his father was born in Kilbride, near Finny.[88] For Patrick Joyce, the figure of Myles Joyce functions as 'a symbol of the reality of British justice in Ireland and of the organised violence of the state generally' – in a genealogy in which James Joyce as well as Waldron are obvious sources. Or, to quote his starker terms, 'the cradle of the British state engendered the grave of Myles Joyce.'[89] Changing to historical fact a story that Waldron had been careful to list as 'tradition', Joyce concludes: 'Myles Joyce's was a culture the difference of which is starkly indicated in the figure of his grieving wife, "keening" outside Galway gaol for nine days after his execution.'[90]

Conversely, in James Murphy's 2014 biography of Earl Spencer and in his discussion of the Maamtrasna controversies, the historiographical emphasis is determinedly less on the individual's fate. Murphy explicitly situates himself against what he sees as 'the triumph of the nationalist narrative concerning Maamtrasna' and, following a detailed survey of government responses to the trials and their aftermath, concludes:

> All of this is not necessarily to make a claim for Myles Joyce's guilt. Indeed, it seems likely that he was innocent. But it helps to recover a sense of the more complex circumstances of the time. This is necessary because the triumph of the nationalist narrative concerning Maamtrasna has meant that it is generally simply accepted as being, to use Robert Kee's phrase, 'one of the most blatant miscarriages of justice in British legal history.'[91]

Murphy's analysis of the significance of Myles Joyce's 'last protestation of innocence' is admirable in its willingness to reinspect a subject so laden with emotional potency. However his comments become remarkably entangled in a knotted issue of formal religion *vis-á-vis* individual beliefs:

> If he [Myles] had not been actually inside the house, he may have believed himself thereby to be innocent. Yet he had said he was not even in the vicinity. If he had known himself to be guilty, would he have wanted, as a Catholic, to have died with a lie on his lips, believing that divine judgement was to follow? But how religious a person was he? The well-known spread of Tridentine Catholicism in nineteenth-century Ireland, with its emphasis on sacraments

such as confession, had made its least and last impact in Gaelic-speaking areas
of the west of Ireland.[92]

And here again traditional lore – in this case relating to the condemned
young Patsy Joyce, as seen through the eyes of the judicial elite – acquires
the status of historical fact: 'Patrick Joyce, survivor of the massacre, was said
never to have heard of God. On the other hand, Myles Joyce may have been
quite religious. A priest attended him on the scaffold.'[93]

While Joyce and Murphy differ sharply in their political evalua-
tions, both deploy the executed figure of Myles Joyce as a symbol at the
bar (to adapt James Joyce's phrase), in a trial where the exercise of state
authority is the deeper matter at stake. From the immediate aftermath of
the Maamtrasna murders down to the present, the events have thus been
incorporated into larger political narratives, most usually nationalist in
character. Within these accounts, the case of Myles Joyce points to the
breakdown, complicity or failure of the British state in its dealings with
Ireland, or (much less commonly) to a view of the state as wrongly accused.
A key and necessary consequence is the continuing notoriety of Myles Joyce,
a man wrongly executed, but emphasis on the shortcomings of the political
administration has also had less welcome repercussions. It has resulted in
a simplified view of social and cultural factors; an underestimation of the
part played by a judicial system ill-equipped to accommodate linguistic and
class difference.

— 8 —

AFTERLIVES

'These wretched heartbroken men'

That your petitioners most humbly beg your Excellency to consider their sentences now, as we are growing old and feeble, and their aid and help would materially assist us and enable us to retain our land and live an industrious life for the future.

> Petition by Julia Joyce (wife of Paudeen and mother of Tom), Julia Joyce (wife of Martin), and Mary Casey (wife of John Casey), September 1898[1]

In December 1882, Martin Joyce, his brother Paudeen, Paudeen's son Tom, Michael Casey and his nephew John Casey began their sentences of penal servitude for life. 'Life' terms then comprised 20 years and, by convention, life prisoners usually received further remission for good behaviour. All such remissions were refused in the case of the Maamtrasna prisoners. Two men died in prison: the elderly Michael Casey in 1895, then in his mid-seventies, and John Casey in 1900 in his early fifties. The three Joyces were released in late October 1902. During these two decades, the men's fates were rarely the subject of public comment or interest and few details of their lives in prison survive. But those that exist, largely in convict reference files or through mentions in contemporary prison reports, give some insight into the isolation of their lives and the hardship they experienced.

Early in 1883, Tim Healy, nationalist and agrarian activist, was serving a six-month sentence in Dublin's Richmond Jail. While there, he encountered a prison warder named Foster who had previously served in Kilmainham Jail:

His stories of the Galway prisoners there, convicted by Dublin special juries under the Crimes Act and sentenced to death, were heartrending. He said none of them could speak English, and that they bewailed their fate in Gaelic, holding up their hands to try to make him understand. They numbered their children on their fingers and by signs tried to show him their ages and heights.[2]

Each prisoner spent the initial nine months of his sentence in solitary confinement before moving to a public works or 'labour' prison.[3] Michael Casey was imprisoned first in Mountjoy Male Prison in December 1882; in August 1884 he was moved to Maryborough (today Portlaoise), where he spent the remaining eleven years of his life. At that time, Maryborough prison catered largely for ailing inmates and prisoners of intermediate (lower-security) class. John Casey was imprisoned initially in Mountjoy and then in Downpatrick Prison, County Down. In December 1886 he was moved to the invalid class in Maryborough and was now in the same prison as his uncle, where he remained for another twelve years. In 1898 he was transferred for medical treatment to Mountjoy Medical Hospital, where he died on 27 February 1900.[4]

Limited contact between the Joyces was possible in the early years of their confinement but subsequently they were separated for many years. All three were first imprisoned in Mountjoy, and then Paudeen was moved to the lighter regime of Maryborough in August 1884. In a letter to his wife sent in September 1884, Martin wrote approvingly: 'He [Paudeen] was sent there [Maryborough] for his own good, through the kindness of the doctor, for he wasn't sick, only a little lonely for leaving us here behind him. It is about 50 miles from here, and a fine healthy place.'[5] Paudeen remained in Maryborough as a member of the invalid class for almost fourteen years; in May 1898, then over 60, he was returned to the much harsher conditions of Mountjoy for four years, until August 1902.[6] Martin Joyce was transferred firstly to Downpatrick Prison in 1884, and when Downpatrick closed in 1891 he was moved to Maryborough as a regular convict.[7] His prison file at Maryborough lists an offence of 'endeavouring to communicate with other convicts', dated 4 April 1891, days after he arrived at the same prison as his brother Paudeen. His punishment was 'to be confined in his cell for one day.'[8] Martin remained in Maryborough until his release in 1902.[9]

Tom, aged only about 20 upon conviction, was confined for most of his sentence in Mountjoy, where he reportedly learned a trade 'as [a] plasterer and slater'. Other attributed occupations were 'shoemaking, labourer, mason and painting'.[10] Tom, who appears to have had some competence in

English before his conviction, learnt to read and write in prison and corresponded with members of his family as well as with Tim Harrington, MP.[11]
By August 1902, all three Joyce men were lodged in Maryborough, from
where they were released in October 1902.

Michael Casey was the only one of the five prisoners not to be exonerated in Patrick Casey's public recantation.[12] Having earlier insisted on
his innocence, he retracted this in a long memorial written on his behalf in
Maryborough on 26 July 1885 and now asserted that he had been forced to
go into the Joyce house against his will, and that he had indeed taken part
in the murders. Most awkwardly for the authorities, Casey declared that he
had, early in December 1882, testified to the innocence of Myles Joyce, his
four fellow prisoners and the approver Philbin and that he had named the
guilty parties:

> Whilst under the sentence of death in Galway gaol, I stated to the magistrate
> that it was John Casey and his son John J. Casey and Pat Lydon (John) that
> murdered [the] Joyce family, and also that it was Thomas Casey and John J.
> Casey that pressed myself to go. I wish to add to this that Burke, who was once
> a policeman but [is] now out on pension, was the interpreter when I made the
> statement, and I have no doubt that he will verify my words. Also, I stated
> to him that Myles Joyce was realy inocent [*sic*], and anything that lay in his
> power to do it for him. And also I told him that Patrick Joyce (John), his son
> Thomas Joyce, and Martin Joyce and John James Casey were realy inocent [*sic*],
> and as for Philbin, that he was not there at all that night.[13]

No record survives of such a statement by Michael Casey in December
1882 but the allegation that it had been made, and with the assistance of
a named police interpreter, gave this memorial a particular urgency. The
prison governor forwarded it to the General Prisons Board in early August
1885 and it is likely to have been one of the documents referred to in the
House of Commons by Chief Secretary Dyke on 10 August. However, it
and other memorials submitted by Michael Casey were unsuccessful, and
the repeated official reply was that the law should 'take its course'.[14]

In the private letters and public memorials written on their behalf, the
other four men strongly asserted their innocence. One of the earliest letters
is one sent from John Casey to his wife Mary, at the end of the first six
months of his confinement: 'Dear Mary, it is very hard to be here for a
crime that I know nothing about. Thanks be to God, I know nothing whatever about it. But I fret more for you and the children then [*sic*] I do for
myself; for you know as well as I do myself that I had no hand in that act.'[15]

The highly formulaic nature of this and other letters suggests that they were translated and written on John's behalf, perhaps by a prison warder, priest or fellow prisoner. On receipt, a local person (possibly the local priest) would have interpreted and read it to his wife Mary. John's communication to his wife continues with reassurance as to the conditions of his imprisonment:

> I received your welcome letter after I came to this prison. I was very happy to find you and children and friends were all right well. I am very well myself, thank God. I am going to school every day and to chapel every day. We have Mass three times a week. I have nothing to complain of; everything is very cleane [*sic*]. I have flannels, and a good bed, and good cloths [*sic*]; write whin [*sic*] you get this and let me know how my mother is, and my brother, my sister, and her family, your father and mother and brothers, and did you here [*sic*] from your sister.[16]

It is clear from the letters that John hoped to be exonerated in time and released. On 27 June 1884 John wrote: 'Keep good courage and I will do the same. I hope everything will come to light hereafter. I don't expect to be always here.'[17]

As the years progressed, the men sent dozens of memorials seeking clemency. What an official in the Chief Secretary's Office termed the 'gigantic wilderness of papers' that was the Maamtrasna file shows that during the years of their confinement numerous pieces of correspondence from 'the Maamtrasna convicts' were submitted to that office.[18] An 1894 document listed 13 memorials, each naming the convicts concerned and the high-ranking official under whose consideration each was to be placed.[19] Many other petitions were sent in subsequent years, and others were submitted either by public parties interested in the case or by relatives of the prisoners. One such memorial, forwarded by Clonbur priest Fr Martin Mellet in 1897, featured a large typescript page giving the reasons as to why an inquiry should take place into the justice of the sentences pronounced on 'John Casey, Martin, Pat, and Thomas Joyce'; over 50 signatures were included, mostly from curates, parish priests and justices of the peace, and commencing with that of Archbishop John McEvilly.[20]

The style of these petitions followed established protocols and modes of address from the petitioner to 'His Excellency, the Lord Lieutenant of Ireland.' An instruction on the petition form ordered: 'The petition, which must be legibly written on the ruled lines and not crossed, must be couched in proper and respectful language, and any complaint must be made as soon as possible after the occurrence which gives rise to it.'[21] The documents that now survive required complex acts of translation behind the scenes, whereby the prisoners' fervent attestations of innocence, expressed in their native Irish, had to be not only translated but also rendered into formal 'officialese'. On some occasions the name of the witnessing warden (who was likely to have also been the translator) was given, and the illiterate prisoner's mark was indicated. Tom Joyce, however, not only signed his name to all memorials but apparently penned all of his own, with the exception of his first individual appeal in 1895.

In spite of the formulaic and mediated nature of these petitions, there are instances where the personal circumstances of the men's lives, their hopes of asserting their innocence, and their dashed aspirations emerge poignantly from between the formal lines. The memorials from Paudeen Joyce repeatedly called attention to the needs of his large family: 'I left a helpless family the nine of them and the tenth were convicted along with me,' he wrote in March 1892.[22] His memorials also continually asserted not only his innocence of the crime but also the prejudiced nature of his trial. For example, in his first memorial (sent in August 1884), he offered testimony that he had not been allowed to present during the Dublin proceedings: 'It was only on the day following the murder that the petitioner received news of the horrible transaction, and he immediately repaired to the scene of the outrage, where he remained until he was arrested.'[23] The petition continued with information as to the motivation behind the Joyce witnesses' testimony: 'Petitioner wishes to convey to your Excellency the fact that the witnesses who gave evidence against him, Anthony Joyce and John Joyce (Patrick), were sworn enemies of his, the petitioner having previously prosecuted them for sheepstealing, and, as natural to expect, were his bitterest foes; they swore falsely against him, not even a particle of truth in the evidence they gave.'[24] And as late as June 1900, his son Tom Joyce similarly wrote that 'he is and has been in a position to exonerate himself from any complicity or participation in the said crime.'[25]

Much of the impetus behind the submission of public letters of appeal and petition came from local Maamtrasna clergy. In June 1894, writing from Carna, County Galway, the parish priest Fr Michael McHugh submitted a lengthy letter pleading that the Lord Lieutenant 'be able to see your way to open the prison door to these wretched, heartbroken men and allow them to return to their little homes and families.' McHugh's role was of particular interest since, as he acknowledged in the letter, he was not only curate

in the district at the time of the murder but also had been instrument
in 'inducing the men now undergoing penal servitude to plead guilty.'[26]
When interviewed by Tim Harrington in 1884 McHugh had equivocated
regarding the men's innocence; now he expressed his deep conviction
regarding the innocence of four of them: 'Since then I have learned a good
deal of the Maamtrasna murders, and I have not the remotest shadow of a
doubt that four of the men now undergoing penal servitude as well as poor
Myles Joyce are as innocent of the crime and all complicity in the crime as
the child yet unborn.'[27]

In the late 1890s, the petitions took on a new urgency, reinforced by the
fact that the men had now served much longer than was customary for life
prisoners. In March 1896, Tom Joyce sought release from 'His Excellency
the lord lieutenant' on the grounds that the 'petitioner may have an opportunity of accompanying a sister of his to America who is emigrating there in
the month of April.'[28] Annexed to the usual memorial forms was a separate
short communication from the governor of Mountjoy on 10 March, who
reported that, the previous December, Tom's mother and sister had visited
him and that his sister was planning to return to America in the spring.[29]
Two years later, in 1898, Tom Joyce sought release on the basis that the
'petitioner's mother, who during all these years has striven to retain the little
holding which she possesses, is now an old woman, and her only hope in life
is that she may have the comfort of seeing [the] petitioner restored to her'[30];
similarly, in 1899 he sought to be restored 'once more to his blighted home
and destitute old parent.'[31]

In 1899, emphasising his 'exemplary prison character' and his seventeen
years in prison, Tom Joyce argued that such a long term of imprisonment
was 'unequalled in the convict records at the present time either in Ireland
or England, for 'in the ordinary course of justice prisoners undergoing life
sentences are liberated after completing fifteen years.'[32] This point was
also made in the many petitions from the prisoners' female relatives. In
September 1898, a petition was forwarded on behalf of Julia Joyce (Judy,
wife of Paudeen and mother of Tom who mentioned her frequently in his
petitions), Julia Joyce junior (Jude, wife of Martin Joyce), and Mary Casey
(wife of John Casey). The document, signed with marks from the three
women, was an appeal on their husbands' behalf that 'the long years they
have been in prison may have satisfied the law.' Plaintively, the petition
besought the Lord Lieutenant 'to consider their sentences now, as we are
growing old and feeble, and their aid and help would materially assist us

and enable us to retain our land and live an industrious life for the future.'[33] In spite of all of these attempts, the men did not receive remission of any kind. The forms of licence for the release of Martin Joyce, Paudeen Joyce, and Tom Joyce were issued only in October 1902.[34]

DEATHS IN PRISON

Prison warder Foster's description of the Maamtrasna men signing their ages and the number of their children, in an effort to be understood, captures graphically the linguistic isolation experienced by them in jail. For much of their time in Maryborough Prison, just one Irish-speaking warder was on staff and this man had been appointed with the express purpose of teaching the men English.[35] The Roman Catholic chaplain in Maryborough at the time, Fr Phelan, did not speak Irish and, in the early 1890s, repeatedly lobbied the prison board for the provision of an Irish-speaking priest to attend them. The board refused each request and claimed that the men could understand English. Phelan stoutly denied this, to the board's increasing vexation. Writing in 1891, he remarked: 'I fear one of them is too old and another unwilling to learn.'[36] A year later, he reported that the 'three Irish-speaking prisoners' (likely to be Paudeen Joyce, John Casey and Michael Casey) had not 'made any progress in their study of the English language. They have not consequently approached the sacraments at Easter time. From one cause or other they have a prejudice against this study, and as a matter of fact, they have not made any real effort to learn it.'[37]

The provision of Irish-speaking warders was a contentious issue within the administration of Irish prisons in the 1880s and 1890s. In October 1883, less than a year after he had participated into the secret inquiry into the execution of Myles Joyce, Richard Kinkead testified as Medical Officer to the Galway Jail to the Royal Commission of Prisons in Ireland. He was examined at some length on the topic of Irish in the prisons by George Sigerson (medical doctor and influential cultural revivalist) and his fellow commissioner the liberal unionist MP Edmond Wodehouse. In response to Wodehouse's question if it were common in Galway Jail to have prisoners speaking only Irish, Kinkead replied: 'Frequently. More among the male prisoners. From Arran and Connemara side they speak sometimes nothing but Irish.'[38] He also reported that Galway Jail then had one Irish-speaking warder on the male side but none on the female side.[39] Other evidence presented to the commission described the case of an Irish-speaking prisoner transferred to Tullamore where none of the prison staff could speak Irish; here, and contrary to official regulations which forbade communication between prisoners, the prison inspector had brought a bilingual speaker to the man's cell to translate for him.[40]

The issue of an Irish-speaking chaplain not being available to the Maamtrasna prisoners came to public attention in 1895 because of the failing health of Michael Casey and expressed concerns about his spiritual welfare. On 10 April, the visiting committee at Maryborough prison wrote to the prison governor, recommending that the executive 'consider the propriety of the release of this convict.' Its report noted that Casey, 'now 73 years of age', appeared to be 'in a very critical state of health' and 'being an Irish speaking prisoner, his position is a very serious one, as an Irish speaking priest has not yet been able to attend to look after these prisoners.'[41] Writing the next day from Dublin Castle, the secretary of the General Prisons Board for Ireland, sought a medical report as to the health of Michael Casey from the governor of Maryborough, John Condon, and requested that measures be taken to 'have an Irish speaking clergyman visit the Irish speaking prisoners without further delay.'[42] The governor's ambiguous reply that 'the convict has been regularly visited by the local clergyman' elicited a terse and firmly worded official response: 'I should like to know the exact date when an Irish speaking priest last visited this prisoner. You note that the local clergymen regularly visit him. Am I to assume from this he is able to go to confession to them? Have they deemed it necessary to admit extreme unction in this case?'[43]

It is clear from this correspondence that the board recognised the urgency of the case, a view not shared by the prison governor. In his reply, Condon stated: 'Convict A619 Michael Casey has not been able to go to confession,' that 'it has not been deemed necessary to administer extreme unction as he was not at any time considered in danger of death,' and that 'the date on which an Irish speaking priest last visited this prisoner was 23rd January 1894' (i.e. some fifteen months earlier).[44] A further minute of the General Prisons Board recorded that arrangements had been made to have the prisoner visited by an Irish-speaking clergyman without delay.[45] However Michael Casey did not receive the ministrations of an Irish-speaking priest before he died. Four months later, on 22 August 1895, he breathed his last at Maryborough prison; the cause of death was recorded as apoplexy. Reporting his death to the Board, the prison governor wrote, in blatant disregard of confessional privacies and strong earlier evidence that Michael did not understand English: 'He spoke English sufficiently to enable Rev. J. Harris to hear his confession to such extent, and which was made with such apparent repentance, as to justify the hope that everything possible was done.'[46]

However, immediately following Michael Casey's death, the private detail of one man's relationship with his spiritual minister gained considerable public notoriety. On 29 August 1895, Tim Healy, now MP for North Louth, raised the issue in the House of Commons, reminding his audience of the 'case of the Maamtrasna prisoners, as to whose conviction, he said, grave doubt existed'. Citing the death of one of the men, Healy described 'some' of the prisoners as Irish-speaking people who were denied 'the ordinary solaces of religion by being confined in a part which was not an Irish-speaking part of the country.'[47] Yet in his subsequent memoir, published in 1928, the now establishment figure Healy, recently retired from his position as the first Governor-General of the Irish Free State, recalled the situation very differently. The details of his reminiscence show a curious mixture of retrospective justification and misremembering; for example, Healy recalled – in error – that 'one or two' prisoners had not been hanged, and that the last had been released in 1903.[48] More invidiously, he argued that the guilt of the 'surviving convict' had been inferred from what he termed 'refusal' to participate in the religious sacraments, a private act now put under very public scrutiny. Here Healy drew from a version of events relayed by prison warders whose veracity for him was unquestionable but which prison records contradict. His comments stage a kind of spiritual mini-trial, complete with moral sentence, and greatly underplay linguistic barriers. They make for distasteful reading and indict their author rather than his stated object:

> The Irish members had not pressed for his release – for a reason which would not strike outsiders. We knew that year after year Gaelic-speaking priests visited Maryboro' jail to enable him to go to confession. The decrees of the Council of Trent bind Catholics annually (at least) to approach the sacraments. This convict, the warders told us, refused to do so. That carried to our mind the inference of guilt, and besides, showed that he was so ignorant of his religion that he distrusted the integrity of priests nominated specially for his benefit. Coupled with the infamous nature of the crime, this restrained us from lifting a finger to hasten his enlargement.[49]

John Casey, nephew of Michael, also died in prison. In November 1886, only four years after the life sentences had begun, the Downpatrick Prison surgeon reported that he considered the life of John to be in danger: 'The surgeon reports that the convict would be likely to derive benefit by removal to an invalid establishment, but that he is not at present in a fit state of health to be at once discharged. This is one of the "Maamtrasna" prisoners.' The official medical recommendation was to remove John Casey to Maryborough Invalid Prison, and 'if not, release [him] on licence'.[50] That same year, three or more petitions were submitted from Downpatrick on the grounds of Casey's failing health. The text of one petition read as follows:

> That petitioner has lost his health recently in prison, and it is in such a precarious state at present that his life is in danger and he may in all likelihood die in a short time. That petitioner has a small farm in Galway, upon which his wife and three young children reside, and he earnestly implores that your Excellency may be graciously pleased to grant him his liberty and thereby afford him the happy consolation of spending the short period that may remain to him of life with his family.[51]

An accompanying surgeon's report diagnosed 'pulmonary haemorrhage,' and provided a number of replies to queries posed by the central prisons board. The question of whether the disease had been caused or aggravated by confinement to prison elicited the following equivocal response: 'I do not think so except so far as the depressing influence of separation from his family may affect him.' In reply to the question as to whether the prisoner was anxious to be discharged, the short answer was 'yes', and as to where he would go if discharged, the reply was 'home to his wife' and their small farm in Derrypark, Co. Galway.[52] But there was to be no release. In mid-December 1886 John Casey was moved to the 'invalid class' at Maryborough, where he remained for twelve years; in 1898, following a report that he was suffering 'chronic and permanent lung disease with general debility', he was transferred for medical treatment to Mountjoy Medical Hospital, where he died on 27 February 1900, with the cause of death recorded as pulmonary tuberculosis.[53]

Within a week of John Casey's death, his demise was the subject of a series of questions in Parliament by MPs, including Patrick 'Pat' O'Brien and William Redmond, who sought to establish whether his medical condition had been brought under the prior notice of the governor; if so, on what dates; whether the prisoner had been asked whether he wished to be transferred to a hospital outside; and why Casey was housed in Mountjoy

Prison rather than in the more suitable invalid facilities at Maryborough Prison.[54] On 7 March 1900, the *Irish Times* gave prominence to the parliamentary intervention by O'Brien, in which he cited the 'strong opinion' of the coroner's jury that 'the man when found to be hopelessly ill should have been released'.[55] An internal, posthumous review of Casey's case acknowledged that his case had only been submitted for central consideration as a health case for the first time in January 1900, 'since which date he was never fit for removal'.[56] These official documents include a postscript relayed by Woodhouse, the prison doctor, and scored in red pen: 'It may be added that the medical member of the board asked him, if his illness were to take a favourable turn, whether he would wish to be transferred to a hospital outside; he said he would not, unless he was going to recover'[57] – a rare instance of reported speech from one of the Maamtrasna prisoners, albeit heavily mediated officially.

FATE OF THE ORPHAN BOYS

The welfare of the orphaned Patsy and Martin Joyce was intermittently the subject of official scrutiny. It is clear that local constables believed that a threat to their lives existed in the lead-up to the trials and also in their aftermath; whether familial support was available to them at home is less clear. The boys travelled to the Crown Witness depot in Ballybough in Dublin in September and then lodged with a local family called the Clements. In early December, following the end of the trials, crown witnesses Anthony, John, and Pat Joyce returned under police protection to Galway and then to their homes.[58] The Chief Secretary papers record that the boys were informed that they too could go to Galway but that they expressed the wish to remain in Ballybough 'for the period'.[59] Martin, however, sought official permission to pay a short visit to his home, for reasons detailed by Sub-Inspector Heard in Dublin to his Clonbur colleague Inspector Stokes: 'Martin is now anxious to go to Maamtrasna for 3 or 4 days to arrange some private matters and has asked me to give him armed escort there about and also funds for the journey. It would appear that he wants to dispose of the cattle and crops which belonged to his late father and to pay some shop bills in the neighbouring village.'[60] The reply from Clonbur recommended a short visit by Martin as 'prudent': 'There is no objection that Martin Joyce should be sent down to Maamtrasna. He will be quite safe under police protection for a few days, but I don't think it prudent that he should be allowed to remain longer. The cattle belonging to his late father have been disposed of, some remnant of a crop remains on the place, and it might be necessary he should come across to dispose of it.'[61] It is moving to read not only of the teenage boy's determination to arrange his late father's affairs but also that he believed himself in significant danger in the weeks after his family's murders; a view shared by the police authorities. Martin returned to Dublin unharmed in early January 1883.

A remarkable aspect of the correspondence regarding the boys' care is the personal interest taken by senior figures in the welfare of Patsy. On 21 November 1882, writing to Queen Victoria of the trials' conclusion, Lord Lieutenant Spencer brought to her attention the situation of 'the little boy who was wounded and recovered' and reminded her of an earlier offer to 'contribute something to him'.[62] Spencer's expressed sympathy also had a much more distasteful element; the letter continues: 'It was shown that the poor child was ignorant of the existence of a God, and evidently was little better than an untaught savage.'[63] He also commented that he 'was thinking of getting the child into some orphanage or home where he will be respectably brought up' and that he had heard of 'a school of that kind' recently established by MacEvilly, the Roman Catholic Archbishop of Tuam.[64] Victoria responded three days later, expressing a willingness to help 'about the boy Joyce in any manner you think best' but also reiterating her strong wish that 'in this atrocious case you will not be memorialised to reprieve the murders.'[65] Her financial contribution (which appears to have been of the order of 20 or 25 pounds) was pledged towards the cost of Patsy's care at Artane Industrial School.[66]

The suggestion of Artane as a home for the boys seems to have been made to Spencer by William Clements and his wife, and both boys moved there in 1883. In October 1883 Spencer wrote in glowing terms to Victoria regarding a visit he had paid that day to the industrial school. As a rare contemporary source regarding the boys' situation, it is worth reproducing in length. As was the convention in the correspondence, Spencer referred to himself in the third person:

> Lord Spencer went today to see the Artane Industrial School, He was very much pleased with it, about 700 boys are there, under the Christian Brothers

they are taught farming and a great many trades, and looked very happy and healthy. The brothers are most loyal and say that they believe true loyalty and the love of order must be brought to the lowest Irish population through the children. They inculcate this very earnestly and your Majesty would have liked the hearty cry in which they sang the National Anthem.

Lord Spencer also saw the two Joyce boys, the little boy about 10 cannot yet speak English, he looks still very delicate and has the mark of the wound on his head. The Doctor says he was well, and he is reported to be very quick, and had rapidly learnt his alphabet. He knows nothing of God in any kind of education.

Martin the elder boy, though not prepossessing in appearance seemed very intelligent and sensible. He acquired English at the place where he had been a servant for two years. He spoke freely to Lord Spencer and was a good deal moved in referring to his home. He says that he has no wishes to go back there, lest they should kill him. He knows nothing of the reason of the murder of his relations. He was away at that time.[67]

According to Spencer, Martin was expected to spend about a year in Artane while Patsy would remain 'until he is fit for some trade.' He concluded that he had made himself 'responsible to the managers for them, and your Majesty's kind contribution will go towards the payment.'[68]

Six years later, in August 1888, Spencer and Queen Victoria again corresponded on the boys' condition. Spencer personally commissioned Patrick Keenan, Resident Commissioner of Education in Dublin, to visit Artane and to report on Patsy and Martin's progress.[69] Keenan observed that Martin 'had proved to be an excellent boy' and had continued in Artane as a workman 'at fourteen shillings a week' for some time (three months previous to Keenan's visit, 'when [Martin's] time was up', he had emigrated to America). He described Patsy as 'a most dutiful and intelligent boy' and 'very deft at the trade of carpenter'.[70] The correspondence also displays Spencer's continuing and material concern for the boys' fate, but, with this, a strong defensiveness regarding the court's treatment of Patsy. Writing to the Queen's Secretary, Henry Ponsonby, on 9 August 1888, almost six years after the events, he was at pains to emphasise again the boys' perceived ignorance: 'Neither boy could speak a syllable of English when they arrived, I believe, and I believe I am not exaggerating when I say that I believe they had no idea of an existence of a God or of any religion.'[71]

Over subsequent years, the boys' uncle Thomas Joyce was the only family member to participate in official discussions regarding their welfare, and this in an increasingly disputatious fashion relating to their claim for compensation. Following a lengthy investigation and many official delays, compensation totalling £500 was awarded to the boys in June 1884. Much official correspondence ensued as to how the award should be administered, who should be appointed as administrator, and where and how the monies should be invested for the two minors.[72]

In the course of these exchanges, Thomas Joyce made a series of applications and his role in the claim became more contentious. In July 1884 a letter headed 'Artane Industrial School' and signed by Artane school manager Thomas Hooper confirmed that the boys would be brought to meet their solicitor that month, and that their uncle Thomas Joyce of Kilbride had been appointed as administrator. Fr Hooper, a Catholic clergyman and the head of Artane Industrial School, would remain officially responsible for the boys' welfare for the rest of the decade. Further extensive correspondence from Thomas Joyce's solicitors claimed considerable costs payable to him for his work as administrator, including the payment of an amanuensis (for work as scribe and translator). In April 1887, a letter written on Thomas' behalf described him as a 'delicate, illiterate man,' and in December 1887 he complained bitterly about the damage to his own 'business' allegedly resulting from his own work as an administrator.[73]

Although Spencer had predicted that Martin would remain in Artane for a year only, he in fact lived there for five years (from early 1883 to early 1888). In April 1887, he was almost 21 and his coming of age brought the issue of payment of compensation to the fore. On 28 April 1887, Thomas Joyce wrote to the Lord Lieutenant's office on his nephew's behalf, asking that his share be paid to him to him to 'allow him [to] go and make his living out of it, being that he is no longer a minor.'[74] Payment was delayed considerably since Martin's age could not be verified.[75] The following January, Martin, who was still in Artane, declined the initial amount offered to him (£126, representing half of the monies) as falling short of the amount of compensation awarded; later that month, a final amount of £209 10s. 2d. was awarded 'in respect of the murder of John Joyce' and presented to Martin at Artane on 30 January.[76]

A year after Martin left Artane, the behaviour of the boys' uncle took an ugly turn with respect to the welfare of Patsy. On 12 February 1889 Dublin Castle received a communication written on Thomas' behalf, which suggested that Patsy had died: 'I have not heard a word from either of them for the last twelve months, and I am informed that Patrick died, and that there is no account at all of Martin.' The letter concluded by asking 'His

Excellency' to cause an inquiry to be made into the whereabouts of the boys 'and how they are situated if living'; the writer also requested information as 'to what has become of the compensation and how has this fund been distributed; my being their uncle, I am interested in the matter.'[77] A query sent to Artane elicited the following immediate and unequivocal response from Fr Hooper: 'There is no truth in what is alleged. Patrick Joyce, as appears from our accounts, is yet in this institution and he is very well. The older boy Martin went to America and was doing well there when he wrote about two months ago.'[78]

By 1890, Patsy was aged 16 and was clearly anxious to join Martin, now living in Cleveland, Ohio;[79] because he had five years remaining as a legal minor, the release of the remaining compensation funds was a complex issue. In March 1890, Fr Hooper wrote to the Lord Lieutenant on the boy's behalf, requesting that the money be paid to him.[80] As the manager of Artane, Hooper reported that Patsy's 'time in the school has been up for some weeks,' and that 'the boy is anxious to emigrate to his brother, who is now a married man settled down in America.'[81] Ensuing inquiries established that Thomas Joyce was now dead, but in March 1890 the Castle received an objection to the release of funds on behalf of Thomas' widow Bridget Joyce of Kilbride: 'The friends of Patrick Joyce believe he is too young to be entrusted with any money.'[82] The official recommendation was that Patsy should be visited by the inspector of reformatory and industrial schools to ascertain the boy's 'capability of taking care of himself,' and that a portion of the money would be forwarded so as to enable the boy to join his brother.[83] A final note from Assistant Under-Secretary Kaye on 31 March 1890 suggested that this step had been implemented.[84]

As a result of searches by descendants of the Joyce family, Patsy's emigration record has been located: in May 1896 he was a listed passenger on the ship *Anchoria*, which travelled from Glasgow via Moville to New York;[85] his later whereabouts are unknown, a sad rupture which also evokes the immense trauma and bereavement experienced by the young boy.[86] Martin's destination, according to Jarlath Waldron's local informants, was Cleveland, Ohio,[87] from where he returned in the mid 1890s, possibly before Patsy's arrival in the United States, and settled in Artane, Dublin. The 1901 census provides valuable social detail regarding the adult life of Martin, whose teenage years had seen such horrific loss. He is described as a 33-year-old general labourer, born in County Galway, bilingual, and able to read and write. Martin had married in America and now rented a two-room house in

Artane South, Drumcondra rural district. His wife Kathleen, born in County Dublin, was listed as 29 and a speaker of English only. The couple had five children (English-speaking) – 11-year-old John (named after Martin's father), 9-year-old Joseph (Joe), 6-year-old Martin, 3-year-old Christopher (Christy), and infant Sarah.[88] A decade later, Martin was listed in the 1911 census as a butcher by trade and now had eight children including, poignantly, a 7-year-old named Patrick.[89] In 1920, two of Martin's sons, Joe and Christy, were members of the senior Dublin GAA football team who were playing in Croke Park, on what became known as 'Bloody Sunday' (21 November) when members of the British Auxiliaries and RIC opened fire on the match crowd and caused the deaths of 14 civilians. Martin's grandson, Johnny Joyce, has played a key role in recent commemorations of the Maamtrasna events and in the campaign for the pardoning of Myles Joyce.[90]

RELEASE FROM PRISON

On Friday, 24 October 1902, Martin Joyce, Paudeen Joyce and Tom Joyce were finally released from prison, having served all but four weeks of their 20-year term (see Images 20–25, p. XI). Martin was in his late fifties, his brother Paudeen in his mid-sixties, and Paudeen's son Tom was now aged about 40. Early that morning they took a train from Maryborough to Dublin and then another train west. Drawn from local stories and recollections, Waldron's account of their arrival to large crowds in Ballinrobe hints at the traumatic dimensions of their return:

> So terrified were the ex-prisoners of the boisterous crowd that they asked to be taken in a covered wagon to the Cavalry Barracks in Ballinrobe … In the Barracks therefore they hid until they felt the crowd had dispersed. Then they crept silently to the pub on the corner of Bridge St where they remained until sometime after mid-night and then, when they saw that not a soul was abroad on this raw October night, they slipped out to the street and, unnoticed, set off to walk the eighteen miles home.[91]

In the newspapers of the day, what might have stayed a low-key, local event was given a political edge. On the day after their release, the *Freeman's Journal* featured a six-column report entitled 'Maamtrasna. Release of the

Joyces. History of the Trial. The Subsequent Revelations. Gross Miscarriage of Justice.'[92] The ensuing article continued, however, in a very different tone and credited the men's release to 'a personal appeal by some of their female relatives to Earl Dudley when he visited Galway County during the past week.' A detailed summary, for the benefit of a new generation of *Freeman* readers, featured details from the November 1882 trials, Myles Joyce's 'dying declaration of innocence,' Thomas Casey's confession, the discovery of the crown brief, Harrington's case and the 1884 parliamentary debates.[93]

On 30 October 1902, the *Ballinrobe Chronicle* extravagantly complimented the role of the Lord Lieutenant and his wife and depicted the situation of the released prisoners in the most sanitised of terms:

> The prompt release of the three Maamtrasna prisoners, Martin Joyce, Pat Joyce, and Thomas Joyce, from Maryborough Jail, where they had been undergoing a sentence of penal servitude for life, is accepted here as an evidence of the keen and genuine interest taken in the people of the West by his Excellency owing to his personal observations during his visit last week. At Maamtrasna the wives of the prisoners threw themselves before his Excellency, and in their expressive Gaelic appealed for the release of their imprisoned husbands. An interpreter was quickly found to make all clear, with the result that on Friday evening the three men arrived by train in Ballinrobe, well clad and looking well after 20 years' incarceration, free once more to return to their native mountains, where we trust a new and happier life awaits them in exercising the habits of industry and control which they must have acquired during the dark days of their imprisonment.[94]

The fate of the men then disappeared from media attention, with the exception of a letter to the *Freeman's Journal* published on 16 November. Authored by 'Sacerdos',[95] it proposed the creation of 'some little fund' on behalf of 'the poor Joyces, lately released from Maryborough Jail':

> We know those poor men were innocent, but we can never know how they suffered during the long years of their imprisonment. We felt for them in the terrible wrong to which they had to submit. Why not show our practical sympathy with them now on their return to their humble homes? Should a fund be set on foot for them, I am sure it would have the support of many.[96]

No evidence exists that such a fund ever emerged.

Tom, the youngest of the three Joyce men, emigrated soon afterwards and no trace exists of his subsequent life.[97] His uncle Martin died on 6 March 1906; the registration of his death, at age of 60, lists the cause as 'debility, three months certified' and refers to his wife Jude being present at his death in Cappanacreha.[98] Paudeen is listed in the 1911 census as being 88 years of age, a monoglot Irish speaker and illiterate. He is also described as a widower and a 'lodger' in the Cappanacreha home of his son John, aged 44; other inhabitants of the house were John's wife Catherine, and their four children aged between 6 months and 9 years.[99] According to Waldron's informants, relations between Paudeen and his son Tom were 'strained' on their release as were relations with his son John (Seán Siobháin) and Paudeen was remembered as having 'lived out his days alone in a deserted house.'[100]

PERSONAL AFTERLIVES: 1901–11

The released men must, in subsequent years, have regularly encountered those who had testified against them in 1882. Anthony Joyce of Cappanacreha – the prosecution's lead witness – lived until April 1910.[101] John died in May 1908, at the age of ninety; according to Waldron he suffered a fall from a horse in the mid-1890s and was confined to bed for many years.[102] His daughter Mary, who had received compliments from Judge Barry on her English-language testimony, continued to live in the family household with her children as did her brother Pat, the other family member to testify, and his children.[103]

They would also have crossed paths with Anthony Philbin, one of the two approvers. Philbin died in 1906 at the age of 65.[104] The Chief Secretary papers show that Philbin had strongly considered emigration in the immediate aftermath of the trials but ultimately chose to stay in Cappaduff.[105] For the first eighteen months after the sentencing of their neighbours, Philbin and Casey received police protection and a financial allowance; this ceased in July 1884.[106] Philbin's census return in 1901 provides an especially vivid contrast between his life after 1882 and the fate of the imprisoned men. Aged 60, and listed as a farmer, bilingual and able to read and write, Philbin was by then the father of a large family with 7 children aged between 2 and 18, almost all of whom were born in the years following the Maamtrasna trial.[107]

The approver Thomas Casey emigrated to America around 1890, but his estranged wife Mary (Philbin) remained at home.[108] Of the seven men who had been alleged by Harrington to be guilty (including the executed men Patrick Joyce and Patrick Casey, the approver Thomas Casey and the prisoner Michael Casey), three remained at large: Pat Leyden, 'Big' John Casey of Bunachrick and his son John.[109] Leyden was by 1884 in England, according to Tim Harrington's account, though Waldron reports that he was believed to have returned from England in later years to the Maamtrasna region. No clear record exists in the 1901 or 1911 censuses of his being in the area. Also, according to Waldron, both 'Big' John Casey and his son continued to live in the area but were estranged from each other, and his son 'lived out his days nearby in abject poverty.'[110]

Little information exists as to the later life of Bridget Joyce, wife of Myles, who seems to have died as a young woman.[111] In the 1940s, John Conoboy (Seánín Bán Ó Conabuí), the husband of Bridget and Myles' daughter Máirín, sought to have his father-in-law's remains returned to the family for burial. A formal request to the Department of Justice brought the following reply: 'Reply states that it would be impossible to identify the remains of any executed person after the lapse of 61 years, as all executed persons were buried in unmarked graves.'[112] A number of Bridget and Myles's children and grandchildren emigrated to America: in April 2018, two granddaughters of Máirin and John, Carolyn and Alice Conaboy, met with President Michael D. Higgins in New York, soon after his granting of pardon to their great-grandfather.[113] In August 2018 they visited Ireland to take part in a commemorative ceremony in Galway Cathedral with Johnny Joyce (great-grandson of the murdered John Joyce), held on the 136th-year anniversary of the murders.[114]

Another poignant case points to the interrelatedness of the families affected by the imprisonments. Julia Casey is listed in the 1911 census as a widow aged 89, and living in Cappanacreha with her daughter, Julia (61), and granddaughter, Mary (29).[115] Mother of Patrick and John Casey, Julia had appeared as defence witness in the Dublin court. The experience of her daughter Siobhán (more usually translated Jude) is salutary: Patrick, Jude's brother, was executed in 1882, having confessed to playing a part in the murders; her brother John (who was one of the four unjustly imprisoned men) died in 1900, two years prior to the end of his sentence. Her husband Martin Joyce, also unjustly imprisoned and for whose reprieve she had petitioned, served 20 years in prison and lived only a few years following release. Jude's daughter Mary was born in March 1882, just months before her father's trial and imprisonment.[116] It is difficult to do justice to the destruction of lives caused by the executions and imprisonments, but to linger a moment on Mary's life hints at its extent. Unless she were able to visit her father in the faraway prisons of Downpatrick or Maryborough/Portlaoise (which was unlikely), Mary would have conversed with him for the first time as a 20-year-old woman when, on his release and in broken health, he returned to live in an impoverished household which the women had struggled to maintain for 20 years, and where he died three and a half years later.

— 9 —

JAMES JOYCE

'Ireland at the bar'

The figure of this dumbfounded old man, a remnant of a civilization not ours, deaf and dumb before his judge, is a symbol of the Irish nation at the bar of public opinion.

James Joyce, 'Ireland at the bar' (1907)[1]

Nationalist MP, barrister and campaigner Tim Harrington was a friend of John Stanislaus Joyce for over 30 years; ties reinforced by their shared loyalty to Parnell but endangered, and finally broken, by John Joyce's continual pecuniary requests.[2] Harrington became an increasingly influential figure in municipal politics in the late 1890s: in 1901 he was elected Mayor of Dublin and was re-elected in 1902 and 1903. John Stanislaus must have read Harrington's 1884 pamphlet about the Maamtrasna murders and is likely to have mentioned it to his writerly son. Key years in the Maamtrasna case are also key Joyce family dates: James was born on 2 February 1882, six months before the murders took place; on 1 December 1902, two months after the release of the prisoners, he left Dublin hoping to pursue medical studies in Paris. He carried with him a letter of recommendation that his father had persuaded Tim Harrington to write. In the letter, dated 29 November 1902, Harrington wrote from the Mansion House and with the signature of Lord Mayor: 'I know the bearer Mr. Joyce since his childhood, and I am also well acquainted with his family. He is a young man of excellent character and whose career as a student has been distinguished by industry and talent. He goes abroad to have an opportunity of further pursuing his studies and I look forward with very great hopes to his having the same brilliant success that he has had at home.'[3]

A year before this, John Stanislaus Joyce completed his decennial census schedule on 31 March 1901. The family comprises husband, wife and their ten children living in no 8, Royal Terrace, Clontarf West, Dublin, and occupying six of the house's eight rooms. John Stanislaus lists himself as 'a government pensioner' and records his two older sons 'James Augustine' aged 19 and 'John Stanislaus' aged 16, both then students, as speakers of 'Irish and English.'

LANGUAGE AND CENSUS: DUBLIN, GALWAY, TRIESTE

The surprising identification of the 19-year-old James as bilingual runs against the usual critical emphasis on the young Joyce's antipathy to the Irish language. According to Stanislaus' biography of his brother, the influence of George Clancy (the model for 'Davin' in *A Portrait*) led James to study Irish 'for a year or two'.[4] Joyce appears to have briefly attended Patrick Pearse's weekly Irish lessons at Newman House in 1899 but gave them up because Pearse 'found it necessary to exalt Irish by denigrating English'.[5] John Stanislaus' emphasis on his sons' knowledge of Irish also runs against his own general profile: John Wyse Jackson and Peter Costello note in their biography that Joyce's father's knowledge of Irish 'was slight' and 'he himself had no interest' in the language.[6] The census entry might therefore best be read as an instance of paternal investment in filial abilities rather than evidence of deep-seated cultural affiliation, but it does demonstrate a higher status for Irish in the young Joyce's early life than is generally recognised.

The 1901 census returns also illuminate the linguistic milieu of the teenage Nora Barnacle (born 1884). The March household return for the Barnacle family, Bowling Green, in the Galway North Urban electoral district shows the generational inverse to that of the Joyces, whereby Annie Barnacle, the 40-year old listed 'head of family', is also listed as a speaker of Irish and English. The blank entries for her six children, including the 18-year-old Norah [*sic*] listed as a seamstress, imply they are speakers of English only, and, interestingly, none of the four 'scholar' children is listed as bilingual. The census return for Nora's baker father – then a boarder with the Walsh family in Faugh East, Oughterard, having been thrown out of the family home some years before – records him as a bilingual, living in a household of bilinguals.[7]

Two local Galway families, the Bodkin and Feeney families, had deceased sons who had been friends of Nora Barnacle; both young men may have influenced the character of Michael Furey in Joyce's 'The Dead'.[8] In these families also, the languages spoken differed between parents and children. The 1901 entries for the Bodkin family, who had a small shop on Prospect Hill and whose son Michael had died the year before, record that the parents, Patrick and Winifred, are bilingual speakers. Their son Leo, an 18-year-old scholar, is listed as an English-speaker only.[9] In cases like the Bodkins and Barnacles it is difficult to determine what level of comprehension of Irish was possessed by children who grew up among bilingual parents and neighbours. Also, parents may have chosen to term their children English-speaking monoglots as a sign of prestige and social status. The case of Michael Feeney (d. 1897), who Brenda Maddox suggests is a closer model for the character of Furey,[10] suggests a more extensive presence of spoken Irish in Nora's teenage life.[11] The likely census return for Michael's family is that of the Feeney family of William Street West, Galway: within it, the 52-year-old mother Mary is listed as a speaker of Irish only, both in 1901 and 1911; her husband, Anthony, a toll collector, and her two listed children are recorded as Irish and English speakers. Thus, living in a neighbourhood that included monoglot Irish speakers among her neighbours and her friends' families, Nora would, at the very least, have needed to comprehend spoken Irish. Years later, in an account of their September 1912 visit to the Aran Islands, Joyce would relate Nora's quite intimate questioning of one of the islanders, suggesting that she served both as a linguistic translator and cultural mediator on his behalf: 'The islander, who is her son, sits next to the fireplace and answers my companion's queries with an embarrassed and humble air … My companion again asks him why there are no women for him, and the islander, taking off his cap, buries his face in the soft wool, confused and smiling.'[12]

In the next national census in 1911, the returns for the Barnacle family listed all five members of the household, including the 53-year old Annie, as English-speakers only, in what is a regular pattern among Irish urban families of the period. By 1911, John Stanislaus Joyce and his two daughters, Florence and Mabel, were listed as boarders with the Sloan family, but the return for James' brother, Charles, now head of his own household, shows an interesting echo of his father's practice in recording his ten-year-old scholar son, John Stanislaus Joachim, as a bilingual speaker.[13]

By 1911 James Joyce and Nora Barnacle were living in Trieste and a surviving census return, as discovered by Erik Schneider, is a fascinating illustration of the language politics surrounding their new home.[14] While officially termed 'The 1910 Census', it was taken in January 1911 and, as the last Trieste census during Austrian-Hungarian rule, was especially contentious with respect to *Umgangssprache* (vernacular language used). As Schneider notes, irredentist activism led to what was perceived by officials as artificial inflation of the size of the Italian-speaking population over Slavic and German-speakers: 'The fraud was so extensive that the Austrian authorities invalidated the first census totals and then completely revised the census in 1911, restoring approximately 20,000 Slavic, German and other language speakers which had been falsely or dubiously certified as Italian-speaking. The census was revised again in 1946, during the Allied occupation of Trieste, resulting in further minor adjustments to the totals.'[15]

Returning to the Joyces in Trieste in 1911, their census form, as authored by James, lists language of use for Nora and he as English but Italian for the two children, Giorgio and Lucia, and maid, Maria Kirn.[16] In fact, following their arrival in Trieste in 1905, both James and Nora had quickly learned the local dialect of Triestino, 'the linguistic glue that bound the city together' in John McCourt's words, and this was the language in which their children were raised.[17] Triestino was a composite of 'many other Italian dialects as well as Armenian, English, Spanish, Turkish, Sicilian, Maltese, German, Hungarian, Slovenian, Croatian, Czech and Greek.'[18] In letters of the period, Joyce would employ both the Triestine dialect and more standard Italian but he had greater spoken fluency in Triestino than in Italian. One of his Triestine contemporaries, writer Silvio Benco, observed in a translated recollection published by Willard Potts in 1979 that the Triestine dialect remained the 'customary language' of the Joyce family long after they had moved from Trieste to Paris.[19]

The Trieste census return vividly documents the tension between official standardising norms and the complexities of individuals' lives. In the columns on place of birth and legal residence, James recorded Nora and he as having been born in Dublin and Galway, Ireland, Great Britain, and as British subjects (*brittanico*). These and other entries were the subject of extensive revisions by an Austrian official: Great Britain is replaced with England and *brittanicio* with *gran inghilterra* which is, as Schneider notes, 'a misnomer in Italian.' The languages carefully delineated by Joyce for the four family members are all struck through and replaced with the letters 'fr.' or the abbreviation for *fremdsprache*, literally 'foreign language' (in official terminology, this denoted a language that was not recognised for the purpose of census-taking). In addition, Maria Kirn's language is changed from Italian to Slovene.

These strong interventions were, Schneider suggests, designed to 'reject the idea that Italian could be the principal language of children of English-speaking parents.'[20] That children should speak a language other than their parents, and be recorded as such, was, as we have seen, not unusual in nineteenth-century Ireland. In Ireland, such language shift within the family, from Irish to English, was welcomed and encouraged by the recording state apparatus. In 1911 Trieste, however, the Joyce family's irregular entry – and its inherent bilingualism – was seen to be 'foreign' and outside of official categories and enumeration. The vehemence of the 'striking out' also shows that this migrant family, transitioning to the spoken, subaltern language of their neighbours and using a language feared as register of nationalist agitation,[21] exemplified to Austrian officials a threatening socio-political instance close to home.

It was in this political and cultural environment that Joyce wrote and published his *Il Piccolo della Sera* articles; a total of nine appeared in Italian in the Trieste newspaper between 1907 and 1912. The third in the series, published as 'L'Irlanda alla sbarra' ('Ireland at the bar'), appeared on 16 September 1907 and is now best known for its reference to the trial and execution of Myles Joyce. Joyce's choice of title, 'Ireland at the bar', derives from Gladstone's famous speech to the House of Commons on 7 June 1886, arguing for the passing of the 1886 Home Rule bill: 'Ireland stands at your bar expectant, hopeful, almost suppliant …'.[22] This peroration was frequently reprinted in the late nineteenth and early twentieth centuries and was, for instance, quoted in Morley's 1903 biography of Gladstone.[23] The continuing campaign for Irish Home Rule was also the context for Joyce's attempt in 1914 to publish the essays in book form. In March 1914 Joyce wrote to the Italian publisher Angelo Fortunato Formiggini offering to reprint these 'signed editorials' as 'a volume of Irish essays' which 'would be of interest to the Italian public'. The contemporary political scene, he argued, made their republication timely: 'This year the Irish problem has reached an acute phase, and indeed, according to the latest news, England, owing to the Home Rule question, is on the brink of civil war … I am an Irishman (from Dublin): and though these articles have absolutely no literary value, I believe they set out the problem sincerely and objectively.'[24] Joyce's letter of proposal (which seems not to have been answered) demonstrates the particular significance of the 'Ireland at the bar' essay in the series: it was to be placed first in the running order and was also suggested as a title for the proposed volume.[25]

The *Piccolo della Sera* articles were written during a period lasting some five years when Joyce was 'exclusively an Italian writer' in terms of his published output, as John McCourt and Giorgio Melchiori have shown.[26] Language politics in early twentieth-century Trieste, as discussed earlier, were especially complex, with Italian being one of three languages current in the city along with the local dialect, Triestino, and German, the language of authority. Its use as a *lingua franca* among Trieste's multilingual community may be understood, as Melchiori observes, as 'an effort by an extremely mixed community to find a new cultural identity. It was the language of exiles finding and founding a new country of their own. For many Triestines Italian was an acquired language, deliberately learned and used in order to establish new cultural roots.'[27] The most famous case in the literary scene was that of Ettore Schmitz, Joyce's friend who was of German origin and who wrote novels in Italian under the pseudonym 'Italo Svevo' (literally 'Italian Swabian'). Joyce's own written Italian was, as Conor Deane has remarked, at first 'often ungrammatical and clumsy' and in the 1907 pieces included 'a tendency to use Dantesque archaisms and Latinate vocabulary.' In later years, 'and particularly by 1912 he had become a reasonably accomplished stylist in the language.'[28] The newspaper *Il Piccolo della Sera* had a distinct pro-Italian political agenda under editor Roberto Prezioso, who was one of Joyce's first English-language students at the Berlitz school in Trieste; his objective in commissioning the series of articles from Joyce was, in the words of Mason and Ellmann, that the 'evils of British imperial rule in Ireland would have its lesson for the imperial ruler of Trieste.'[29]

'IRELAND AT THE BAR' (1907): 'DEAF AND DUMB BEFORE HIS JUDGE'

'L'Irlanda alla sbarra' begins with Joyce's account of 'a sensational trial' which took place 'several years ago' in Ireland:

> In a lonely place in a western province, called Maamtrasna, a murder was committed. Four or five townsmen, all belonging to the ancient tribes of the

Joyces, were arrested. The oldest of them, the seventy year old Myles Joyce, was the prime suspect. Public opinion at the time thought him innocent and today considers him a martyr. Neither the old man nor the others accused knew English. The court had to resort to the services of an interpreter. The questioning, conducted through the interpreter, was at times comic and at times tragic. On one side was the excessively ceremonious interpreter, on the other the patriarch of a miserable tribe unused to civilized customs, who seemed stupefied by all the judicial ceremony. The magistrate said:

'Ask the accused if he saw the lady that night.' The question was referred to him in Irish, and the old man broke out into an involved explanation, gesticulating, appealing to the others accused and to heaven. Then he quieted down, worn out by his effort, and the interpreter turned to the magistrate and said:

'He says no, "your worship".'[30]

Following this imaginative reconstruction, Joyce adds his now much-quoted editorial comment: 'The figure of this dumbfounded old man, a remnant of a civilization not ours, deaf and dumb before his judge, is a symbol of the Irish nation at the bar of public opinion. Like him, she is unable to appeal to the modern conscience of England and other countries.'[31] He goes on to indict English newspapers for their poor role as 'interpreters' between Ireland and the English electorate and for their persistent figuring of the Irish as 'criminals, with deformed faces'. In the second half of the article, which is much less frequently cited by critics, Joyce addresses the 'entangled' and 'still unresolved Irish question', chiefly in relation to Irish agrarian unrest. The ending of the article is rightly termed by Hans Walter Gabler as 'anti-climactic';[32] Joyce's target here is the contemporary judgement that Ireland is 'undergoing a period of unusual crime' and the erroneous representation by the London press, disseminated internationally, of Ireland as undergoing an 'agrarian revolt'.[33] Joyce's article then closes with a deft rhetorical strategy in which he details the prevalence of ravages on cattle by 'bestial, maddened criminals' – in England – and a contemporary miscarriage of British justice is invoked. Here Joyce refers to the recent exoneration of George Edalji (in May 1907), who had been wrongly convicted of participating in the 'Great Wryley' outrages in a case that had received much coverage in the *Times* of that year.[34]

The essay contains a number of significant errors with respect to the details of the Maamtrasna trials; inaccuracies that can be explained, at least in part, by Joyce's distinctive authorial interests.[35] The 'interrogation' is presented in very vague terms legalistically but would seem closest in historical detail to the August 1882 hearing by the resident magistrate in

Cong.[36] This direct questioning of the prisoner would not have occurred in a criminal court in 1882: until the Criminal Evidence Act of 1898, the accused in a criminal case was considered an 'incompetent' witness (as was her or his spouse) and therefore not permitted to testify or be examined.[37] Direct errors of fact include the number of those arrested, the names of the accused (not all Joyces), the age of Myles Joyce (who was close to 40), and the description of all the accused as monoglot speakers of Irish. While Joyce's account of the execution relays the infamous detail of Marwood's role, it suggests a public location attended by crowds of people rather than the secluded and restricted space within the Galway Jail where the hangings took place.[38]

Such errors are acknowledged passingly by later editors but in a curious double-play whereby Joyce's reliability is also to be reaffirmed. Kevin Barry, in the more recent edition of Joyce's critical and political writings, acknowledges that Joyce knew the trial 'inaccurately and by hearsay' and refers readers to Harrington's pamphlet for more information. Barry then continues: 'However the role of the interpreter for the Gaelic-speaking defendants was as Joyce describes it,' but no evidence is provided by Barry for this confident assertion.[39] For Jeanne Flood and for other commentators, the appeal of the story for Joyce can be explained by a symbolic if not actual kinship suggested by shared surnames and by the compelling fact that the 'incestuous tangle' of victims, accused and informers were all Joyces. This attraction was reinforced by the coincidence of the murders happening in the year of James Joyce's birth.[40] Other critics have speculated on Joyce's historical sources: as was discussed in the chapter on Myles Joyce's execution, John Garvin suggests that the folk version of Myles Joyce's fate 'was known to Nora Barnacle 20 years previously, that she related it to Joyce, as her most memorable association with his name before she met him and that he used the praying crowd scene and the hangman's allegedly brutal *coup de grace* for his 1907 journalism.'[41] The direct influence of Tim Harrington seems most apparent in Joyce's version of the 'story' or 'legend' of the execution. In his 1884 pamphlet, Harrington provided an especially vivid account of the scene: 'The rope caught in the wretched man's arm, and for some seconds it was seen being jerked and tugged in the writhing of his last agony. The grim hangman cast an angry glance into the pit, and then, hissing an obscene oath at the struggling victim, sat on the beam, and kicked him into eternity.'[42]

A more productive approach to understanding the significance of 'Ireland at the bar', rather than identifying factual errors, is to explore what fuelled Joyce's interest in the case; his own amplifications and additions are especially revealing in this regard. The most significant is his extensive fabrication of the role of the interpreter in the trial of Myles Joyce. As we have seen in Chapter 5, the only one of the accused men to receive the services of an interpreter (for the translation of crown witness testimony) was the last, Michael Casey, and for a very short period of time. Unlike the more typical occlusion of the role of the interpreter in judicial records, when one such exists,[43] 'Ireland at the bar' foregrounds him as a central, shaping presence. Joyce's recurring preoccupation with *l'interrogatorio* (questioning, cross-examination or interrogation) is very much to the fore in this early article, in which the key structural alignment is that of interpreter and patriarch (rather than legal counsel or judge): *l'interprete formalista* 'on one side' and *il patriarca della misera tribù* 'on the other'.[44] The essay also demonstrates Joyce's authorial interest in the power of a false mediator who wrongly translates, who actively edits and fatally filters the information presented. This process of wilful misapprehension persists to the execution scene, in the final grotesque failure by the instrument of the state to make itself understood to its victim (*neppure il carnefice potesse farsi comprendere dalla vittima e*).[45] As the rest of the article makes clear, false and damaging interpretations have continued into the present time of writing through the agency of English journalists who, in Joyce's words, retain 'something of the laconic quality of the interpreter mentioned above.' These false brokers continue to lead their readers into thinking of the Irish as 'highwaymen with distorted faces' in implicit contrast to the eloquent journalist and truthful 'messenger' who authors the piece.[46]

Yet on a closer reading of the tropes of language and speech within Joyce's representation of Myles Joyce, a much less sympathetic perspective emerges. The early description of Myles as 'patriarch of a miserable tribe' unused to *usanze civili* (customs, 'civilised' or 'civic') reads more like a phrase from the most critical of newspaper editorials on the Maamtrasna events.[47] His 'involved explanation' (*spiegazioni intricate*)[48] is then rendered through indirect discourse and through reference to a language of the body, of gesticulation and gesture. It is worth noting that the retrieval of the linguistic detail of Myles' protest – the rendering in even a word or phrase of what he originally said (in Irish) – is beyond the capacity, or more accurately the interest, of Joyce's imaginative reconstruction. In the next lines, an account of the 'old man' being 'almost beside himself' (*quasi fuori di sé*, meaning literally 'almost out of himself'), excess of language passes over to unintelligibility.[49] The subsequent switch of register from historical event to allegory – 'the figure of this dumbfounded old man, a remnant of a civilization not ours, deaf and dumb before his judge'[50] – brings not only the final silencing of Myles' voice but also the removal of his ability to speak and hear. The change in adjectives in the original Italian text shows this process clearly: from *istupidito* to *inebetito* to *sordomuto*.[51]

The phrase 'remnant of a civilization not ours' is a riddling one, and its emphatic rejection of a connection sits oddly with the ties of lineage and consanguinity with the 'ancient tribe of the Joyces' invoked in the opening lines.[52] However the line becomes more comprehensible if Myles Joyce represents a language and *civiltà* unable to render itself audible or to be rendered intelligible (*di non capire e di non farsi capire*) within the Joycean text. As an imaginative restaging of the 1882 trial and execution, which also draws attention to the scene's cultural difference and distance from the present, the 'Ireland at the bar' article is therefore curiously equivocal. Its dramatised critique of the interpreter's role suggests a strong sympathy with the accused, the author's name-sake, and this is the interpretation most commonly given to James Joyce's invocation of Myles Joyce. However, the article itself has a very different narrative effect, re-enacting the power of a dominant voice to reduce the complexity of speech in another language, firstly to monosyllables and ultimately to silence.

It is all the more interesting, then, that the reported 'voice' of Myles Joyce should function as an emblematic political instance for critic Luke Gibbons in his 2015 book *Joyce's Ghosts*. From the outset, Gibbons reads the essay as a positive treatment of Irish: 'Though James Joyce is often presented as an adversary of the Cultural Revival and the Irish language, his article "Ireland at the bar" gives a sympathetic account of the fate of a native tongue struck mute by colonial power.'[53] In Gibbons' reading of the passage, Myles himself is heard to speak through the lingering acoustic trace 'your worship':

> It is characteristic of Joyce's finely tuned ear that he should pick up the barely silenced put-down of the colloquialism 'your worship' in the doomed speech from the dock. The magistrate might well have thought that the fawning deference emanated from the translator himself had not the presence of reported speech been indicated through a shift in intonation, signaled in print by Joyce's reproduction of the original gauche Hiberno-English in the Italian version ('*afferma di no*, "your worship"'). It may be that the 'officious inter-preter'[54] is mocking the hapless defendant, but it is clear that Joyce does not share in this condescension.[55]

Gibbons' argument is circuitous in form but its flourish is that the colloquialism 'your worship' functions as the 'only vestige of Myles Joyce's voice retained in the act of translation.'[56] He goes on to acknowledge some of the linguistic ambiguities of the text (whether we are to hear Myles' original words as Irish or Hiberno-English) but his preference for a reading of the phrase as politically oppositional is evident:

> The obsequious 'your worship' in Joyce's account of the Maamtrasna trial, the only vestige of Myles Joyce's voice retained in the act of translation, is ambiguous on more than one count, for though given as reported speech, it is also unclear whether the original was meant to be in Irish or Hiberno-English. 'Your worship' was a comic staple of peasant speech in Irish fiction throughout the nineteenth century, though, as its ingratiating excess suggested, it was not to be taken at face value and more often than not hinted at thinly disguised contempt.[57]

From a critical perspective, an attractive aspect of Gibbons' reading is the greater linguistic agency attributed to Myles Joyce. The implication of his analysis is that Myles Joyce may have had mastery of some Hiberno-English idiom and that his choice of this phrase could mark a subversive imitation of judicial authority (an argument in turn reminiscent of post-colonial readings of Maria Edgeworth's Thady Quirk,[58] exemplifying 'sly civility' in Homi Bhabha's famous term).[59] Gibbons' reference to the 'doomed speech from the dock' situates Myles in a lineage extending back to Robert Emmet and others. However, despite the appeal of these arguments, another, and more persuasive, alternative lingers, namely that the phrase 'your worship' is that employed by the 'ceremonious' interpreter, the target of Joyce's ire and of his sardonic ear, and also of his greater authorial interest.[60]

PORTRAITS OF LANGUAGES CROSSING

In April 1907, some five months before the publication of 'Ireland at the bar', Joyce delivered 'Ireland: Island of saints and sages', his first of three lectures at the Università Populare in Trieste.[61] In it, he provided a somewhat sardonic account of the success of the language revival movement in Dublin, an appraisal not far removed from the sceptical views of Gabriel Conroy in 'The Dead' and with details that must have resonated with an audience well experienced in matters of linguistic politics:

> Ten years ago it [the Irish language] was spoken only by peasants in the western province, on the Atlantic coast, and a little on the small islands that stand like pickets at the advance outpost of Europe facing the western hemisphere. Now the Gaelic League has revived its use ... The League organises festivals, concerts, debates and social gatherings at which the speaker of *Beurla* [*sic*] (that is, English) feels like a fish out of water, lost in the midst of a crowd chatting away in a harsh, guttural tongue. Often on the streets groups of young people may be seen to pass speaking Irish perhaps a little more emphatically than is really necessary. The members of the League correspond in Irish and on many occasions, the poor postman, unable to read the address, has had to turn to the head of his section for help in unraveling the problem.[62]

Later in the lecture, in a less frequently cited remark, Joyce gestures to the future: 'It would be interesting, but beyond the aims I have set myself this evening, to see what the probable consequences would be of a resurgence of this people; to see the economic consequences of the appearance of a rival, bilingual, republican, self-centred and enterprising island next to England, with its own commercial fleet and its ambassadors in every port throughout the world.'[63] His summoning to mind of a 'bilingual' as well as 'republican, self-centred and enterprising island' now reads as quite the 'what-might-have-been' of Irish twentieth-century culture.

Other textual moments in Joyce's mid-career point to his continuing interest in the interplay between the English and Irish languages, and what it is notable about these passages is their mischief. This interplay is a recurring preoccupation in the last chapter of *A Portrait of the Artist as a Young Man*, including the fragments of Stephen's diary which end the novel; passages that resonate in interesting ways with the 'Ireland at the bar' essay.[64] *A Portrait*'s most famous engagement with the subject of language is undoubtedly the 'funnel/tundish' conversation that occurs during Stephen's encounter with the Dean of Studies in the Physics Theatre in Newman House. Stephen's rhetorical conclusions ('The language in which we are speaking is his before it is mine ...')[65] are some of *A Portrait*'s most frequently-quoted lines. This exchange is very often, however, read out of context, but within the novel it is preceded and succeeded by other lively meditations on the subject of language and difference.

Just before his meeting with the Dean, Stephen recollects a confidence shared with him by 'the young peasant' and Irish-speaker Davin, whom 'the gossip of his fellow students ... loved to think of' as 'a young fenian': 'His nurse had taught him Irish and shaped his rude imagination by the

broken lights of Irish myth.'[66] Stephen is deeply flattered by the revelation
that Davin's story was 'never told' to 'a living soul' and he is further won
'over to sympathy by the speaker's simple accent.' This reported near-se-
duction takes place somewhere in the Ballyhoura hills, 'better than ten
miles from Kilmallock', as Davin is walking home from a hurling match
in Buttevant.[67] Although it is not clear what language is spoken by Davin
and by the woman whom he meets, his account to Stephen carries a strong
inflection of Irish-language idiom and syntax. In rendering the encounter,
Joyce deliberately employs a heightened Hiberno-English register, resulting
in a passage that we might now think more characteristic of authors such as
Synge and Gregory. Here, Joyce matches, if not mocks, his revivalist peers
through his storytelling:[68]

> Well, I started to walk and on I went and it was coming on night when I got
> into the Ballyhoura hills; that's better than ten miles from Kilmallock and
> there's a long lonely road after that. You wouldn't see the sign of a christian
> house along the road or hear a sound. It was pitch dark almost. Once or twice
> I stopped by the way under a bush to redden my pipe and only for the dew was
> thick I'd have stretched out there and slept. At last, after a bend of the road, I
> spied a little cottage with a light in the window ... [69]

As the 'last words of Davin's story sang in his memory', Stephen walks
along Grafton Street – refusing the importuning of a flower-girl – and
then through Stephen's Green to Newman House and its physics theatre.
Following on from Davin's encounter, Stephen's exchange with the Dean
brings again to the fore the question of socio-linguistic difference: 'a funnel'
is called 'a tundish in Lower Drumcondra, said Stephen laughing, where
they speak the best English.' The burden of an 'acquired speech' is given
(now famous) words as follows:

> He felt with a smart of dejection that the man to whom he was speaking was
> a country-man of Ben Jonson, He thought:

> —The language in which we are speaking is his before it is mine. How different
> are the words *home*, *Christ*, *ale*, *master*, on his lips and on mine. I cannot speak or
> write these words without unrest of spirit. His language, so familiar and so for-
> eign, will always be for me an acquired speech. I have not made or accepted its
> words. My voice holds them at bay. My soul frets in the shadow of his language.[70]

Stephen's internal musings are quite sententiously articulated, reflecting that
less than attractive quality in his character. However, the subsequent return

of the 'language issue' in the closing paragraphs of *A Portrait* is significantly more playful and represents a form of 'speaking back' to the earlier conversations. Diary entries on Stephen's findings regarding the word 'tundish' and on John Alphonsus Mulrennan's visit to the west of Ireland occur in immediate succession (the Syngean echoes now a more evident pastiche):

> 13 *April*: That tundish has been on my mind for a long time. I looked it up and find it English and good old blunt English too. Damn the dean of studies and his funnel! What did he come here for to teach us his own language or to learn it from us? Damn him one way or the other!

> 14 *April*: John Alphonsus Mulrennan has just returned from the west of Ireland. (European and Asiatic papers please copy.) He told us he met an old man there in a mountain cabin. Old man had red eyes and short pipe. Old man spoke Irish. Mulrennan spoke Irish. Then old man and Mulrennan spoke English. Mulrennan spoke to him about universe and stars. Old man sat, listened, smoke, spat. Then said:
> —Ah, there must be terrible queer creatures at the latter end of the world.[71]

The revelation that tundish is indeed 'good old blunt English' confounds Stephen,[72] and the enigmatic question ensues: 'What did he come here for to teach his own language or to learn it from us?'[73] The demarcations of language by region or nation that were invited in the earlier conversation – Dublinese or 'Englishness' – are now teasingly refused as is, more seriously, any simplistic model of cultural influence. Furthermore, any lingering traces of a 'monolingual paradigm'[74] are finally banished by the mischievous account of the old man and Mulrennan's encounter: 'Old man spoke Irish. Mulrennan spoke Irish. Then old man and Mulrennan spoke English.'[75] Unlike Myles Joyce, this putative monoglot Irish speaker proves to be a more than able bilingual, well-skilled in what Doris Sommers has termed the bilingual 'everyday arts of manoeuvring and self-irony.'[76] Notably, and in a further sign of Joyce's mischief-making, it is this bilingual peasant who voices one of Joyce's richest and most playful instances of Hiberno-English: 'Ah, there must be terrible queer creatures at the latter end of the world.'[77]

FINNEGANS WAKE: 'A'COTHRAIGE, THINKINTHOU GAILY?'

One way to trace the continuing relevance of Irish-speaking in Joyce's writings is to note the recurrence of discomfiting questions relating to 'having
Irish'. These range from Miss Ivors' taunt to Gabriel in 'The Dead' ('And
haven't you your own language to keep in touch with – Irish?'),[78] to the challenge by Davin to Stephen in *Portrait* ('Why don't you learn Irish?'),[79] to the
opening chapter of *Ulysses* and Buck Mulligan's teasing response to the milk
woman's misrecognition of Haines' Irish as French ('Irish, Buck Mulligan
said. Is there Gaelic on you?'),[80] and, finally, to the wonderful homonymic
question in *Finnegans Wake*: 'O thaw bro norm, A'Cothraige, thinkinthou
gaily?'[81] The Irish-language phrase *tá brón orm* or 'I'm sorry' is hinted at in
'O thaw bro norm' but in Joyce's telling, the apology precedes the question *an dtuigeann tú Gaeilge?* ('do you understand Irish?') In conversations
about language today, such an apology is much more likely to be uttered
in defensive response. As a consequence, the weight of linguistic politics
both in Joyce's day and ours makes 'thinkinthou gaily?' a wickedly unlikely
homonym for *an dtuigeann tú Gaeilge?*[82]

Early in the *Wake*, the Cad's question, 'Guinness thaw tool in jew me
dinner ouzel fin?', launches the legal proceedings; translatable, perhaps, as
Conas tá tú inniu mo dhuine uasal fionn? ('How are you today my noble fair-
haired fellow?').[83] In the later 'Festy King' episode, references to Maamtrasna abound:

> a child of Maam, Festy King, of a family long and honourably associated with
> the tar and feather industries, who gave an address in old plomansch Mayo
> of the Saxons in the heart of a foulfamed potheen district, was subsequently
> haled up at the Old Bailey on the calends of Mars, under an incompatibly
> framed indictment of both the counts ...[84]

The prisoner appears in the 'dry dock' wearing 'beside stains, rents and
patches, his fight shirt, straw braces, souwester and a policeman's corkscrew
trowswers, all out of the true (as he had purposely torn up all his cymtry-
manx bespokes in the mamertime), deposing for his exution with all the
fluors of sparse in the royal Irish vocabulary ...'.[85] As the legal accused, his
deposition features an oxymoronic blend of floweriness and sparseness;
some pages later, explicit reference is made to Pegger Festy's 'Brythonic
interpreter', who may be already implicitly present in the verbal play of
'Royal Irish Constabulary' and 'royal Irish vocabulary'.[86]

The crown's case against Festy includes an allegation of disguise, made by rubbing 'some pixes of any luvial peatsmoor' and 'clanetourf' on his face: 'it was attempted by the crown (P. C. Robort) to show that King, *elois* Crowbar, once known as Meleky, impersonating a climbing boy, rubbed some pixes of any luvial peatsmoor o'er his face, plucks and pussas, with a clanetourf as the best means of disguising himself'.[87] Here Joyce writes into the Festy King episode one of the crucial details from the Maamtrasna case and the argument central to Tim Harrington's appeal on behalf of Myles Joyce and others, namely that the murder party, as seen by the young Joyce boys, had 'dirt on their faces' and therefore could not be identified clearly by the Joyce witnesses. Early in his 1884 pamphlet, Harrington had declared in resounding terms: 'Nice distinctions as to distances, minute examination of circumstances, contrasts and comparisons, may all be dismissed from consideration when I announce to my readers that beyond all question of doubt the men who murdered John Joyce and his family were disguised, had blackened faces, and wore white flannel vests, called among the peasantry of the West *bawneens*.'[88] Harrington also argued repeatedly that this detail had been deliberately suppressed by the prosecution in order to bolster the crown case and its campaign.[89] It is therefore possible that his influential pamphlet, or at least its central argument, would have been remembered by Joyce and its trace made visible in the *Wake*, given Harrington's friendship with John Stanislaus Joyce.

The Festy King trial ends some pages later:

> But a new complexion was put upon the matter when to the perplexedly uncondemnatory bench (whereon punic judgeship strove with penal law) the senior king of all, Pegger Festy, as soon as the outer layer of stuccko-muck had been removed at the request of a few live jurors, declared in a loudburst of poesy, through his Brythonic interpreter on his oath, mhuith peisth mhuise as fearra bheura muirre hriosmas, whereas take notice be the relics of the bones of the story bouchal that was ate be Cliopatrick (the sow) princess of parked porkers ... he did not fire a stone either before or after he was born down and up to that time.[90]

The removal of 'the outer layer of stuccko-muck' leads to Festy's outburst 'of poesy', delivered through 'his Brythonic interpreter on his oath'. That the witness fluently speaks in 'loudburst',[91] or more 'fluors of sparse'[92] might be read as a revisiting of, even recompense for, the earlier 'deaf-mute' figure of Myles Joyce in 'Ireland at the bar'. In further contrast to the 1907 article is an apparent attempt by the narrator to render Festy's Irish-language words, although the transliteration 'mhuith peisth mhuise as fearra bheura muirre hrisomas' is largely incomprehensible and the final homonym 'bheura muirre hrisomas' may well be 'very merry Christmas'. In other words, what teasingly appears to be Irish – and another alluring vestige of the accused's original voice – is more likely to be transliterated Hiberno-English.

Soon after in the *Wake*'s 'Festy King' episode, we read that:

> the four justicers laid their wigs together, Untius, Muncius, Punchus and Pylax but could do no worse than promulgate their standing verdict of Nolans Brumans whereonafter King, having murdered all the English he knew, picked out his pockets and left the tribunal scotfree, trailing his Tommeylommey's tunic in his hurry, thereinunder proudly showing off the blink patch to his britgits to prove himself (an't plase yous!) a rael genteel.[93]

King's 'true' act of murder is a linguistic one, of having 'murdered all the English he knew' (perhaps even in the mangled phrase 'mhuith peisth mhuise ...').[94] As Susan Swartzlander has usefully remarked, 'Joyce's technique in this passage is to present the details of a court proceeding in such a way that the reader is left only with confusion.' Through 'a series of misunderstandings', that encompass witness, prosecutor, defendant, judges and reader, the narrative 'becomes a parody of blind (and deaf) justice.'[95] Yet for all these parodic strains and given the many textual resonances of the Maamtrasna trials, it is striking that this accused, Festy King, is acquitted and leaves the tribunal 'scotfree.'[96]

Festy King's mock trial, and its echoes of the 'Ireland at the bar' article, has been commented upon in detail by Joseph Valente in his *James Joyce and the Problem of Justice* (1995). Valente's observations on Joyce's 1907 essay differ from those of most other critics in identifying the 'sociocultural distance' established by the young journalist between himself and the figure of Myles Joyce. This difference, for Valente, is crucially related to mastery of language: 'the vital trait enabling Joyce to portray the tragic-farcical proceedings against his namesake so eloquently – his mastery not only of the language in which they were held but a whole spectrum of European languages, such as Italian – insists upon his dramatic sociocultural distance from the figure memorialised.'[97] Valente's reading includes some pithy formulations of the parallels between the 1907 and 1939 texts: 'Where Myles knew no English and so was murdered, James "murdered all the English he knew" in response.'[98] But what becomes problematic in this 'fluor' of critique is the repeated contrast between what Valente sees as Myles Joyce's 'deficiency of language' and his name-sake's 'proficiency'. Once again this involves occlusion of the language in which Myles Joyce was proficient (Irish), through which James Joyce's mastery of (some) languages can shine even more brightly.[99] The endpoint of Valente's critique is a troubling relativism regarding law and language:

> What Joyce's Wakean parody serves to reveal, then, is that in appealing for justice in a foreign language, the language of otherness, Myles Joyce not only symbolised the Irish nation at the bar, he exemplifed the appeal for justice as such, insofar as this appeal can only be answered by that *in* language which is most foreign *to* language, by the otherness of language to itself. All of this is to say that the appeal for justice can never really be answered at all, which is why it must be repeated endlessly and in endlessly variable forms.[100]

In these diverse readings of James Joyce on Myles Joyce, the 'figure' of Myles is translated further into symbol or theoretical exemplar, be it of a Bhabha-type colonial resistance (Gibbons) or a post-structuralist vanishing-point (Valente); in one he is 'made to speak', in the other, he is fully silenced. What receives little attention here is the language in which Myles Joyce actually spoke, as was the case in Joyce's own first engagement with the case of Maamtrasna. In his later writings, Joyce would turn away from the silenced monoglot figure to embrace playful bilinguals. But a continuing motif in his work, more sympathetically rendered in later writings, is an interest in communicative failure, or breaks in verbal exchange, which result from the (often wilful) miscomprehension of listeners.

An excess of interpretative zeal, generated by one early essay, is of course a practice invited by and inaugurated by Joyce himself: 'The figure of this dumbfounded old man, a remnant of a civilization not ours, deaf and dumb before his judge, is a symbol of the Irish nation at the bar of public opinion ... .'[101] As an essay first written in Italian, possibly intended by Joyce to be circulated later to an English-speaking readership, and subsequently disseminated through different English translations, 'Ireland at the bar' continues to pose compelling questions regarding law and language, justice and interpretation, translation and its relation to the 'original' voice or text. The more vexing issue has to do with the article's status as the potential 'last word' on the historical figure Myles Joyce. For Joyce, the article was intended a form of 'speaking-back' not only to historical misinterpretation but also to contemporary misrepresentation. For many of his readers, this is their first and only encounter with the story of Myles Joyce and Maamtrasna, read through an English-language translation and with a now complex critical apparatus; but the article is at its most revealing when read within the dual context of Joyce's life-long fascination with the Maamtrasna case and the events' broader cultural history.

CONCLUSION

Maithiúnas

... the phenomena that interest me are precisely those that blur these boundaries [between language, dialect, idiom], cross them, and make their historical artifice appear, also their violence, meaning the relations of force that are
concentrated there and actually capitalise themselves there interminably.

Jacques Derrida, Monolingualism of the Other[1]

Táim co saor leis an leanbh atá 'san gcliabhán.
I am as innocent as the child in the cradle.

Last words of Myles Joyce, as reproduced by Frederick Higginbottom[2]

The dying words of Myles Joyce, uttered on 15 December 1882, reverberated
strongly on 4 April 2018 when President Michael D. Higgins delivered his
presidential pardon (*maithiúnas*) at Áras an Uachtaráin in the company of
Minister for Justice and Equality Charlie Flanagan. The assembled audience
included direct descendants of the Joyce victims (relatives, too, of Myles
Joyce); relatives of the Casey family; author Seán Ó Cuirreáin, who had
campaigned for many years to secure this outcome; the former Attorney
General Máire Whelan and members of the Department of Justice; Fr
Kieran Waldron (brother of the late Jarlath Waldron); the documentary
makers and actors in TG4's *Murdair Mhám Trasna*; and many journalists.
In reading the official pardon (see Appendix II), President Higgins cited
the conclusion of the 'final and authoritative review of the case', namely
that the conviction in the case was 'unsafe according to the standards of the

time' and that the 'deficiencies in the conviction warrant the Government advising the President that he exercise his right of pardon.'[3] And in his accompanying words, he reminded us of the historical irony of our setting: Áras an Uachtaráin was formerly the Viceregal Lodge, from where Earl John Spencer sent his telegram on 14 December ordering that the law 'should take its course'.[4]

Dying declarations are a central part of the Maamtrasna narrative, as is the history of their being suppressed or ignored. Michael and Patsy's testimony that the murder party had 'soot on their faces', taken while Michael was dying and Patsy severely injured, strongly challenged a prosecution case that rested on the guilty men being visible and each identifiable from afar. The deeming of Patsy's words to be 'worthless' and the prevention of his testimony in court were, as Tim Harrington rightly recognised, critical events, and strongly impugn the justice of the legal proceedings.

Statements by Patrick Joyce and Patrick Casey when facing execution were also kept from view; encountering them all these decades later, in the immense sheaf of papers that constitute the National Archives' 'Maamtrasna file', was an especially powerful moment in my own years of research. The veracity of a confession spoken before death, or in the face of death, is almost sacrosanct: in traditional belief, a dying person would not perjure her or himself and risk damnation; and a dying declaration has long had a special status in law. But that these statements did not, along with other contemporary sources of disquiet, prompt further investigation into a man's wrongful execution and others' wrongful imprisonment is another grim indictment of the Maamtrasna trials and verdicts.

Myles Joyce's words of protest from the scaffold reach us through translation and mediation: first transcribed by a local reporter present at his execution, and passed on both orally and in print form. Even in the days immediately following, changes in their phrasing took place: from the personal idiom of *leis an leanbh atá 'san gcliabhán,* 'as innocent as the child in the cradle' (spoken by a man who had very young children at home), to the more conventionally rhetorical register of 'as innocent as the child unborn'.[5] In one of the most frequently cited invocations of his fate, that by the young James Joyce, Myles is allowed no words at all. And while their reproduction in this book, via the English journalist Frederick Higginbottom (see Image 31, p. XV) carries new resonances in the light of the Irish presidential pardon, they also remind us of what cannot be fully known of a man's inner anguish and, crucially, what cannot be undone.[6]

*

Maamtrasna continues to be of interest to many, as is evident in the range of cultural engagements that have occurred over the decades with regards to the 1882 murders, trials and executions. The events feature in Anthony Trollope's last novel *Landleaguers*, where the gruesome murders are seen to mark a turning point in public attitudes to agrarian violence.[7] Echoes occur in Bram Stoker's 1890 novel *The Snake's Pass* in the choice of Joyce as surname for the heroine's family and more indirectly in topographical descriptions.[8] An unlikely successor to Stoker is the priest and novelist Andrew M. Greeley whose 2001 novel *Irish Love* is set both in contemporary Connemara and in 1880s Joyce Country.[9] Dramatic versions include the 2012 play 'Green Street', staged in the original Green Street courthouse,[10] and *An Taibhdhearc's* 2015 bilingual production staged in Galway.[11] Waldron's 1992 local history book/study has been especially influential, prompting radio programmes, documentaries and history podcasts,[12] and was a central source for Seán Ó Cuirreáin's Irish-language account, *Éagóir* (2016).[13] Ó Cuirreáin's work, including new findings from newspaper archives and prison registers, led in turn to the vivid and very well-received drama-documentary, *Murdair Mhám Trasna*, broadcast on television on 4 April 2018, the same day as the official pardon.

For people living in the Maamtrasna area, including those descended from the various protagonists, this public fascination must at times seem an intrusion. Yet any history of what occurred in 1882 must also acknowledge the ferocity of local violence that was at the heart of the events, whereby three adults and two children were brutally murdered, and two children left orphans, by the actions of a group of their neighbours. Who committed the murders, why, and whether the guilty were convicted are questions very often posed by those who hear of the Maamtrasna case for the first time, but to seek answers involves a disturbing encounter not only with the immense damage wrought by legal injustice but also with a legacy of bitterness that has lasted for generations.[14] The charge by Tim Harrington, reinforced by the later confession of Thomas Casey, that three guilty men remained at large, is sobering and persuasive. His interviews with locals at the time suggest that one of them, John Casey of Bunachrick, was a 'strong man' in the community, that he was in bitter enmity with John Joyce, and that he led a party of six other men to threaten, injure and ultimately to murder John Joyce and four others of his family.

Antagonisms regarding land, grazing rights and also status and power within the local community seem to have fuelled the actions of the murder party and also to have influenced the testimony of the chief prosecution witnesses. Breandán Mac Suibhne's microhistory of agrarian animosities and their long aftermath in western Donegal offers a powerful valuable parallel, though his study comes to a somewhat more optimistic conclusion than the Maamtrasna histories yield:

> This story, if sordid, illuminates differences in feeling and understanding, not simply between people in that distant time, but between the long dead and their lineal descendants. Telling this story allows faint outlines of bright futures lost in the mid-nineteenth century to emerge. But the story also points to dark futures averted. In that regard, it reveals poor countrypeople – a class too easily and too often imagined as impotent in the face of massive socio-economic change – to have themselves, in small measure but in a moment of significance, combined to moderate the forces remaking their world.[15]

The phrase 'faint outlines' is especially salient, given that, by retelling the story of Maamtrasna, one is seeking to uncover experiences distant in time, belonging to people with a very different social and economic standing, and very often lived using a subaltern language. Pádraig Ó Néill's admonitions in 1816 (quoted in Chapter 4) as to the dangers of a court's seeking to translate the figurative idiom of Irish (its 'own proper colours') into English 'legalese' return to mind here and are more broadly salutary.[16] During the key events comprising the Maamtrasna case – arrests, trials, executions or life imprisonment – who spoke what language, and by whom they were understood, mattered significantly in determining the accused's fates. Those who had competence in English had the potential for negotiation with the legal and political system; those who had little or none were especially vulnerable in a judicial process that cast doubt on whether an Irish monoglot even existed. Irish-speaking prisoners were hugely isolated in the prison system. The particular vulnerability before the law of being a monoglot Irish speaker might appear to be a key 'moral' of the Maamtrasna events, and yet as Chapter 2 has shown, one of the immediate consequences of these fateful occurrences may have been, in the short term at least, a tightening of private communication within this Irish-speaking area and with it an intensification of monolingualism.

A closer look at the social fabric within which the Maamtrasna events occurred reveals the subtle processes of language continuance as well as language change, manifest in the comprehension, whether in totality or in part, of two languages. Thus, it challenges us to rethink our assumptions regarding the linguistic and cultural landscape of late nineteenth-century Ireland, particularly in those areas dismissed as 'remote' by metropolitan observers. My hope is that the study of Maamtrasna will also help to generate more dynamic models of linguistic change in Irish cultural studies that can attend to how individuals use language as a mobile resource, and often in creative bilingual manoeuvres that subvert an outdated mono-glot ideology.[17] Within this more complex dynamic, how speakers move between languages and how languages cross in social and official inter-action is especially telling, as are the instances where such crossings fail, where the necessary mediating, translating and interpreting supports are not available or refused. This is where the contemporary valence of Maamtrasna may be at its most significant.

*

The Maamtrasna murders is a story of violence, which includes the violence practiced by the state. In April 2017, while a visiting scholar at the University of Virginia, I was invited to give a lecture on my research into the case. That same week, some newspapers carried accounts of the lethal execution of Kenneth Williams, the fourth man to be executed by the state of Arkansas within a week. Williams was pronounced dead at the end of a 13-minute lethal injection that resulted in what eye witnesses termed 'disturbing signs of distress on the part of the prisoner'[18] and featured the use of the sedative midazolam which has a horrific history in American executions. The state's governor greeted news of the execution with the following comment: 'The long path of justice ended tonight. Arkansans can reflect on the last two weeks with confidence that our system of laws in this state has worked.'[19] 'The state must and wants to *see die* the condemned one', Jacques Derrida has remarked on the death penalty. 'And moreover it is at that moment, in the instant at which the people having become the state or the nation-state *sees die* the condemned one that it best sees itself.'[20]

The injustices that arise from a state's failure to recognise languages other than those officially sanctioned also have dual historic and contempo-rary relevance, and recent asylum cases offer disturbing instances. One such case, detailed by Jan Blommaert, relates to an application in the United Kingdom in which the government was demonstrably culpable in failing to assess properly the complexity of the applicant's case. The applicant (a refugee from Rwanda) displayed proficiency in English and Runyankole, rather than the expected Kinyarwanda and French, and, as a result, his deportation to Uganda was ordered.[21] Here, the individual's complex linguistic repertoire, the result of familial displacement, failed to fit official and simplistic assumptions of equivalence between language usage and political territorial boundaries: in other words, he was perceived to speak the 'wrong' language. These gross errors and misapprehensions occur, as Bloomaert demonstrates, when language competences are viewed only 'as indicative of *origins,* defined within stable and static ('national') spaces and not of biographical trajectories that develop in actual histories and topographies.'[22] In the context of migration and movement at an unprecedented scale, individuals' lives and trajectories grow more and more complex, and existing categories of cultural assessment are less able to acknowledge this.

A further consequence of such migration and mobility is that the role of public service interpreters has gathered in urgency; yet recent international studies highlight the paucity and poor quality of many of these services. With respect to the UK, Marina Rabadán-Gómez observes that 'there is little or no national regulation of the industry and most interpreting service users set their own standards and criteria for the level of qualification and experience of the interpreters they use.'[23] A recent survey of legal interpreting in Greece (as part of a European Social Fund project initiated in 2012) has investigated the experiences of 200 non-Greek-speaking persons who have been arrested and detained in Greek prisons, with stark results. Almost 60 per cent of prisoners stated that there had not been an interpreter present during their encounter with the police and legal system; at least two out of five of the interpreters who were appointed did not speak the language of the defendant; almost half of the respondents said that they did not understand the interpreter and three out of five responded that that they did not receive any information about the interpreting process.[24] This occurs, despite, under the European Convention of Human Rights, the clear-stated right of an accused to have the free assistance of an interpreter if he or she does not have sufficient understanding of the language of their legal proceedings (reinforced by later directives).[25]

In Ireland today, the arrival of new immigrants from a wider range of backgrounds than heretofore necessitates a significant expansion of translation and interpretation services in the judicial system; yet these needs are poorly addressed, where recognised, at service or policy level. Translation scholar Michael Cronin has highlighted the particular weakness of contemporary provision for court interpreting, and the regrettable failure of the state in this area:

> There is absolutely no requirement that these interpreters be properly trained or that they have demonstrable proficiency in any of these languages they purport to master. The situation is one of a high degree of disorganisation and a marked absence of regulation. Many existing practices are highly unethical, such as having young children interpreting for their parents in maternity hospitals. Ireland is not unique in this respect. The situation in many parts of Europe is not much better but the Irish case is all the more disappointing in that one would have thought that a country which has been bilingual since its inception would display a fair degree of sensitivity to language and translation issues.[26]

Research by Kate Waterhouse on the operation of interpreters in Ireland's district court supports Cronin's remarks.[27] Her work uncovers the problems that have arisen from a profit-making system in which out-sourced interpreters are required to aid immigrant defendants with limited competence in English: in the cases which she reviewed, some did not speak at all during court proceedings, others interpreted only a portion, and a 'startling' number of interpreters had evident difficulties in English. As she succinctly notes, 'in the Irish District Court, once an interpreter is provided to a defendant who needs or claims to need one in criminal proceedings, there is an assumption that the duty of the court to the defendant has been fulfilled.'[28] Thus, in a recent discussion of international court reporting, the case of Ireland functions as a 'cautionary' tale because of its inadequate and poorly managed system of outsourcing – one consequence of which has been that many experienced interpreters have now left the profession.[29]

To conclude, our contemporary moment is one in which large-scale mobility (forced or voluntary) is occurring within a seemingly globalised society but individual migrants can find poor accommodation from judicial systems and legal processes. Given the immense numbers of those experiencing migration and displacement, one can only begin to imagine the fateful encounters that are now taking place between the monolingual, or reluctantly bilingual, practices of our judicial and legal systems and the tremendously complex biographical trajectories of those seeking refuge and citizenship.[30] New systems of interpretation, translation and brokerage will be needed to facilitate and support such 'crossings over' in many states. At the same time, what Yildiz has termed the 'monolingual paradigm'[31] continues – and arguably is strengthening – as a national ideal, in the face of increasing plurilingual practice. In Ireland as elsewhere, language loyalties and affiliation are remerging in some arenas as potent sites for exclusivist ambition or for the denial of cultural diversity. For those people today whose lives attest to 'language crossings' – whether as migrants or refugees or others politically and culturally dispossessed – standing at the bar of judicial process and of public opinion remains a perilous place.

Appendix I

KEY PERSONAGES IN THE MAAMTRASNA CASE

I. The Joyce family of Maamtrasna (the Máirtíns):
- John Joyce (Seán Mháirtín Antoine Seoighe), aged about 50 at time of death.
- Bridget/Breege Joyce, his second wife (née Casey, and formerly O'Brien), aged about 45 at time of death. John and Bridget married on 13 February 1879.
- Margaret Joyce, John's mother, aged about 80 at time of death.
- Michael Joyce, John's son, aged about 17 at time of death.
- Margaret Joyce (Peggy), John's daughter, aged about 14 at time of death.
- Patsy Joyce (who recovered from his injuries), aged about 8 in August 1882.
- Martin Joyce (absent from the house that evening), aged 16 in August 1882.

II. The Ten Maamtrasna Accused

The 'Shauns' of Cappanacreha
- Myles Joyce (Maolra Sheáin Seoighe),[1] aged around 40 in August 1882 and executed 15 December 1882. Myles was a monoglot Irish speaker and illiterate. Civil records give birth details for six children (four daughters and two sons)[2] born to Myles Joyce and Bridget Lydon/Lyden: Mary, born on 11 March 1870; Bridget, born on 17 November 1871; John, born on 1 June 1874 (died 29 June 1877); Michael, born on 10 February 1877; Sarah, born on 22 July 1879 and Honor, born on 11 April 1882.
- Martin Joyce (Máirtín Sheáin Seoighe), aged in his late thirties in August 1882, brother of Myles and Paudeen, released from prison on 24 October

223

1902 and died in March 1906. Martin was a monoglot Irish speaker and illiterate. His wife Jude (original Irish, Siobhán, and variously translated as Julia/Judith) was a sister of John and Patrick Casey and niece of Michael Casey. A civil marriage record exists for Martin and Judith Casey of Derrycasey in 1875; Martin was then 30 years of age and a widower, while his new wife was 27 years old. Surviving birth records include entries for a number of children born to Martin and Jude, including a child, Pat, registered on 14 February 1879, and a daughter, Mary, born on 23 March 1882.

- Paudeen/Pat Joyce (Páidín Sheáin Seoighe), aged around 45 in August 1882, brother of Myles and Martin, released from prison on 24 October 1902. Paudeen was a monoglot Irish speaker and illiterate. He was married to Siobhán (Judy) O'Brien and contemporary sources suggest that they had ten children, including Tom.
- Thomas Patt/Tom Joyce (Tomás Pháidín Sheáin Seoighe), aged around 20 in August 1882, son of Paudeen, nephew of Myles and Martin, and single.[3] He was released from prison on 24 October 1902 and emigrated soon afterwards. Tom may have had some limited competence in English in 1882 and became literate in English while in prison.

The Caseys of Derry
- Michael Casey (Mícheál Ó Cathasaigh), aged about 60 in August 1882, died in Maryborough (Portlaoise) Prison on 22 August 1895. Michael was a monoglot Irish speaker and illiterate; he was married with children.
- John Casey (Seáinín Beag Ó Cathasaigh), nephew of Michael and brother of Patrick, in his mid-thirties in August 1882. John was married with three children. He died in Mountjoy Prison on 27 February 1900. John was a monoglot Irish speaker and illiterate.
- Patrick Casey (Pádraig Shéamuis Ó Cathasaigh), brother of John and nephew of Michael, in his mid-twenties in August 1882, executed on 15 December 1882. Patrick was a bilingual speaker and was illiterate. Patrick Casey was not married and, at the time of the murders, lived at home with his mother Julia Casey.

Pat Joyce, Shanvalleycahill (unrelated to any of the other accused), in his early twenties in August 1882, executed 15 December 1882. Patrick was a bilingual speaker and was able to read and write; he was newly married without children.

The Approvers
- Anthony Philbin of Cappaduff (Antoine Mac Philibín), aged about 40 in August 1882, turned Queen's evidence in November 1882. Philbin was a bilingual speaker and was literate. He was Thomas Casey's brother-in-law. Anthony Philbin married Catherine Quinn, his second wife, in June 1878; the marriage record describes him as a widower of 35 years of age and his wife, a

'spinster (previously unmarried') of 20. In 1882 he had a young son, Stephen, as well as children from his first marriage.

- Thomas Casey of Glensaul (Tomás Ó Cathasaigh), aged in his late thirties in August 1882, turned Queen's evidence in November 1882. Casey was a bilingual speaker and literate. In January 1867, Thomas Casey married Mary Philbin, sister of Anthony; by 1882 they had six children.

III. Chief Crown Witnesses (the 'Maolra' Joyces)

- Anthony (Antoine Mhaolra Seoighe) of Cappanachreha, aged around 50 in August 1882. Anthony was a monoglot Irish speaker in 1882 and recorded as such in the 1901 census.
- John Joyce (Seánín Mhaolra Seoighe) of Derry, in his late fifties in August 1882. John was a monoglot Irish speaker in 1882 and recorded as such in the 1901 census.
- Patrick 'Pat' Joyce (Páidín Mhaolra Seoighe) of Derry, John's son, in his late teens in August 1882. Patrick was a monoglot Irish speaker in 1882, though recorded as bilingual in the 1901 census.
- Mary Joyce (Máire Mhaolra Seoighe) of Derry, John's daughter, aged around 20 in August 1882. Mary was bilingual in 1882 and testified in English at the November trials; she was also recorded as bilingual in the 1901 census.

Prison Records

The fullest surviving descriptions of the ten men accused of the murders come from the contemporary prison registers, in which aspects of their physical appearance were carefully itemized.[4] The records of Galway Jail in August 1882, when the accused men were first committed there, describe each man's age, height, hair and eye colour, and complexion, as well as the trade or occupation, religion and degree of education of each, though not their ability to speak English or Irish. Register entries also exist in relation to the men's stay in Dublin's Kilmainham Jail, from early October to November 1882. Further entries in the Galway prison ledgers in November 1882, recording the men's return from the trials in Dublin, supplement the earlier detail by adding details of weight on admission.

Myles Joyce was described in August 1882 as a 40-year-old farm laborer, 5 feet 5 ½ inches in height, with brown hair, blue eyes, and a sallow complexion; on return to Galway Jail in November 1882, he was recorded as 9 stones 10 lbs. in weight. Myles's brother Martin was also described as 40 years of age, and his brother Paudeen was 45 year of age; both brothers were smaller (5 feet 4 inches in height) but of sturdier build (Martin was 11 stones 8 lbs. in weight, Paudeen was 4 pounds lighter). Paudeen's son Tom (whose name was recorded as Thomas Patt) was recorded as 20 years in age and lighter in weight than his father (10 stones 10 lbs.). All four of the Joyces were described as laborers and Catholics with 'nil' degrees of education.

In the same register, the Casey brothers from Derry, Patrick and John, were described as 26 and 36 years of age respectively, and their uncle Michael as 60 years old. Patrick was 5 feet 4½ inches in height and, in November 1882, 10 stones 13 lbs. in weight; his older brother John was two inches shorter in stature and lighter in weight (9 stones) while their uncle Michael was the sturdiest in build of all the accused (5 feet 6 inches in height, and 12 stones 5 lbs. in weight). As was the case with the Joyce family, all three of the Caseys were listed as laborers and Catholics with 'nil' degrees of education. The eighth accused man, Patrick Joyce of Shanvalleycahill, was, at 23 years of age, the second youngest of the accused, the tallest (5 feet 9 inches in height) but of slight build (9 stones 4 lbs.). He too was listed as a laborer and a Catholic. Patrick Joyce was the only one of the convicted men who was reportedly able to both read and write.

According to the Galway prison register in August 1882, Thomas Casey from Glensaul and Anthony Philbin of Cappaduff were described as 38 and 40 years old respectively. Casey was 5 feet 7 inches in height and Philbin (his brother-in-law) was shorter at 5 feet 3¼ inches. Both men were listed as Catholic, Casey as a laborer and Philbin as a farmer; Casey's degree of education was denoted as 'nil', whereas Philbin was able to read. In the Kilmainham register, the entries for Philbin and Casey's education were significantly different: both men were described as able to read and write (in English) along with Patrick Joyce. The Dublin prison entries for trade and occupation also differed: Philbin was once again described as 'farmer' as were Thomas Casey, Michael Casey and the Joyce brothers Martin and Paudeen, while Myles and Tom Joyce, Patrick Joyce of Shanvalleycahill, and Patrick and John Casey were once again described as labourers.

Appendix II

PARDON

WHEREAS Mr Myles Joyce of Maamtrasna, Co. Galway was convicted before a special jury in Dublin in December 1882 for the murder of Ms. Margaret Joyce and sentenced to death:

AND WHEREAS on the 14th day of December 1882 the said Myles Joyce was refused clemency by John Spencer, the Lord Lieutenant:

AND WHEREAS on the 15th day of December 1882 the said Myles Joyce was executed by hanging in Galway Gaol:

AND WHEREAS upon consideration of a final and authoritative review of the case, carried out at the direction of the Taoiseach, and in light of the conclusion of that review that the conviction in the case was unsafe according to the standards of the time, the Government has accepted the recommendation of the Minister for Justice and Equality that the deficiencies in the conviction warrant the Government advising the President that he exercise his right of pardon:

AND WHEREAS the Government has therefore advised the President to grant to the said Myles Joyce a pardon in respect of the said conviction:

NOW I, MICHAEL D. HIGGINS, President of Ireland, do hereby, on the advice of the Government, pardon the said Myles Joyce in respect of the said conviction, and wholly remit the sentence imposed as if he had not been so charged or convicted.

GIVEN under my Official Seal

This the 4th day of April, 2018

Uachtarán na hÉireann

MAITHIÚNAS

<u>DE BHRÍ</u> gur ciontaíodh an tUasal Maolra Seoighe as Mám Trasna, Co. na Gaillimhe, os comhair giúiré speisialta i mBaile Átha Cliath i mí na Nollag 1882 i ndúnmharú Mhairéad Bean an tSeoighigh agus gur cuireadh pianbhreith bháis air:

<u>AGUS DE BHRÍ</u>, ar an 14ú lá de Nollaig 1882, gur dhiúltaigh John Spencer, Fear Ionaid na Banríona, trócaire don Mhaolra Seoighe sin:

<u>AGUS DE BHRÍ</u>, ar an 15ú lá de Nollaig 1882, gur cuireadh an Maolra Seoighe sin chun báis trína chrochadh i bPríosún na Gaillimhe:

<u>AGUS DE BHRÍ</u>, ar athbhreithniú críochnaitheach údarásach ar an gcás, a rinneadh ar ordachán ón Taoiseach, a bhreithniú, agus i bhfianaise chonclúid an athbhreithnithe sin gur chiontú neamhshábháilte de réir chaighdeáin an ama a bhí sa chiontú sa chás, go bhfuil an Rialtas tar éis glacadh leis an moladh ón Aire Dlí agus Cirt agus Comhionannais go ndlitear leis na heasnaimh sa chiontú go gcomhairleodh an Rialtas don Uachtarán a cheart maithiúnais a fheidhmiú:

<u>AGUS DE BHRÍ</u> go bhfuil an Rialtas, dá bhrí sin, tar éis comhairliú don Uachtarán maithiúnas a thabhairt don Mhaolra Seoighe sin i leith an chiontaithe sin:

<u>ANOIS</u> DÉANAIMSE, MICHEÁL D. Ó hUIGÍNN, Uachtarán na hÉireann, leis seo, ar chomhairle an Rialtais, maithiúnas a thabhairt don Mhaolra Seoighe sin i leith an chiontaithe sin, agus an phianbhreith a forchuireadh air a loghadh go hiomlán amhail is nach rabhthas tar éis é a chúiseamh nó a chiontú amhlaidh.

ARNA THABHAIRT faoi mo Shéala Oifigiúil

An 4ú lá seo d'aibreán, 2018

Uachtarán na hÉireann

NOTES

1 Maamtrasna was later transferred to County Mayo under official adjustments to county boundaries in 1898. A common variant spelling is 'Maumtrasna' and the Irish-language name is *Mám Trasna*.

2 In the aftermath of the murders, a civil engineer employed by the crown prosecution took these measurements.

3 The dying declaration of Patrick (Patsy) Joyce was recorded in the brief assembled by the Crown for its prosecution case: see Crown Briefs, 1882, National Archives, Dublin (hereafter CB, 1882, NA): County Galway-Dublin Commission Court, October 1882. *The Queen vs Anthony Philbin and Others. Murder of the Joyces at Maamtrasna*, p. 46.

4 Testimony by John Joyce to Petty Sessions District of Clonbur, 20 August 1882, CB, 1882, NA, *The Queen vs Anthony Philbin and Others*, p. 15.

5 Detail from deposition by Constable John Johnston, 5 September 1882, CB, 1882, NA, *The Queen vs Anthony Philbin and Others*, p. 7.

6 Variant spellings are used for the boy's name in contemporary coverage (Patsy /Patsey).

7 Variant spellings exist in the official record for many of the townland names e.g. Finny/Finney and Cappanacreha/Cappanacreeha (in Irish *Ceapaigh na Creiche*). The term *ceapach* means 'tillage plot' and *creiche* comes from the Irish word for 'raid' so the placename itself carries a history of violence and dispossession: 'land taken by force'. An alternative interpretation of the placename, given in the 1838 Ordnance Map, is *Ceapa na Croiche* or 'Plot of the Gallows'. See https://www .logainm.ie/. Differing spellings for Patrick Joyce's address, in the trial transcript

and prison registers, include Shanvallycahill and Shanballychoill, both phonetic renderings of the Irish-language placename *Sean Bhaile Chathail* (meaning 'old home of Charles'). See Jarlath Waldron, *Maamtrasna: The Murders and the Mystery* (Dublin, 1992), p. 332; also https://www.logainm.ie/.

8 In the official records, the men's names are sometimes given with the man's first name and the name of his father in brackets, following local practice in Irish of using both a person's first name and that of the person's father in the genitive case, e.g. Thomas Joyce (Pat) to denote *Tomás Pháidín* (Thomas, the son of Pat). His father – formally recorded as 'Patrick (John) Joyce' – would have been known locally as *Páidín Sheáin Seoighe*. For ease of reference and to differentiate the men involved, they will be referred to as 'Tom Joyce' and 'Paudeen Joyce.'

9 See for example *Ballinrobe Chronicle*, 19 August 1882.

10 It is estimated that, between 1879 and 1888, a total of 76 Land War–related fatalities (including seven legal executions) took place; see Marc Mulholland, 'Land war homicides', in Senia Paseta (ed.), *Uncertain Futures: Essays about the Irish Past for Roy Foster* (Oxford, 2016), pp 81–96. Historian Seán Connolly has shown, however, that agrarian violence in the late nineteenth century 'contrary to what is often assumed, accounted for only a small part of total Irish deaths by violence.' In the decade 1871–80, 68 out of 486 murders were classified as agrarian and, also contrary to general perception, only 24 per cent of these involved attacks on landlords or their servants; 32 per cent related to disputes within families and 32 per cent between neighbours or between tenants and sub-tenants. See Seán Connolly, 'Unnatural deaths in four nations: Contrasts and comparisons', in Seán Connolly (ed.), *Kingdoms United? Great Britain and Ireland since 1500: Integration and Diversity* (Dublin, 1999), p. 207. See also Ian O'Donnell, 'Lethal violence in Ireland, 1841 to 2003', in *British Journal of Criminology*, 2005, 45, pp 671–95. My thanks to Professor Ian O'Donnell for these references.

11 Myles Dungan's chapter on the Maamtrasna trials (which he discusses as one of seven key Irish political trials) is a valuable overview and includes extracts from Lord Lieutenant Spencer's contemporary correspondence; see Myles Dungan, *Conspiracy: Irish Political Trials* (Dublin, 2009).

12 My models here, in seeking to tell the larger story of significant social change through a micro-history, include from Irish examples such works as Angela Bourke's splendid *The Burning of Bridget Cleary: A True Story* (London, 1999) and Terence Dooley's compelling *The Murders at Wildgoose Lodge* (Dublin, 2007). Key international models include Natalie Zemon–Davis's influential *The Return of Martin Guerre* (Cambridge, 1983) and Janet Malcolm, *Iphigenia in Forest Hills: Anatomy of a Murder Trial* (CT, 2011), the latter is of particular relevance given its contemporary subject of a murder trial and the continuing limits of legal interpretation and linguistic understanding.

13 Following general practice in sociolinguistics, I use 'monoglot' to denote an

individual who is capable of speaking only a single language and 'monolingual' to refer to an individual or community that uses only one language.

14 According to contemporary prison records and newspaper accounts, Myles Joyce was about 40 years of age in 1882. See Irish Prison Registers, 1790–1924: General Prisons Register, Galway Gaol, August 1882; accessible at https://www.findmypast.ie/.

15 The census of 1881 listed a total of nine counties in which over 20 per cent of the population could speak Irish: these ranged from Limerick (20.8 per cent) to Galway (64.9 per cent) and also included (in ascending order) Sligo, Donegal, Cork, Clare, Kerry, Waterford and Mayo (Census of Ireland, 1881: *General Report*, PP 1882 [3365], p. 14). See Brian Ó Cuív, 'Irish language and literature, 1845–1921', in W. E. Vaughan (ed.), *A New History of Ireland Volume VI: Ireland under the Union, II, 1870–1921* (Oxford, 1996), pp 385–435. Gearóid Ó Tuathaigh's contribution to the Famine Folio series offers a rich overview: '*I mBéal an Bháis': The Great Famine and the Language Shift in Nineteenth-Century Ireland*, *Famine Folios* series (CT and Cork, 2015).

16 The figure of monoglot speakers in Connaught given by the *1881 General Report* is 33,335.

17 The term 'monolingual *habitus*' is taken from the work of Ingrid Gogolin and describes the 'deep-seated habit of assuming monolingualism as the norm in a nation'; see her article 'The "Monolingual *Habitus*" as the common feature in teaching in the language of the majority in different countries', in *Per Linguam*, 2013, 13:2, pp 38–49.

18 Monica Heller, 'Bilingualism as ideology and practice', in Monica Heller (ed.), *Bilingualism: A Social Approach*, Palgrave Advances in Linguistics (Houndmills, UK, 2007), pp 2, 13. Key discussions of Irish bilingualism include Máirtín Ó Murchú, *Urlabhra agus Pobal: Language and Community* (Baile Átha Cliath, 1970), on its implications for language policy, and Liam Mac Mathúna's literary study, *Béarla sa Ghaeilge. Cabhair Choigríche: An Códmheascadh Gaeilge/Béarla i Litríocht na Gaeilge 1600–1900* (Dublin, 2007).

19 Heller, 'Bilingualism as ideology and practice', p. 2.

20 Jan Blommaert, *The Sociolinguistics of Globalization* (Cambridge, 2010), p. 180.

21 Ibid., p. 197.

22 Ibid., p. 103.

23 Richard Howard (ed.), Richard Howard and Annette Lavers (trans.) Roland Barthes, *Mythologies*, new edn., (1957: New York, 2012), p. 49.

CHAPTER I

1 Patrick S. Dinneen, *Foclóir Gaedhilge agus Béarla: An Irish-English Dictionary*, new edn (Dublin, 1927), p. 705.

2 In a later deposition, recorded on 5 September, Constable Johnston named these men as 'John Joyce, Michael Joyce, John O'Brien, Tom O'Brien (Dan),

Nicholas O'Brien, Michael O'Brien, John Collins, Martin Collins, Patrick Lydon, Peter Lydon, and Andrew Joyce, all of whom live at Maamtrasna in the county of Galway.' His deposition, along with testimonies by other eyewitnesses to the scene and the dying declarations of the Joyce boys, were preserved in the crown prosecution brief: see Crown Briefs, 1882, National Archives, Dublin (hereafter CB, 1882, NA): County Galway–Dublin Commission Court, October 1882, *The Queen vs Anthony Philbin and Others. Murder of the Joyces at Maamtrasna*, p. 8.

3 According to the Royal Irish Constabulary (hereafter RIC) list and directory for the six months of July to December 1882, sunrise on Friday, 18 August, was at 4.46 a.m.; sunset the previous evening was at 7.22 p.m. and the moon rose at 8.49 p.m. on 17 August.

4 Deposition by John Collins to the inquest held at Maamtrasna, 19 August, CB, 1882, NA, *The Queen vs Anthony Philbin and Others*, p. 2.

5 RIC service records suggest that John Johnston (service number 42920) entered the police service in 1877 at the age of 17 and was posted to Kilafin, Gort (Galway West Riding district). In the early 1880s he appeared regularly as complainant in the Galway petty sessions. He retired in 1910 at sergeant rank. Lenihan's biography is more difficult to trace: the records show a Thomas Lenihan (service number 40086) who was stationed in Mayo between 1874 and 1882. See RIC Service Records (hereafter RIC SR), 1816–1922, http://www.findmypast.co.uk.

6 Variant spellings are given for the constable and sub-constable's names but, checking against constabulary records, the correct names are 'Johnston' and 'Lenihan.' RIC SR, 1816–1922, http://www.findmypast.co.uk.

7 Deposition by Constable John Johnston to the inquest held at Maamtrasna, 19 August, CB, 1882, NA, *The Queen vs Anthony Philbin and Others*, pp 2–3.

8 This is a mistranslation from the interpreter: Michael's original words may have been *an lá roimhe* (day previous) or *arú inné* (the day before yesterday). Tuesday, 15 August, was a Catholic holy day (the Feast of the Assumption of the Blessed Virgin Mary) which required Mass attendance.

9 Dying declaration of Michael Joyce, taken 18 August 1882, CB, 1882, NA, *The Queen vs Anthony Philbin and Others*, p. 24. John O'Brien was one of the 11 men who reported the crime to the RIC men in Finny. Neither he nor Malley were among those suspected of the murders.

10 The Irish word for 'married', *pósta*, can also mean 'closely united'.

11 Dying declaration of Patrick (Patsy) Joyce, taken 18 August 1882, CB, 1882, NA, *The Queen vs Anthony Philbin and Others*, p. 46. In two instances, the original language of the boy's testimony is preserved and these two untranslated nouns 'kippeen' (*cipíní* referring to the sticks of bog deal) and 'boneens' (*báinín*, the term for a jacket made of homespun woollen cloth) are rendered in quotation marks in the surviving transcript.

12 I am indebted to Breandán Mac Suibhne for his insights here, and elsewhere; see his *The End of Outrage: Post-Famine Adjustment in Rural Ireland* (Oxford, 2017), pp 147–9. For a useful survey of the historic origins of this legal exception, and a discussion of its contemporary status, see the Irish Law Reform Commission's consultation paper *Hearsay in Civil and Criminal Cases*, LRC CP 60–2010 (Dublin, 2010). The commission 'provisionally' recommended that dying declarations as an existing inclusionary exception be retained, p. 169.

13 Deposition by Andrew (Andy) Joyce to the inquest held at Maamtrasna, 19 August, CB, 1882, NA, *The Queen vs Anthony Philbin and Others*, p. 2.

14 The Chief Secretary's Office Registered Papers, National Archives (hereafter CSORP, NA), document the interactions between the Lord Lieutenant (in 1882, Earl Spencer), the Chief Secretary for Ireland (in 1882, George Otto Trevelyan), the Dublin Castle administration and the British state. Two distinct officers represented the British state in Ireland at this period: the Lord Lieutenant or Viceroy, who ordinarily did not sit at cabinet, and the Chief Secretary who, while nominally subordinate to the Lord Lieutenant, was the government officer with responsibility for Ireland and answered to parliament. Due to the weakness of Trevelyan as Chief Secretary, Spencer effectively combined both roles for much of his second tenure as Lord Lieutenant (1882–1885). My thanks to Martin Maguire for this information.

15 The brief was prepared by Bolton and his colleagues for the opening of the murder trials at Dublin Commission Court and was completed in October. See CB, 1882, NA, *The Queen vs Anthony Philbin and Others. Murder of the Joyces at Maamtrasna.* p. 46.

16 *Freeman's Journal* (hereafter *FJ*), 21 August 1882.

17 Ibid.

18 Ibid. In the second instance, the transliteration of the Irish-language word was misprinted as 'more'.

19 Record of post-mortem examinations by Dr John Hegarty, Surgeon H. J. Tugham and Coroner C. G. Cottingham, Maamtrasna, 19 August, CB, 1882, NA, *The Queen vs Anthony Philbin and Others*, pp 3–4.

20 *FJ*, 21 August 1882.

21 Ms 236, Coimisiún Béaloideasa Éireann (hereafter CBÉ), ll, pp 176–9. Spellings have not been standardised.

22 My translation: 'Well they went out, outside the door then, and they stood outside the door. And the old woman asked the young woman – who was his wife – his mother asked the woman if she recognised the men who did the murder. And she said that she recognised each and every one of them. The men returned inside then, they murdered them all except for one young lad who hid himself in a barrel.'

23 Ms 931, CBÉ, ll, pp 3–9, 45–7. Spellings have not been standardised. Ó Duithche's account also includes details of the questioning of locals, including

that of his own father, and the story of a local man who was exonerated by the officials because of a local policeman's testimony that the man had eaten a large breakfast: *"Ní íosfat sé" adeir sé "'an feed' a d'ith sé, dhá mbeadh aon 'skill' insa 'murdar aige."* My translation: 'The officer asked him [the local policeman] how did he come to know that. He wouldn't eat the feed that he did eat if, he said, he'd had any "skill" in the murder' [policeman's reply].

24 Waldron gives two Irish translations: *Loch an Fuaiche* (which is the more common translation, meaning 'lake of the winnowing winds') and *Loch na Fuaithe* (which he translates as 'the lake of the hatred'). See Jarlath Waldron, *Maamtrasna: The Murders and the Mystery* (Dublin, 1992), p. 10.

25 Waldron, *Maamtrasna*, pp 9–10. For Dunlop's comment, see his memoir *Fifty Years of Irish Journalism* (London and Dublin, 1911), p. 60.

26 Convict Reference Files (hereafter CRF) (1902), J13, folder 23; CSORP, NA. This large box of files, newly conserved and arranged in 31 folders, is known as 'The Maamtrasna file' and includes many of the prison records and memorials relating to the Maamtrasna accused up to 1902, as well as correspondence between the Chief Secretary's Office and local RIC officials from 1882 to 1884. It also contains many documents related to the lead-up to the executions in December 1882 and an internal inquiry requested by the Lord Lieutenant's Office in 1884, following Thomas Casey's 'confession.' Folder 29 in the file contains the full trial transcript.

27 CRF (1902), J13, folder 23; CSORP, NA.

28 *Galway Vindicator*, 19 August 1882.

29 This contemporary rendition, 'Maam Trasna', was a rare acknowledgement of the place name's two-word Irish origin, *Mám Trasna*.

30 *Ballinrobe Chronicle* (hereafter *BC*), 19 August 1882.

31 *Galway Express*, 19 August 1882.

32 In his memoir of the trial (published in 1887), Bolton accounted for the murders as follows: 'enough transpired to satisfy us that an extensive secret Society existed in the district; and it was stated that John Joyce was treasurer to the local branch, and was accused of having applied some £11 of the funds to his own use and that, when pressed for the money, he threatened to give information to the police' (in relation to the Huddy murder). Bolton also cited the local supposition that Joyce's mother had already given information, based on a recent newspaper report of an 'old woman residing on the mountain overlooking Lough Mask, who, when gathering firewood, saw the bodies thrown into the lake. The description of this woman corresponded with that of old Mrs Joyce, who, just before the bodies were found, had been living with one of her sons at a place commanding a full view of the lake.' See George Bolton, *A Short Account of the Discovery and Conviction of the 'Invincibles' and of Some Trials of Which the Writer Had Charge in 1881, 1882, 1883 and 1884 with a Few Observations on Preliminary Investigations in Criminal Cases* (Dublin,

1887), pp 34–5.

33 Andrew Dunlop, *Fifty Years of Irish Journalism*, (London and Dublin, 1911), p. 182–91. See Felix Larkin, 'Green shoots of the new journalism in the *Freeman's Journal* 1877–1890', in Karen Steele and Michael de Nie (eds), *Ireland and the New Journalism* (New York and London, 2014), pp 35–55; here Larkin persuasively argues for a new departure in the *FJ*'s social reporting, commencing with William O'Brien's reports of rural poverty in County Tipperary in 1877–8.

34 Two days later, on Wednesday, Dunlop and fellow journalists returned to the scene of the murder for the purposes of attending the adjourned inquest but on their return visit they travelled by car to Clonbur, then travelled by boat 'rowed by two stalwart peasants, up the southern inlet of Lough Mask' and landed at Finney from where they had a 'stiff walk' of several miles 'including the crossing of the mountain ridge', Dunlop, *Fifty Years of Irish Journalism*, p. 191. See Chris Morash's engaging discussion of Dunlop in his article 'Ghosts and wires: The telegraph and Irish space', in Steele and de Nie (eds), *Ireland and the New Journalism*, p. 25.

35 The Wheatstone Universal Electric Telegraph was patented in 1858 and recorded telegram text on a punched tape in Morse code. The instrument consisted of a perforator which punched the tape holes and grouped them in combinations of code, a transmitter which converted them into electrical signals, and a receiver which received the signals and noted them on paper.

36 Dunlop, *Fifty Years*, p. 188.

37 Ibid., pp 188–9.

38 *FJ*, 21 August 1882. This article, published on Monday, seems to have also featured contributions from journalist Edward 'Doc' Byrne, who, according to Waldron, was on holiday in nearby Ballinrobe at the time. Byrne had worked as editor for the *Belfast Morning News* and would become editor of the *Freeman's Journal* in 1884. This was the article that highlighted issues relating to the treatment of Irish-language testimony at the coroner's inquest, as discussed: nuances much more likely to be captured by the Tuam-born Byrne than the Scottish-born Dunlop. See Waldron, *Maamtrasna*, p. 34.

39 These ages for Michael and Margaret (Peggy) are at odds with the post-mortem records that estimated Michael's age as about 17 and Peggy's as about 14. Other records suggest that Patrick (Patsy) was aged eight at the time of the murders.

40 *FJ*, 21 August 1882.

41 Ibid., 22 August 1882.

42 *Daily Express* (hereafter *DE*), 21 August 1882.

43 *FJ*, 22 August 1882. The *DE* continued its interest in Patsy's fate, reporting on Wednesday that he 'is happily, gradually though slowly recovering' but not such as 'to enable him to do more than articulate a single word or two at a

time'. See *DE*, 23 August 1881.

44 The graveyard is named in *FJ*, 22 August 1882, as 'Crooka Chample' (Chapel Hill).

45 *DE*, 23 August 1881.

46 In nineteenth-century law, an 'information' had the specific legal meaning of 'a complaint, before a magistrate, that a crime had been committed'; see W. E. Vaughan, *Murder Trials in Ireland, 1836–1914* (Dublin, 2009), p. 60. On the distinction between 'deposition' and 'information', Vaughan writes: 'The word "information" tended to be used indiscriminately to describe all sworn statements made before magistrates and coroners but there was in fact a difference between "depositions" and "informations": the term "information" is applied to the statement grounding the charge, taken in the absence of the accused; the term "deposition" means each written and sworn statement taken at the inquiry in the presence of the accused', p. 80.

47 Anthony Joyce's information is signed with an x as his mark (a signature is not specified in the case of John's), and a footnote to both documents record that they were taken in the presence of Gardiner 'having been first duly read and interpreted to the witness, who is an Irish-speaking one, and the interpreter having been first duly sworn.' CB, 1882, NA, *The Queen vs Anthony Philbin and Others*, p. 11.

48 Ibid. Information given by Anthony Joyce, Finny, 19 August 1882.

49 Ibid.

50 The Irish term *sráid* means both street and village (*sráidbhaile*).

51 CB, 1882, NA, *The Queen vs Anthony Philbin and Others*, p. 11.

52 Information given by John Joyce, Finny, 19 August 1882, CB, 1882, NA, *The Queen vs Anthony Philbin and Others*, p. 15.

53 Ibid., p. 15.

54 Ibid., pp 12–14, 16–19.

55 The image appeared on the cover of the *Illustrated Police News*, 25 November 1882, soon after the conclusion of the trials.

56 Special (Parnell) Commission: 1888–9, a verbatim copy of the Parnell Commission Report, vols I–XI evidence, I, pp 1–5; National Library of Ireland.

57 Ibid.

58 Ibid.

59 Ibid., p. 28–30.

60 *Congested Districts Board for Ireland Baseline Reports* (Dublin, 1892–8): 'Partry', pp 385–91; 'Joyce Country', pp 439–42.

61 *Congested Districts Board for Ireland Baseline Reports*: 'Partry', pp 385–91.

62 Ibid., p. 389.

63 Ibid., pp 439–42.

64 *Belfast Newsletter*, 16 December 1882.

65 Ibid.

66 *Census of Ireland, 1881,* part 1, vol. IV (hereafter *CI, 1881,* 1.IV), pp 170–9, 181–8.

67 The only parish in Galway to have a higher percentage of illiteracy was Ballinrobe (83.2 per cent) while the neighbouring parish of Ross (which included the townland Maamtrasna) was not far behind at 73.4 per cent. *CI, 1881,* 1.IV, pp 181–8.

68 Of the 66 men in the Ballinchalla parish who were aged 40 and upwards (a cohort which included some of the accused men), 55 were illiterate, three could read and write, and 8 could read only; of the 64 women aged 40 and upwards, one could read and write, one could read only, and 62 were illiterate. Of Ballinchalla's population of 530 people, 524 persons were Catholic and six were Protestant Episcopalian. Three out of the four Protestant males could read and write and one was illiterate; the two recorded Protestant females could read and write. Of the 524 Roman Catholics recorded, 15 men and 12 women were able to read and write; 42 men and 32 women could read only; and 200 men and 223 women (together comprising 81 per cent of the local Catholic population) were illiterate. *CI, 1881,* 1.IV, p. 170.

69 Mac Suibhne's illuminating micro-study *The End of Outrage* (2017) takes as its subject a comparable example from 1850s west Donegal.

70 *Congested Districts Board for Ireland Baseline Reports,* pp 443.

71 John Henry Ryan (1846–1929) studied engineering in TCD and, following graduation, worked for a decade as a railway engineer in the United States. On his return to Ireland in 1880, he set up a private practice in Dublin and became one of the leading Irish consulting engineers of the day; he was chief engineer to a number of large railway projects in Ireland (Tralee and Dingle railway, west Kerry railway) and the United States (Hudson's Bay and Pacific railway). See *Dictionary of Irish Architects, 1720–1940* (Dublin, 2018), https://www.dia.ie/.

72 The map is included in CRF (1902), J13, folder 28; CSORP, NA.

73 *FJ,* 21 August 1882.

74 Spencer to Queen Victoria, 18 September 1882, Althorp Papers, Add 76831, British Library.

75 Statement of Honor Joyce, 28 August 1882, CB, 1882, NA, *The Queen vs Anthony Philbin and Others,* p. 34.

76 Deposition by Constable John Johnston, 5 September 1882, CB, 1882, NA, *The Queen vs Anthony Philbin and Others,* pp 7–8.

77 Family names are very helpfully differentiated in Seán Ó Cuirreáin, *Éagóir: Maolra Seoighe agus Dúnmharuithe Mhám Trasna* (Baile Átha Cliath, 2016), pp 36–40.

78 During the trial, Ryan calculated this distance to be 'about 114 or 120 yards'. See *The Dublin October Commission. 13th November, 1882. County of Galway. The Maumtrasna Massacre,* trial transcript, p. 8; contained in CRF (1902), J13, folder 29: CSORP, NA. The townland of Derry comprised three villages: Derrycasey

(or *Barr na gCathasach*, reputedly named as such because of the many inhabitants named Casey), Derrypark, and Bunachrick (or *Bun an Chnoic*, meaning 'bottom of the hill'); Waldron, *Maamtrasna*, p. 28.

79 It would appear from the Crown Brief that 'Big' John Casey was briefly questioned by the local police in late August. In his information he acknowledged that there was a history of bad relations between him and the murdered man. He also stated that he had not gone to the wake or funeral: 'I did not go look at the murdered people at all'. CB, 1882, NA, *The Queen vs Anthony Philbin and Others*, p. 33.

80 Ryan measured the distance between the home of the murdered Joyces and that of Anthony Joyce as two and a quarter miles. The houses of the two other accused, Anthony Philbin and Thomas Casey, lie outside the map area in Cappaduff and Glensaul (Glensaul being approximately four miles from the scene of the murders). See evidence tendered by Ryan, *The Dublin October Commission*, pp 7–9.

81 Tim Harrington, *The Maamtrasna Massacre: Impeachment of the Trials* (Dublin, 1884), p. 12: 'But the strangest fact of all, perhaps, is this – that the house of the murdered family was in the middle of a row of some ten houses, extending along the path or "street," as one of the witnesses called it, and these houses are nearly all occupied by Joyces and O'Briens, cousins of the murdered man and his wife.'

82 Ibid.

83 Their Catholic parish was Kilbride/Finny.

84 The population of Maamtrasna townland was 94 in the pre-Famine census of 1841 and fell to 78 persons in 1851; it then rose gradually in later decades to 88 in 1861, 103 in 1871, and 108 in 1881. See *Census of Ireland, 1881, Part 1, Areas, Houses and Population: also the ages, civil or conjugal condition, occupations, birthplaces, religion, and education of the people.*, vol. IV. Province of Connaught (hereafter *CI, 1881, 1, AHP*) (Dublin, 1882), p. 104.

85 In 1881 the parish of Ballinchalla comprised 98 houses, with a population of 530 and valuation of £150 and 13 shillings. See *CI, 1881, 1, AHP*, p. 101.

86 The townland of Derry experienced a sharp decrease in population in the famine period, from 227 in 1841 to 132 in 1851, but then rose swiftly to 223 in 1861 (222 in 1871), and finally exceeded its pre-Famine population in 1881 (241 inhabitants). Ibid.

87 *Griffith's Valuation: Primary Valuation of Tenements*, (1847–1864), Parish of Ross, p. 104, http://www.askaboutireland.ie/griffith-valuation, 20 January 2017. The cancelled valuation books are available for viewing at the Valuation Office, Irish Life Centre, Dublin. My thanks to Brigid Clesham and Joanne McEntee for these references.

88 In 1865 a Landed Estates Court conveyance records the transfer of Maumtrasna and Glenbeg East and West, part of the estate of the assignees of James Knox

Gildea, to the Earl of Leitrim for £2,620, subject to the right of the tenants of Maumtrasna and Glenbeg East to cut turf, for their own use only, on the 1,373 acres of common or mountain of Maumtrasna for the duration of their tenancies. See listing in A. P. W. Malcolmson, *The Clements Archive* (Dublin, 2010), p. C/2, 8 June 1865.

89 Cancelled Valuation Book (1866–1923), Maumtrasna (townland), Ross (parish), Ross (barony), Owenbrin (electoral division), Ballinrobe (union), Mayo (county); Valuation Office, Irish Life Centre, Dublin (hereafter CVB, Maumtrasna).

90 A civil death record exists for a 59-year-old widow named Catherine Joyce of 'Montrassna' who died on 2 March 1870; the informant being John Joyce, a householder of 'Montrassna'. These and other parish records (birth and baptismal, marriage and death) have been accessed through the online gene-alogical sources, https://www.findmypast.ie/ and http://www.rootsireland.ie.

91 John Joyce's neighbour Michael O'Brien, for example, held a lease for nine acres but with a land valuation of £2 3s. Joyce's valuation consisted of £1 8s. for land and 7s for buildings. See CVB, Maumtrasna.

92 Witnesses to John Joyce and Bridget O'Brien's marriage were Hubert J. McNally and Mary Sarsfield. The civil record of their marriage can be accessed at http://www.rootsireland.ie.

93 Civil records provide details of the death of a 35-year-old woman called Mary Joyce, wife of John Joyce of 'Maarntrassa' [*sic*], on 20 April 1874, who may be John's wife and mother of his four children. A baptismal record for Patrick Joyce, son of John Joyce and Mary O'Brien, dated 17 February 1874, is likely to be that for Patsy and this would suggest that Mary died within months of his birth. Civil death records and church baptismal records can be accessed at http://www.rootsireland.ie. My warm thanks to Gemma Kelleher for her invaluable assistance.

94 A civil death record exists for Daniel O'Brien of 'Montrassa' [*sic*], Bridget's first husband, who died on 10 March 1874, aged 75. See http://www.rootsire-land.ie.

95 See, for example, *FJ*, 21 August 1882.

96 Here I differ from Waldron who also describes John Joyce as having lived without a holding of his own prior to his second marriage; Waldron, *Maamtrasna*, p. 30.

97 CVB, Maumtrasna.

98 In 1891 the leaseholder's name was changed to Thomas O'Brien and in 1895 to 'John J. Joyce (Michael)', who continued to hold the lease in records dated 1909; in 1923 the lease for the same holding was held by a Bridget Joyce. See CVB, Maumtrasna.

99 Ibid.

100 This lease had been transferred to him in 1874 and had formerly been held

by Patrick Lydon, who was likely the father of Myles's wife, Bridget Lydon. In 1890 the lease was transferred to a Thomas Joyce. See CVB, Maumtrasna and CVB (1866-1923), Cappanacreha (townland), Ballinachalla (parish), Ross (barony).

101 Waldron, *Maamtrasna*, pp 28–9. The implications of these land 'striping' events in 1866, in which pieces of land had been taken from some of the sons of Shaun Joyce and given to Anthony and John, sons of Maolra Joyce, bear suggestive comparison with the consequences of land-squaring compellingly described by Breandán Mac Suibhne in *The End of Outrage* (2017).

102 Waldron, *Maamtrasna*, p. 27.

103 Ibid., p. 40; see an account of the Clonbur petty sessions case published by the *BC*, 30 October 1880. Myles' place of birth and address in the 1880 jail register are given as 'Fair Hill', the literal English-language translation for *An Fhairce* or Clonbur village.

104 Harrington, *The Maamtrasna Massacre*, p. 26.

105 CB, 1882, NA, *The Queen vs Anthony Philbin and Others*, p. 33. Casey also stated that he had not gone to the wake or funeral: 'I did not go look at the murdered people at all'.

106 *FJ*, 9 September 1884. I am greatly indebted to Johnny Joyce, great-grandson of John Joyce, for this reference and his generous assistance.

107 Ibid.

CHAPTER 2

1 Lady Morgan (Sydney Owenson), *The O'Briens and the O'Flahertys: A National Tale* (London, 1827, 1988), p. 402.

2 See Brian Ó Cuív, 'Irish language and literature, 1845–1921', in W. E. Vaughan (ed.), *A New History of Ireland Volume VI: Ireland under the Union, II, 1870–1921* (Oxford, 1996), pp 385–435, and Garret FitzGerald, 'The decline of the Irish language, 1771–1871', in Mary Daly and David Dickson (eds), *The Origins of Popular Literacy in Ireland* (Dublin, 1990), pp 59–72.

3 *Census of Ireland* (hereafter *CI*), 1891, part II, General Report (hereafter GR), pp 72–3.

4 *CI, 1881*, part II, GR, pp 73–4.

5 *CI, 1881*, part I, vol. IV, Province of Connaught (Dublin, 1882), p. 188.

6 Important exceptions to this neglect include the work of historians Niall Ó Ciosáin and Gearóid Ó Tuathaigh, and Liam Mac Mathúna's enlightening study of Irish and English code-mixing in Irish-language literature: Liam Mac Mathúna, *Béarla sa Ghaeilge. Cabhair Choigríche: An Códmheascadh Gaeilge/Béarla i Litríocht na Gaeilge 1600–1900* (Dublin, 2007). In his 2005 article 'Gaelic culture and language shift,' Ó Ciosáin called for 'a more detailed ethnography of language use' – what historian Gearóid Ó Tuathaigh has suggestively termed the lost 'acoustic imprint' of nineteenth-century

Ireland. Niall Ó Ciosáin, 'Gaelic culture and language shift', in Laurence Geary and Margaret Kelleher (eds), *Nineteenth-Century Ireland: A Guide to Recent Research* (Dublin, 2005), p. 141; personal conversation with Professor Gearóid Ó Tuathaigh. See also Gearóid Ó Tuathaigh, *'I mBéal an Bháis': The Great Famine and the Language Shift in Nineteenth-Century Ireland*, Famine Folios series (CT and Cork, 2015); and James Kelly and Ciarán Mac Murchaidh (eds), *Irish and English: Essays on the Irish Linguistic and Cultural Frontier, 1600–1900* (Dublin, 2012). Nicholas Wolf's valuable work has greatly illuminated the continuing use of Irish in a public sphere in the late eighteenth and nineteenth centuries: see Nicholas Wolf, *An Irish-Speaking Island: State, Religion, Community, and the Linguistic Landscape in Ireland, 1770–1870* (Wisconsin, 2014), discussed in more detail later. Aidan Doyle's chapter in the *Cambridge History of Ireland* provides a general survey, though more informative on the historical complexities of literacy than of language in the period: Aidan Doyle, 'Language and literacy in the eighteenth and nineteenth centuries', in James Kelly (ed.), *Cambridge History of Ireland* (Cambridge, 2018), pp 353–79. For a useful overview on the history of the Irish language, see Vincent Morley's contribution to Richard Bourke and Ian McBride (eds), *Princeton History of Modern Ireland* (Princeton, 2016), pp 320–42.

7 William Wilde, *Irish Popular Superstitions* (Dublin, 1852).

8 Ibid., p. 27.

9 For example Diarmuid Ó Giolláin, *Locating Irish Folklore: Tradition, Modernity, Identity* (Cork, 2000), p. 17.

10 Wilde, *Irish Popular Superstitions*, p. 27.

11 See Ríonach Uí Ogáin's biography, *Immortal Dan: Daniel O'Connell in Irish Folk Tradition* (Dublin, 1995); Wolf, *An Irish-Speaking Island*, p. 177.

12 Monica Heller, 'Bilingualism as ideology and practice', in Heller (ed.), *Bilingualism: A Social Approach: Palgrave Advances in Linguistics* (Basingstoke, 2007), p. 13.

13 Niall Ó Ciosáin, *Print and Popular Culture in Ireland, 1750–1850* (Hampshire, 1997), p. 6. Máirtín Ó Murchú's working paper *Urlabhra agus Pobal: Language and Community* (Baile Átha Cliath, 1970) focuses on the implications of a diglossia approach for language policy. For a useful critique of the term 'diglossia' as applied to nineteenth-century Irish society, see Wolf, *An Irish-Speaking Island*, pp 44–7. Wolf's critique is in turn disputed in part by Ó Ciosáin: Niall Ó Ciosáin, 'Gaelic and Catholic: Review of *Irish-speaking Ireland*', in *Dublin Review of Books*, July 2015, 69, http://drb.ie.

14 *Census of Ireland for the Year 1851. Part VI. General Report*, PP 1856 [2134], (Dublin, 1856), p. xlvi.

15 John Windele, 'Present extent of the Irish language', in *Ulster Journal of Archaeology*, 1854, 5, pp 243–5.

16 Whitley Stokes, *Projects for Re-establishing the Internal Peace and Tranquillity*

of Ireland (Dublin, 1799), p. 45.

17 Daniel Dewar, *Observations on the Character, Customs, and Superstitions of the Irish; and on some of the causes which have retarded the moral and political improvement of Ireland* (London, 1812), p. 88; see discussion of the circulation of Dewar's observations by the Baptist Irish Society in Pádraig de Brún, *Scriptural Instruction in the Vernacular: The Irish Society and Its Teachers, 1818– 1827* (Dublin, 2009), pp 10–12.

18 Wolf, *An Irish-Speaking Island*, p. 3.

19 Garret FitzGerald, 'Estimates for baronies of minimum level of Irish-speaking amongst successive decennial cohorts, 1771–1781 to 1861–1871', in *Proceedings of the Royal Irish Academy*, 1984, 84, pp 117–55; Garret FitzGerald, 'Irish-speaking in the pre-Famine period: A study based on the 1911 census data for people born before 1851 and and still alive in 1911', in *Proceedings of the Royal Irish Academy*, 2003, 103C, pp 191–283.

20 Garret FitzGerald, 'Estimates for baronies', p. 126.

21 Ibid., pp 127–8. Linking these trends to the lives of the Maamtrasna accused, Myles Joyce was born sometime between 1837 and 1842. According to 1881 census information for the barony of Ross, of Myles Joyce's cohort of men aged 40 and under 50, 121 were monoglot Irish speakers and 185 were bilingual; 232 women of the same age were monoglot and 153 bilingual. *CI, 1881*, part I, vol. IV, p. 181.

22 James Kelly, 'Introduction', in Kelly and Mac Murchaidh (eds), *Irish and English*, p. 38.

23 FitzGerald, 'Estimates for baronies', p. 121.

24 '*Dátheangachas forleathan pobail a spreag an macarónachus abhus agus ba chomhartha é ar chlaochlú ó bhonn a bheith tagtha ar an suíomh sochtheangeolaíochta*' ('It was widespread public bilingualism that generated this macaronic writing, a sign of the fundamental transformation that had taken place in the socio-linguistic scene'); see Mac Mathúna, *Béarla sa Ghaeilge*, p. 217, pp 187–8 (Chapter 5).

25 E. Ronayne, *Ronayne's Reminiscences* (Chicago, 1900). For a fascinating discussion of Ronaye's life, see Kerby A. Miller and Ellen Skerrett, with Bridget Kelly, 'Walking backward to Heaven?: Edmund Ronayne's pilgrimage in famine Ireland and gilded age America', in Enda Delaney and Breandán Mac Suibhne (eds), *Ireland's Great Famine and Popular Politics* (New York, 2016), pp 80–141.

26 Ronayne, *Ronayne's Reminiscences*, p. 27.

27 Ibid., p. 35.

28 Ibid., pp 41–2.

29 Ibid., p. 297.

30 Ibid., pp 320–1.

31 For more information on Ó Súilleabháin's biography, see Desmond McCabe's

entry in *Dictionary of Irish Biography* VII (Dublin and Cambridge, 2009), pp 953–5. The original manuscript of the diary is held by the Royal Irish Academy.

32 Proinsias Ó Drisceoil, '*Cín Lae Amhlaoibh*: Modernization and the Irish language', in Jim Kelly (ed.), *Ireland and Romanticism: Publics, Nations and Scenes of Cultural Production* (Basingstoke, 2011), p. 17.

33 Siobhán Kilfeather, 'Terrific register: The gothicization of atrocity in Irish romanticism', in *Boundary 2*, 2004, 31:1, pp 49–71.

34 Lesa Ní Mhungaile, 'Bilingualism, print culture in Irish and the public sphere', in Kelly and Mac Murchaidh, *Irish and English*, p. 221; Ní Mhungaile quotes from Vincent Morley, *Irish Opinion and the American Revolution* (Cambridge, 2002), p. 2. See also his more recent *The Popular Mind in Eighteenth-Century Ireland* (Cork, 2017).

35 Ó Drisceoil, '*Cín Lae Amhlaoibh*: Modernization and the Irish language', p. 13.

36 Irish-language quotations are taken from Tomás de Bhaldraithe, *Cín Lae Amhlaoibh*, abridged edn (Dublin, 1970); English-language translations are from Michael McGrath's edition for the Irish Texts Society (London, 1936–7), volumes XXX–XXXIII. Quoted text: de Bhaldraithe, p. 9; McGrath, I, p. 55, 14 May 1827. 'Suaidléirí' is a derogatory Irish-language term for Methodists.

37 McGrath, I, p. 51, 11 May 1827, footnote 1, and quoted by Ó Drisceoil, '*Cín Lae Amhlaoibh*: Modernization and the Irish language', p. 20; the manuscript addition is not included by de Bhaldraithe.

38 De Bhaldraithe, pp 84–5; McGrath, III, p. 33.

39 De Bhaldraithe, p. 101; McGrath, III, p. 165. The Ballyhale assembly and its relation to the 'Carrigshock incident' of 1831 are discussed by Gary Owens in *Cultural and Social History*, 2004, 1, pp 36–64.

40 De Bhaldraithe, p. 90. Translation of Irish: 'A fine, sunny, thinclouded, calm day. The Shelloe and the Keating children left my school. I closed it. I have now no school'; from McGrath, III, p. 73.

41 De Bhaldraithe, p. 104. Translation of Irish: 'An inspector of police (Major Brown) came to examine people against the policeman who shot the horse yesterday'; from McGrath, III, p. 205.

42 See E. Margaret Crawford's invaluable *Counting the People: A Survey of the Irish Censuses, 1813–1911: Maynooth Research Guides for Irish Local History* (Dublin, 2003).

43 Dominique Arel, 'Language categories in censuses; Backward- or forward-looking?', in David I. Kertzer and Dominique Arel (eds), *Census and Identity: The Politics of Race, Ethnicity, and Language in National Censuses* (Cambridge, 2002), p. 94.

44 See E. J. Hobsbawn, *Nations and Nationalism Since 1790: Programme, Myth, Reality* (Cambridge, 1990), p. 97. The 1860 Congress decided that the language question should be optional, 'each state deciding whether it had or had not any "national significance"'; the 1873 Congress recommended its inclusion in

all censuses. Neither Arel nor Hobsbawn cites the early incidence of a census language question in Ireland.

45 The excellent collection of essays Gwenfair Parry and Mari A. Williams (eds), *The Welsh Language and the 1891 Census* (Cardiff, 1991), demonstrates the many controversies regarding how the question was to be phrased and the resulting returns to be interpreted.

46 Sample schedules can be viewed at https://www.census.gov/.

47 A sample Canadian census schedule for 1901 can be viewed at http://www.collectionscanada.ca/. In a comparative study of census questions on language, Extra and Gorter show that, comparative to other countries (e.g. Australia, South Africa and the UK), Canada has an especially high number of questions; see Guus Extra and Durk Gorter, *Multilingual Europe: Facts and Policies* (Berlin and New York, 2008), p. 21.

48 Letter from Edward Singleton to Thomas Larcom, 11 November 1850, Ms 7,527LP, NLI.

49 Considerable agitation had surrounded the inclusion and wording of a census question on 'language spoken'; when a clarification was sought from the Registrar General regarding 'how much English was required in order to enable a person to claim to be bilingual,' the official reply was 'Any person who is able to give evidence in English in a court of law should (if he also knows Welsh) be returned as speaking 'both' languages.' Geraint H. Jenkins, 'The Historical Background to the 1891 Census', in Parry and Williams (eds), *The Welsh Language and the 1891 Census*, pp 1–30.

50 *Census of England and Wales 1891*, vol. IV, GR, 81: Section IX 'Languages in Wales and Monmouthshire.'

51 See Arel, 'Language Categories in Censuses', pp 98–108.

52 Ibid., pp 100–2; see also Mark Cornwall, 'The struggle on the Czech-German language border, 1880–1940', in *English Historical Review*, 1994, 109, pp 914–51.

53 Arel, 'Language Categories in Censuses', p. 106.

54 Ibid., pp 99–100.

55 Instructions to Superintendents III. 4, reproduced in *CI, 1851*, GR, appendix, p. cxxvii.

56 Arel notes that the 'statistical fate of those claiming to speak two languages equally' preoccupied some German and Prussian statisticians, and 'a bilingual category appeared on a few censuses in Germany and Prussia in the 1850s and 1860s … Eventually, as elsewhere in Central and Eastern Europe, the assumption was made that, in all cases, one language had to predominate at the individual level, and consequently a single primary language was assigned to the professed bilinguals', Ibid., p. 98.

57 *Freeman's Journal*, 25 March 1851.

58 Ibid.

59 Letter from MacAdam to O'Donovan, 29 January 1851, Windele Papers, Royal

Irish Academy (hereafter WP, RIA) 4B 10/116 (emphasis in the original).

60 Letter from O'Donovan to Windele, 31 January 1851, WP, RIA 4B 10/117. On 28 July 1851, in a letter to Windele, Thomas Swanton observed: 'You are aware I suppose that McAdam [*sic*] was the cause of the Gaelic enquiry in the Census', WP, RIA 4B 11/62.

61 Thomas Aiskew Larcom (1801–79) was Assistant Supervisor of the Ordnance Survey of Ireland (1828–48) and Under-Secretary of State for Ireland (1853–69); he played a key role in the organisation of the 1841 census but was not directly involved in 1851 due to illness. See letter from Larcom to Farr, 10 October 1850, Ms 7,527 Larcom Papers, National Library of Ireland (hereafter LP, NLI).

62 Letter from Singleton to Larcom, 11 November 1850, Ms 7,527 LP, NLI.

63 Much of the extensive literature on the challenges to census accuracy posed by self-reporting derives from Stanley Lieberson's work, for example 'How can we describe and measure the incidence and distribution of bilingualism?', in L. G. Kelly (ed.), *Description and Measurement of Bilingualism* (Toronto, 1969), pp 286–95. See also John de Vries, 'Some methodological aspects of self-report questions on language and ethnicity', in *Journal of Multilingual and Multicultural Development*, 1985, 6.5, pp 347–68. The results of the Welsh census in 1891 were highly contentious and led to official allegations of revivalist over-reporting of Welsh speakers: see Parry and Williams (eds), *The Welsh Language and the 1891 Census*.

64 Letter from MacAdam to Windele, 14 March 1851, 12L 12/24, WP, RIA.

65 Ibid.

66 Letter from John O'Donovan to Windele, 17 March 1851, 12L 12/18, WP, RIA (emphasis in the original). The O'Donovan-Reeves correspondence, held in University College Dublin, includes a 21 March letter from O'Donovan making a similar point, noting 'Mac Hale is an exception because he finds the language useful to him in the remoter regions where they have little or no English, but the younger town or village priests will compel the learning of English.' UCD Library Special Collections, JOD L 42.

67 Windele to Registrar General, 27 February 1851, 12L 12/23, WP, RIA.

68 Ibid.

69 See *CI, 1851*, GR, appendix, p. cxxvii.

70 Instructions to Superintendents III. 4, reproduced in *CI, 1851*, GR, appendix, p. cxxvii.

71 Reproduced in *CI, 1851*, GR, appendix, p. cix.

72 See for example Ms 5249, National Archives, Dublin (hereafter NA), in which 22 of 79 surviving miscellaneous individual returns provide information about monoglot Irish or bilingual households.

73 Ms 5249 (1), NA.

74 Ms 5249 (27) and (18), NA.

75 Ms 5249 (12), NA. Other famine-related deaths are recorded in the schedule for the Downing family who lost three members between 1849 and 1850: the father, whose cause of death is listed as 'decline', and two daughters whose causes of deaths are listed as 'influencsy' and 'smallpox'; see Ms 5249 (18), NA.

76 In relation to education levels in the area, more specific regional information survives for the Tibohine parish, rural area, in which the figure for males who could read and write was 1,613, read only 663, and neither read nor write 3,494; the corresponding figures for females were 708,650 and 4,348 (these are not broken down into decennial cohorts, however). *CI, 1851*, GR, County Tables, pp 586–7.

77 Peter O'Brien, *The Reminiscences of the Right Honourable Lord O'Brien*, Georgina O'Brien (ed.) (New York and London, 1916), p. 136. In his memoir O'Brien describes his 'old nurse Kelly' as a 'typical old-fashioned Irish servant, very faithful, and devoted to us. She was with us until she died, and was always *seventy-four* when the census came round, though she was much nearer ninety-four!', pp 6–7.

78 Ibid., pp 136–7; his daughter's account also runs counter to O'Brien's self-parading of his lack of knowledge of Irish through an anecdote told at a literary fund dinner in 1911. Having complimented a 'Russian lady' on her children's knowledge of many languages, he was asked by her if he too was a linguist: 'The gratified mother turned to me, and looking at me—not wholly without interest, as I thought—asked me whether I was not a good linguist. "Alas, madam!" I replied, with tears in my voice, "I do not speak even the language of my own country."' p. 111.

79 See entry on William Wilde by J. Lyons in *Dictionary of Irish Biography VII*, vol. IX, pp 936–7.

80 Angela Bourke, *The Burning of Bridget Cleary: A True Story* (London, 1999), p. 32.

81 Ibid., pp 32–3.

82 Peter Froggatt, 'Sir William Wilde and the 1851 census of Ireland', in *Medical History*, 1965, 9.4, pp 305–27.

83 Terence de Vere White, *The Parents of Oscar Wilde* (London, 1967), pp 219–20.

84 Ibid., p. 287.

85 'Our Portrait Gallery, Second Series: no. 16', in *Dublin University Magazine* May 1875, 85, pp 570–89.

86 Robert MacAdam, 'Six hundred Gaelic proverbs collected in Ulster', in *Ulster Journal of Archaeology*, 1858, 6, pp 172–83, 172.

87 G. B. Adams, 'The validity of language census figures in Ulster, 1851–1891', in *Ulster Folklife*, 1979, 25, pp 113–122, 116.

88 Adams, 'The validity of language census Figures', p. 121.

89 Windele, 'Present extent of the Irish language', p. 243.

90 Ibid.

91 Ibid., p. 244.

92 MacAdam, 'Six hundred Gaelic proverbs', p. 173.

93 E. G. Ravenstein, 'On the Celtic languages in the British Isles: A statistical survey', in *Journal of the Statistical Society of London*, September 1879, 42.3, pp 579–643, 581.

94 *Nation*, 24 February 1877, p. 10.

95 Ravenstein, 'On the Celtic languages in the British Isles', p. 581.

96 See William Wilde, 'On the ancient races of Ireland; Extracts from the address to the Anthropological Section of the British Association' (Belfast, 1874), in Lady Wilde (ed.) *Ancient Legends, Mystic Charms and Superstitions of Ireland* (London, 1888), p. 342.

97 These figures are drawn from FitzGerald's 'Estimates for baronies', p. 140. See also Brian Ó Cuív, 'Irish language and literature, 1845–1921', p. 386.

98 In Reg Hindley, *The Death of the Irish Language: A Qualified Obituary* (London, 1990), the author suggests that the level of under-estimation in earlier censuses could have been as high as 40 per cent, making for a revised 1851 figure of 2,134,000 Irish speakers (15). While agreeing that the 1881 increase in Irish-speakers is mostly attributable to the change in form layout, G. B. Adams also observes that 'it is also possible that public attitudes to the Irish language were changing and that there was greater readiness to claim an ability to speak it'; see G. B. Adams, 'Language census problems, 1851–1911', in *Ulster Folklife*, 1975, 21, pp 68–72, 68.

99 This is discussed in FitzGerald, 'Estimates for baronies', p. 139, footnote 2.

100 1,649 men and 2,065 women were recorded as monoglot Irish-speakers in 1881; 1,842 men and 1,794 women as bilingual. *CI, 1881*, part I, vol. IV (Connaught), p. 188.

101 Irish-speakers constituted over three-quarters of Ballnahinch's population of 20,569 in 1891. See *CI, 1891*, part I, vol. IV (Connaught), p. 188.

102 In 1881 1,649 men were self-declared monoglots as were 2,065 women; in 1891 the figure for men was 2,641 and women 2,615. The corresponding figures for bilingual speakers were 1,842 men and 1,794 women (1881) and 1,353 men and 1,356 women (1891). See *CI, 1881*, part I, vol. IV, p. 188 and *CI, 1891*, part I, vol. IV, p. 188.

103 Ibid. The total of 121 Irish-speaking men aged between 40 and 50 in 1881 increased to 197 monoglots aged between 50 and 60 in 1891, a percentage increase of almost 63 per cent (female monoglots in those age groups decreased from 232 to 142).

104 For example, the 1881 census lists 478 boys and 459 girls as aged under ten and Irish-only speaking in 1881, but in 1891 the figures for those aged over ten and under 20 are 875 males and 907 females. Ibid.

105 See *CI, 1901*, NA, http://www.census.nationalarchives.ie/. In the 1901 census, D. E. D.s (district electoral divisions) replaced baronies as the unit of measurement for language-use. Estimates by Garret FitzGerald give a figure of 57 per

cent monoglot speakers for those aged over 60 in the D. E. D. of Owenbrin in 1901 (to which Maamtrasna belonged); this was one of the highest figures in the country, surpassed only by areas such as Lettermore (*Leitir Mór*) and Gorumna Island (*Garmna*) with figures of 80 and 84 per cent. The nearby area of Ross had a figure of 42 per cent, and Cong also 57 per cent. See FitzGerald, 'Irish-speaking in the pre-Famine period: A study based on the 1911 census data for people born before 1851 and still alive in 1911', in *Proceedings of the Royal Irish Academy*, 103C, 2003, 248, pp 253–4. I am indebted to Cormac Ó Gráda for these 1901 findings.

106 Hyde's address was first delivered before the Irish National Literary Society, Dublin, 25 November 1892, and a published version appeared two years later in Charles Gavan Duffy, *The Revival of Irish Literature: Addresses by Sir C. G. Duffy, George Sigerson, Douglas Hyde* (London, 1894), pp 115–61. See Liam Mac Mathúna, 'From manuscripts to street signs via *Séadna*: The Gaelic League and the changing role of literacy in Irish, 1875–1915', in Betsey Taylor FitzSimon and James H. Murphy (eds), *The Irish Revival Reappraised* (Dublin, 2004), pp 49–63, 52.

107 Hyde, 'The necessity for de-Anglicising Ireland', p. 137.

108 See Neville, '"He spoke to me in English. I answered him in Irish": Language shift in the folklore archives' in Jean Brihault (ed.), *L'Irlande et ses Langues* (Rennes, 1992), pp 19–32.

109 For an online version of Hyde's text, see http://www.spinnet.eu/images /2014-05/hydenecessity.pdf, 10 May 2016. This passage is also discussed by Mac Mathúna in *Béarla sa Ghaeilge*, pp 224–6.

110 Mac Mathúna, 'From manuscripts to street signs via *Séadna*', p. 52.

111 Neville, 'He spoke to me in English. I answered him in Irish', p. 22.

112 Ibid., p. 25.

113 Anita Pavlenko, *The Bilingual Mind and What It Tells Us about Language and Thought* (Cambridge, 2014), pp 1–39, 20–1.

114 Ibid., p. 23.

115 Ibid., p. 39.

116 Doris Sommer, *Bilingual Aesthetics: A New Sentimental Education* (Durham, North Carolina, 2004), p. 6. The full quotation is as follows: 'It is time we noticed that working—and also underemployed—bilinguals sparkle too, and for similar reasons to elite codeswitchers. Both know the risks of language and the magic of making contact when communication could have misfired. With an exquisite consciousness of conventions, and a keen skepticism about what can or should be said, bilinguals develop the everyday arts of manoeuvring and self-irony.'

117 Pavlenko, *The Bilingual Mind*, p. 24. Quoting from the influential work of Grosjean, she observes: 'a bilingual is not the sum or two complete or incomplete monolinguals in one body but rather a specific speaker-hearer with a

unique—but nevertheless complete—linguistic system, whose competencies are developed to the extent required by his or her needs and those of the environment.'

118 'Membership in bilingual communities of practice,' Romaine also observes, 'may be defined not so much by active use of two or more languages, but primarily in terms of passive competence and shared norms of understanding.' See Suzanne Romaine, 'The bilingual and multilingual community', in Tej. K. Bhatia and William C. Ritchie (eds), *The Blackwell Handbook of Bilingualism* (Oxford, 2004), pp 385–405, 386.

119 Ibid., p. 387; Romaine draws here from Nancy Dorian's study of bilingual speakers in Scotland, *Language Death: The Life Cycle of a Scottish Gaelic Dialect* (Philadelphia, 1981).

120 Arel, 'Language categories in censuses', p. 93.

121 Joseph Lee, *Ireland 1912–1985: Politics and Society* (Cambridge, 1989), p. 662–3. Similarly in his 2005 article 'Gaelic culture and language shift', Niall Ó Ciosáin has highlighted the continuing inadequacy of theories which account only for the acquisition of one language and not the loss of the other. See Niall Ó Ciosáin, 'Gaelic culture and language shift', in Laurence Geary and Margaret Kelleher (eds), *Nineteenth-Century Ireland: A Guide to Recent Research* (Dublin, 2005), pp 136–69, 141.

122 Tony Crowley, 'English in Ireland: A complex case study', in Terttu Nevalainen and Elizabeth Closs Traugott (eds), *The Oxford Handbook of the History of English* (Oxford, 2012), pp 470–80, 478.

123 See the illuminating closing section on 'identity' in Joseph Lee, *Ireland 1912–1985: Politics and Society* (Cambridge, 1989), pp 658–86.

124 Lee, *Ireland 1912–1985*, p. 664. Lee further notes that Irish 'was spoken by as many, if not more, people in the early nineteenth century than Flemish, or Dutch (or Dutch and Flemish combined), or Danish, or Norwegian, or Swedish, or Finnish, or Basque, or Welsh.'

125 Ibid., p. 663–4. The longer history of Finnish agitation in the nineteenth century for the enhanced status of the language and the replacement of Swedish in the education system, public administration and civic society could offer a fuller and instructive comparison with Ireland, especially in the light of Joep Leerssen's apt comment that Finnish 'had the status in 1800 that Saami has nowadays: known to exist, but not used in other than dialect-vernacular situations.' Joep Leerssen, *National Thought in Europe: A Cultural History* (Amsterdam, 2006), pp 167–8.

126 An influential early work on this topic, published in English, was Robert Auty's 'Language and society in the Czech national revival', in *Slavonic and East European Review*, December 1956, 35.84, pp 241–8.

127 See Hugh LeCaine Agnew, *The Czechs and the Lands of the Bohemian Crown* (Stanford, 2004), pp 124–45, 130.

128 Ibid., p. 143, 137–8.

129 Ibid., p. 149.

130 Lee, *Ireland 1912–1985*, p. 665

131 Ibid., p. 665–6.

132 Wolf, *An Irish-Speaking Island*, p. 19. Wolf concludes firmly that 'in the century before 1870 … Ireland was not by any means an Anglicized kingdom and, indeed, was quite capable of articulating the forms of modernity—whether religious, political or economic—in the Irish language', p. 269.

133 These terms are drawn from Tony Crowley's work: 'in order for a particular type of language change to occur, there must be a form of cultural hegemony that leads people to begin actively to adopt one language rather than another (attraction must be added to advantage)'; Crowley, 'English in Ireland: A complex case study', p. 479.

134 See also Margaret O'Callaghan, 'New ways of looking at the state apparatus and the state archive in nineteenth-century Ireland: "Curiosities from that phonetic museum"—Royal Irish Constabulary reports and their political uses, 1879–1891', in *Proceedings of the Royal Irish Academy*, 2004, Section C, vol. 104.2, pp 37–56; and Niall Ó Ciosáin, *Ireland in Official Print Culture 1800-1850: A New Reading of the Poor Inquiry* (Oxford, 2014), pp 167–73.

CHAPTER 3

1 Included in Crown Briefs, 1882, National Archives, Dublin (hereafter CB, 1882, NA): County Galway–Dublin Commission Court, October 1882. *The Queen vs Anthony Philbin and Others. Murder of the Joyces at Maamtrasna*, p. 46.

2 According to the *Freeman's Journal* (hereafter *FJ*), 21 August 1882, 15 arrests were made but only the ten men named in Anthony and John Joyces' statements were remanded for sending to Galway Jail.

3 These depositions, along with information regarding the investigation of alibis, survive in the 49-page crown prosecution brief, a key document in the crown's preparation for trial, and which was completed in October 1882. See CB, 1882, NA, *The Queen vs Anthony Philbin and Others*.

4 Ibid., p. 34.

5 Ibid., p. 22.

6 An ensuing italicised note in the Crown Brief commented that 'the trousers had been washed, but faint indications of blood were found on them' and supporting evidence for this was tendered by Dr Davy of the Royal College of Surgeons. CB, 1882, NA, *The Queen vs Anthony Philbin and Others*, pp 22–3.

7 Ibid., p. 28.

8 Ibid.

9 Waldron speculates that Tom 'had some smattering of English' and that he later acted as the conduit of communication between the accused men and their defence solicitor. See Jarlath Waldron, *Maamtrasna: The Murders and the Mystery*, (Dublin, 1992), p. 125.

10 CB, 1882, NA, *The Queen vs Anthony Philbin and Others*, p. 8.

11 *Ballinrobe Chronicle*, 30 October 1880.

12 CB, 1882, NA, *The Queen vs Anthony Philbin and Others*, p. 13.

13 Ibid., p. 17.

14 Details from General Prisons Register, Galway gaol August 1882. Information is also provided in the Kilmainham register, October 1882, and (on the men's return to Galway) again in the Galway register, November 1882. These registers can be accessed through the database of Irish Prison Registers, 1790–1924, https://www.findmypast.ie/.

15 Martin is also entered as 40 years of age, though he was younger than Myles and probably in his late thirties. Paudeen is described as 45 years old, and his son Tom (whose name was recorded in the register as Thomas Patt) as 20 years of age. The Casey brothers, Patrick and John, are described as 26 and 36 years of age respectively, and their uncle Michael was 60 years old. Thomas Casey is recorded as being 38 years old and Anthony Philbin as 40. Irish Prison Registers, 1790–1924, https://www.findmypast.ie/.

16 In January 1867, Thomas Casey married Mary Philbin; by 1882 they had six children. Anthony Philbin had married Catherine Quinn, his second wife, in June 1878; the marriage record describes him as a widower of 35 years of age and his wife, a 'spinster (previously unmarried') of 20. In 1882 he had a young son, Stephen, as well as children from his first marriage. See https://www.rootsireland.ie/ and https://www.findmypast.ie/.

17 Deposition by Constable John Johnston, 5 September 1882, CB, 1882, NA, *The Queen vs Anthony Philbin and Others*, p. 7.

18 The practice is now called Concanon and Meagher solicitors. I have followed the practice of the 1880s court and press reporters in using the spelling Concannon.

19 Death notice for Edmund Concannon (Concanon), *Tuam Herald*, 25 October 1902. Henry, his son, died in 1930; see his death notice in *Tuam Herald*, 22 February 1902.

20 Waldron, *Maamtrasna*, p. 53.

21 Ibid.

22 In Bolton's words, 'to get at the truth, and to completely put a stop to the possibility of false alibis, we had to examine and take informations or statements from 643 witnesses'; he also claimed that 'several affected not to understand English'. See George Bolton, *A Short Account of the Discovery and Conviction of the "Invincibles" and of some trials of which the writer had charge in 1881, 1882, 1883 and 1884 with a few observations on preliminary investigations in criminal cases* (Dublin, 1887), pp 35, 38. In 1884, Bolton was suspended temporarily as Crown Solicitor because of threatened bankruptcy proceedings; when these did not transpire, he then regained his position. He was also involved in a series of high-profile libel cases against the nationalist paper *United Ireland*.

See Patrick Tynan, *The Irish National Invincibles and Their Times* (London, 1894), pp 501–2.

23 Waldron, *Maamtrasna*, p. 31.

24 The case that immediately preceded the Maamtrasna trials in the Dublin court was the infamous Lydon case in which two brothers, Patrick Walsh and Michael Walsh, were found guilty of the murder of a man named Martin Lydon and also of a leading prosecution witness Constable Kavanagh. This case is discussed in Tim Robinson, *Connemara: The Last Pool of Darkness* (Dublin, 2008).

25 The *Royal Irish Constabulary List and Directory*, which listed constabulary departments, resident magistrates, Dublin Metropolitan Police leaders, and other officials, was published at six-monthly intervals. Prior to the RIC's reorganization of grades in 1883, the non-commissioned ranks extended from sub-constable to constable to head constable, while the commissioned ranks were ordered from sub-inspector and county inspector to provincial inspector and inspector general.

26 *Royal Irish Constabulary List and Directory*, July to December 1882, 82, p. 81. The 1881 census recorded 4 barracks in the petty-sessions district of Clonbur and 19 RIC men; this represented a lower than usual ratio of constabulary staff to barracks, the more typical ratio being 6 staff members per barrack. *Census of Ireland, 1881*, part 1, vol. IV, Province of Connaught (Dublin, 1882), p. 10.

27 The eight protection posts were located at Churchfield, Cloughbrack, Doon, Creggdotia, Glantraigue, Petersburgh, Rosshill, and Ebor Hall, the most remote from Clonbur being Glantraigue (10 miles), Churchfield (10 miles), and Doon (11.5 miles). See *Royal Irish Constabulary List and Directory*, pp 148, 151. The working and living conditions for junior constabulary members were often horrendous, particularly in these temporary accommodations erected during the Land War period. In his history of the Irish constabularies from 1822 to 1922, Donal O'Sullivan observes that 'several hundred RIC men died in the years that followed the Land War from tuberculosis, bronchitis, pleurisy, and other bronchial diseases, and only in 1907 was a fund set up to support medical treatment for RIC men with these conditions': see Donal J. O'Sullivan, *The Irish Constabularies, 1822–1922: A Century of Policing in Ireland* (Dingle, 1999), pp 160–1.

28 In Julia's statement Mary is referred to twice as 'a little girl' but later her age is given as 20, suggesting an overly literal translation of *giorseach* (*girseach, cailín*). CB, 1882, NA, *The Queen vs Anthony Philbin and Others*, p. 39.

29 Ibid.

30 Ibid., p. 38.

31 Ibid., p. 40.

32 Ibid., p. 28.

33 Ibid., pp 33–9. These statements, made under oath, were recorded as having been signed with a mark, as was the case for almost of all of the witnesses

recorded in the brief, although, once again, the use of an interpreter is erratically specified.

34 Ibid., p. 35.

35 Ibid., pp 35–6.

36 Ibid., pp 43–5. Mary Ann's alibi for her husband, Patrick Joyce, rested on the argument that a large group of people was in the house that night, including her mother-in-law, sister-in-law, uncle John Lynch, and John Coyne, a man recently returned from America. But all those named, with the exception of her sister-in-law, denied their ever having been in the Joyce house that evening.

37 Ibid., p. 34.

38 Ibid.

39 Ibid.

40 Ibid.

41 The resident magistrates travelled on occasion to the accused's homes to take statements: for example, Mary Casey, mother-in-law of John Casey, was interviewed in John Casey's home on 29 August. Ibid., p. 40.

42 Ibid., p. 37.

43 Ibid., p. 46.

44 Ibid.

45 The terms *callagh* and *collagh* are anglicised versions of *cúil-leaba* ('recess bed').

46 CB, 1882, NA, *The Queen vs Anthony Philbin and Others*, p. 47.

47 Ibid., p. 49.

48 Ibid., p. 48.

49 *Weekly Irish Times*, 26 August 1882. Breandán Mac Suibhne writes illuminatingly on the contemporary deployment of incidences of agrarian violence as arguments against Irish self-government in his article on James MacFadden in Gerald Moran (ed.), *Radical Priests, 1660–1970* (Dublin, 1998), pp 146–84. See also his introduction to the memoir Hugh Dorian, *The Outer Edge of Ulster: A Memoir of Social Life in Nineteenth-Century Donegal* David Dickson and Breandán Mac Suibhne (eds) (Dublin, 2000) and Angela Bourke, *The Burning of Bridget Cleary: A True Story* (London, 1999).

50 *Ballinrobe Chronicle*, 26 August 1882. The same day, the English police weekly, *Illustrated Police News*, in its first report on the Maamtrasna murders, also referred to the local suspicion that Joyce had given information with respect to the murder of the two Huddys.

51 *Galway Express*, 19 August 1882. This account was taken up by the Dublin-based *Daily Express* (hereafter *DE*), 21 August 1882; the paper later published a retraction and apology.

52 Ibid., p. 26 August 1882.

53 *Irish World*, 23 September 1882.

54 Janet Malcolm, *Iphigenia in Forest Hills: Anatomy of a Murder Trial* (New Haven, CT and London, 2011), p. 129.

55 *FJ*, 23 August 1882. This article was reproduced by the *Galway Vindicator* three days later.

56 Ibid.

57 Dunlop, *Fifty Years of Irish Journalism*, p. 191.

58 *DE*, 21 August 1882.

59 Ibid., 23 August 1882.

60 This tour is also the subject of a chapter in Dunlop's memoir; see Andrew Dunlop, *Fifty Years of Irish Journalism* (London and Dublin, 1911), pp 192–206.

61 *FJ*, 15 September 1882.

62 Ibid.

63 Ibid.

64 Waldron, *Maamtrasna*, pp 57–9.

65 CRF (1902), J13, folder 21; CSORP, NA.

66 These statements are included in 'The Maamtrasna file': CRF (1902), J13, folder 21; CSORP, NA.

67 Ibid.

68 Although the Galway prison register described Casey as unable to read and write, and Philbin as able to read only, the register for the men in Kilmainham described both men as able to read and write in English, and similarly described Patrick Joyce of Shanvalleycahill as literate. See General Prisons Register, Galway gaol, August 1882 and Kilmainham register, October 1882; Irish Prison Registers, 1790–1924, https://www.findmypast.ie/.

69 The surviving document in the Maamtrasna file at the National Archives in Dublin seems to be a transcription of an original note, and whether the original was penned by Casey himself cannot be definitely verified. See CRF (1902), J13, folder 21; CSORP, NA. In a later interview with Tim Harrington, Casey stated that on the Friday or Saturday, 'I wrote the note to Mr Bolton asking him to come to see me.' See Tim Harrington, *The Maamtrasna Massacre: Impeachment of the Trials* (Dublin, 1884), p. 29.

70 The circumstances of these statements were the subject of particular attention from the Lord Lieutenant's office following Thomas Casey's public recanting in 1884. Bolton, responding to queries in 1884, noted 'On the 13th of November, it was communicated to Casey, through the Governor that his evidence would be accepted, and he made a statement to Mr A. N. Brady, R. M., which the latter took down in his own handwriting, and signed.' CRF (1902), J13, folder 21; CSORP, NA.

71 In an interview with Tim Harrington in 1884, Casey explained that 'Kelly' and 'Nee' were 'false names' used to disguise the identities of Pat Leyden and 'young John' Casey, two of the three members of the murder party who were never charged. Harrington, *The Maamtrasna Massacre*, p. 24.

CHAPTER 4

1 Patricia Palmer, *Language and Conquest in Early Modern Ireland: English Renaissance Literature and Elizabethan Imperial Expansion* (Cambridge, 2001), p. 193.

2 *Freeman's Journal* (hereafter *FJ*), 2 November 1882.

3 Ibid.

4 Jarlath Waldron, *Maamtrasna: The Murders and the Mystery* (Dublin, 1992), pp 57–8.

5 The correspondence regarding Kelly, and his attempted substitution by Duffy, may be found in Convict Reference File (hereafter CRF) (1902) J13, folder 24, National Archives (hereafter NA).

6 Letter from P. Duffy, Crown Witness House, Ballybough, to Dublin Castle, 15 September 1882; CRF (1902) J13 folder 24, NA.

7 Letter from Head Constable Heard, Clontarf Barracks, to Dublin Castle, 22 September 1882; CRF (1902) J13 folder 24, NA.

8 See Vaughan's summary of the legal difference between 'depositions' and 'informations': an information applies 'to the statement grounding the charge, taken in the absence of the accused', while a deposition is 'each written and sworn statement taken at the inquiry in the presence of the accused'; see W. E. Vaughan, *Murder Trials in Ireland, 1836–1914* (Dublin, 2009), p. 80.

9 Chief Secretary's Office Registered Papers, National Archives (hereafter CSORP, NA) 1890/5749 (Joyce compensation file).

10 Royal Irish Constabulary (hereafter RIC) service records document the record of a Patrick Kelly (service number 20753), born in Roscommon, who was appointed in 1856 at the age of 19. Kelly, a Roman Catholic, served in Mayo as Sub-Constable from 1874 to 1882, and moved to Galway West Riding in June 1882. In December 1882, Kelly was made a Police Constable; he became a pensioner in 1886 and died in Galway in 1892. See RIC Service Records, 1816–1922: http://www.findmypast.co.uk.

11 Unlike local courts and many county courts in the 1880s, the Special Commission Court did not employ a paid interpreter; for the Maamtrasna trials and others of its proceedings, the *ad hoc* services of members of the RIC were deployed instead. For a discussion of nineteenth-century interpretative practice in local courts, see Mary Phelan's doctoral thesis 'Irish language court reporting 1801–1922' (DCU, 2013).

12 The reported motive for the murders of Martin Lydon and his father John was that they farmed land previously held by Patrick Walsh's father and from which the Walsh family had been evicted. For reference to Evans, see *Irish Times* and *FJ*, 22 August 1882.

13 According to RIC records, Constable Thomas Evans was appointed at the age of 22 in 1854 and was stationed in the 1870s in Hollymount and Killateeaun RIC stations in Mayo. His service number was 18813 and he is identified

as Protestant in the service register, with native county of 'Mayo/Galway'. In 1873 he married Mary Jane Colvin of Spiddal and both are described as 'congregationalist' in the record of their marriage in the *Galway Express* of 3 January 1874 (the ceremony was performed by James Mecredy, member of the evangelical wing of the Church of Ireland). Evans' membership of a Protestant Evangelical branch may have been a reason for his knowledge of Irish. He ended his constabulary service as a head constable in Longford in 1888 and died in 1909. See RIC Service Records, 1816–1922: http://www.findmypast.co.uk.

14 Waldron, *Maamtrasna*, p. 58.

15 *Ballinrobe Chronicle* (hereafter *BC*), 10 November 1877. In the proceedings the resident magistrate McSheehy praised Evans for having 'got out of his sickbed on the day that he [McSheehy] had been in the mountains to take the injured man's depositions, and even acted as interpreter on the occasion.'

16 In later commentaries on the Maamtrasna case, the role of the interpreter, if mentioned, is usually the generalised object of opprobrium, one example being Patrick Joyce's short comment in *The State of Freedom*: 'The court interpreters used were either unwilling or unable to convey the impassioned stories of the accused, who were convicted on the basis of the evidence of paid informers.' Patrick Joyce, *The State of Freedom: A Social History of the British State since 1800* (Cambridge, 2013), p. 305.

17 *Reg. v. Burke*, in Edward W. Cox, *Reports of Cases in Criminal Law, Argued and Determined in all the courts in England and Ireland*, vol. 8: 1858–61, 24 vols (London, 1843–1916), pp 44–65.

18 *Reg. v. Burke*, pp 46–7. This case is discussed briefly in W. E. Vaughan, *Murder Trials in Ireland, 1836–1914* (Dublin, 2009), pp 238–9.

19 *Reg. v. Burke*, pp 44–65.

20 Ibid., p. 64. Limerick-born Thomas Langlois Lefroy (1776–1869) was an influential judge and Lord Chief Justice of Ireland from 1852 to 1866; he is best known, however, as a love interest of the young Jane Austen and perhaps as inspiration for the character of Darcy in *Pride and Prejudice* (1813).

21 Ibid., p. 54. Christian also noted, more sardonically: 'and certainly if every lady who sings an Italian song is to be taken on that account to have a perfect knowledge of the Italian language, I can only say that a great number of ladies may very easily find themselves placed in a very unpleasant position indeed.' Ibid., p. 55.

22 Ibid., p. 56. In his closing comment, also, Christian highlighted the frequency of legal testimony being given in Irish in contemporary western courts: 'I venture to say that if every case during the last assizes in which a witness insisted on being examined in Irish, and his knowledge of English was suggested, there had been witnesses examined *pro* and *con*, it is a matter of very serious doubt to me whether the spring assizes for the province of Connaught would be over at the present moment.'

23 Edward Parkyns Levinge, *The Justice of the Peace for Ireland: A Treatise on Summary Jurisdiction, Preliminary Proceedings as to Indictable Offences, with an Appendix of the Most Useful Statutes and an Alphabetical Catalogue of Offices*, third edn (Dublin, 1872), p. 90.

24 Richard Nun and John Edward Walsh, *The Powers and Duties of Justices of the Peace in Ireland: And of Constables as Connected Therewith: With an Appendix of Statutes and Forms*, vol. 2 (Dublin, 1842), appendixes, p. 1174. My thanks to Nicholas Wolf for these references.

25 National Library of Ireland Ms G 236; the 1886 notebook is bound with the manuscript papers of Charles Kendal Bushe (1767–1843), Lord Chief Justice of Ireland from 1822 to 1841.

26 See Nicholas Wolf, *An Irish-Speaking Island: State, Religion, Community, and the Linguistic Landscape in Ireland, 1770–1870* (Wisconsin, 2014), Chapter 5, pp 149–80. See also Lesa Ní Mhungaile's study of the use of Irish and of paid interpreters in the Irish courts in the eighteenth and earlier nineteenth centuries, 'The legal system in Ireland and the Irish language 1700–c. 1843', in Michael Brown and Seán Donlan (eds), *The Laws and Other Legalities of Ireland, 1689–1850* (Abington, 2016), pp 325–57, especially pp 329–39. Phelan's doctoral thesis 'Irish language court reporting 1801–1922' examines the provision of salaried court reporters in nineteenth-century assizes and quarter sessions, drawing from newspaper records, the Chief Secretary's Office Registered Papers and grand jury presentment books.

27 Wolf, *An Irish-Speaking Island*, p. 149.

28 Richard McMahon, 'The courts of petty sessions and the law in pre-Famine Galway' (MA thesis, NUI, Galway, 1999), p. 51; quoted by Ní Mhungaile, 'The legal system', pp 329–30. See also Richard McMahon, 'Manor courts in the west of Ireland before the Famine', in Desmond Greer and Norma Dawson (eds), *Mysteries and Solutions in Irish Legal History* (Dublin, 2001), pp 115–59.

29 Wolf, *An Irish-Speaking Island*, p. 155. The quarter sessions were county courts that met four times a year; more serious cases were then committed to the assizes courts. The petty sessions dealt with the majority of lesser legal cases, both civil and criminal. On the operation of petty sessions courts, see Richard McMahon, 'The courts of petty sessions and society in pre-Famine Galway', in Raymond Gillespie (ed.), *The Re-making of Modern Ireland: Essays in Honour of J. C. Beckett* (Dublin, 2003), pp 101–37.

30 Wolf, *An Irish-Speaking Island*, p. 155. An instance of this is cited by William Thackeray in his *Irish Sketchbook 1842* (1843; Dublin, 1990), p. 216; see Ní Mhungaile, 'The legal system', p. 332.

31 *BC*, 23 July 1898.

32 *Old Bailey Proceedings Online*, April 1852, trial of Francis Sullivan, Cornelius Ronan, John Sullivan, Michel [*sic*] Harding, Matthew Canty, Mary Donovan,

Mary Canty, Honora Sullivan (t18520405-424), https://www.oldbaileyonline
.org/, version 7.2, 3 July 2017. My thanks to Carolina Amador Moreno for this
reference.

33 Ní Mhungaile, 'The legal system', pp 334–6.

34 Ibid. Here Ní Mhungaile quotes the 1867–8 memoir of Maurice Lenihan,
Limerick journalist and court reporter, who claimed that judges such as Barry
Yelverton (d. 1805) and Baron Smith (d. 1836), who were dedicated antiquarians, had learned Irish 'in order not to be dependent on the fidelity of interpreters in cases where witnesses could not speak English', pp 334–5.

35 Pádraig Ó Néill's writings are quoted in Eoghan Ó Néill, *Gleann an Óir*
(Dublin, 1988), p. 139; also quoted in Ní Mhungaile, 'The legal system', p. 335.

36 Ó Néill, *Gleann an Óir*, pp 139–40.

37 *Times* (London), 11 April 1894; quoted by Wolf, *An Irish-Speaking Island*, p. 158.

38 Ní Mhungaile, 'The legal system', p. 337.

39 Ibid.; also on this topic, see Wolf, *An Irish-Speaking Island*, pp 160–1, and
Terence Dooley, *The Murders at Wildgoose Lodge: Agrarian Crime and
Punishment in pre-Famine Ireland* (Dublin, 2007), p. 187.

40 Wolf, *An Irish-Speaking Island*, p. 164.

41 *Census of Ireland* (hereafter CI), *1891. Part II. General Report* (hereafter GR),
with illustrative maps and diagrams, tables, and appendix, House of Commons
Sessional Papers, 1892, XC.1, p. 570.

42 See Wolf, *An Irish-Speaking Island*, p. 158 and note p. 317. The existence of
a female interpreter is cited in the provinces of Munster, Connaught and
Leinster.

43 *CI, 1891. Part II. GR* [C.6780] H. C. 1873, p. 444.

44 *CI, 1871. Part I. Area, houses, and population: Also the ages, civil condition, occupations, birthplaces, religion, and education of the people.* Vol. III. Province of Ulster
[C.964]. H. C. 1874, p. 444.

45 *CI, 1901. Part I. Area, houses, and population: Also the ages, civil condition, occupations, birth places, religion, and education of the people.* Vol. III. Province of
Ulster [C.1123]. H. C. 1902, p. 125.

46 See http://www.ainm.ie/, 12 July 2017; cited by Wolf, *An Irish-Speaking Island*,
p. 157. In the overall census tallies of listed occupations for males in Munster
in 1901, however, no entry exists for interpreter. See *CI, 1901, Part I*, vol. II,
Province of Munster [Cd. 1058], H. C. 1902, p. cxxiv.

47 Palmer, *Language and Conquest in Early Modern Ireland*, p. 191. As she illustrates,
within a period of military and cultural conquest, 'the interpreter is a necessarily
hybrid figure, straddling, linguistically at any rate, two cultures', p. 193.

48 For example, in June 1871, prior to commencement of proceedings at
Claremorris Quarter Sessions, Judge John Richards referred to the recent
death of 'Mr. Rush, interpreter' and stated that he had 'fourteen applications
for the office,' each of which with good testimonies. A man named Peter

Rippingham of Ballinrobe was appointed as 'the most eligible'; see *Tuam Herald*, 1 July 1871.

49 *Connaught Telegraph*, 29 March 1879.

50 See *BC*, 4 March 1882; *Connaught Telegraph* report of Castlebar petty sessions court, 31 August 1895; *BC* report of local quarter sessions, 24 October 1896; and *Connaught Telegraph* report of Mayo assizes, 19 March 1898.

51 *BC*, 13 April 1872.

52 *Skibbereen Eagle*, 14 October 1882. Donovan's case was later dismissed. In the 1881 census, the barony of Ibane and Barryroe, where Donovan lived, recorded 581 monoglot speakers of Irish and 7,091 bilingual speakers. *CI, 1881. Part I. Area, houses, and population: Also the ages, civil condition, occupations, birthplaces, religion, and education of the people.* Vol. II. Province of Munster. [C.3148]. H. C. 1882, p. 395.

53 Crown Office Papers 1893, Mayo correspondence, Interpreters Papers: National Archives Dublin, IC-78–51.

54 Ibid.

55 Ibid.

56 Ibid.

57 Ibid. To support his application, Kane included a testimonial from 'Martin May, Ballygarris, Certificated Teacher of the Irish Language under Board of National Education' who attested that 'Having examined John Kane in the Irish Language I hereby certify that he can speak it fluently and also interpret it from a witness to the satisfaction of the County Court judge.' The script and style of the supporting letter from Kane himself suggest quite limited literacy in English, and of a standard markedly inferior to other applicants: 'I enclose you tesimonials [*sic*] and also beg to state that I understand the Irish language well and can also translate it.' [emphasis in original]

58 Ibid.

59 *Annual report of the Local Government Board for Ireland, being the eleventh report under 'the Local Government Board (Ireland) Act,' 35 & 36 Vic., c. 69; with appendices*, House of Commons Sessional Papers, 1892, XXIX.1, pp 205–6. Into the late 1890s, discriminatory spending by local authorities on interpreters was allowed but within clear limits: the 1898 rules and schedules for local government authorised the spending of 'any sum not exceeding five pounds that may be recommended by the judge of assize at any spring or summer assizes for an interpreter at such assizes.' *Orders by Lord Lieutenant in Council, and Orders, Rules and Schedules by Local Government Board for Ireland, under Local Government and Registration (Ireland) Acts, 1898*, 19th Century House of Commons Sessional Papers 360, LXXXIII Pt.II.1, p. 82.

60 One example, dated 18 December 1883, relates to the petty sessions at Dungloe, County Donegal, in a prosecution case brought by Sergeant Potter against William Boyle for selling illicit spirits to a man named Patrick O'Donnell.

The services of Thomas Kenny were needed for the examination of O'Donnell, an Irish speaker, and he was awarded a fee of ten shillings for this and other police cases. An inquiry to Letterkenny from the Inspector General regarding the scale of the fees yielded more information regarding Kenny; resident magistrate Edmund Yates Peel attested that he was a small farmer, summons server, and a 'poor man', whose 'services as interpreter are indispensable; at least, if he did not interpret, some one else would have to be paid to do so.' CSORP, NA 1884/5663; Kenny was finally awarded 5 shillings in payment.

61 Documents survive from 1896 regarding the employment of John Faherty as an interpreter in Spiddal. See CSORP, NA 1896/6073. Faherty appears to have been especially enterprising and his correspondence attests not only to the continuing need for interpreter services in the Spiddal court at that period but also to central government resistance to any initiative towards professionalising the post of petty sessions interpreter. On 8 April 1896 he wrote to the Under-Secretary at Dublin Castle proposing the printing of new 'more convenient' forms for interpreters at petty sessions and enclosing two kinds of certificate for official approval; his letter was signed 'John Faherty, Interpreter at P (Petty) Sessions'. The simpler certificate provided a means for an interpreter to list easily the number of cases and number of witnesses interpreted; the more complicated return provided a column for 'complainants', 'defendants' and number of witnesses examined in cases 'in which the parties under examination were unable to speak in English, and in which the services of an Irish interpreter were required.' Faherty's proposals received a tart reprimand from Under-Secretary David Harrel who instructed the Inspector General's office as follows: 'Please have it explained to this man by one of your local officers that his proposal to have forms printed for use in Petty Sessions is not one that can be sanctioned, and that he is quite unauthorized to sign himself "Interpreter at Petty Sessions".' See also CSORP, NA 1896/6073.

62 For example, a query sent by the Gaelic League to the Clerk of the Peace for County Waterford in July 1898 seeking to ascertain if an Irish interpreter had been appointed, produced a reply saying that the Grand Jury for the County had decided 'not to make a permanent appointment, as there is seldom anything to be done' and that should an 'occasion' occur, the Irish interpreter from the Dungarvan Quarter Sessions would be employed. *FJ*, 19 July 1898; see Wolf, *Irish-Speaking Island*, p. 158. In August 1904, the *Tuam Herald*'s report of the Milltown Petty Sessions recounted how the resident magistrate himself had to act as interpreter in a case against a number of people summoned for non-payment of poor rates. According to the newspaper account, 'a good deal of amusement was caused by one of the defendants, a very old man, who could speak nothing but Irish, coming up to defend his case, and Mr McDonogh himself had to act as interpreter.' See *Tuam Herald*, 20 August 1904.

63 Reports of the case, usually entitled 'Judge Dane and the Irish language', included the *Evening Herald*, 27 October 1899; *FJ*, 27 October 1899; *The Cork Examiner*, 28 October 1899; and *The Western People*, 4 November 1899.

64 *Connaught Telegraph*, 28 October 1899. As in a number of other instances cited here, the bar for comprehension of English in the courtroom was set by judge and interpreter at a very low level.

65 According to *BC*, 4 November 1899, one councillor reported hearing the interpreter 'one evening, when on his way home, admit that he *was not a competent Irish speaker*, and that he did on several occasions misconstrue the questions put by counsel' (emphasis in original).

66 According to Costello, 'the interpreter right enough came on the table and said he was speaking that morning to the man in English, and thereupon the poor man protested that he could not speak English, and, as a matter of fact, the only single word of English he could say was intermixed with Irish is the phrase "fair-play".' Costello also told the council meeting that he 'knowing Irish—for fortunately he was not ashamed of the language of his country' had on a previous occasion told the judge that 'the interpreter was misrepresenting counsel's questions and the witness's replies.' See *BC*, 4 November 1899.

67 Maguire's letter was also published in *FJ*, 30 October 1899.

68 *BC*, 4 November 1899.

69 Joep Leerssen, *National Thought in Europe: A Cultural History* (Amsterdam, 2006), p. 263.

70 Roland Barthes, *Mythologies*, new edn, Richard Howard (ed.), Richard Howard and Annette Lavers (trans.) (1957: New York, 2012), pp 48–52. The Dominici trial is compared with the events of Maamtrasna in an insightful article by Stiofán Ó Cadhla, 'Tiontú an Chultúir: Affaire Dominici agus Maolra Seoighe', in *Études Irlandaises*, 2010, 35.2, pp 35–50. See Margaret Atack's fascinating account of the trial, its contemporary status as *fait divers* and its cultural (including cinematic) afterlives in 'L'Affaire Dominici: Rural France, the State and the nation', in *French Cultural Studies*, October 2001, 12.3, pp 285–301.

71 Barthes, *Mythologies*, p. 49. The Dominici affair was also the subject of an (unfinished) episode in Orson Welles' ground-breaking 1955 television travelogue series *Around the World with Orson Welles*, entitled 'The tragedy of Lurs', and footage of Welles' documentary and partial reconstruction of the murder features in the British Film Institute's 2015 DVD reissue of the *Around the World* series.

72 Gerald Griffin, *The Collegians* (1829; republished Belfast, 1992), pp 251–7.

73 Ibid., p. 256.

74 Ibid., p. 256.

75 Wolf, *An Irish-Speaking Island*, p. 84.

76 Ibid., p. 89.

77 Ibid., p. 102.

78 Somerville and Ross's diaries record their spending three days in Cashel, County Galway (Wednesday 14 August to Friday 16 August 1901) as the guest of 'Johnny O'Loghlen', proprietor of the Zetland Arms Hotel in Cashel, having travelled by train from Ballinahinch to Recess, and then by car about five miles to Cashel. See MS. 17/874, Somerville and Ross Papers, Queen's University Belfast. My grateful thanks to Maura Farrelly and colleagues at Special Collections, QUB, for their expert assistance. For a fuller treatment of this essay, see Margaret Kelleher, 'An Irish problem: Bilingual manoeuvres in the work of Somerville and Ross', in Anna Pilz and Whitney Standlee (eds), *Irish Women's Writing: Advancing the Cause of Irish Liberty, 1878–1922* (Manchester, 2016), pp 121–36.

79 'An Irish problem' was published, for a fee of 20 pounds, in the conservative journal *National Review* and soon after included in their 1903 essay collection *All on the Irish Shore* (London, 1903), pp 182–92.

80 Somerville and Ross, 'An Irish problem', pp 182–3. The depiction of Darcy compares interestingly with some of the detail of James Joyce's 1907 pen portrait of Myles Joyce.

81 Ibid., p. 186.

82 Ibid., p. 184.

83 Ibid., p. 185.

84 Ibid., p. 183.

85 Ibid., pp 191–2. *Méar* is the Irish word for finger, and *méar coise* one of the Irish words for 'toe.'

86 Somerville and Ross, 'An Irish problem', pp 197–8.

87 Kwai Hang Ng, *The Common Law in Two Voices: Language, Law and the Post-Colonial Predicament in Hong Kong* (California, 2009), p. 5.

88 Ibid., p. 28.

89 Ibid., p. 258.

90 Elizabeth Mertz, *The Language of Law School: Learning to 'Think Like a Lawyer'* (New York, 2007), p. 131.

91 A key early volume in defining the field is Franz Pöchhacker and Miriam Shlesinger (eds), *Interpreting Studies Reader* (London, 2002). On translation studies, see the invaluable series by Michael Cronin, including *Translating Ireland: Translation, Languages and Identity* (Cork, 1996); *Across the Lines: Travel, Language, Translation* (Cork, 2000); *Translation and Globalization* (London, 2003) and *Translation in the Digital Age* (London, 2013).

92 Ruth Morris, 'The gum syndrome: Predicaments in court interpreting', *Forensic Linguistics*, 1999, 6.1, pp 6–29.

93 Ibid., p. 7.

94 Cecilia Wadensjö, *Interpreting as Interaction: On Dialogue-Interpreting in Immigrant Hearings and Medical Encounters* (Linköping, 1992). See also

Susan Berk-Seligson, *The Bilingual Courtroom: Court Interpreters in the Judicial Process* (Chicago, 1990; new edn, 2002), in particular the new chapter (Chapter 10, pp 219–40) added to the 2002 edn. Sandra Hale, *The Discourse of Court Interpreting: Discourse Practices of the Law, the Witness and the Interpreter* (Amsterdam, 2004); Morris, 'The gum syndrome'; Philipp Sebastian Angermeyer, 'Translation style and participant roles in court interpreting', in *Journal of Sociolinguistics*, 2009, 13.1, pp 3–28.

95 Hale, *The Discourse of Court Interpreting*, p. 236.

96 On treatment of Aboriginal peoples by the Australian law system, see chapters by Michael Walsh and Diane Eades in John Gibbons (ed.), *Language and the Law* (Harlow, 1994), pp 217–33 and 234–64 and articles by D. Mildren and Michael Walsh in the *Forensic Linguistics* special issue on law and interpreters (1999, 6.1), pp 137–60 and 161–95. On the treatment of Spanish speakers in the United States, see Berk-Seligson, *The Bilingual Courtroom*; on the conflict between Anglo-American law and the Hopi tribal court, see Justin B. Richland, *Arguing with Tradition: The Language of Law in Hopi Tribal Court* (Chicago, 2008).

97 'Court interpreters are linguistic marshals who police the boundary separating English evidence from Cantonese utterances': Ng, *The Common Law in Two Voices*, p. 121.

98 Angermeyer, 'Translation style', p. 24.

CHAPTER 5

1 Roland Barthes, *Mythologies*, new edn, Richard Howard (ed.), Richard Howard and Annette Lavers (trans.) (1957; New York, 2012), p. 52.

2 Emmet's famous 1803 speech from the dock was delivered in Green Street, with its ringing lines 'If I stand at the bar of this court and dare not vindicate my character, what a farce is your justice. If I stand at this bar and dare not vindicate my character, how dare you calumniate it!' See Robert Emmet, *The Life, Trial and Conversations of Robert Emmet, Esq.* (New York, 1845), p. 114. 'Cyclops' features two direct references to court activities in Green Street. See James Joyce, *Ulysses* (1922; Harmondsworth, 1982), pp 297, 321.

3 *Graphic* (London), 2 December 1882.

4 This can be inferred from details in the court transcript: see in particular the trial of Michael Casey. *The Dublin October Commission. 13th November, 1882. County of Galway. The Maumtrasna Massacre*, Convict Reference Files (hereafter CRF) (1902), J13, folder 29, National Archives (hereafter NA), p. 221.

5 *Belfast Newsletter* (hereafter *BN*), 14 November 1882; *Freeman's Journal* (hereafter *FJ*), 17 November 1882.

6 The trial transcript is available in CRF (1902), J13, folder 29, NA.

7 Barthes, *Mythologies*, p. 49.

8 See, for example, the testimony of John Collins, *The Dublin October Commission*, p. 11.

9 Elizabeth Mertz, *The Language of Law School: Learning to 'Think Like a Lawyer'* (New York, 2007), p. 131.

10 See trial accounts in *Irish Times* (hereafter *IT*), 16 November 1882, and *Daily Express* (hereafter *DE*), 16 November 1882.

11 *FJ*, 14 November 1882.

12 *IT*, 15 November 1882.

13 Witnesses for the defence of Patrick Joyce included his neighbours Michael Joyce (Irish-speaking and examined through an interpreter) and Patrick Keenahan (English-speaking); *The Dublin October Commission*, pp 59–60. Patrick Casey's witnesses included his Irish-speaking mother, Julia Casey, and his cousin Mary Casey; see *The Dublin October Commission*, pp 123–7.

14 Until the passing of the Criminal Evidence Act of 1898, prisoners and their spouses were excluded from examination or cross-examination in criminal cases and were regarded as 'incompetent' witnesses with a special interest. Prisoners could make only unsworn statements from the dock following the delivery of sentences. See W. E. Vaughan, *Murder Trials in Ireland, 1836-1914* (Dublin, 2009), pp 175–6.

15 See report in *IT*, 1 November 1882.

16 Malley was called to the bar in 1843 and became Queen's Counsel in 1868. In 1884 he unsuccessfully contested a parliamentary seat as Conservative candidate in South Mayo; his opponent, the former Fenian prisoner, J. F. X. O'Brien secured 99 per cent of the vote. Malley later became senior Crown Prosecutor for Galway and Father of the Connaught Bar before his death in 1900. See death notice, *IT*, 12 September 1900.

17 See F. Elrington Ball, *The Judges in Ireland 1221–1921*, vol. ii (London, 1926), p. 38. A useful general resource is Maurice Healy, *The Old Munster Circuit* (London, 1939).

18 *IT*, 13 November 1882.

19 Costs for all witnesses, prosecution and defence, were paid by the Crown. See George Bolton, *A Short Account of the Discovery and Conviction of the 'Invincibles' and of some trials of which the writer had charge in 1881, 1882, 1883 and 1884 with a few observations on preliminary investigations in criminal cases* (Dublin, 1887), pp 38–9. According to Bolton, the defence solicitor served notice of the names of 'twenty witnesses, two to provide alibis for each of the accused' and that those witnesses were in court during the trials, including Peter Lyden and Mary Conboy who were alibi witnesses for Myles Joyce.

20 Under the provisions of the 1882 Prevention of Crime (Ireland) Act, a special jury could be convened rather than a common jury, and was considered by the prosecution more likely to convict. All the Maamtrasna trials were heard by special juries, i.e. selected from among the special (and usually more affluent) jurors listed in the jurors book; see Vaughan, *Murder Trials in Ireland*, pp

17–18, 129. Chapter 4 of Vaughan's work provides an excellent discussion of nineteenth-century procedures for empanelling juries.

21 *BN*, 14 November 1882. Niamh Howlin observes that the number of jurors ordered to 'stand by' at the commencement of Patrick Joyce's trials (37) was exceptionally high for the period. This was a right, open to the Crown, which permitted the exclusion of jurors without stating cause, and was widely seen as a form of 'jury-packing' to secure an outcome favourable to the prosecution. See Niamh Howlin, *Report on the Trial of Myles Joyce, November 1882*, prepared for the Irish Government, July 2017, pp 16–7; http://www.justice.ie /en/JELR/Report_by_Dr_Niamh_Howlin_Maamtrasna_Murders.pdf/Files /Report_by_Dr_Niamh_Howlin_Maamtrasna_Murders.pdf.

22 *FJ*, 14 November 1882. In the later cases of Patrick Casey and Myles Joyce, the jury's occupations were not specified in the *Freeman's* report.

23 *The Dublin October Commission*, p. 11.

24 In the next trial, that of Patrick Casey, two days later, Collins' evidence is rendered only in the third person (as it is for all subsequent appearances). His conversation with Michael receives only passing attention from O'Brien and no reference is made to Collins' conversation with Patsy. *The Dublin October Commission*, p. 85.

25 *The Dublin October Commission*, pp 12–13.

26 Philipp Sebastian Angermeyer, 'Translation style and participant roles in court interpreting', in *Journal of Sociolinguistics*, 2009, 13.1, pp 3–28. See also Philipp Sebastian Angermeyer, *Speak English or What?: Codeswitching and Interpreter Use in New York City Courts* (Oxford, 2015), Chapter 4, pp 69–100.

27 Angermeyer, 'Translation style', pp 5–6.

28 Ibid.

29 *The Dublin October Commission*, p. 15.

30 As Angermeyer notes, official transcripts of trials today 'generally include only translations, but not the original utterances made in a language other than the official language of the court'; see his 'Translation style', p. 5. Interestingly, while contemporary newspapers employed a variety of reporting strategies, the majority of journalists chose to reproduce the Joyces' examination and cross-examination in the first person, increasing dramatic effect but in effect performing a further act of translation from Evans' third-person formal interpretation.

31 According to Waldron, Mary was 'sent to school and learned her English there', the school in question being the Churchill (Protestant-run) school in Derrypark; see Jarlath Waldron, *Maamtrasna: The Murders and the Mystery* (Dublin, 1992), p. 67.

32 *The Dublin October Commission*, p. 28.

33 Ibid., p. 146.

34 Ibid., pp 123–7.

35 Ibid., 124–5.

36 Ibid., 146–7.

37 Ibid., p. 30.

38 Ibid., p. 29.

39 Ibid., p. 178.

40 In Stritch's closing speech for the defence of Patrick Joyce, this argument reached an almost farcical level: 'Their story [that of Philbin and Casey] is merely a repetition of the story they heard at least six or seven times repeated by the witnesses swearing against them. The witnesses for the crown, who were Irish-speaking, were examined before the prisoners, when the depositions were taken. It was given in Irish and translated and written down by the magistrates. Therefore it was told twice and then read by the magistrates, turned into Irish again, and the two witnesses, Casey and Philbin, for the second time heard the story', *The Dublin October Commission*, p. 61.

41 Ibid., p. 39.

42 Ibid.

43 Ibid.

44 Ibid., p. 134.

45 Janet Malcolm, *Iphigenia in Forest Hills: Anatomy of a Murder Trial* (New Haven, CT, 2011), p. 56.

46 *The Dublin October Commission*, p. 49.

47 *DE*, 15 November 1882. In its first coverage of the case in August, that newspaper had reported on the boy's 'blood-marked and bandaged head' (*DE*, 21 August 1882).

48 *DE*, 15 November 1882.

49 Dying declaration of Patrick (Patsy) Joyce, taken 18 August 1882, Crown Briefs, 1882, National Archive, Dublin: *The Queen vs Anthony Philbin and Others*, p. 46.

50 *The Dublin October Commission*, p. 156.

51 Chief Secretary's Office Registered Papers, National Archives 1890/5749 (Joyce compensation file).

52 *Spectator*, 18 November 1882.

53 *Evening Mail* (hereafter *EM*), 20 November 1882.

54 *The Dublin October Commission*, p. 27.

55 Ibid., p. 125.

56 Evans also received much praise from court reporters: *FJ*, 15 November 1882, in its coverage of day two of the trial, cited the 'surprising clearness' with which 'the Irish speaking witnesses give their evidence through the interpreter.' The *DE*, 16 November 1882, expressed its regret that, due to 'the strict rules of the constabulary force,' Evans would not 'receive remuneration for his skilled services rendered in this case to the judge and jury.'

57 *The Dublin October Commission*, p. 55.

58 Ibid., p. 137.

59 Ibid., p. 143.

60 In the court transcript the response of the prisoner to the guilty verdict was merely recorded as follows: 'The prisoner – I am not guilty.' *FJ*, 16 November 1882; *IT*, 16 November 1882.

61 O'Brien's memoir was completed and edited by his daughter Georgina: Peter O'Brien, Georgina O'Brien (ed.), *The Reminiscences of the Right Honourable Lord O'Brien* (New York and London, 1916), p. 48.

62 Vaughan, *Murder Trials in Ireland*, p. 294. Earlier Vaughan discusses Barry's record as a 'hanging judge' and shows it was third in order of severity in comparison to his contemporary judges: in a ten-year period Barry pronounced 11 sentences of death (his fellow judges William O'Brien and Richard Moore delivered 16 and 18 respectively); see Vaughan, *Murder Trials in Ireland*, pp 258–9.

63 *The Dublin October Commission*, p. 147.

64 *FJ*, 18 November 1882.

65 Ibid.

66 Ibid. The court transcript does not record this exchange.

67 *EM*, 17 November 1882.

68 *FJ*, 18 November 1882. The analogy also featured a misattribution by the journalist, who confused the recent conviction of Patrick Walsh for the murder of Martin Lydon in Letterfrack with the conviction of his brother Michael for the murder of prosecution witness Constable Kavanagh. Patrick Walsh was hanged in Galway Jail on 22 September 1882; in October his brother Michael was found guilty of the murder of Constable Kavanagh but was not executed.

69 *Weekly Freeman*, 25 November 1882.

70 *The Dublin October Commission*, p. 149.

71 Ibid., pp 151–2.

72 For example, *FJ*, 18 November 1882.

73 *FJ*, 18 November 1882. At the commencement of Myles' trial, the Crown ordered 27 men to stand by. Myles' defence counsel, exercising his right to challenge jurors, sought to exclude one juror who had been present during the previous trials but was unsuccessful; this man was instead made foreman of the jury. See *The Dublin October Commission*, pp 152–4.

74 *FJ*, 20 November 1882.

75 *The Dublin October Commission*, p. 157.

76 Ibid., p. 162; later that day, in his summing up, Barry commented on the linguistic specificity of this answer: 'He is asked did he know Myles Joyce, and he replied I knew him since I knew anyone – a peculiar phrase they use in Ireland', p. 208.

77 *The Dublin October Commission* p. 165; baptismal records from the parish suggest that Myles and his wife, Bridget, had five children living, aged between 3 and 12 at the time of the trial.

78 At this time, jurors had the right to question witnesses and often exercised that right.

79 *The Dublin October Commission*, p. 170.

80 *BN*, 20 November 1882. Later that day, Malley's cross-examination of Philbin would establish publicly, for the first time in the trial, and with some reluctance from the witness, that besides being a brother-in-law of Thomas Casey, he was a first cousin of John and Patrick Casey.

81 *The Dublin October Commission*, p. 165.

82 Ibid., p. 189.

83 Ibid., p. 190.

84 In his memoir, Bolton makes much of the fact that the defence did not call Peter Lydon and Mary Conaboy, who had stated that 'they slept in Myles Joyce's house, and that he was not absent from it on that night', claiming that 'it was known that they could not stand the test of cross-examination.' See Bolton, *A Short Account*, p. 39.

85 *The Dublin October Commission*, p. 196.

86 Ibid., pp 196–7. The National Folklore Collection (NFC) includes many references to this belief, namely that the corpse of a murdered man bleeds in the presence of, or if touched by, the murderer; see NFC 41, pp 251, 309 (collected by Seán Mac Mathshamhna in County Clare) and NFC 908, pp 339–41 (collected by Seosamh Ó Dálaigh from Peig Sayers, Dún Chaoin).

87 *The Dublin October Commission*, p. 197.

88 Ibid.

89 Ibid., p. 199.

90 Ibid., p. 203.

91 Ibid., pp 209–10.

92 Ibid., pp 207–8.

93 Ibid., p. 210.

94 The square brackets are included in the court transcript. Ibid.

95 Ibid.

96 Vaughan records the instance of Patrick Lydane in Galway in 1858 whose scaffold speech in Irish was translated by the jail's chaplain, his statement that he was 'as innocent as the child unborn' causing 'a sensation': Vaughan, *Murder Trials in Ireland*, p. 344. An example of fictional usage occurs in Carleton's 'The Donagh; or The Horse Stealers', a much-anthologised story first published in his second series, *Traits and Stories of the Irish Peasantry* (Dublin, 1833). Another famous instance of this protest is credited to the Donegal man Charlie Sharpe, who was alleged to be a Molly Maguire and to have been implicated in an 1863 murder in the United States; Sharpe was executed in 1879 and his scaffold protest, of being 'as innocent as the babe unborn' was widely reported: see Breandán Mac Suibhne, *The End of Outrage: Post-Famine Adjustment in Rural Ireland* (Oxford, 2017), pp 231–2.

97 *FJ*, 20 November 1882.

98 Ibid. This account of court reactions to the verdict was reproduced in the *Nation*, 25 November 1882. Myles Joyce's protestations of innocence also featured prominently in other newspaper accounts including the *IT*, 20 November 1882, and the *BN* of the same day. The *BN* correspondent chose to render Myles' words in the first person, though in more standard English prose.

99 *DE*, 20 November 1882.

100 Ibid.

101 *The Dublin October Commission*, p. 209.

102 Ibid., p. 210.

103 Ibid.

104 Ibid.

105 *IT*, 20 November 1882.

106 *FJ*, 21 November 1882.

107 *DE*, 21 November 1882.

108 *Dublin Evening Mail*, 20 November 1882.

109 *IT*, 21 November 1882.

110 *The Dublin October Commission*, p. 211.

111 *FJ*, 21 November 1882.

112 Ibid.

113 *The Dublin October Commission*, p. 221.

114 Vaughan, *Murder Trials in Ireland*, pp 175–6.

115 *The Dublin October Commission*, p. 221.

116 Ibid.

117 *BN*, 21 November 1882.

118 *FJ*, 22 November 1882.

119 *The Dublin October Commission*, p. 241.

120 See Tim Harrington, *The Maamtrasna Massacre: Impeachment of the Trials* (Dublin, 1884), p. v: 'he, by pointing out to them that if they were innocent, their vindication might come in good time, induced them to accept the terms held out to them.'

121 Ibid., p. 35.

122 *Graphic*, 25 November 1882.

123 See, for example, *FJ*, 22 November 1882.

124 *FJ*, 22 November 1882. In the court transcript, Barry's delivery of the death sentence to the five accused was followed by a rare moment of descriptive comment by the court reporter in what were the closing lines of the 243-page document: 'The prisoners, huddled together in front of the dock, evinced every anxiety to understand what had been said, but evidently failed'; see *The Dublin October Commission*, p. 243.

125 *The Dublin October Commission*, p. 243.

126 Counsel for the crown included many of the same personnel from the Maamtrasna trial (James Murphy, Peter O'Brien as well as Bolton, the State Solicitor) while the men's defence included the firm of Teeling and Adams, and established local solicitor P. J. B. Daly of Ballinrobe. The judge was Justice William O'Brien who soon after presided over the trial of the 'Invincibles' for the Phoenix Park murders of May 1882.

127 'Long' was an adjective added colloquially to his name, and this epithet was generally used in coverage of the case.

128 These details are drawn from the *Freeman's Journal* account of the Huddy trials, 8 December 1882.

129 The *FJ* coverage of the case noted that 'Head-Constable Evans, who acted as interpreter during the Maamtrasna murder trials, was again sworn as interpreter between the English speaking witnesses and the Irish speaking prisoner', 8 December 1882. In fact, as we've seen, Evans had performed this role for the accused only briefly during the Maamtrasna trials, during the short trial of Michael Casey; otherwise his main task was to translate for the Irish-speaking crown witnesses.

130 See *FJ*, 15 December 1882; *BN*, 19 December 1882.

131 *FJ*, 8 December 1882.

132 Ibid.

133 *FJ*, 8 December 1882.

134 *FJ*, 22 November 1882.

135 Howlin, *Report on Myles Joyce*, p. 2.

136 Ibid., p. 28.

137 Ibid., pp 31–2.

CHAPTER 6

1 Jacques Derrida, *The Death Penalty*, vol. 1, in *The Seminars of Jacques Derrida*, vol. 9, Peggy Kamuf (trans.) (2012; Chicago, 2014), First Session, p. 25.

2 *Freeman's Journal* (hereafter *FJ*), 27 November 1882.

3 Marwood (1818–83) served as executioner for the British government from 1874 until his death in 1883; during those nine years he hanged a total of 176 people in Britain and Ireland, including five members of the 'Invincibles' found guilty of the Phoenix Park Murders. He was also notorious for his development of the 'long drop' hanging method which was designed to break a prisoner's neck at the drop's end rather than the 'slow drop' method of death by strangulation. See Howard Engel, *Lord High Executioner: An Unashamed Look at Hangmen, Headsmen, and Their Kind* (Ontario, 1996), pp 59–70.

4 *Irish Times* (hereafter *IT*), 7 December 1882.

5 Letter from Barry to Spencer, 29 November 1882. See Convict Reference File (hereafter CRF), 1902, J13, folder 10, National Archives (hereafter NA).

6 In subsequent correspondence with Queen Victoria, Spencer expressed

personal regret that the mitigation proved necessary, and criticised the 'law officers' for not being 'more guarded' in their dealings with the prisoners' counsel; Victoria's deep displeasure that the full 'penalty of the law' was not carried out was expressed in a handwritten reply. See Earl Spencer to Queen Victoria, 11 December 1882, and Queen Victoria to Earl Spencer, 9 January 1883, Althorp Papers, Add 76831 and 76832, British Library.

7 The correspondence between the *Freeman's Journal* newspaper office and Dublin Castle can be found in CRF, 1902, J13, folder 18, NA.

8 Ibid.

9 *FJ*, 13 December 1882.

10 CRF, 1902, J13, folder 18, NA.

11 Ibid.

12 Ibid., folder 21, NA.

13 Ibid.

14 In his second statement, Joyce elaborated on this claim, stating that 'the man (unnamed) in whose house they had met' was a relative of John Joyce's wife, who had told him that her husband 'had gone two nights to this man's barn "asking to get opportunity to kill him,"' and that this was the reason 'why he had got John Joyce killed.' Ibid. Harrington's pamphlet would identify the man unnamed by Patrick Joyce as 'Big' John Casey who remained uncharged. Tim Harrington, *The Maamtrasna Massacre: Impeachment of the Trials* (Dublin, 1884), p. ix.

15 Patrick Casey also appears to have made a statement to Magistrate Brady: The files include a two-page unwitnessed document in which he alleged that 'the first and second days we were in the dock in Dublin' he had been asked by Thomas Casey to 'turn witness to the Crown.' Curiously Casey's statement exonerated his brother John by implication but not explicitly. CRF, 1902, J13, folder 21, NA.

16 The line 'Myles is no relation … if he is hanged' appears to be in another's hand but Patrick Joyce's own signature follows. Ibid.

17 The same report also conveyed, without comment, the official response by Kaye to the Myles Joyce memorial: 'that his Excellency, after a careful consideration of all of the circumstances of the case, had felt it his painful duty to decide that the law must take its course'; see *FJ*, 15 December 1882.

18 The statements can be found in a file held by Under-Secretary W. B. Kaye, to whom Mason forwarded the documents on 13 and 14 December. See CRF, 1902, J13, folder 21, NA.

19 In *Discipline and Punish*, Foucault notes that, in comparative international terms, 'England was one of the countries most loath to see the disappearance of the public execution'; see Michel Foucault, *Discipline and Punish: The Birth of the Prison* (1975; London [trans.], 1977), p. 14. For some recorded uses of Irish on the executioner's platform between the 1820s and 1850s, see Nicholas

Wolf, *An Irish-Speaking Island: State, Religion and the Linguistic Landscape in Ireland 1770–1870* (Madison, 2014), pp 52–3.

20 See V. A. C. Gattrell, *The Hanging Tree: Execution and the English People 1770–1868* (Oxford, 1994), p. 46. The closing lines of Gatrell's 600-page work provide a powerful rejoinder to any reader's assumption that the history of execution closed in 1868: 'Appeals to humanity encased their policy, but the state's retributive power continued to override imaginative compassion, and the horror continued behind prison walls for a century yet … within the secret prison power was to be – and is – wielded more efficiently than ever it had been at Tyburn', pp 610–11.

21 John Stuart Mill, 'Civilisation: Signs of the times', in *London and Westminister Review*, 1836, XXV, pp 1–28.

22 Gattrell, *The Hanging Tree*, pp 610–11.

23 Derrida, *The Death Penalty*, vol. 1, p. 25.

24 Dunlop provided a brief account of the execution in his 1911 memoir *Andrew Dunlop, Fifty Years of Irish Journalism* (London and Dublin, 1911), pp 207–10. Later in the memoir, he acknowledges that he 'knew not a word' of Irish, p. 216. Dunlop remained equivocal about Myles Joyce's innocence, arguing that the statement by the two other executed men 'implying that Joyce was innocent … probably only meant that he was not one of the actual perpetrators of the crime', p. 208.

25 Gattrell, *The Hanging Tree*, p. 267.

26 *IT*, 15 December 1882.

27 Ibid., 12 December 1882.

28 The correspondent for the *Evening Telegraph* highlighted the curious absence of relatives in the vicinity of the jail: 'In vain I looked for a single relative of the wretches who had that morning risen never to sleep again, but not one of their kinsmen had come to learn the mournful tidings which the black flag conveyed.' *Evening Telegraph*, 15 December 1882. Friends and relatives of Myles Joyce had campaigned to the last days for his release.

29 As Elaine Scarry has remarked in her study of 'the structure of torture', 'What assists the conversion of absolute pain into the fiction of absolute power is an obsessive, self-conscious display of agency. On the simplest level the agent displayed is the weapon.' See Elaine Scarry, *The Body in Pain: The Making and Unmaking of the World* (New York and Oxford, 1985), p. 27.

30 *Galway Vindicator and Connaught Advertiser* (hereafter *GVCA*), 16 December 1882.

31 *Galway Express* (hereafter *GE*), 16 December 1882.

32 *GVCA*, 16 December 1882; these two men are likely to have been the prison chaplain, Greaven, and an Irish-speaking warder named Coen.

33 *GE*, 16 December 1882.

34 Ibid. One of the most distinctive features of this *Galway Express* article is the journalist's phonetic transcription in Irish of one of Myles' repeated phrases,

Arrah thawmay glimmacht. The Irish phrase, phonetically transcribed (original: *táim ag imeacht*), was italicised for dramatic effect in the newspaper printing and accompanied by a parenthetical translation, 'I am going'. The translation, however, removes the power of the opening vocal exclamation, *Arrah*.

35 Ibid.

36 *GE*, 16 December 1882.

37 Ibid.

38 Ibid.

39 Ibid.

40 Ibid.

41 Ibid.

42 Ibid.

43 *FJ*, 16 December 1882.

44 Ibid.

45 *Evening Telegraph*, 15 December 1882.

46 *Belfast Newsletter*, 16 December 1882.

47 Chief Secretary's Office Registered Papers, National Archives (hereafter CSORP, NA) 1883/189.

48 Account reproduced in *New Zealand Herald*, Saturday, 31 March 1883.

49 James Joyce, 'Ireland at the bar' (1901), reproduced in Ellsworth Mason and Richard Ellmann (eds), *The Critical Writings of James Joyce* (New York, 1959), pp 197–8. The variant translations of this essay will be discussed in detail in Chapter 9.

50 The records from this investigation survive in the CSORP, NA, files but have not previously been examined by commentators on Maamtrasna. They are available in CSORP, NA 1883/189.

51 The impact of the Maamtrasna case on the career of Spencer, including his reactions to the convicted men's appeals, is examined in detail in the recent biography by James Murphy, *Ireland's Czar: Gladstonian Government and the Lord Lieutenancies of the Red Earl Spencer, 1868–1886* (Dublin, 2014). While Spencer's papers in the British Library (Althorp Papers) and Royal Archives, along with some contemporary newspapers, are the subject of close investigation by Murphy, this and other significant CSORP, NA, files relating to Spencer's work as Lord Lieutenant are not discussed.

52 The practice of the *Athenaeum* was not to print anonymous communications; see, for example, the note in its issue of 30 December 1882, 2879, p. 908: 'No notice can be taken of anonymous communications.'

53 CSORP, NA 1883/189.

54 These nine witnesses were the prison governor Mason, the sub-sheriff Redington, chaplain Fr Greaven, medical doctor Rice, and five prison warders named Evans, St. George, McGann, Coen, and Sammon. CSORP, NA 1883/189.

55 Richard Kinkead (1858–1928) was appointed surgeon of Galway Jail in 1879 and was also Professor of Midwifery at Queen's College Galway (appointed 1876). He was unable to attend the execution due to a summons to attend the assizes in Sligo as a crown witness and nominated the more junior Rice in his stead. Patrick M. Rice was a private practitioner and consulting sanitary officer to Galway Urban District. Kinkead did not support Rice's findings. CSORP, NA 1883/189.

56 Ibid.

57 Ibid.

58 This view was echoed by other witnesses; Sub-Sheriff Redington, for example, testified that the reason for the 'hitch' was 'the excitement of Myles Joyce.' Ibid.

59 Ibid.

60 Ibid.

61 The last third of this passage had originally read: 'the Executioner had considerable difficulty in getting it again placed into proper position. If he had not succeeded in doing so without delay it is possible that a serious failure in carrying out the execution might have occurred.' The manuscript in CSORP, NA 1883/189 shows that this text was struck out by Spencer and reworded by him from the phrase 'the executioner felt it necessary' onwards.

62 According to the Dictionary of National Biography's entry on Higginbottom, he remained as special correspondent in Ireland for almost ten years and his reporting during that period 'established the Press Association as the principal supplier of Irish news for the London and provincial press.' Dilwyn Porter, 'Higginbottom, Frederick James (1859–1943)', in *Oxford Dictionary of National Biography* (Oxford, 2004); http://www.oxforddnb.com/, 8 January 2017.

63 A notable example is the London *Daily News*, Saturday, 16 December 1882, which ran a lengthy eye-witness report on the executions and on the subsequent contentious inquest.

64 See Frederick J. Higginbottom, *The Vivid Life: A Journalist's Career* (London, 1934), p. 38. Higginbottom (1859–1943) would subsequently become a journalist with the *Pall Mall Gazette* (1900–19), where he briefly served as editor (1909–12), and journalist with the *Daily Chronicle* (1919–30). He commented on Irish affairs on occasion in later years, including a contribution to the *Empire Review and Magazine*, vol. 23 (1914), pp 93–9.

65 For example, the translation of *Go maithid Dia do'n mhuintir* in Higginbottom's volume as 'God forgive them' omits the particular charge of *muintir* (meaning 'household, community, family'). *Táim co saor leis an leanbh* is translated as 'I am as innocent as the child', but *saor*, while meaning 'blameless' and 'innocent', has the primary meanings of 'free', 'independent', or 'noble.' Higginbottom, *The Vivid Life*, p. 42.

66 Higginbottom, *The Vivid Life*, p. 43.

67 See Erll and Rigney's work on 'memorial dynamics', situated by them as part of a wider shift within memory studies from the study of 'sites of memory' to an examination of 'dynamics' and processes of circulation. Astrid Erll and Ann Rigney (eds), *Mediation, Remediation and the Dynamics of Cultural Memory* (Berlin and Boston, 2012), p. 3.

CHAPTER 7

1 Tim Harrington, *The Maamtrasna Massacre: Impeachment of the Trials* (Dublin, 1884) p. 43.

2 *Spectator*, 11 November 1882; my thanks to Ciarán O'Neill for this reference.

3 See article from 'The Globe', reproduced in the *Freeman's Journal*, 22 December 1882.

4 According to Healy, Harcourt could not pronounce the word 'Maamtrasna', and always called it 'Manstrasma.' See T. M. Healy, *Letters and Leaders of My Day* (London, 1928), p. 188.

5 House of Commons Debates (hereafter HC Deb), 26 April 1883, 3.278, c. 1137.

6 Ibid. As discussed in the previous chapter, the statement by Patrick Joyce as signed by Brady included the closing line: 'Myles is no relation of mine in the world – it is the greatest murder in Ireland that ever was if he is hanged', and other statements by Joyce and Casey, taken immediately prior to the executions, had termed Myles 'as innocent as the child unborn of the crime.'

7 'Arabi' refers to the Egyptian nationalist Colonel Ahmed 'Urabi, known as 'Arabi Pasha' who was tried for rebellion in December 1882 and whose death sentence was commuted to banishment for life. The reference to 'Suleiman' is probably a reference to Sultan Sulaiman II, Malay ruler of the Dutch protectorate Riau-Lingga, who died in 1883.

8 HC Deb, 13 August 1883, 3.283, cc 284–390, 294–5. Harrington went on to argue that Myles Joyce was disadvantaged by the holding of his trial in Dublin since his counsel was unable to bring witnesses necessary to his defence and that he was tried by a packed jury.

9 HC Deb, 13 August 1883, 3.283, cc 284–390, 297.

10 O'Shea was the husband of Katharine (Kitty) O'Shea, who later became the wife of Charles Stewart Parnell.

11 HC Deb, 13 August 1883, 3.283, cc 284–390, 302.

12 Ibid., 17 August 1883, 3.283, cc 1022–81, 1035–6.

13 Ibid., cc 1044–5.

14 *Freeman's Journal* (hereafter *FJ*), 11 August 1884.

15 In chapter 18 of his 1911 *Reminiscences*, entitled 'A Third Visit to Maamtrasna', Dunlop provides another account of his travels west, this time to interview Casey and Philbin, and again the difficulties of the journey are given the most detailed attention. See Andrew Dunlop, *Fifty Years of Irish Journalism*

(London and Dublin, 1911), pp 207–18. Philbin, the journalist recollected, 'would say nothing, indeed, on the subject which had led me to visit him until Father Corbett spoke to him in Irish – doubtless making him aware that I knew not a word of that language', p. 216. His encounters were not enough to persuade him of the veracity of Casey or Philbin's new testimony: at the end of the chapter, Dunlop warmly praises Spencer's August 1884 rebuttal to McEvilly and confidently (and quite erroneously) concludes that 'the agitation on the subject' then ceased and 'there was no mention afterwards of the Maamtrasna case either in Parliament or in the Press', p. 218.

16 *FJ*, 11 August 1884.

17 Ibid.

18 Ibid.

19 *FJ*, 11 August 1884.

20 Ibid., p. 12 August 1884.

21 Ibid.

22 The Chief Secretary papers include extensive correspondence relating to the internal inquiry ordered by Spencer. These include a detailed confidential report from RIC District Inspector Read of Athlone in August 1884 who suggested that money was a large motivation for Casey's actions along with his wife 'wanting revenge on the Joyce witnesses' for implicating Anthony Philbin, her brother. The file also includes a number of affidavits from local RIC members (some of whom understood Irish) who reported conversations overheard between Anthony Philbin and his relatives in which Philbin provided conflicting accounts as to his own movements on the evening of 17 August 1882 but unequivocally asserted Myles Joyce's innocence. See Convict Reference File, 1902, J13, folder 20, National Archives. On Spencer's view of the McEvilly intervention, see James Murphy, *Ireland's Czar: Gladstonian Government and the Lord Lieutenancies of the Red Earl Spencer, 1868–1886* (Dublin, 2014), pp 316–17.

23 That Tim Harrington was the likely author is suggested by the author's self-identification as a friend of Fr Corbett; also the author explicitly distanced himself from the sceptical perspective adopted by the earlier 'energetic reporter' (Dunlop).

24 *FJ*, 6 September 1882.

25 Ibid.

26 Meaning an itinerant or wandering person.

27 This is the newspaper's style of transcription for *cóta mór*.

28 The *FJ* coverage was widely disseminated; for example the *Illustrated Police News*, 13 September 1884, quoted at length from the 6 September interview.

29 Healy, *Letters and Leaders*, p. 187.

30 Ibid.

31 A less well-known contemporary, and anonymously-authored, publication, entitled *The Mysteries of Ireland*, detailed events at Maamtrasna from

a pro-prosecution perspective. The three-hundred page book had a lengthy subtitle: 'giving a graphic and faithful account of Irish secret societies, and their plots, from the rebellion of 1798 to the year 1882, with the sketches of the lives of the leaders, their last speeches before condemnation, and the history of recent murders in Ireland'. This would appear to have been published in London c. 1883–4 and provided an 18-page account of the 1882 murders, trials and executions.

32 Harrington had published eight letters in the *FJ* on 20, 23, 25, 27 September; 2, 7, 10 and 15 October 1884, respectively. The Chief Secretary papers include a 24-page memorandum prepared by George Bolton for Under-Secretary Kaye in direct response to Harrington's *Freeman's* letters.

33 Bunachrick (spelt by Harrington Bun-na-cnic, a closer transliteration of the Irish *Bun an Chnoic*) was one of three villages in the townland of Derry, the others being Derrypark and Derrycasey. Thomas Casey, who was not related to the Caseys of Bunachrick, was from the village of Glensaul. John Casey was known locally as 'Big' John, a signal of his status of local 'strongman'.

34 Harrington, *The Maamtrasna Massacre*, p. 1.

35 Ibid.

36 Ibid., p. 2.

37 Ibid., pp 3–4.

38 Ibid. Harrington is alluding here to the notebooks kept by members of the Crime Branch Special Detective Force established in 1882.

39 See Patrick Maume, 'Harrington, Timothy Charles', in James McGuire and James Quinn (eds), *Dictionary of Irish Biography* (Cambridge, 2009); http://dib.cambridge.org/viewReadPage.do?articleId=a3816.

40 Harrington, *The Maamtrasna Massacre*, p. 4.

41 Ibid.

42 Ibid., p. 2.

43 Ibid.

44 Ibid., pp 14–15.

45 Ibid., p. 15.

46 Harrington uses the term loosely to refer to a secret local agrarian group.

47 Ibid., p. 26. The interview is reproduced on pp 23–31.

48 Ibid., pp 37–8.

49 Ibid., p. 16.

50 Ibid., p. 24.

51 Ibid., p. 38.

52 Ibid., p. 39.

53 Ibid., p. 40. The four depositions in question comprised those of John Collins, Constable Johnston, the dying declaration of Michael Joyce, and the dying declaration of Patrick Joyce, the last of which, as Harrington rightly noted, was 'hidden away in the last page of the crown brief, as if stowed out of sight.'

54 Ibid., p. 42.

55 Ibid., pp 42–3.

56 Ibid., p. 43.

57 HC Deb, 23 October 1884, 3.293, cc 127–49.

58 HC Deb, 23 October 1884, 3.293, c. 137.

59 Ibid., 24 October 1884, 3.293, cc 168–235, 186–7.

60 Ibid., c. 225. Trevelyan quoted in some detail from *United Ireland*'s initial expression of welcome for the verdict which reads as follows: 'The Maamtrasna trials are over, and such of the miserable creatures as did not turn approvers have been sentenced to be hanged. We believe the public are satisfied that a disgusting butchery has been avenged upon convincing evidence by juries comparatively fairly chosen.' *United Ireland*, 25 November 1882.

61 HC Deb, 27 October 1884, 3.293, cc 266–339, 268.

62 Ibid., cc 272–3.

63 Ibid., 28 October 1884, 3.293, cc 357–435, 383.

64 In his 1938 biography, Hammond suggests that Gladstone was 'less at ease about the case than his Attorney General and his Home Secretary' and also that the Prime Minister was open to the suggestion made by Gorst and Russell, in the immediate aftermath of the debate, that a retrial of three of the men was possible, on a different charge (i.e. by trying them for the murder of one of the other victims). This suggestion was firmly opposed by Spencer. See J. L. Hammond, *Gladstone and the Irish Nation* (New York, 1938), p. 321. For a refutation of Hammond's criticism of Spencer's 'short sightedness', see Murphy, *Ireland's Czar*, p. 320.

65 HC Deb, 17 July 1885, 3.299, c. 1064. The implications of Parnell's 1885 motion for Spencer are discussed by Murphy, *Ireland's Czar*, pp 350–2.

66 Ibid., cc 1101–1102.

67 Ibid., 10 August 1885, 3.300, c. 1572.

68 Ibid., 14 February 1895, 4.30, cc 782–806, 787. By then Harrington was a qualified barrister as well as MP; he was appointed to the Irish Bar in 1887 and served as Counsel for Parnell and colleagues at the Special Commission, 1888–9.

69 Ibid., c. 803. These petitions will be discussed in more detail in the next chapter.

70 Michel Foucault, *Discipline and Punish: The Birth of the Prison* (1975; London, 1977), p. 66.

71 'Lamentable lines on the execution of the Maamtrasna murderers', broadsheet ballad, National Folklore Collection, University College Dublin.

72 This line was famously issued from the dock in October 1867 by the Fenian Edward O'Meagher Condon, whose sentence was commuted on the eve of his execution. The speech is reproduced in T. D. Sullivan, A. M. Sullivan and D. B. Sullivan, *Speeches from the Dock; or, Protests of Irish Patriotism* (New York, 1904) pp 265–7.

73 'Lamentable lines', broadsheet ballad.

74 *Full Report of the Appearance of the Ghost of Myles Joyce in Galway Jail* (Dublin, 1883). The broadsheet was folded into an eight-page pamphlet and was printed by Nugent and company, High Street, Dublin.

75 *FJ*, 11 January 1883. In the newspaper article, 'tall mystic figure' is placed in quotation marks and the line reads: 'they state that the figure is Myles Joyce in the spirit'.

76 *Illustrated Police News*, 27 January 1883.

77 *FJ*, 13 September 1884.

78 Ibid., 17 August 1885.

79 John Garvin, *James Joyce's Disunited Kingdom and the Irish Dimension* (Dublin, 1976), p. 164.

80 Ibid., pp 164–5.

81 Ibid., p. 165. In addition, Nuns' Island, the home of Gretta's grandmother in 'The Dead' and where Gretta and Michael Furey meet for the last time, was also the location of Galway Jail; see James Joyce, *Dubliners* (1914; Dublin, 2012), p. 253. My thanks to Victor Luftig for this observation.

82 The *Freeman's Journal*, 10 February 1883, featured a long account of the trial and an editorial comment on the trial's outcome on 12 February.

83 T. P. O'Connor, *The Parnell Movement, with a Sketch of Irish Parties since 1843* (London, 1886), pp 501–5. The other case named by O'Connor is that of Patrick Higgins, who was one of the men convicted of the Lough Mask murders. In the 1887 'popular' edition of *The Parnell Movement*, the reference to Myles Joyce was condensed to one sentence: 'There was a strong feeling in Ireland that Myles Joyce – one of the men hanged for participation in the hideous Maamtrasna massacre – was innocent, and also some others who were still in penal servitude', p. 268.

84 Michael Davitt, *The Fall of Feudalism in Ireland, or The Story of the Land League Revolution* (London and New York, 1904), p. 381. See Carla King, *Michael Davitt after the Land League, 1882–1906* (Dublin, 2016), p. 58.

85 Garvin credits his source for Myles Joyce's last words as 'a local journalist who knew Irish' and 'took down his last words on the scaffold'; Garvin, *James Joyce's Disunited Kingdom*, p. 167. He may have drawn from Higginbottom as an intermediary source but their English translations differ slightly: for example, Higginbottom's 'I had neither hand or foot in the murder' changes in Garvin to 'I had neither hand or foot in the killing' and Higginbottom's line 'It is a poor thing to die on a stage' is, in Garvin, 'It's a poor thing to die on the scaffold' (the Irish term in Higginbottom's facsimile image is '*ar an g-croich*'); see Higginbottom, *The Vivid Life*, p. 42; Garvin, *James Joyce's Disunited Kingdom*, p. 167.

86 Jarlath Waldron, *Maamtrasna: The Murders and the Mystery* (Dublin, 1992), back cover. Waldron's version, which may draw on local retellings, is much

shorter than Higginbottom's: for example the line, 'It is a poor thing to die on a stage for what I never did' is omitted. Textual variants include Waldron's use of the more legal term '*neamhchiontach*' (literally, 'not guilty') rather than '*saor*' to denote innocence.

87 Ibid., p. 155.
88 See Patrick Joyce, 'The Journey West', in *Field Day Review*, 2014, 10, pp 60–91.
89 Patrick Joyce, *The State of Freedom: A Social History of the British State since 1800* (Cambridge, 2013), p. 307.
90 Ibid., pp 305–6.
91 Murphy, *Ireland's Czar*, p. 236. Kee supplied a foreword to Waldron's book in which he drew an explicit parallel between the comments by Judge Barry and the infamous 'appalling vista' remarks in the context of his refusal of the 1979 appeal by the 'Birmingham Six.'
92 Ibid., p. 235.
93 Ibid.

CHAPTER 8

1 Convict Reference Files (hereafter CRF) (1902), J13, folder 12, National Archives (hereafter NA).
2 T. M. Healy, *Letters and Leaders of My Day*, (London, 1928), p. 186.
3 The details that follow, including the prisoners' records and memorials, are drawn from CRF (1902), J13, NA and five General Prison Board (hereafter GPB), NA files, one for each of the five prisoners. Following a standard template, the penal record for each prisoner includes special remarks, a weekly record of marks and gratuities, a list of prison offenses, a record of petitions and applications by the prisoner, a roll of letters received, and a statement of visits accorded; see CRF (1902), J13. The five GPB files include fuller medical records as well as a list of letters written and received (recorded by the prison schoolmaster), and a list of visits. The imprisoned men received, on average, one or two letters a year mostly from their wives, and a handful of visits during their imprisonment. It is not specified how the letters were written or read, but the GPB file for Martin Joyce details petitions by him in Downpatrick in 1888 to gain assistance in letter-writing from a prisoner 'who understands Irish'; the official response was to grant help from 'an officer who understands Irish.' See GPB/PEN/1902/68, NA.
4 John's listed occupations in prison were initially 'picking rope junk', 'winding yarn' and 'shoemaking', and, after 1886, 'invalid'. See GPB/PEN/1900/118, NA.
5 Letter by Martin Joyce to Julia Joyce, 5 September 1884, reproduced in Tim Harrington, *The Maamtrasna Massacre: Impeachment of the Trials* (Dublin, 1884), p. 6.
6 Paudeen's listed occupation was 'light labour'; see GPB/PEN/1902/69, NA. His last outgoing letter is dated March 1900 and his GPB file includes a letter

sent by his wife 'Mrs Julia Joyce Patt' in January 1902 pleading for information regarding her husband, 'not having heard from him in a long time'. See GPB/PEN/1902/69, NA.

7 In November 1885, Martin Joyce had secured sufficient good behavior marks to be promoted to the first class of convict, but an obstacle to his promotion was his inability to read and write. The Downpatrick governor wrote positively on his behalf noting that Martin had 'been attending school and every effort has been made to teach him, but, with little effect, as he can only speak an odd word of English.' He also observed: 'The prisoner himself appears very anxious to learn but he cannot overcome the great disadvantage he labors under – not being able to speak English; and it is no fault of his, in my opinion, that he is not able to read and write.' See GPB/PEN/1902/68, NA.

8 GPB/PEN/1902/68, NA. The file shows also that in March 1895 Martin received a visit from Tim Harrington, a month after the MP had failed to gain parliamentary support for an inquiry into the conviction of the prisoners.

9 Martin's listed 'trade or occupation in prison' was woodcutting. See GPB/PEN/1902/68, NA. In the annual governor reports, Martin's conduct was listed as 'satisfactory', 'good', or 'very good' with the observation in 1890 that 'this prisoner has had very fair health since his admission to this prison.' CRF (1902), J13, folder 6, NA and GPB/PEN/1902/68.

10 See GPB/PEN/1902/70, NA.

11 The GPB file lists letters sent by Tom to Harrington in 1895, 1899 and 1900 (with one letter to Harrington suppressed in 1897), and many petitions sent by him after 1895. Family recipients included his sisters Kate and Margaret in America. Tom received a total of three visits in prison: one in November 1884 from Tim Harrington, one in August 1893 from Fr Mellet, and one in December 1895 from his mother Julia and sister Bridget. Following his transfer to Maryborough in 1898, he appears to have traded visit privileges for letter and petition writing. See GPB/PEN/1902/70, NA.

12 An 1885 penal record relating to the prisoner Michael Casey documented various aspects of the elderly man's first three years of incarceration. Under special remarks it was stated that his 'conduct in separate confinement was very satisfactory', and that he had received 'first class for chairman's order' on 15 August 1883. The page for prison offenses had two entries, both for June 1885, in each case that of 'refusing to work in laundry', for which the punishment of 'stop one supper' was ordered. In the two-year period from early 1883 to early 1885 Michael Casey received seven letters, two from his wife and five from his daughter; he sent six letters, four to his daughter Margaret and two to James Connors/O'Connor of Derrypark, Cappaduff. The page entitled 'statements as to visits of convicts' is blank. See CRF (1902), J13, folder 2, NA and GPB/PEN/1895/155.

13 CRF (1902), J13, folder 2, NA.

14 Ibid., folders 2 and 3.

15 Letter by Michael Casey to Mary Casey, 15 June 1883, reproduced in Harrington, *The Maamtrasna Massacre*, p. 5.

16 Ibid.

17 Letter of 27 June 1884, reproduced in ibid., pp 5–6.

18 This comment was made in a handwritten memo dated 17 September 1895; see CRF (1902), J13, folder 8, NA.

19 Martin Joyce authored at least two memorials from prison, one addressed to Lord Ashbourne in October 1888 and the second to Lord Zetland in November 1890. His brother Paudeen sent many petitions, beginning in 1884 and continuing to 1902, including a petition submitted jointly with his son Tom in 1901. Tom was the last to petition and his first personal submission was in 1895; thereafter he petitioned for release very frequently, with some seven memorials forwarded between 1895 and 1898. See CRF (1902), J13, folders 7, 9, 11–13, NA. Many, though not all of these petitions, are cited in an official list contained in CRF (1902), folder 7, J13, NA.

20 CRF (1902), J13, folder 11, NA.

21 Many examples exist in CRF (1902), folder 2 and 5, J13, NA. For a list of some of the petitions forwarded by the men or on their behalves see CRF (1902), folder 7, J13, NA.

22 CRF (1902), J13, folder 7, NA.

23 It's notable that the prosecution brief had not specified the circumstances of Paudeen's arrest, unlike others arrested.

24 CRF (1902), J13, folder 7, NA.

25 Ibid., folder 14, NA.

26 Ibid., folder 7, NA.

27 The fifth man is Michael Casey.

28 CRF (1902), J13, folder 9, NA.

29 Ibid. See also GPB/PEN/1902/70.

30 CRF (1902), J13, folder 12, NA.

31 Ibid., folder 13, NA. Tom repeated these attempts to secure a release in a series of pleas forwarded between 1897 and 1902, with arguments based on the exceptional length of his sentence, his young age on conviction, his 'exemplary character,' and the 'long years of mental torture he has suffered'. See CRF (1902), J13, folders 12 and 13, NA.

32 CRF (1902), J13, folder 13, NA.

33 In 1900 a rough handwritten note was forwarded in the name of Julia Joyce, with respect to her son Tom and her husband 'Patt'; it also mentioned her brother-in-law Martin Joyce in Maryborough Prison. In the appended note she cited the 'poverty and distress' of her 'five sones [*sic*] and daughters' and entreated 'your Honour for the love of God to do something to release them.' CRF (1902), J13, folder 14, NA.

34 See Prison Board files for Martin, Paudeen (Patrick John) and Tom (Thomas Patrick) Joyce held in National Archives: GPB/PEN/1902/68–70.

35 *Twelfth report of the General Prisons Board*, Ireland, 1889/90 [C.6182] (1890), pp 118–19. My thanks to Ciara Breathnach for this reference.

36 *Thirteenth report of the General Prisons Board*, Ireland, 1890/1 [C.6451] (1891), p. 120.

37 *Fourteenth report of the General Prisons Board*, Ireland, 1891/2 [C.6789] (1892), p. 118.

38 *Royal Commission on Prisons in Ireland*, vol. 1 (Dublin, 1884), p. 101.

39 Later in the course of the commission, Sigerson determinedly returned in his questioning to the absence of a female Irish-speaking warder in Galway Jail. He posted the situation of a monoglot Irish-speaking female prisoner, with a 'disease of an internal organ' and treated by a doctor 'speaking no Irish', who would then need to communicate through a male warder: 'Do you think it is a proper thing that a female prisoner should be deprived of all possibility of speaking of her disease, in its incipient stage, except through the medium of a male warder, when delicacy of feeling may prevent her from having recourse to such a medium?' His interviewee, Pierce Joyce (owner of the Galway Mervue estate and a prison inspector from 1879 to 1906) responded that the existence of a female officer was desirable; pushed further by Sigerson as to why he had never made a report on the subject, he replied that he 'had never known a case to arise of such a thing'. *Royal Commission on Prisons in Ireland*, vol. 2 (Dublin, 1884), p. 145.

40 Ibid., p. 55. In 1889 Martin applied, unsuccessfully, for a transfer to Mountjoy from Downpatrick on the basis that he could not attend confession since the English-speaking chaplain did not know Irish. The prison governor's response in Downpatrick, unlike Maryborough, was to sanction the provision of an Irish-speaking clergyman, a Father Egan, to assist the prison chaplain. See. GPB/PEN/1902/68, NA.

41 CRF (1902), J13, folder 8, NA. The committee also noted that Fr Mellet, the local priest from Clonbur, had been expected to visit but was prevented by illness.

42 CRF (1902), J13, folder 8, NA.

43 On 16 April an internal report on the health of Michael Casey declared him to be 'feeble but regaining health' and detailed his daily diet as follows: '2 oz whiskey, 1 bottle porter, rice boiled in milk, arrowroot, tea, milk – 2.5 pints, 3 eggs, bread – 1lb – and beef or mutton or bottom.' The note concluded: 'He eats it all.' See CRF (1902), J13, folder 8, NA. For an illuminating account of prison conditions and prison diet during the period, see Ciara Breathnach, 'Medical officers, bodies, gender and weight fluctuation in Irish convict prisons, 1877–95', in *Medical History*, 2014, 58.1, pp 67–86.

44 CRF (1902), J13, folder 8, NA.

45 Ibid.

46　See GPB/PEN/1895/155. Hours before Michael died, a note from the medical officer, forwarded to Dublin Castle, stated that 'the convict has taken epileptic seizures, which are at present of a mild nature, but are very frequent'; a reply by the Prison Board encouraging consultation with the resident medical officer as to whether 'further containment is likely to endanger the convict's life' – is dated 23 August, the day after Michael Casey had died. CRF (1902), J13, folder 8, NA.

47　HC Deb, 29 August 1895, 4.36, c1225.

48　Healy, *Letters and Leaders of My Day*, pp 188–9.

49　Ibid.

50　CRF (1902), J13, folders 3 and 14, NA. See also GPB/PEN/1900/118.

51　CRF (1902), J13, folder 14, NA.

52　Ibid.

53　Ibid.

54　Responding to the latter of these queries, Attorney-General Atkinson argued that the transfer of Casey to Mountjoy only 18 months previously was 'due to structural alterations in that prison' and that in both prisons Casey had been 'classed as a hospital patient, and treated accordingly.' CRF (1902), J13, folder 14, NA.

55　Ibid.

56　Ibid.

57　Ibid.

58　Chief Secretary's Office Registered Papers(hereafter CSORP), NA 1882/46032.

59　See correspondence in Ibid.

60　Letter by Heard, 21 December 1882, in ibid.

61　Letter from Stokes to Heard, 23 December 1882 in ibid. On 29 December Clifford Lloyd, the resident magistrate for Galway, instructed that 'a responsible constable' be placed 'in charge of an escort of four men fully armed, who are never to leave him while in the district.'

62　Earl Spencer to Queen Victoria, 21 November 1882, Althorp Papers (hereafter AP) Add 76831, British Library (hereafter BL).

63　Ibid.

64　Ibid.

65　On 11 Dec, Spencer wrote to Victoria in deeply apologetic terms, informing her of the commuting of five of the death sentences and observing that he 'had he been at liberty to do so, would probably have allowed the law to take its course'. Queen Victoria responded in a handwritten note on 9 January, saying that this was 'much to be regretted'; AP Add 76831, BL.

66　Queen Victoria to Earl Spencer, 24 November 1882, ibid. References to this donation also exist in Queen Victoria's correspondence held in the Royal Archives (hereafter RA), Windsor Castle: see RA VIC/ADDA12/768 and RA PPTO/PP/QV/MAIN/1888/18355.

67 Earl Spencer to Queen Victoria, 11 January 1883, AP Add 76832, BL.

68 Ibid.

69 Letter from Earl Spencer to Sir Henry Ponsonby, 9 August 1888, RA PPTO/PP/QV/MAIN/1888/18355.

70 Patrick Keenan, 'The Joyce boys of Maamtrasna' (1888), RA PPTO/PP/QV/MAIN/1888/18355.

71 Letter from Earl Spencer to Sir Henry Ponsonby, 9 August 1888, RA PPTO/PP/QV/MAIN/1888/18355. The comment re Martin's not knowing English is at odds with Spencer's own observations in January 1883 quoted earlier.

72 See CSORP, NA 1890/5749. This compensation file has not featured in earlier studies of Maamtrasna. It contains much correspondence from George Lyster, solicitor for the boys, who initiated their application in October 1882 (when both Irish-speaking boys had successfully testified under oath). Official action was slow to take place: in May 1883 Lyster inquired about the fate of the claims, and he did so again in March 1884. The official investigation of their claims was conducted by Gerald Fitzgerald; his inquiry involved quite extensive interviews with members of the Royal Irish Constabulary (RIC), including Matthew Rudden, Thomas Stokes, and Sergeant Johnston. Fitzgerald's verdict was that the crime had indeed arisen 'out of unlawful association', thus rendering the boys eligible for compensation under the Prevention of Crime Act. But Fitzgerald recommended that compensation be paid only in the case of the murder of their father, and not for those of other family members, because, he argued 'the substantial loss occurred to the applicants through the murder of John Joyce.'

73 CSORP, NA 1890/5749.

74 Ibid.

75 In September Fr Mellet wrote from Clonbur to Assistant Under-Secretary Kaye to explain that he had checked the parish register and could not find Martin's name on it, but that Martin's uncle could testify on oath as to the year of his birth being 1866. Efforts to find a civil registration for Martin's birth were also unsuccessful. See CSORP, NA 1890/5749.

76 Ibid. In his 1888 report, Patrick Keenan noted that Martin had 'touched no part' of his earnings while employed at Artane or any of the compensation money (£250 from which £41 of costs were deducted) and that the money was being kept by Hooper on Martin's behalf. (Keenan, 'The Joyce boys of Maamtrasna', RA PPTO/PP/QV/MAIN/1888/18355). However, in a letter dated 22 February 1890 Hooper stated that he had 'handed over all his money to him'; CSORP, NA 1890/5749.

77 CSORP, NA 1890/5749.

78 Ibid.

79 See Jarlath Waldron, *Maamtrasna: The Murders and the Mystery* (Dublin, 1992), p. 317; and information provided by Johnny Joyce, Martin's grandson.

80 CSORP, NA 1890/5749.

81 Ibid.

82 Letter from Bridget Joyce, widow of 'Thomas Joyce Martin', to W. J. B. Kaye, sent from Kilbride, Clonbur Post Office, 25 March 1890, CSORP, NA 1890/5749

83 CSORP, NA 1890/5749.

84 Ibid.

85 This information is taken from 'Ellis Island and other New York passenger lists, 1820–1957', accessed via https://www.myheritage.com/. Patsy is described as a labourer, 22 years of age, with one piece of baggage, and with a destination of Cleveland, Ohio. According to family sources, Patsy went to Liverpool following his departure from Artane in 1890 and worked in Fr Murphy's Industrial School there for some time. I am indebted to Johnny Joyce for this information.

86 Waldron notes that he emigrated to England shortly after leaving Artane (Waldron, *Maamtrasna*, p. 317) but the evidence from Artane correspondence suggests that his ultimate destination was the United States. See CSORP, NA 1890/5749.

87 Waldron, *Maamtrasna*, p. 317.

88 See http://www.census.nationalarchives.ie/. Joseph, born in Cleveland in June 1892, is the father of Johnny Joyce.

89 Census information has been accessed from http://www.census.nationalarchives.ie/.

90 The efforts by Johnny Joyce, and his family to trace the fate and possible descendants of Patsy are, at time of writing, still unsuccessful. Martin Joyce died in Artane in 1933.

91 Waldron, *Maamtrasna*, p. 309. The personal information included here is drawn both from Waldron's oral sources and from my own research in the Census Records of 1901 and 1911, digitised by NA. See these records at http://www.census.nationalarchives.ie.

92 *Freeman's Journal* (hereafter *FJ*), 25 October 1902.

93 Ibid.

94 In his memoir, *Letters and Leaders of My Day*, T. M. Healy added another layer of folklore to the story of the men's release, miscrediting the 1903 visit of 'the late Queen Alexandra and King Edward to Connemara' (which took place nine months after their release): 'The wife of the surviving convict (at the Marble Quarries in Galway) fell on her knees before the Royal pair, sobbing that she was lonely for her man. Guilty or innocent, he had been twenty years in jail, and the Queen, touched by her sorrow, asked the King to telegraph a pardon. Next day the prisoner was set at large.' T. M. Healy, *Letters and Leaders of My Day* (London, 1928), p. 188.

95 This was the penname of John Bannon (1829–1913), an Irish Jesuit priest who had served as a Confederate chaplain during the Irish Civil War and was a regular *FJ* correspondent.

96 *FJ*, 16 November 1882.

97 Waldron, *Maamtrasna*, p. 315.

98 Waldron gives cause of Martin's death as tuberculosis; Waldron, *Maamtrasna*, pp 315–16.

99 In 1911 all of Paudeen's family members, including his son, daughter-in-law and grandchildren, are listed as speakers of Irish only, with the exception of 9–year-old Mary, a 'scholar' who is entered as bilingual. See http://www.census.nationalarchives.ie/.

100 Waldron, *Maamtrasna*, p. 316.

101 The 1901 census describes Anthony as a monoglot Irish speaker and farmer of 73 years of age who could not read or write. Anthony's wife Margaret was then aged 60 and bilingual, as were his three children Martin (24), Maggie (20) and Pat (19), this last child born around the time of the Maamtrasna events and when Anthony was 40 or so years of age. The older son Martin is described as unable to read, as is his mother, while the younger two children are recorded as able to read and write. In 1911 Anthony's widow Margaret lived with her unmarried sons Martin and Patrick. See http://www.census.nationalarchives.ie/.

102 John is recorded in the 1901 census as a 79-year-old widower and farmer who is a monoglot Irish speaker and unable to read. By 1901 his son Pat, a farm labourer, was bilingual and illiterate. Curiously Mary, a bilingual speaker, is recorded in 1901 as literate but in 1911 as unable to read. John's recorded cause of death was 'debility, five years, no medical attendant' and the informant was his daughter Mary who was present at his death. 1901 and 1911 details are drawn from http://www.census.nationalarchives.ie/.

103 In 1901 Mary's married name was Connor but her husband was not resident in the house. The inhabitants of the house were Mary, her brother Pat, her father John, Mary's 12-year-old son (Pat), and Pat's two daughters (Mary and Kate); the three children were bilingual and the two school-going children able to read and write. See http://www.census.nationalarchives.ie/.

104 Philbin was, by then, a widower; the cause of death recorded was 'retention of urine, certified six days.' See the registration of his death in Cappaduff, Ballinrobe, April 1906: https://civilrecords.irishgenealogy.ie/.

105 See CRF (1902), J13, folders 22 and 24, NA.

106 See CRF (1902), J13, folder 24, NA.

107 See http://www.census.nationalarchives.ie/.

108 Waldron, *Maamtrasna*, p. 307.

109 Ibid., p. 315.

110 Ibid.. The 1901 census records a 40-year-old man called John Casey, a monoglot Irish-speaking farmer who 'cannot read', living in Derry with his wife, Bridget, and five sons, and a 60-year-old John Casey, also of Derry, also a monoglot Irish-speaker who cannot read, living with his wife, Mary, four

children and a nine-year-old grandson named Pat Lydon. Both of these men are recorded in the 1911 censuses as aged 52 and 75 respectively and both remain monoglot Irish speakers at that date. See http://www.census.nationalarchives.ie/.

111 Family information from her great-grandchildren suggests that Bridget died in the late 1880s and that Máirín reared the other children with the assistance of her uncle John Lydon. In the 1901 census Máirín (Mary) is listed as married to John Conoboy, and living with her uncle John Lydon, Bridget's brother, in the Joyce home at Cappanacreha, Owenbrin. My thanks to Gemma Kelleher for this information.

112 Department of Justice files (1943), 90/16/408, NA.

113 See coverage in *New York Times*, 6 April 2018: https://www.nytimes.com /2018/04/06/world/europe/irish-hanged-pardon.html.

114 See *Irish Times* report of their visit to Ireland, during which they received a copy of the Irish pardon granted to their great-grandfather by President Higgins and also called for a dismissal of the case by the British government. See https://www.irishtimes.com/news/ireland/irish-news/maamtrasna -murders-relatives-call-on-britain-to-dismiss-case-1.3600964. The commemorative event was organised by Seán Ó Cuirreáin, author of *Éagóir*.

115 All three women spoke Irish only and were described as illiterate in 1911. See http://www.census.nationalarchives.ie/.

116 Information drawn from http://www.findmypast.ie/, https://www.rootsireland .ie/ and https://www.irishgenealogy.ie/en/.

CHAPTER 9

1 Ellsworth Mason and Richard Ellmann (eds), *The Critical Writings of James Joyce* (New York, 1959), p. 198.

2 John Wyse Jackson and Peter Costello, *John Stanislaus Joyce: The Voluminous Life and Genius of James Joyce's Father* (London, 1997). In 1907 John Stanislaus unsuccessfully sought to sue Tim Harrington and Daniel Hishon over monies he believed to be owing to him; Jackson and Costello, *John Stanislaus Joyce*, p. 292.

3 Ibid., p. 243.

4 Stanislaus Joyce, *My Brother's Keeper: James Joyce's Early Years*, Richard Ellmann (ed.) (1958; London, 1982), p. 175.

5 See Richard Ellmann, *James Joyce: New and Revised Edition* (Oxford, 1982), p. 61. This detail is drawn from a personal conversation with Joyce relayed by Frank Budgen in his memoir *Further Recollections of James Joyce* (London, 1955). Pearse is also the model for the unflattering portrait of teacher Hughes in Joyce's *Stephen Hero* (1944). In March 1901 Joyce was in the second year of his BA degree; the previous April he had published 'Ibsen's New Drama' in the *Fortnightly Review* and the following October he would publish 'The Day

of the Rabblement', his denunciation of the Irish as 'the most belated race in Europe' (Ellmann, *James Joyce*, p. 89).

6 Jackson and Costello, *John Stanislaus Joyce*, p. 233.

7 On Thomas Barnacle's expulsion from the family home, see Brenda Maddox, *Nora: The Real Life of Molly Bloom* (Boston, 1988), p. 14. For a more benign reading of family relations in the Barnacle household, see Pádraic Ó Laoi's short biography *Nora Barnacle Joyce: A Portrait* (Galway, 1982).

8 See Maddox, *Nora*, pp 15–18.

9 These entries can be accessed at http://www.census.nationalarchives.ie/.

10 Maddox, *Nora*, pp 15–18. According to Maddox, Nora's 'first serious crush, when she was approaching thirteen' was on Michael Feeney who was aged sixteen, p. 15.

11 Barry McCrea also discusses Nora Barnacle's cultural and linguistic environment briefly; in his *Languages of the Night: Minor Languages and the Literary Imagination in Twentieth-Century Ireland and Europe* (New Haven and London, 2015), p. 28.

12 See James Joyce, 'The Mirage of the Fisherman of Aran', translated from *Il Piccolo della Sera*, 5 September 1912, in Kevin Barry (ed.), *James Joyce: Occasional, Critical and Political Writing*, Conor Deane (trans.) (Oxford, 2000), p. 204. My grateful thanks to Anne Fogarty for this reference.

13 See http://www.census.nationalarchives.ie/.

14 Erik Schneider, 'Towards *Ulysses*: Some unpublished Joyce documents from Trieste', in *Journal of Modern Literature*, summer 2004, 27.4, pp 1–16. Sam Alexander provides an elegant reading of Joyce's preoccupation with demography and his use of the census as a literary model in his 'Joyce's census: Character, demography and the problem of population in *Ulysses*', in *Novel: A Forum on Fiction*, 2012, 45.3, pp 453–4. My thanks to Sam Alexander for both references.

15 Schneider, 'Towards *Ulysses*', p. 6, drawing from the work of Castro Diego de Castro.

16 Schneider, 'Towards *Ulysses*', p. 9.

17 John McCourt, *The Years of Bloom: James Joyce in Trieste, 1904–1920* (Dublin, 2000), p. 51. This is an invaluable resource for Joyce's years in Trieste.

18 Ibid. McCourt also comments: 'In this respect the language of *Finnegans Wake* is like an exaggerated, exploded version of *Triestino*', pp 52–3.

19 Quoted by McCourt, *The Years of Bloom*, p. 53.

20 Schneider, 'Towards *Ulysses*', pp 9–10; for more on Maria Kirn, see McCourt, *The Years of Bloom*, pp 171–8.

21 See McCourt's discussion of Joyce's relationship with Triestine irredentism in *The Years of Bloom*, pp 98–121.

22 The term 'Ireland at the bar' derives from Gladstone's speech to the House of Commons on 7 June 1886, arguing for the passing of the 1886 Home Rule bill:

'Ireland stands at your bar expectant, hopeful, almost suppliant. Her words are the words of truth and soberness. She asks a blessed oblivion of the past, and in that oblivion our interest is deeper than even hers.' HANSARD (CCCVI [3d Ser.], pp 1215–40, 1239, June 7 1886). See Andrew Gibson, *The Strong Spirit: History, Politics and Aesthetics in the Writings of James Joyce, 1898–1915* (Oxford, 2013), p. 101. Gibson, however, misquotes the original Gladstone line as 'Ireland stands at the bar, expectant, hopeful.'

23 John Morley, *The Life of William Ewart Gladstone* (New York, 1903), p. 340.

24 Giorgio Melchiori, 'The language of politics and the politics of language', in *James Joyce Broadsheet*, February 1981, 4, p. 1.

25 Joyce's other more politically-engaged articles such as 'Home Rule comes of age' and 'The Home Rule comet' were also to be placed early in the volume, with the articles on 'Fenianism' and 'The shadow of Parnell' completing the book; see Barry (ed.), *James Joyce: Occasional, Critical and Political Writing*, pp xi–xiii.

26 McCourt, *The Years of Bloom*, pp 79–136; Melchiori, 'The language of politics', p. 1.

27 Melchiori, 'The language of politics', p. 1.

28 Deane, 'Translator's Introduction', in Barry (ed.), *James Joyce: Occasional, Critical and Political Writing*, pp xxxiii–xxxv.

29 Mason and Ellmann (eds), *The Critical Writings of James Joyce*, p. 187. The newspaper *Il Piccolo* was founded in 1881, its title (lit. 'small' or 'little') referring to its being a single two-sided page; the evening edition had, John McCourt notes, 'a less openly political agenda' than the day paper and published more national and international news. See McCourt, *The Years of Bloom*, pp 95–107.

30 This translated text is reproduced from Mason and Ellmann (eds), *The Critical Writings of James Joyce*, pp 197–8.

31 Ibid., p. 198.

32 Hans Walter Gabler, 'James Joyce *Interpreneur*', in *Genetic Joyce Studies*, spring 2004, 4, p. 3, http://www.geneticjoycestudies.org/, 28 August 2018.

33 Mason and Ellmann (eds), *The Critical Writings of James Joyce*, pp 199–200.

34 Ibid. For a discussion of Joyce's interest in the Great Wyrley case, see Adrian Hardiman, 'Joyce, Great Wryley and the necessity of judicious doubt', in *Dublin James Joyce Journal*, 2012, 5, pp 1–15. Hardiman usefully notes that 'Ireland at the bar' is Joyce's 'first published engagement with the topic of notorious crimes' (the Maamtrasna and Wyrley cases), a recurring preoccupation, as Hardiman illustrates, in both *Ulysses* and *Finnegans Wake*; p. 3. See also Adrian Hardiman, *Joyce in Court: James Joyce and the Law* (London, 2017).

35 For an illuminating discussion of Joyce's lifelong interest in the law, see Hardiman, *Joyce in Court*. Hardiman discusses the Maamtrasna murders on pp 52–67, drawing from earlier studies of the case by Jarlath Waldron and Myles Dungan.

36 Mason and Ellmann (eds), *The Critical Writings of James Joyce*, p. 198.

37 At the Cong inquiry, the accused were allowed to cross-examine the Joyce prosecution witnesses (though Myles Joyce declined to do so); the accused were not questioned themselves.

38 Joyce's description is as follows: 'The story was told that the executioner, unable to make the victim understand him, kicked at the miserable man's head in anger to shove it into the noose'; see Mason and Ellmann (eds), *The Critical Writings of James Joyce*, p. 198.

39 Kevin Barry (ed.), *James Joyce: Occasional, Critical and Political Writing* (Oxford, 2000), p. 326. Ellmann and Mason misidentify the murder victims as 'a man named Joyce, his wife and three of his four children', Mason and Ellmann (eds), *The Critical Writings of James Joyce*, p. 197. More usefully, in a later footnote they direct readers to 'a description of the hanging by one of the few eyewitnesses' in *The Vivid Life* by Frederick Higginbotham [*sic*], p. 198.

40 Jeanne A. Flood, 'Joyce and the Maamtrasna murders', in *James Joyce Quarterly*, summer 1991, 28:4, pp 879–88.

41 John Garvin, *James Joyce's Disunited Kingdom and the Irish Dimension* (Dublin, 1976), p. 165.

42 Tim Harrington, *The Maamtrasna Massacre: Impeachment of the Trials* (Dublin, 1884), p. vi.

43 The interpreter 'usually exists only by implication, a medium who leaves no message to posterity'; see Patricia Palmer, *Language and Conquest in Early Modern Ireland: English Renaissance Literature and Elizabeth Imperial Expansion* (Cambridge, 2001), p. 191.

44 The rhetorical flourishes that enliven Joyce's account – such as the disparity between the old man's 'involved explanation' and the interpreter's 'dry' translation – partake in a long tradition of Irish courtroom humour extending back, as previously discussed in Chapter 4, to texts such as Griffin's *Collegians* (1829). In Griffin's account, however, and in many such comic portrayals, the wiliness of the testifying (bilingual) witness is the source of reassuring comedy; in Joyce's essay, the stark process of judicial censorship is sardonically re-enacted in a manner that is at once comic and discomfiting.

45 Mason and Ellmann (eds), *The Critical Writings of James Joyce*, p. 198; Italian text from Barry, *James Joyce: Occasional, Critical and Political Writing*, p. 218.

46 Barry (ed.), *James Joyce: Occasional, Critical and Political Writing*, p. 198.

47 Mason and Ellmann (eds), *The Critical Writings of James Joyce*, p. 197; Italian text from Barry, *James Joyce: Occasional, Critical and Political Writing*, p. 217.

48 Ibid.

49 Ibid.

50 Gabler observes that the text of 'Ireland at the bar' is 'essentially structured like an emblem, where the story corresponds to the emblematic image and the peroration to the moralizing subscription obligatory in pictorial emblematic

art' and that this 'emblematic story-telling' – which characterises some of the *Piccolo della Sera* pieces – is of 'the family of the *Dubliners* stories (perhaps their minor relations),' see Gabler, 'James Joyce *Interpreneur*', p. 3.

51 In the Italian original, this reads: *La figura di questo vecchio inebetito, avanzo di una civiltà non nostra, sordomuto dianzi il suo giudice, è la figura simbolica della nazione irlandese alla sbarra dell'opnione pubblica.* See Barry (ed.), *James Joyce: Occasional, Critical and Political Writing*, p. 218. *Inebetito* (from *ebete*, 'stupid, dull, foolish', and thus *inebetito,* 'made obtuse, dazed, stunned') is translated by Mason and Ellmann as 'dumbfounded', linking to the translation of *sordomuto* as 'deaf and dumb'; Mason and Ellmann (eds), *The Critical Writings of James Joyce*, p. 198. In the new translation included in Kevin Barry's edition, Conor Deane chooses the more temperate word, 'bewildered' ('the figure of this bewildered old man'), and translates Joyce's term *sordomuto* more literally as 'deaf-mute'. See Barry (ed.), *James Joyce: Occasional, Critical and Political Writing*, pp 145–7. For more on the complex and contested textual history of the essay, see *James Joyce Archive: Notes, Criticism, Translations, and Miscellaneous Writings (A Facsimile of Manuscripts and Typescripts)*, vol. 1, Hans Walter Gabler (preface and arrangement) (New York and London, 1979); and also Gabler, 'James Joyce *Interpreneur*', pp 1–4. (New York and London, 1979), pp 653–703. Questions of literary authorial attribution by digital methodologies, with respect to Joyce's non-fiction writings, are the subject of the engaging essay, Kevin Barry et al., 'Is it Joyce we are reading?: Non-fiction, authorship, and digital humanities', in Katherine Ebury and James Alexander Fraser (eds), *Joyce's Non-Fiction Writings: Outside His Jurisfiction* (Switzerland, 2018), pp 93–107.

52 Mason and Ellmann (eds), *The Critical Writings of James Joyce*, p. 198.

53 Luke Gibbons, *Joyce's Ghosts: Ireland, Modernism, and Memory* (Chicago, 2015), p. 79.

54 Gibbons uses the translation by Conor Deane for his English source text.

55 Gibbons, *Joyce's Ghosts*, p. 80.

56 Ibid.

57 Within Gibbons' ensuing and enlightening chapter on 'vernacular modernism', the line 'He says no, your worship' comes to serve as an illustrative instance of 'previously silenced voices' breaking into 'dominant or consensual narrative forms.' See Ibid., pp 80–2, and other references to Myles Joyce, pp 92, 101.

58 Maria Edgeworth, *Castle Rackrent* (London, 1800).

59 Homi Bhabha, 'Sly civility', in *October*, autumn 1985, 34, pp 71–80.

60 In Joyce's original Italian text, the phrase 'your worship' was placed in quotation marks, thus denoting the insertion of an English 'foreign' idiom, and serving as a further instance of the interpreter's intrusive presence. In Mason and Ellmann's version, 'your worship' is also placed in quotation marks, p.197; these are omitted in the Barry-Deane version which reads 'He says no, your worship', p.145.

61 See Barry (ed.), *James Joyce: Occasional, Critical and Political Writing*, pp 108–26.

62 Ibid., p. 109.

63 Ibid., p. 125.

64 My thanks to John Paul Riquelme for suggesting this comparison.

65 James Joyce, *A Portrait of the Artist as a Young Man* (New York, 1916; Oxford, 2000), p. 159.

66 Ibid., p. 152.

67 W. J. McCormack has suggested that this is an area likely to have been Irish-speaking at that period; however the 1901 census records for the 23 homesteads in the townland of Ballyhoura show that only five of these were recorded as having bilingual speakers, and the Irish-speaking inhabitants of two of these were over 65. See W. J. McCormack, 'James Joyce, cliché, and the Irish language', in Bernard Benstock (ed.), *James Joyce: The Augmented Ninth* (Syracuse, 1988), p. 332; and http://www.census.nationalarchives.ie/. The language columns within individual schedules contain a number of crossings out and erasures, presumably by the enumerators, but suggest that, at a maximum, two young women in that townland spoke Irish in 1901.

68 McCormack notes that here 'the language of the novel swings toward a form of English in which Irish influence is perceptible'; see McCormack, 'James Joyce, cliché, and the Irish language', p. 332.

69 James Joyce, *A Portrait of the Artist as a Young Man*, p. 153.

70 Ibid., p. 159.

71 Ibid., p. 212.

72 Ibid. Anne Fogarty has noted that as a Middle English and Shakespearean word, 'tundish' is also an example of the fossilised vocabulary of Irish-English. Conversation with the author.

73 The enigmatic conclusion of *Castle Rackrent* comes to mind here: 'Did the Warwickshire militia, who were chiefly artisans, teach the Irish to drink beer? Or did they learn from the Irish to drink whiskey?' Maria Edgeworth, *Castle Rackrent* (Dublin, 1800), p. 182.

74 See Yasemin Yildiz, *Beyond the Mother Tongue: The Postmonolingual Condition* (New York, 2012).

75 James Joyce, *A Portrait of the Artist as a Young Man*, p. 212.

76 'With an exquisite consciousness of conventions, and a keen skepticism about what can or should be said, bilinguals develop the everyday arts of manoeuvring and self-irony.' Doris Sommer, *Bilingual Aesthetics: A New Sentimental Education* (Durham, North Carolina, 2004), p. 6.

77 For a fascinating reading of this passage in relation to H. G. Wells' *The War of the Worlds* (1897), see Katherine Ebury, '"Mulrennan spoke to him about universe and stars": Astronomy in *A Portrait of the Artist as a Young Man*', in *Dublin James Joyce Journal*, 2013–4, 6 & 7, pp 90–108, 101–5.

78 James Joyce, *Dubliners* (1914; Dublin, 2012), p. 189. '*Beannacht libh*', Miss Ivors' departing and taunting Irish phrase to Gabriel, has received some critical

scrutiny: McCormack argues that Miss Ivors' final salutation 'enact[s] a significant grammatical error,' since as the person leaving, she should have said '*Beannacht agaibh.*' See McCormack, 'James Joyce, cliché, and the Irish language', pp 330, 332. This argument is discounted by McCrea and others, but in my view has some persuasive force since this is a typical grammatical rule insisted upon in early language lessons and easily made the object of ridicule by a bright, disgruntled learner.

79 Joyce, *A Portrait of the Artist as a Young Man*, p. 170.

80 Part of the joke here is that Mulligan's awkward English is almost a direct translation from the Irish phrase *An bhfuil Gaeilge agat*, *agat* being the prepositional pronoun for *ag* (denoting spatial location, 'by'; or temporal location, 'at'; or possession).

81 James Joyce, *Finnegans Wake* (hereafter *FW*) (1939; London, 1999), 54.14.

82 See Roland McHugh, *Annotations to Finnegans Wake* (Baltimore, 2006), p. 54 who translates the phrase as 'I am sorry St Patrick do you understand Irish?' Diarmuid Curraoin notes that the construction mirrors a well-known nineteenth-century folk song, '*A Dhónaill uí Chonaill an dtuigeann tú Gaelainn*'; see Diarmuid Curraoin, '*I know that I have broken every heart*': *The Significance of the Irish Language in Finnegans Wake and in Other Works by James Joyce* (Palo Alto, CA, 2014), p. 118. The *Wake* paragraph ends with another partial phrase in Irish: 'Mercy, and you? Gomagh,thak' (an abbreviation of '*go maith*' or 'good', following the French 'merci'); *FW* 54.18–19.

83 *FW*, 35.15–16. According to William York Tindall in his *Reader's Guide to Finnegans Wake* (Syracuse, 1969), p. 59, 'the Cad speaks sinister Gaelic', but the origins of Tindall's epithet 'sinister' are unclear. Christine O'Neill-Bernhard draws from the work of Jarlath Waldron to construct a perceptive reading of the Festy King episode: Christine O'Neill-Bernhard, 'Symbol of the Irish nation, or of a foulfamed potheen district: James Joyce on Myles Joyce', in *James Joyce Quarterly*, spring-summer, 1995, 32.3 & 4, pp 712–21.

84 *FW*, 85.22–8. See O'Neill, 'Symbol of the Irish nation', pp 719–21, for a comprehensive list of possible allusions, and also Garvin, *James Joyce's Disunited Kingdom*, pp 165–6, 168–9.

85 *FW*, 85.32–86.1.

86 *FW*, 91.3–4. McHugh glosses 'fluors of sparse' as 'flowers of speech' and notes the Latin verb 'fluor' meaning 'to flow', *Annotations to Finnegans Wake*, p. 86.

87 Ibid., 86.6–11.

88 Harrington, *The Maamtrasna Massacre*, p. 16.

89 For example, Harrington, *The Maamtrasna Massacre*, pp 38–43.

90 *FW*, 90.34–91.13.

91 *FW*, 91.3.

92 *FW*, 86.1.

93 Ibid., 92.35–93.5.

94 See also *FW*, 63.20–2: 'on his first time of hearing the wretch's statement that, muttering Irish, he had had had o'gloriously a'lot too much'; Ibid., 498.15–16: 'all murdering Irish, amok and amak'; and James Joyce, *Ulysses* (1922; London, 1982), 200.14–16: 'In words of words for words ... Murthering Irish.'

95 Susan Swartzlander, 'Multiple meaning and misunderstanding: The trial of Festy King', in *James Joyce Quarterly*, summer 1986, 23:4, pp 465–76. Swartzlander persuasively reads Festy King and Pegger Festy as the same character and as Shem figures; more contentiously, she reads the trial as a metaphor for authorial 'trials', i.e. 'the complaints leveled against him and his work', p. 474.

96 *FW*, 93.3.

97 Joseph Valente, *James Joyce and the Problem of Justice: Negotiating Sexual and Colonial Difference* (Cambridge, 2009), p. 253.

98 Ibid., p. 255.

99 Ibid., pp 254–6. One of the consequences of Valente's argument is a curious restaging of the trial of Myles Joyce, in which he is made complicit in his own victimisation: 'Via the complexities of tribal consanguinity and incestuous rivalry, the ultimate victim of the piece, Myles Joyce, was in some sense implicated in his own victimization, much as the Earwickers are all implicated in one another's "sins," and much as the Irish people at large (whom Myles Joyce personifies in "Ireland at the bar") were always to some degree responsible for their own colonization – a point Joyce stresses throughout his career', p. 254.

100 Ibid., p. 256.

101 Mason and Ellmann (eds), *The Critical Writings of James Joyce*, p. 198.

CONCLUSION

1 Jacques Derrida, *Monolingualism of the Other; or, The Prosthesis of Origin*, Patrick Mensah (trans.) (Stanford, CA, 1998), p. 9.

2 Frederick J. Higginbottom, *The Vivid Life: A Journalist's Career* (London, 1934), facing p. 42.

3 The pardon granted to Myles Joyce was the first arising from a case that had occurred prior to the founding of the Irish state. The decision to grant was supported by Dr Niamh Howlin's expert review of the case and by legal advice from the Attorney General affirming its jurisdiction. It was the second instance of a posthumous award, the first granted to Harry Gleeson in December 2015. The text of Howlin's report can be accessed at http://www.justice.ie/en/JELR/Pages/PR18000112.

4 See https://www.president.ie/media-library/speeches/.

5 See discussion in Chapter 6.

6 In his study of the death penalty in Ireland, and writing specifically of the posthumous pardon granted to Harry Gleeson in 2015, Ian O'Donnell makes the following important point: 'While the sentiment expressed is laudable,

the language used is somewhat unfortunate. Although it is clear that the effect of the action is to wipe the slate clean, it is nevertheless the case that one cannot be pardoned for what one has not done. A pardon implies guilt, it simply frees the guilty from the legal consequences of their crimes. It is anomalous to pardon someone for being innocent.' See Ian O'Donnell, *Justice, Mercy, and Caprice: Clemency and the Death Penalty in Ireland* (Oxford, 2018), pp 261–2.

7 *Landleaguers* was uncompleted at the time of Trollope's death in December 1882. He visited Ireland twice in 1882 to gather material for the novel, including a journey in August with his niece Florence Bland, and details from the early news reports of the Joyce murders can be identified in his text. Chapter 48 of the published novel, entitled 'The new aristocracy fails,' briefly alludes to the 'awful horror' of a family murder whereby 'six unfortunates' were sacrificed to 'stop the tongue of one talkative old woman.' In Trollope's account, the family are victims of 'loaded pistols and black-visaged murderers', his use of the term 'black-visaged' is especially striking, given the suppression of this detail during the November trials. See Anthony Trollope, *The Landleaguers* (New York, 1883), pp 253–4.

8 Bram Stoker, *The Snake's Pass: A Critical Edition*, Lisabeth Buchelt (ed.) (1890; Syracuse, 2015); for more on Stoker and Maamtrasna, see Nicholas Daly, *Modernism, Romance and the Fin de Siècle: Popular Fiction and British Culture, 1880–1914* (Cambridge, 1999), pp 71–5.

9 In the final author's note, Greeley refers to (unsuccessful) efforts by Micheál MacGréil S.J. in 1882 to place a cross at the Joyce house: *Irish Love* (New York, 2001) p. 201.

10 The three-part play, authored by Sarah Binchy, Gill McGaw, Geoff Power and Pauline Shanahan, featured extracts from the 1882 trial, along with the 1803 trial of Robert Emmet and the 1976 capital murder trial of Marie and Noel Murray, and was staged in the original Green Street courthouse.

11 *Maum* (director Diarmuid de Faoite, July 2015) was a bilingual production in which the original language of the speaker was retained, so for example the character of Myles Joyce and other accused spoke in Irish; the prosecution counsel in English. However, this bilingual staging, while conceptually powerful, proved somewhat flat in performance, with a blunting both of the linguistic 'messiness' and the emotional force of the events. For example, the play's trial scene omitted the court interpreter, occluding the historical fact that an interpreter was deployed in court to serve the prosecution witnesses and also removing the startling moment of his being stood down for the trial of Myles Joyce. A more dramatically effective device was the play's emphasis on differing generational competences within the lives of both legal personnel and the accused: the older defence lawyer is characterised as bilingual and his young, ambitious son an English monoglot, while the accused Tom Pháidín

Sheáin (Tom Joyce) is clearly bilingual and his father Páidín Sheáin and uncle Myles Sheáin are Irish monoglots. Sighle Ní Chonaill (Meehan), *Maum*, Macdara Ó Fátharta (trans.), National Irish Language Theatre, Galway.

12 The valuable Irish History podcast series includes three episodes on the Maamtrasna murders: https://irishhistorypodcast.ie/category/podcast/the-maamtrasna-murders/.

13 Ó Cuirreáin has been a key campaigner for greater public and governmental recognition of the mistrial of Myles Joyce; he was one of the organisers of a commemoration held in Galway in 2012, marking the 130th anniversary of the hangings, and which featured a wreath-laying attended by President Higgins. Initiatives developed by the organisers of the commemoration included making available to the public, for the first time, a collection of prison photographs of the accused taken by a former British Army officer, Captain J. J. Dunne, who later worked as a prison warder. His photograph album was donated to the National Library by his grandson and is included in the National Library of Ireland (hereafter NLI) Invincible Files (MS ALB40, NLI)

14 In 1992 Waldron, drawing from his knowledge as local priest, observed that the events of 1882 had 'divided the Valley into two hostile camps. Every inhabitant of the place was related by blood or marriage to somebody on one side or the other'. He also remarked that 'thankfully, however, all this is changing. The event, now removed from the passage of over a hundred years, can be addressed with more calm, reason and objectivity.' Jarlath Waldron, *Maamtrasna: The Murders and the Mystery* (Dublin, 1992) p. 11.

15 Breandán Mac Suibhne, *The End of Outrage: Post-Famine Adjustment in Rural Ireland* (Oxford, 2017), p. 17.

16 Quoted in Eoghan Ó Néill, *Gleann an Óir* (Dublin, 1988), p. 139.

17 I am indebted here to Jan Blommaert, *The Sociolinguistics of Globalization* (Cambridge, 2010), p. 180.

18 Quoted in *Guardian*, 28 April 2017.

19 Ibid. Three of the men executed had, according to the Fair Punishment Project at Harvard Law School, strong claims for mitigation. Kayla Greenwood, whose father Michael was killed by Williams, wrote to the governor asking that his execution not take place and, having read of a public appeal for funds to support families who were not able to cover the financial costs of the executed men's funerals, paid for Williams' daughter and granddaughter to visit him before his execution.

20 Jacques Derrida, *The Death Penalty, Vol. 1*, in *The Seminars of Jacques Derrida, vol. 9*, Peggy Kamuf (trans.) (2012; Chicago, 2014), First Session, p. 25.

21 Blommaert, *The Sociolinguistics of Globalization*, p. 171.

22 Ibid.

23 'General introduction', in Théopile Munyangeyo, Graham Webb and Marina Rabadán-Gómez (eds), *Challenges and Opportunities in Public Service Interpreting*

(London, 2016), p. 3. My grateful thanks to Professor Mina Karavanta for this reference and to Cara Brophy-Browne.

24 Stefanos Vlachopoulos, Periklis Tagkas, Themistoklism Gogas, Eleftheria Dogoriti and Theodoros Vyzas, 'Foreigners before Themis: Legal interpreting in Greece', in *Challenges and Opportunities in Public Service Interpreting*, pp 213–33.

25 Ibid.

26 Michael Cronin and Clíona Ní Ríordáin, 'Interview with Michael Cronin', in *Études Irlandaises*, 2010, 4, pp 35–2; http://etudesirlandaises.revues.org/1939, 28 January 2017.

27 See Kate Waterhouse, 'Profits on the margins: Private language service providers and limited-English-proficient immigrants in Irish courts', in David C. Brotherton, Daniel L. Stageman, Shirley P. Leyro (eds), *Outside Justice: Immigration and the Criminalizing Impact of Changing Policy and Practice* (New York, 2013), pp 179–97, and Kate Waterhouse, *Ireland's District Court: Language, Immigration and Consequences for Justice* (Manchester, 2014).

28 Waterhouse, 'Profits on the margins', p. 190.

29 Here Waterhouse quotes from Ruth Morris' comparative study of court interpreting in *MonTI (Monographs in Translation and Interpreting)*, 2010, 2, pp 47–70, 57–9; Waterhouse, *Ireland's District Court*, p. 76. Morris' work draws heavily from Mary Phelan's insightful comments in 'Court interpreters in the news (for the wrong reasons)', in *ITIA Bulletin*, October 2007, pp 4–5.

30 See for example recent work by Adrian Blackledge and Angela Creese on the flexible use of linguistic resources by bilinguals and the value of 'translanguaging' or language crossing as a cultural and cosmopolitan competence: Adrian Blackledge and Angela Creese, 'Translanguaging in the bilingual classroom: A pedagogy for language and teaching?' in *The Modern Language Journal*, 2010, 94.1, pp 103–15; unpublished 2016 conference paper. See also Blommaert's recent work on language and 'superdiversity' in *Ethnography, Superdiversity and Linguistic Landscapes: Chronicles of Complexity* (Bristol, 2013) and in Karel Arnaut, Jan Blommaert, Ben Rampton and Massimiliano Spotti (eds), *Language and Superdiversity* (New York, 2016).

31 In her study *Beyond the Mother Tongue*, Yildiz reminds readers that it is 'monolingualism, not multilingualism, that is the result of a relatively recent, albeit highly successful, development.' 'But,' as she observes, 'a monolingual paradigm, which first emerged in late eighteenth-century Europe, has functioned to obscure from view the widespread nature of multilingualism, both in the present and in the past. Monolingualism is not just a term denoting the presence of just one language but instead it constitutes a key structuring principle that organises the entire range of modern social life. According to this paradigm, individuals and social formations are imagined to possess one "true" language only, their "mother tongue"; and through this possession to

be organically linked to an exclusive, clearly demarcated ethnicity, culture, and nation.' Yasemin Yildiz, *Beyond the Mother Tongue: The Postmonolingual Condition* (New York, 2012), p. 2.

APPENDIX I

1 In these registers all family names (personal and surnames) are given in standard English-language forms.

2 In the course of his evidence as leading prosecution witness, Anthony Joyce testified that he thought Myles Joyce had 'five in family', and that 'they are small and they are weak'.

3 The age attributed to Tom Joyce is broadly in line with the evidence of the Catholic parish registers, which recorded the baptism of 'Tom, son of Pat Joyce and Judy O'Brien' on 26 November 1860, making him 21 at the time of the murders. Source is Microfilm 04214/07, baptisms December 1853 to September 1881 for Catholic parish of Kilbride (and Finney), in the archdiocese of Tuam; digitised by National Library of Ireland.

4 Digital copies of the prison registers for Galway and Kilmainham are available in the Irish Prisons Register collection at www.findmypast.ie (accessed 24 January 2017): see IRE-PRISR-RS00018280-4492674-00762, IRE-PRIS R-RS00018280-4492674-00744 and IRE-PRISR-RS00018280-4492674-00744.

BIBLIOGRAPHY

PRIMARY ARCHIVAL SOURCES

Census Papers

Census of Ireland, 1851. Area, houses, and population: also the ages, civil condition, occupations, birthplaces, religion, and education of the people. Part IV, Report on Ages and Education [C.2053], PP 1856 (Dublin: Thom, 1856).

Census of Ireland, 1851. Area, houses, and population: also the ages, civil condition, occupations, birthplaces, religion, and education of the people . Part VI, General Report [C.2134], PP 1856 (Dublin: Thom, 1856).

Census of Ireland, 1871. Area, houses, and population: also the ages, civil condition, occupations, birthplaces, religion, and education of the people. Part I. Vol. III. Province of Ulster [C.964], PP 1874 (Dublin: Thom, 1882).

Census of Ireland, 1881. Areas, Houses and Population: also the ages, civil or conjugal condition, occupations, birthplaces, religion, and education of the people. Part I. Vol. IV. Province of Connaught [C. 3268], PP 1882 (Dublin: Thom, 1882).

Census of Ireland, 1881: General Report [C. 3365], PP 1882 (Dublin: Thom, 1882).

Census of Ireland, 1891. Areas, Houses and Population: also the ages, civil or conjugal condition, occupations, birthplaces, religion, and education of the people. Part I. Vol. IV, Province of Connaught [C. 6685], PP 1892 (Dublin: Thom, 1892).

Census of Ireland, 1891: General Report [C. 6780], PP 1892 (Dublin: Thom, 1892).

Census of England and Wales 1891: Volume IV. General Report, 81. Section IX 'Languages in Wales and Monmouthshire'.

National Archives, Dublin
Chief Secretary's Office Registered Papers including:
CSORP 1882/46032 (disposal of Crown witnesses)
CSORP 1883/189 (inquiry into execution of Myles Joyce)
CSORP 1890/5749 (Joyce compensation file)
CSORP/Library Cases/Box 24 (prosecution materials)

Convict Reference Files (1902), J13, 31 folders ('The Maamtrasna File')

Crown Office Papers: Crown Briefs, 1882. Dublin: County Galway–Dublin
   Commission Court, October 1882. *The Queen vs Anthony Philbin and Others.*
   Murder of the Joyces at Maamtrasna. Brief on behalf of the Crown. For
   George Bolton, Crown Solicitor (Dublin: Thom, October 1882).

Crown Office Papers 1893, Mayo correspondence, Interpreters Papers: National
   Archives Dublin, IC-78–51.

Department of Justice files (1943), 90/16/408 (request for exhumation of remains
   of Myles Joyce)

The Dublin October Commission. 13th November, 1882. County of Galway. The
   Maumtrasna Massacre, trial transcript, contained in Convict Reference Files
   (1902), J13, folder 29

General Prison Board reports: GPB/PEN/1895/155 (Michael Casey); GPB/
   PEN/1900/118 (John Casey); GPB/PEN/1902/68–70 (Martin, Patrick/
   Paudeen and Thomas Joyce)

Miscellaneous Census Returns from 1851, Ms 5249

National Library of Ireland
Congested Districts Board for Ireland Baseline Reports (Dublin: Thom, 1892–1898)

Harrington Papers, Ms 8576

Invincibles Album, ALB 40 (also digitised)

Larcom Papers, Ms 7, 524–7257

Microfilm 04214/07, baptisms from December 1853 to September 1881 for the
   Catholic parish of Kilbride (and Finney) in the archdiocese of Tuam;
   digitised by the National Library of Ireland

Registers for Derrypark RIC area, 1879–1897, Ms 2193

Special (Parnell) Commission: 1888–9, a verbatim copy of the Parnell Commission
   Report, vols I–XI evidence, XII index

Prison Reports
Report of the Royal Commission on Prisons in Ireland, vols 1 and 2 (Dublin: Thom, 1884)
Twelfth report of the General Prisons Board, Ireland, 1889/90 [C.6182], 1890
Thirteenth report of the General Prisons Board, Ireland, 1890/1 [C.6451], 1891
Fourteenth report of the General Prisons Board, Ireland, 1891/2 [C.6789], 1892

Queen's University Belfast Special Collections
Somerville and Ross Papers, MS. 17/874

Royal Irish Academy
Windele papers, 4B and 12L

British Library
Althorp (Earl Spencer) Papers, K349, Add 76831

Royal Archives, Windsor Castle (Queen Victoria correspondence)
RA VIC/ADDA12/768
RA PPTO/PP/QV/MAIN/1888/18355

UCD Archive and Special Collections
'Lamentable Lines on the Execution of the Maamtrasna Murders', broadsheet
ballad, National Folklore Collection
O'Donovan-Reeves correspondence, UCD Library Special Collections, JOD L 42
National Folklore Collection, MS 41, 236, 908, 931

Valuation Books
Griffith's Valuation: Primary Valuation of Tenements, Parish of Ross (1847–1864),
cancelled valuation books, Valuation Office, Irish Life Centre, Dublin.

Newspapers
Belfast Newsletter, 1882
Connaught Telegraph, 1882
Daily Express, 1882
Daily News (London), 1882
Dublin Evening Mail, 1882
Freeman's Journal, 1882–1902
Galway Express, 1882
Galway Vindicator, 1882
Graphic (London, illustrated), 1882
Illustrated Police News (London), 1882
Irishman, 1882
Irish Times, 1882

Irish World (New York), 1882
Nation, 1882
Spectator (London), 1882
Times (London), 1882
Tuam Herald, 1882
United Ireland, 1882
Weekly Freeman (illustrated), 1882
Weekly Irish Times (illustrated), 1882

Online Databases
British Parliamentary Papers, http://parlipapers.proquest.com.ucd.idm.oclc.org/parlipapers/search/basic/hcppbasicsearch/

British Parliamentary Papers on Ireland (Enhanced), http://www.dippam.ac.uk/eppi/

Census of 1901 and 1911, National Archives, http://www.census.nationalarchives.ie/

Census of 2011, Central Statistics Office, Dublin, http://www.cso.ie/en/census/census2011reports/census2011thisisirelandpart1/

Census of 2011, Northern Ireland Statistics and Research Agency, http://www.nisra.gov.uk/Census/key_report_2011.pdf/

Civil and church records:

> https://civilrecords.irishgenealogy.ie/churchrecords/civil-search.jsp/
>
> http://www.findmypast.co.uk/
>
> https://registers.nli.ie/
>
> http://www.rootsireland.ie/

Dictionary of Irish Biography VII (Dublin and Cambridge: RIA and Cambridge University Press, 2009), http://dib.cambridge.org/

Griffith's Valuation (1847–64), http://www.askaboutireland.ie/griffith-valuation/

Hansard House of Commons Debates, http://hansard.millbanksystems.com/

Irish Newspapers Archives, http://archive.irishnewsarchive.com/Olive/APA/INA.Edu/Default.aspx#panel=home/

Irish Prisons Register collection, http://www.findmypast.ie/

Nineteenth-century British Library Newspapers Database, http://www.bl.uk/reshelp/findhelprestype/news/newspdigproj/database/

Oxford Dictionary of National Biography (Oxford: Oxford University Press, 2004), http://www.oxforddnb.com/

Royal Irish Constabulary Service Records, 1816–1922, http://www.findmypast.co.uk/

SECONDARY SOURCES

Adams, G. B., 'Language census problems, 1851–1911', in *Ulster Folklife*, 21, 1975, pp 68–72.

___, 'The validity of language census figures in Ulster, 1851–1891', in *Ulster Folklife*, 25, 1979, pp 113–22.

Agnew, Hugh LeCaine, *The Czechs and the Lands of the Bohemian* Crown (Palo Alto: Stanford University Press, 2004).

Alexander, Sam, 'Joyce's census: Character, demography and the problem of population in *Ulysses*', in *Novel: A Forum on Fiction*, 45.3, 2012, pp 433–54.

Angermeyer, Philipp Sebastian, 'Translation style and participant roles in court interpreting', in *Journal of Sociolinguistics*, 13.1, 2009, pp 3–28.

___, *'Speak English or What?': Codeswitching and Interpreter Use in New York City Courts* (Oxford: Oxford University Press, 2015).

Anonymous, *Full Report of the Appearance of the Ghost of Myles Joyce in Galway Jail* (Dublin: Nugent, 1883).

Anonymous, *Mysteries of Ireland: Giving a Graphic and Faithful Account of Irish Secret Societies, & Their Plots, From the Rebellion of 1798, to the Year 1882, with Sketches of the Lives of the Leaders, Their Last Speeches Before Condemnation, and the History of Recent Murders in Ireland* (London: Milner & Co., 1883–4).

Anonymous, 'Our portrait gallery, second series: no, 16', in *Dublin University Magazine*, 85, May 1875, pp 570–89.

Aranoff, Mark and Janie Rees-Miller, eds, *Blackwell Handbook of Sociolinguistics* (Oxford: Blackwell, 1997).

Arel, Dominique, 'Language categories in censuses; Backward- or forward-looking?', in David I, Kertzer and Dominique Arel, eds, *Census and Identity: The Politics of Race, Ethnicity, and Language in National* Censuses (Cambridge: Cambridge University Press, 2002), pp 1–42.

Arnaut, Karel, Jan Blommaert, Ben Rampton and Massimiliano Spotti, eds, *Language and Superdiversity* (New York: Routledge, 2016).

Atack, Margaret, '*L'Affaire dominici*: Rural France, the state and the nation', in *French Cultural Studies*, 12.3, October 2001, pp 285–301.

Auty, Robert, 'Language and society in the Czech national revival', in *Slavonic and East European Review*, 35.84, December 1956, pp 241–8.

Ball, Elrington F., *The Judges in Ireland, 1221–1921* (London: John Murray, 1926).

Barthes, Roland, *Mythologies*, ed. Richard Howard, trans. Richard Howard and Annette Lavers (New York: Hill and Wang, 2012 [1957]).

Berk-Seligson, Susan, *The Bilingual Courtroom: Court Interpreters in the Judicial Process* (Chicago: University of Chicago Press, 2002).

Blackledge, Adrian and Angela Creese, 'Translanguaging in the bilingual classroom: A pedagogy for language and teaching?', in *The Modern Language Journal*, 94.1, 2010, pp 103–15.

Blommaert, Jan, *The Sociolinguistics of Globalization* (Cambridge: Cambridge University Press, 2010).

___, *Ethnography, Superdiversity and Linguistic Landscapes: Chronicles of Complexity* (Bristol: Multilingual Matters, 2013).

Bolton, George, *A Short Account of the Discovery and Conviction of the 'Invincibles' and of some trials of which the writer had charge in 1881, 1882, 1883 and 1884 with a few observations on preliminary investigations in criminal cases* (Dublin: Hodges and Figgis, 1887).

Bourke, Angela, *The Burning of Bridget Cleary: A True Story* (London: Pimlico, 1999).

Breathnach, Ciara, 'Medical officers, bodies, gender and weight fluctuation in Irish convict prisons, 1877–95', in *Medical History*, 58.1, 2014, pp 67–86.

Casanova, Pascale, *The World Republic of Letters*, trans. M. B. DeBevoise (Cambridge, MA: Harvard University Press, 2004).

Connolly, Seán, 'Unnatural deaths in four nations: Contrasts and comparisons', in *Kingdoms United? Great Britain and Ireland since 1500: Integration and Diversity*, ed. Seán Connolly (Dublin: Four Courts Press, 1999), pp 200–14.

Connolly, Thomas E., *The Personal Library of James Joyce: A Descriptive Bibliography* (Buffalo, NY: University at Buffalo, 1957).

Cornwall, Mark, 'The struggle on the Czech-German language border, 1880–1940', in *English Historical Review*, 109, 1994, pp 914–51.

Cox, Edward W., *Reports of Cases in Criminal Law, Argued and Determined in all the courts in England and Ireland*, 24 vols, vol. 8, 1858–1861 (London: Crockford, 1843–1916).

Crawford, Margaret E., *Counting the People: A Survey of the Irish Censuses, 1813–1911* (Dublin: Four Courts, 2003).

Cronin, Michael, *Translating Ireland: Translation, Languages and Identity* (Cork: Cork University Press, 1996).

___, *Across the Lines: Travel, Language, Translation* (Cork: Cork University Press, 2000).

___, *Translation and Globalization* (London: Routledge, 2003).

___, *Translation in the Digital Age* (London: Routledge, 2013).

Cronin, Michael and Clíona Ní Ríordáin, 'Interview with Michael Cronin', in *Études Irlandaises*, 35.2, 2010, pp 1–7.

Crowley, Tony, 'English in Ireland: A complex case study', in *The Oxford Handbook of the History of English*, ed. Terttu Nevalainen and Elizabeth Closs Traugott (Oxford: Oxford University Press, 2012), pp 470–80.

Curraoin, Diarmuid, *'I know that I have broken every heart': The Significance of the Irish Language in* Finnegans Wake *and in Other Works by James Joyce* (Washington DC: Academia Press, 2014).

Daly, Nicholas, *Modernism, Romance and the Fin de Siècle: Popular Fiction and British Culture, 1880–1914* (Cambridge: Cambridge University Press, 1999).

Davitt, Michael, *The Fall of Feudalism in Ireland, or The Story of the Land League Revolution* (London and New York: Harper, 1904).

de Brún, Pádraig, *Scriptural Instruction in the Vernacular: The Irish Society and Its Teachers, 1818–1827* (Dublin: School of Celtic Studies, Dublin Institute for Advanced Studies, 2009).

Delaney, Enda and Breandán Mac Suibhne, eds, *Ireland's Great Famine and Popular Politics* (New York: Routledge, 2016).

Derrida, Jacques, *Monolingualism of the Other, or, the Prosthesis of Origin*, trans. Patrick Mensah (Palo Alto: Stanford University Press, 1998).

___, *The Death Penalty, Vol. 1, The Seminars of Jacques Derrida*, vol. 9, trans. Peggy Kamuf, 2012 (Chicago: University of Chicago Press, 2014).

de Vere White, Terence, *The Parents of Oscar Wilde* (London: Hodder and Stoughton, 1967).

de Vries, John, 'Some methodological aspects of self-report questions on language and ethnicity', in *Journal of Multilingual and Multicultural Development*, 6.5, 1985, pp 347–68.

Dewar, Daniel, *Observations on the Character, Customs, and Superstitions of the Irish; and on some of the causes which have retarded the moral and political improvement of Ireland*, 8 vols (London, 1812).

Dinneen, Patrick S., *Foclóir Gaedhilge agus Béarla: An Irish-English Dictionary*, 2nd edn (Dublin: Irish Texts Society, 1927).

Dixon, Hepworth W., ed., *Lady Morgan's Memoirs: Autobiography, Diaries and Correspondence*, 2 vols (London: Allen, 1862).

Dooley, Terence, *The Murders at Wildgoose Lodge: Agrarian Crime and Punishment in Pre-Famine Ireland* (Dublin: Four Courts Press, 2007).

Dorian, Hugh, *The Outer Edge of Ulster: A Memoir of Social Life in Nineteenth-Century Donegal*, eds David Dickson and Breandán Mac Suibhne (Dublin: Lilliput Press, 2000).

Doyle, Aidan, 'Language and literacy in the eighteenth and nineteenth centuries', in *Cambridge History of Ireland*, ed. James Kelly (Cambridge: Cambridge University Press, 2018), pp 353–79.

Duffy, Charles Gavan, *The Revival of Irish Literature: Addresses by Sir C. G. Duffy, George Sigerson, Douglas Hyde* (London: Fisher Unwin, 1894).

Dungan, Myles, *Conspiracy: Irish Political Trials* (Dublin: Royal Irish Academy, 2009).

Dunlop, Andrew, *Fifty Years of Irish Journalism* (London and Dublin: Simpkin and Marshall and Hanna and Neale, 1911).

Dunne, Tom, 'Voices of the vanquished: Echoes of language loss in Gaelic poetry from Kinsale to the Great Famine', in *Journal of Irish Scottish Studies*, 1.1, September 2007, pp 25–44.

___, '"On the boundaries of two languages": Representing Irish in novels in English, 1800–1950', in *Culture and Society in Ireland since 1752: Essays in*

Honour of Gearóid Ó Tuathaigh, eds John Cunningham and Niall Ó Ciosáin, (Dublin: Lilliput Press, 2015), pp 44–63.

Ebury, Katherine, '"Mulrennan spoke to him about universe and stars": Astronomy in *A Portrait of the Artist as a Young Man*', in *Dublin James Joyce Journal*, 6 & 7, 2013–4, pp 90–108.

Ebury, Katherine and James Alexander Fraser, eds, *Joyce's Non-Fiction Writings: 'Outside his Jurisfiction'* (London: Palgrave Macmillan, 2018).

Edgeworth, Maria, *Castle Rackrent* (Dublin: Wogan et al, 1800).

Ellmann, Richard, *James Joyce: New and Revised Edition* (Oxford: Oxford University Press, 1982).

Emmet, Robert, *The Life, Trial and Conversations of Robert Emmet, Esq.* (New York: Coddington, 1845).

Engel, Howard, *Lord High Executioner: An Unashamed Look at Hangmen, Headsmen, and Their Kind* (Ontario: Key Porter, 1996),

Erll, Astrid and Ann Rigney, eds, *Mediation, Remediation and the Dynamics of Cultural Memory* (Berlin and Boston: De Gruyter, 2012).

Extra, Guus and Durk Gorter, eds, *Multilingual Europe: Facts and Policies* (Berlin and New York: Mouton de Gruyter, 2008).

FitzGerald, Garret, 'Estimates for baronies of minimum level of Irish-speaking amongst successive decennial cohorts, 1771–1781 to 1861–1871', in *Proceedings of the Royal Irish Academy*, 84, 1984, pp 117–55.

___, 'Irish-speaking in the pre-Famine period: A study based on the 1911 census data for people born before 1851 and still alive in 1911', in *Proceedings of the Royal Irish Academy*, 103C, 2003, pp 191–283.

___, 'The decline of the Irish language, 1771–1871', in Mary Daly and David Dickson, eds, *The Origins of Popular Literacy in Ireland* (Dublin: TCD and UCD, 1990), pp, 59–72.

Flood, Jeanne A, 'Joyce and the Maamtrasna Murders', in *James Joyce Quarterly*, 28.4, summer 1991, pp 879–88.

Fogarty, Anne, '"Where Wolfe Tone's statue was not": Joyce, 1798 and the politics of memory', in *Études Irlandaises*, 24.2, 1999, pp 19–32.

Fogarty, Anne and Fran O'Rourke, eds, *Voices on Joyce* (Dublin: University College Dublin Press, 2015).

Foucault, Michel, *Discipline and Punish: The Birth of the Prison*, trans. Alan Sheridan (London: Penguin, 1977).

Froggatt, Peter, 'Sir William Wilde and the 1851 census of Ireland', in *Medical History*, 1.9.4, 1965, pp 305–27.

Gabler, Hans Walter, 'James Joyce *Interpreneur*', in *Genetic Joyce Studies*, 4, spring 2004, pp 1–4; electronic journal, available at http://www.geneticjoycestudies .org/.

Gal, Susan, 'Diversity and contestation in linguistic ideologies: German speakers in Hungary', in *Language in Society*, 22.3, September 1993, pp 337–59.

Garvin, John, *James Joyce's Disunited Kingdom and the Irish Dimension* (Dublin: Gill and Macmillan, 1976).

Gattrell, V. A. C, *The Hanging Tree: Execution and the English People, 1770–1868* (Oxford: Oxford University Press, 1994).

Geary, Laurence and Margaret Kelleher, eds, *Nineteenth-Century Ireland: A Guide to Recent Research* (Dublin: University College Dublin Press 2005).

Gibbons, John, *Language and the Law* (Harlow: Longman, 1994).

Gibbons, Luke, *Joyce's Ghosts: Ireland, Modernism, and Memory* (Chicago: University of Chicago Press, 2015).

Gibson, Andrew, *The Strong Spirit: History, Politics and Aesthetics in the Writings of James Joyce, 1898–1915* (Oxford: Oxford University Press, 2013).

Gifford, Don, *Joyce Annotated: Notes for* Dubliners *and* A Portrait of the Artist as a Young Man (Berkeley: University of California Press, 1982).

Gogolin, Ingrid, 'The "monolingual *habitus*" as the common feature in teaching in the language of the majority in different countries', in *Per Linguam*, 13.2, 2013, pp 38–49.

Goldman, Jonathan, ed., *Joyce and the Law* (Gainesville: University of Florida Press, 2017).

Greeley, Andrew, *Irish Love* (New York: Forge Books, 2001).

Griffin, Gerald, *The Collegians* (Belfast: Appletree Press, 1992 [1829]).

Hale, Sandra, *The Discourse of Court Interpreting: Discourse Practices of the Law, the Witness and the Interpreter* (Amsterdam: Benjamins, 2004).

Hammond, J. L., *Gladstone and the Irish Nation* (New York: Longmans Green, 1938).

Hardiman, Adrian, 'Joyce, Great Wryley and the necessity of judicious doubt', in *Dublin James Joyce Journal*, 5, 2012, pp 1–15.

___, *Joyce in Court: James Joyce and the Law* (London: Head of Zeus, 2017).

Harrington, Tim, *The Maamtrasna Massacre: Impeachment of the Trials* (Dublin: Nation Office, 1884).

Healy, Maurice, *The Old Munster Circuit: A Book of Memories and Traditions* (London: Michael Joseph, 1939).

Healy, T. M., *Letters and Leaders of My Day* (London: Thornton Butterworth, 1928).

Herlihy, Jim, *The Royal Irish Constabulary: A Complete Alphabetical List of Officers and Men, 1816–1922* (Dublin: Four Courts Press, 1999).

Heller, Monica, ed., *Bilingualism: A Social Approach*, Palgrave Advances in Linguistics (Basingstoke: Palgrave Macmillan, 2007).

Higginbottom, Frederick J., *The Vivid Life: A Journalist's Career* (London: Simpkin Marshall, 1934).

Hindley, Reg, *The Death of the Irish Language: A Qualified Obituary* (London: Routledge, 1990).

Hobsbawn, E. J., *Nations and Nationalism Since 1790: Programme, Myth, Reality* (Cambridge: Cambridge University Press, 1990).

Howlin, Niamh, *Report on the Trial of Myles Joyce, November 1882*, prepared for the Irish Government, July 2017, 32 pp; http://www.justice.ie/en/JELR/Report _by_Dr_Niamh_Howlin_Maamtrasna_Murders.pdf/Files/Report_by_Dr _Niamh_Howlin_Maamtrasna_Murders.pdf/.

Irish Law Reform Commission, *Hearsay in Civil and Criminal Cases*, LRC CP 60–2010 (Dublin: Law Reform Commission, 2010).

Jackson, John Wyse and Peter Costello, *John Stanislaus Joyce: The Voluminous Life and Genius of James Joyce's Father* (London: Fourth Estate, 1997).

Jenkins, Geraint H., 'The historical background to the 1891 census', in *The Welsh Language and the 1891 Census*, eds, Gwenfair Parry and Mari Williams (Cardiff: University of Wales Press, 1999), pp 1–30.

Joyce, James, *Dubliners* (Dublin: O'Brien Press, 2012 [1914]).

___, *Finnegans Wake* (London: Penguin, 1999 [1939]).

___, *Ulysses* (London: Penguin, 1982 [1922]).

___, *The Critical Writings of James Joyce*, ed., Ellsworth Mason and Richard Ellmann (New York: Viking, 1959).

___, *James Joyce Archive: Notes, Criticism, Translations, and Miscellaneous Writings (A Facsimile of Manuscripts and Typescripts)*, vol. I, prefaced and arranged by Hans Walter Gabler (New York and London: Garland, 1979).

___, *James Joyce: Occasional, Critical and Political Writing*, ed., Kevin Barry, trans. Kevin Barry (Oxford: Oxford University Press, 2000).

Joyce, Patrick, *The State of Freedom: A Social History of the British State since 1800* (Cambridge: Cambridge University Press, 2013).

Joyce, Stanislaus, *My Brother's Keeper: James Joyce's Early Years*, ed., Richard Ellmann (London; Faber, 1982 [1958]).

Kelleher, Margaret and Philip O'Leary, eds, *The Cambridge History of Irish Literature* (Cambridge: Cambridge University Press, 2006).

Kelleher, Margaret, 'An Irish problem: Bilingual manoeuvres in the work of Somerville and Ross', in *Advancing the Cause of Liberty: Irish Women's Writing, 1878–1922*, eds, Anna Pilz and Whitney Standlee (Manchester: University of Manchester Press, 2016), pp 121–36.

___, '"Tá mé ag imeacht": The execution of Myles Joyce and its afterlives', in *The Body in Pain Irish Literature and Culture*, eds, Fionnuala Dillane, Naomi McAreavey and Emilie Pine (New York: Springer, 2016), pp 99–115.

___, 'Census, history and language in Ireland & Canada: The origins of the language question', in *Ireland and Quebec: Multidisciplinary Perspectives on History, Culture and Society*, eds, Margaret Kelleher and Michael Kenneally (Dublin: Four Courts Press, 2016), pp 97–112.

Kelly, James and Ciarán Mac Murchaidh, eds, *Irish and English: Essays on the Irish linguistic and cultural frontier, 1600–1900* (Dublin: Four Courts Press, 2012).

Kilfeather, Siobhán, 'Terrific register: The gothicization of atrocity in Irish Romanticism', in *Boundary 2*, 31.1, 2004, pp 49–71.

King, Carla, *Michael Davitt after the Land League, 1882–1906* (Dublin: University College Dublin Press, 2016).

Laird, Heather, *Subversive Law in Ireland: From 'Unwritten Law' to the Law Courts* (Dublin: Four Courts Press, 2005).

Larkin, Felix, 'Green shoots of the new journalism in the *Freeman's Journal*, 1877–1890', in *Ireland and the New Journalism*, eds, Karen Steele and Michael de Nie (New York and London: Palgrave Macmillan, 2014), pp 33–55.

Le Blanc, Jim, 'More on "Derevaun Seraun"', *James Joyce Quarterly*, 35.4/36.1, summer/fall 1998, pp 849–51.

Lee, Joseph, *Ireland 1912–1985: Politics and Society* (Cambridge: Cambridge University Press, 1989).

Leerssen, Joep, *National Thought in Europe: A Cultural History* (Amsterdam: University of Amsterdam Press, 2006).

Levinge, Edward Parkyns, *The Justice of the Peace for Ireland: A Treatise on Summary Jurisdiction, Preliminary Proceedings as to Indictable Offences, with an Appendix of the Most Useful Statutes and an Alphabetical Catalogue of Offices*, 3rd edn (Dublin: Hodges, Foster, 1872).

Lieberson, Stanley, 'How can we describe and measure the incidence and distribution of bilingualism?', in *Description and Measurement of Bilingualism*, ed., L. G. Kelly (Toronto: University of Toronto Press, 1969), pp 286–95.

MacAdam, Robert, 'Six hundred Gaelic proverbs collected in Ulster', in *Ulster Journal of Archaeology*, 6, 1858, pp 172–83.

Mac Mathúna, Liam, *Béarla sa Ghaeilge, Cabhair Choigríche: An Códmheascadh Gaeilge/Béarla i Litríocht na Gaeilge 1600–1900* (Dublin: An Clóchomhar, 2007).

——, 'From manuscripts to street signs via Séadna: the Gaelic League and the changing role of literacy in Irish, 1875–1915', in *The Irish Revival Reappraised*, eds, Betsey Taylor FitzSimon and James H. Murphy (Dublin: Four Courts Press, 2004), pp 49–63.

Mac Suibhne, Breandán, *The End of Outrage: Post-Famine Adjustment in Rural Ireland* (Oxford: Oxford University Press, 2017).

——, *Subjects Lacking Words?: The Gray Zone of the Great Famine*, Famine Folios Series (Hamden, CT and Cork: Quinnipiac University Press and Cork University Press, 2017).

Maddox, Brenda, *Nora: The Real Life of Molly Bloom* (Boston: Houghton Mifflin, 1988).

Maher, John C., *Multilingualism: A Very Short Introduction* (Oxford: Oxford University Press, 2017).

Malcolm, Janet, *Iphigenia in Forest Hills: Anatomy of a Murder Trial* (New Haven: Yale University Press, 2011).

Malcolmson, A. P. W., *The Clements Archive* (Dublin: Manuscripts Commission, 2010), C/2, 8 June 1865.

McCormack, W. J., *From Burke to Beckett: Ascendancy, Tradition and Betrayal in Literary History* (Cork: Cork University Press, 1994 [1984]).

___, 'James Joyce, cliché, and the Irish language', in *James Joyce: The Augmented Ninth*, ed., Bernard Benstock (New York: Syracuse University Press, 1988), pp 323–36.

McCourt, John, *The Years of Bloom: James Joyce in Trieste, 1904–1920* (Madison: University of Wisconsin Press, 2000).

McCrea, Barry, *Languages of the Night: Minor Languages and the Literary Imagination in Twentieth-Century Ireland and Europe* (New Haven and London: Yale University Press, 2015).

McHugh, Roland, *Annotations to* Finnegans Wake (Baltimore: Johns Hopkins, 2006).

McMahon, Richard, 'The courts of petty sessions and society in pre-Famine Galway', in *The Re-making of Modern Ireland: Essays in Honour of J. C. Beckett*, eds, Raymond Gillespie (Dublin: Four Courts, 2003), pp 101–37.

McMahon, Richard, 'Manor courts in the west of Ireland before the Famine', in *Mysteries and Solutions in Irish Legal History*, eds, Desmond Greer and Norma Dawson (Dublin: Four Courts Press, 2001), pp 115–59.

McMahon, Timothy G., *Grand Opportunity: The Gaelic Revival and Irish Society, 1893–2010* (New York: Syracuse University Press, 2008).

Melchiori, Giorgio, 'The language of politics and the politics of language', in *James Joyce Broadsheet*, 4, February 1981, pp 107–14.

Mertz, Elizabeth, *The Language of Law School: Learning to 'Think Like a Lawyer'* (New York: Oxford University Press, 2007).

Mildren, D, 'Redressing the imbalance: Aboriginal people in the criminal justice system', in *Forensic Linguistics*, 6.1, 1999, pp 137–60.

Mill, John Stuart, 'Civilisation: Signs of the times', in *London and Westminster Review*, XXV, 1836, pp 1–28.

Miller, Kerby A., and Ellen Skerrett, with Bridget Kelly, 'Walking backward to heaven?: Edmund Ronayne's pilgrimage in Famine Ireland and Gilded Age America', in *Ireland's Great Famine and Popular Politics*, eds, Enda Delaney and Breandán Mac Suibhne (New York: Routledge, 2016), pp 80–141.

Miller, Joshua, *Accented America: The Cultural Politics of Multilingual Modernism* (Oxford: Oxford University Press, 2011).

Moran, Gerard, ed., *Radical Irish Priests* (Dublin: Four Courts Press, 2009).

Morash, Chris, 'Ghosts and wires: The telegraph and Irish space', in *Ireland and the New Journalism*, eds, Karen Steele and Michael de Nie (New York and London: Palgrave Macmillan, 2014), pp 21–34.

Morgan, Lady (Sydney Owenson), *The O'Briens and the O'Flahertys: A National Tale* (London: Pandora Mothers of the Novel Series, 1988 [1827]).

Morley, John, *The Life of William Ewart Gladstone* (New York: Macmillan, 1903).

Morley, Vincent, *Irish Opinion and the American Revolution* (Cambridge: Cambridge University Press, 2002).

___, 'The Irish language', in *Princeton History of Modern Ireland*, eds, Richard Bourke and Ian McBride (Princeton: Princeton University Press, 2016), pp 320–42.

___, *The Popular Mind in Eighteenth-Century Ireland* (Cork: Cork University Press, 2017).

Morris, Ruth, 'The gum syndrome: Predicaments in court interpreting', in *Forensic Linguistics*, 6.1, 1999, pp 6–29.

Muholland, Marc, 'Land war homicides', in *Uncertain Futures: Essays about the Irish Past for Roy Foster*, ed., Senia Paseta (Oxford: Oxford University Press, 2016), pp 81–96.

Munyangeyo, Théopile, Graham Webb and Marina Rabadán-Gómez, eds, *Challenges and Opportunities in Public Service Interpreting* (London: Palgrave, Macmillan, 2016).

Murphy, James, *Ireland's Czar: Gladstonian Government and the Lord Lieutenancies of the Red Earl Spencer, 1868–1886* (Dublin: University College Dublin Press, 2014).

Neville, Grace, '"He spoke to me in English, I answered him in Irish": Language shift in the folklore archives', in *L'Irlande et ses Langues*, ed., Jean Brihault (Rennes: Presses Universitaires de Rennes, 1992), pp 19–32.

Ng, Kwai Hang, *The Common Law in Two Voices: Language, Law and the Post-Colonial Predicament in Hong Kong* (Palo Alto: Stanford University Press, 2009).

Ní Mhungaile, Lesa, 'Bilingualism, print culture in Irish and the public sphere', in *Irish and English: Essays on the Irish linguistic and cultural frontier, 1600–1900*, eds, James Kelly and Ciarán Mac Murchaidh (Dublin: Four Courts Press, 2012), pp 224–37.

___, 'The legal system in Ireland and the Irish language 1700–c, 1843', in *The Laws and Other Legalities of Ireland, 1689–1850*, eds, Michael Brown and Seán Donlan (Abington: Routledge, 2016 [2011]), pp 325–57.

Nun, Richard and John Edward Walsh, *The Powers and Duties of Justices of the Peace in Ireland: and of Constables as Connected Therewith: with an Appendix of Statutes and Forms*, 2 vols (Dublin: Hodges and Smith, 1842).

O'Brien, Peter, *The Reminiscences of the Right Honourable Lord O'Brien*, ed., Georgina O'Brien (New York and London: Longmans, Green and Arnold, 1916).

Ó Cadhla, Stiofán, 'Tiontú an chultúir: *Affaire dominici* agus Maolra Seoighe', in *Études Irlandaises*, 35.2, 2010, pp 35–50.

O'Callaghan, Margaret, 'New ways of looking at the state apparatus and the state archive in nineteenth-century Ireland: "Curiosities from that phonetic museum" – Royal Irish Constabulary reports and their political uses, 1879–1891', in *Proceedings of the Royal Irish Academy*, Section C, 104.2, 2004, pp 37–56.

Ó Ciosáin, Niall, *Print and Popular Culture in Ireland, 1750–1850* (Dublin: Lilliput Press, 2010 [1997]).

___, 'Gaelic culture and language shift', in *Nineteenth-Century Ireland: A Guide to Recent Research*, eds, Laurence Geary and Margaret Kelleher (Dublin: University College Dublin Press 2005), pp 136–69.

___, *Ireland in Official Print Culture 1800–1850: A New Reading of the Poor Inquiry* (Oxford: Oxford University Press, 2014).

O'Connor, T. P., *The Parnell Movement, with a Sketch of Irish Parties since 1843* (London: Kegan Paul, 1886).

Ó Cuirreáin, Seán, *Éagóir: Maolra Seoighe agus Dúnmharuithe Mhám Trasna* (Baile Átha Cliath: Cois Life, 2016).

Ó Cuív, Brian, 'Irish language and literature, 1695–1845', in *A New History of Ireland Volume IV: Eighteenth-Century Ireland, 1691–1800*, eds, T. W. Moody and W. E. Vaughan (Oxford: Clarendon, 1986), pp 374–423.

___, 'Irish language and literature, 1845–1921', in *A New History of Ireland Volume VI: Ireland under the Union, II, 1870–1921*, ed., W. E. Vaughan (Oxford: Clarendon, 1996), pp 385–435.

O'Donnell, Ian, 'Lethal violence in Ireland, 1841 to 2003', in *British Journal of Criminology*, 45, 2005, pp 671–95.

___, *Justice, Mercy, and Caprice: Clemency and the Death Penalty in Ireland* (Oxford: Oxford University Press, 2018).

Ó Drisceoil, Proinsias, '*Cín Lae Amhlaoibh*: Modernization and the Irish language', in *Ireland and Romanticism: Publics, Nations and Scenes of Cultural Production*, ed., Jim Kelly (Basingstoke: Palgrave Macmillan, 2011), pp 13–25.

Ó Giolláin, Diarmuid, *Locating Irish Folklore: Tradition, Modernity, Identity* (Cork: Cork University Press, 2000).

Ó Hehir, Brendan, *A Gaelic Lexicon for* Finnegans Wake *and Glossary for Joyce's Other Works* (Berkeley: University of California Press, 1967).

Ó Laoi, Padraic, *Nora Barnacle Joyce: A Portrait* (Galway: Kenny's Bookshop, 1982).

O'Leary, Philip, *The Prose Literature of the Gaelic Revival, 1881–1921: Ideology and Innovation* (University Park: Penn State Press, 1994).

Ó Murchú, Máirtín, *Urlabhra agus Pobal: Language and Community* (Baile Átha Cliath: Oifig an tSolathair, 1970).

Ó Néill, Eoghan, *Gleann an Óir* (Dublin: An Clóchomhar, 1988).

O'Neill-Bernhard, Christine, 'Symbol of the Irish nation, or of a foulfamed potheen district: James Joyce on Myles Joyce', in *James Joyce Quarterly*, 32.3 & 4, spring/summer 1995, pp 712–21.

Ó Riagáin, Pádraig, *Language Policy and Social Reproduction: Ireland, 1893–1993* (Oxford: Clarendon, 1997).

Ó Súilleabháin, Amhlaoidh, *Cín Lae Amhlaoibh*, ed., Michael McGrath, Irish Texts Society, vols XXX–XXXIII (London: I. T. S., 1928–1937).

___, *Cín Lae Amhlaoibh*, ed., Tomás Bhaldraithe (Dublin: An Clóchomhar, 1970).

O'Sullivan, Donal J., *The Irish Constabularies, 1822–1922: A Century of Policing in Ireland* (Dingle, Co, Kerry: Brandon, 1999).

Ó Tuathaigh, Gearóid, *'I mBéal an Bháis': The Great Famine and the Language Shift in Nineteenth-Century Ireland*, Famine Folios Series (Hamden, CT and Cork: Quinnipiac University Press and Cork University Press, 2015).

Owens, Gary, 'The Carrickshock incident, 1831: Social memory and an Irish *cause célèbre*', in *Cultural and Social History*, 1, 2004, pp 36–64.

Palmer, Patricia, *Language and Conquest in Early Modern Ireland: English Renaissance Literature and Elizabeth Imperial Expansion* (Cambridge: Cambridge University Press, 2001).

___, *The Severed Head and the Grafted Tongue: Translating Violence in Early Modern Ireland* (Cambridge: Cambridge University Press, 2013).

Parry, Gwenfair and Mari A. Williams, eds, *The Welsh Language and the 1891 Census* (Cardiff: University of Wales Press, 1991).

Pavlenko, Anita, *The Bilingual Mind and What It Tells Us about Language and Thought* (Cambridge: Cambridge University Press, 2014).

Phelan, Mary, 'Irish language court reporting, 1801–1922', unpublished PhD thesis, Dublin City University, 2013.

___, 'Court interpreters in the news (for the wrong reasons)', in *ITIA Bulletin*, October 2007, pp 4–5.

Pöchhacker, Franz and Miriam Shlesinger, eds, *Interpreting Studies Reader* (London: Routledge, 2002).

Ravenstein, E. G. 'On the Celtic languages in the British Isles: A statistical survey', in *Journal of the Statistical Society of London*, 42.3, September 1879, pp 579–643.

Richland, Justin B., *Arguing with Tradition: The Language of Law in Hopi Tribal Court* (Chicago: University of Chicago Press, 2008).

Romaine, Suzanne, 'The bilingual and multilingual community', in *the Blackwell Handbook of Bilingualism*, eds, Tej K. Bhatia and William C. Ritchie (Oxford: Blackwell 2004), pp 385–405.

Ronayne, Edmund, *Ronayne's Reminiscences* (Chicago: Free Methodist Publishing House, 1900).

Royal Irish Constabulary List and Directory, containing lists of the constabulary departments, Dublin metropolitan police, resident magistrates, coast guards, &c, No 82 (July to December 1882).

Scarry, Elaine, *The Body in Pain: The Making and Unmaking of the World* (New York and Oxford: Oxford University Press, 1985).

Schneider, Erik, 'Towards *Ulysses*: Some unpublished Joyce documents from Trieste', in *Journal of Modern Literature*, 27.4, summer 2004, pp 1–16.

Somerville, Edith and Martin Ross, *All on the Irish Shore* (London: Longmans Green, 1903).

Sommer, Doris, *Bilingual Aesthetics: A New Sentimental Education* (Durham, North Carolina: Duke University Press, 2004).

___, ed., *Bilingual Games: Some Literary Investigations* (New York: Palgrave Macmillan, 2003).

Stoker, Bram, *The Snake's Pass: A Critical Edition*, ed., Lisabeth Buchelt (New York: Syracuse University Press, 2015 [1890]).

Stokes, Whitley, *Projects for Re-Establishing the Internal Peace and Tranquility of Ireland* (Dublin, 1799).

Sullivan, T. D., A. M. Sullivan and D. B.Sullivan, *Speeches from the Dock; or, Protests of Irish Patriotism* (New York: Kenedy, 1904).

Swartzlander, Susan, 'Multiple meaning and misunderstanding: The trial of Festy King', in *James Joyce Quarterly*, 23.4, summer 1986, pp 465–76.

Tigges, Wim, '"Deveraun Seraun!": Resignation or escape?', in *James Joyce Quarterly*, 32.1, fall 1994, pp 102–4.

Tindall, William York, *Reader's Guide to* Finnegans Wake (New York: Syracuse University Press, 1969).

Todorov, Tzvetan, 'Dialogism and schizophrenia', in *An Other Tongue: Nation and Ethnicity in the Linguistic Borderlands*, ed., Alfred Arteaga (Durham: Duke University Press, 1994), pp 203–14.

Trollope, Anthony, *The Landleaguers* (New York: George Munroe, 1883).

Uí Ogáin, Rionach, *Immortal Dan: Daniel O'Connell in Irish Folk Tradition* (Dublin: Geography Publications, 1995).

Valente, Joseph, *James Joyce and the Problem of Justice: Negotiating Sexual and Colonial Difference* (Cambridge: Cambridge University Press, 2009).

Vaughan, W. E., *Murder Trials in Ireland, 1836–1914* (Dublin: Four Courts, 2009).

Wadensjö, Cecilia, *Intepreting as Interaction: On Dialogue-Interpreting in Immigrant Hearings and Medical Encounters* (Linköping: Linköping Studies in Arts and Sciences, 1992).

Waldron, Jarlath, *Maamtrasna: The Murders and the Mystery* (Dublin: Edmund Burke, 1992).

Walsh, Michael, 'Interpreting for the transcript: Problems in recording land claim proceedings in Northern Australia', in *Forensic Linguistics*, 6.1, 1999, pp 161–95.

Waterhouse, Kate, 'Profits on the margins: Private language service providers and limited-English-proficient immigrants in Irish courts', in *Outside Justice: Immigration and the Criminalizing Impact of Changing Policy and Practice*, eds, David C. Brotherton, Daniel L. Stageman, Shirley P. Leyro (New York: Springer-Verlag: 2013), pp 179–97.

___, *Ireland's District Court: Language, Immigration and Consequences for Justice* (Manchester: Manchester University Press, 2014).

Wilde, William, *Irish Popular Superstitions* (Dublin: McGlashan, 1852).

___, 'On the ancient races of Ireland; Extracts from the address to the anthropological section of the British Association', Belfast, 1874, in Lady Wilde, *Ancient Legends, Mystic Charms and Superstitions of Ireland*, 2 vols, (London: Ward and Downey, 1888), pp 329–47.

Windele, John, 'Present extent of the Irish language', in *Ulster Journal of Archaeology*, 5, 1857, pp 243–45.

Wolf, Nicholas, *An Irish-Speaking Island: State, Religion, Community, and the Linguistic Landscape in Ireland, 1770–1870* (Madison: University of Wisconsin Press, 2014).

Yildiz, Yasemin, *Beyond the Mother Tongue: The Postmonolingual Condition* (New York: Fordham University Press, 2012).

Zemon-Davis, Natalie, *The Return of Martin Guerre* (Cambridge, MA: Harvard University Press, 1983).

INDEX

Adams, G. B. 46–7
agrarian crimes 10, 15, 66, 72, 99, 105, 162, 166, 171, 201, 217–18
Alton, David xxi
Angermeyer, Philipp Sebastian 99, 106–7
approvers *see* Casey, Thomas; Philbin, Anthony
Ardilaun, Lord 11, 17
Arel, Dominique 55
Artane Industrial School 186–7
Ashbourne, Lord 167
asylum cases 219–20
Athenaeum 145
Australian Aboriginals in Australian courts 98–9
Avebury, Baron (Eric Lubbock) xxi

Balfour, Arthur 165
Ballinchalla parish/electoral division 18, 20, 24–5
Ballinrobe Chronicle 10–11, 64, 72–3, 82, 86, 89, 102, 191
Ballynahinch barony, language in 52
Barnacle, Annie 196
Barnacle, Nora 170, 196–7, 202
    language knowledge 197

Barrett, Michael 137
Barry, Judge Charles Robert 101, 104, 109, 113–15, 121, 123, 127–8, 130, 132, 135–6, 158, 165
Barry, Kevin 202
Barthes, Roland xxiii, 93, 100, 102
Belfast Newsletter 101–2, 120, 130, 138–40, 144
Benco, Silvio 198
bilingualism ix–x, xix–xx, xxii–xxiii, 28–55, 84–6, 89, 108, 110, 113, 146, 151, 155, 182, 189, 192, 196, 217, 219
    'balanced' 54
    in communities 54–5
    degrees of xix–xx, xxiii, 54, 94
    dominant 54
    and humour 94–5
    in legal systems: 93–9; Australia 98; Hong Kong 97; US 98
    James Joyce and bilingualism 196–9, 206, 208, 212
    passive 53–4
    stable 30
    transitional xxii, 29–31, 52–5
Blommaert, Jan xxii–xxiii, 219–20
Bodkin family 197

Bohemia 57
Bolton, George 6, 66, 76–8, 156
Bourke, Angela 45
Bourke, Charles J. 145–7
Boyle, Tom 68–9
Bloody Sunday 190
Brady, A. Newton 5, 13, 64, 76, 78, 137, 152–3
Brien, Constable 62
Bulwer, James 155
Burke, Thomas Henry xviii

Cantonese 97
Capital Punishment Amendment Act (1868) 137–8
Cappanacreha 23–5, 44
Carnarvon, Lord 167
Casey, 'Big' John (Bunachrick) 23–4, 27, 159, 162–3, 193, 217
Casey, John Jr (Bunachrick), 159, 193
Casey, Malachy 68
Casey, Mary (Thomas' wife) (Glensaul) 68–9, 192
Casey, Thomas (Glensaul) xvi, 14, 135–7, 192–3, 217, *I*
    alibi 68
    approver xvii, 77–8, 159
    arrest 61, 64
    interviews 155–7, 162–3
    language xix, 30, 33, 64, 77–8, 110
    recantation 152, 155–8, 191
    testimony 110–11, 119
Casey family (Derry) 27
    John: xvi, 14, 23, 136, 177–8, *I*;
      arrest 61–2; death 176, 184–5;
      ill-health 184; imprisonment
      175–6; language xix, 30, 63, 161,
      181; reprieve 134–5; trial 101, 130–1
      (verdict 131)
    Julia (Judy, mother of Patrick and
      John) xvi, 67–8, 108, 193
    Mary (cousin of Patrick and John)
      67, 108–9, 180

Michael: xvi, 14–15, 23, 136, 159;
    arrest 61, *I*; death xvii, 175, 182–3;
    ill-health 182; imprisonment
    175–7; language xix, 30, 63, 82, 129,
    181; petitions 177; reprieve 134–5;
    trial 101, 128–31
Patrick: xvi, 14, 23, 67–8, 77–8,
    136, 139, 159, 216, *I*; arrest 61;
    description of 103; execution
    xvii, 140–1; inquest 142–3, 145;
    language xix, 30, 63, 161; trial 101,
    108, 114 (verdict 115–17)
relationships 24
Cavendish, Lord Frederick xviii
censuses, international 37–9
    Trieste 198–9
censuses, Irish
    (1851) 30, 37, 39, 42–9, *XII*
    (1861) 39, 48, 84
    (1871) 39, 48
    (1881) 20, 24, 29, 32–3, 48–52
    (1891) 28, 48–52
    (1901) 52, 189–90, 192, 196–7
    (1911) 192, 197
    interpreters listed in: 88–9
    language question: 37–8, 48–9;
      checking 49; wording 38–43
Charlemont, Earl of 25
Christian, Judge Jonathan 84
Churchill, Randolph 165, 167
Clancy, George 196
Clements family 185–6
Clonbur
    district 16–17
    petty sessions 15, 17–18, 26, 89
Coen, Patrick 146
Collins, Sub-Constable 67–8, 80–1
Collins, John xv–xvi, 24, 163, 165
    evidence 3–4, 7, 105; translation 7
Comerford, Vincent 28
Conaboy, Alice 193
Conaboy, Carolyn 193

Conaboy, John (variant Conoboy) 193
Conaboy, Kitty 70
Conaboy, Mary 61, 70–1, 121
Conaboy, Patrick 70–1
Concannon, Edmund ('Mun') 66
Concannon, Henry J. 66, 77, 103, 119
Condon, John 182
Congested Districts Board 18
Connaught Telegraph 89, 92
Cooke, Head Constable Richard 80
Corbett, Fr James 155, 157, 160–2
Costello, Peter 196
Coucke and Goethals trial 93
court(s) *see also* Irish Court for Crown
  Cases Reserved, legal systems,
  manor courts, petty sessions, Special
  Commission Court
    children's evidence in 112
    district 221
    interpreters in 19th-century
      courts: xxii, 44, 79–99, 100–33,
      153–4; in contemporary
      Australian courts 98–9; in
      contemporary Hong Kong
      courts 97–8; in contemporary
      Greek courts 220; in
      contemporary US courts 98; in
      contemporary Irish courts 220–2
    language in 44
Criminal Evidence Act (1898) 202
Croker-King, Charles 145–7
Cromwell, Oliver 36
Cronin, Michael 220–1
Crowley, Tony 56
Czech 57

Daily Express 11, 13, 75, 101, 103, 111–12,
  119, 126–8
Daly, P. J. B. 66
Dane, Judge 92
Davitt, Michael 171–2
de Vere White, Terence 45

Deane, Conor 200
Deasy, Patrick 90
death penalty 134, 137–9, 219
Derrida, Jacques 134, 138, 215, 219
Derrig, Katherine 68
Derry, County Galway 23–4
Derrypark district/townland 11, 17, 23–5
Dewar, Daniel 32
Dobrovský, Josef 57
Dominici, Gaston xxiii, 93
Donnelly, William 40, 45
Downpatrick Prison 176, 184
Drummond family murders 93
Drummond-Wolff, Henry 165
Dublin Evening Mail 72, 101, 112, 117, 129
Dublin University Magazine 46
Dudley, Earl 191
Duffy, crown witness depot 80–1
Dunlop, Andrew 10–12, 74, 138,
  144, 155–6
dying declarations 5–6, 159, 161,
  164–5, 216
Dyke, William Hart 167, 177

Edalji, George 201
Edgeworth, Maria 204
Edinburgh, Duke of 169
Ellmann, Richard 200
emigration 33–4, 56–7 *see also*
  immigration, migration
Emmet, Robert 204
Ennis, Edward 158
European Convention on Human
  Rights 220
Evans, Richard 136, 140
Evans, (Head) Constable Thomas
  79–82, 103, 106–8, 113, 116, 120–1, 125,
  129, 132
Evening Telegraph 101, 138, 144

Faherty, James 81
Feeney family 197

Finnish 56–7
FitzGerald, Garret 28, 32–3
Flanagan, Charlie 215
Flemish movement 93
Flood, Jeanne 202
Flynn, Michael 132
Formiggini, Angelo Fortunato 199
Foucault, Michel 168
Freeman's Journal xxi, 27, 39–40, 66, 135,
    155–7, 169, 190–1
    reports: executions 137–8, 143, 169
    reports: murders 6–8, 10–13, 21,
        72–4, 76, 79
    reports: trials 101–3, 105, 116–19,
        124–31, 133, 159
Froggatt, Peter 45

Gabler, Hans Walter 201
Gaelic League 206
Gaeltacht 28
Gaelic Journal (*Irisleabhar na Gaedhilge*)
    152
Galway Express 11, 73, 138, 140–2
*Galway Vindicator and Connaught
    Advertiser* 10, 140
Ganby, Fr William 16–17, 20
Gardiner, J. C. 14, 65, 80
Garvin, John 170, 172, 202
Gatrell, V. A. C. 138–9
Gavin, James 69
General Prisons Board 177, 182
Gibbons, Sub-Inspector 10, 63, 76
Gibbons, Luke 204–5
Gladstone, William 166, 199
Gleeson, Harry xxi
Globe (North American) 151–2
Gorst, John Eldon 165–7
Graphic (London) 100–1, 109, 111, 131
Gray, Edmund Dwyer 135
Great Famine 32, 46
Greaven, Fr 139, 146
Greeley, Andrew M. 217

Green Street courthouse, Dublin 79, 81,
    100, 104, 158, 216
Griffin, Gerard 93–4
Griffith's Valuation 24–5

Hale, Sandra 98
Hamilton, R. G. C. 157
Hammond, John Lawrence xviii
Harcourt, William 152
Harrington, Tim xxi, 24, 26–7, 144,
    151–7, 164–7, 171, 179, 195–6, 202,
    210, 216–17
    Impeachment of the Trials 159–64
Harris, Rev. J. 183
Healy, Tim xviii, 158, 175–6, 183
Heard, Head Constable 80–1
Hegarty, Dr John 61, 121
Heller, Monica xxii
'Hibernicus' 47
Hiberno-English 54, 124, 204, 207
Higginbottom, Frederick 138, 147–8,
    172, 216, *XV*
Higgins, Michael D. xvii, xxi, 193,
    215–16
Higgins, Thomas (Tom) 132
Higgins (Long), Patrick 132, 171
Home Rule
    bill (1886) 199
    movement xviii, 199–200
Hong Kong 97
Hooper, Fr Thomas 188–9
Howlin, Niamh xvii, xxi, 133
Huddy, John xvi, 11, 132
Huddy, Joseph xvi, 11, 132
Huddy murders 72–3
    trials 66, 132–3
Hughes, Patrick 90
Hyde, Douglas 53
Hynes, Francis 171

illiteracy 20, 42–3
Illustrated Police News 16, 169

immigration 54, 220–2 *see also*
    emigration, migration
informers (approvers) *see* Casey,
    Thomas; Philbin, Anthony
International Statistical Congress
    (1853) 38
interpreters xxii, 42, 85–92, 95–9, 220–2
    see also court(s), Maamtrasna murders
Irish Court for Crown Cases
    Reserved 82
Irish Folklore Commission 8
Irish Parliamentary Party 166–7, 171
Irish Times 101, 103–4, 115, 128–9, 134,
    138–9
Irish World 73
Irishman 102
Irisleabhar na Gaedhilge (*Gaelic
    Journal*) 152

Jackson, John Wyse 196
James, Sir Henry 166
Jenkinson, Edward George 10
Johnson, William Moore 104
Johnston, Constable John 4–6, 22, 26,
    63–6, 106, 158, 163
Joyce, Andrew (Andy) 6
Joyce, Charles 197–8
Joyce, Florence 197
Joyce, Giorgio 198
Joyce, James xix–xxi, 100, 144, 170, 173,
    195–213
    articles (*Il Piccolo della Sera*)
        xx, 199–200; on Myles Joyce
        199–205, 211–13, 216
    bilingualism 196
    'The Dead' 197, 209
    Finnegans Wake xxi, 209–13
    lectures 205–8
    *A Portrait of the Artist as a Young
        Man* 196, 206–8
    Ulysses 209
Joyce, John Stanislaus Jr 198

Joyce, John Stanislaus Sr 195–7
Joyce, Johnny 190, 193
Joyce, Lucia 198
Joyce, Mabel 197
Joyce, Patrick (historian) xviii, 173
Joyce Country xix, 9, 18, 21, 66, 75, 217
Joyce families, relationships 22–7, 120,
    122, 127
Joyce family (the accused; the 'Shauns'
of Cappanacreha)
    Bridget (Myles's wife) 26, 135,
        172–3, 193, *XV*; statement 61, 70–1
    census return for Cappanacreha
        (1851) 44
    family homes in Cappanacreha 22,
        24
    Honor (daughter of Paudeen and
        Judy) 22, 69
    Julia (Siobhán, Jude or Judy, wife
        of Martin) 68, 180, 193–4
    Máirín (daughter of Myles and
        Bridget) 193
    Martin: xvi, 14, 24, 68, 77, 136;
        arrest 61, 63, *II*, *XI*; death 191–2;
        imprisonment 175–6; language
        161; petitions 180–1; release from
        prison xvii, 190–1; reprieve 134–5;
        trial 101, 130–1
    Mary (daughter of Martin and
        Julia) 193–4
    Mary (daughter of Paudeen and
        Judy) 62, 69–70
    Myles xvi, 14, 22, 24, 26, 64–5, 77–8,
        137, 139, 177, *II*; alibi 70–1; arrest
        61, 63; campaign for miscarriage
        of justice xxi, 190; execution xvii,
        xxiv, 138, 140–2, 145, 168; family
        215; 'ghost' 169–70; illiteracy
        118; imprisonment (Galway)
        26; inquest 142–7; landholdings
        26; language xix–xxi, 30, 82,
        117–18, 123, 153–4, 212; last words

140–2, 147–8, 156, 171, 191, 215–16, *XV*; petitions 135; posthumous pardon xvii, xxi, 215–16; symbolism 173–4, 212; trial 101, 117–23, 133; verdict and response 124–8; *see also* Joyce, James

Paudeen: xvi, 22, 24, 26, 69, 78, 136, 192, *II, XI*; arrest 61, 63; descendants 192; illiteracy 192; imprisonment 175–6; language 30, 181; petitions 179–81; release from prison xvii, 190–1; reprieve 134–5; trial 101, 130–1

Siobhán (Judy, née O'Brien, wife of Paudeen) 75, 180, 193

Thomas (Tom): xvi, 14, 22, 24, 26, 69, 136, 192, *II, XI*; arrest 61, 63; imprisonment 175–7; language xix, 177; petitions 179–81; release from prison xvii, 190–1; reprieve 134–5; trial 101, 130–1

Joyce family (prosecution witnesses; the 'Maolras')
Anthony: xvi, 22–24, 26, 69, 129, 136, 156, 161–2, 192; initial cross-examination 64–5; initial statement 14–15, 61; language xix, 77; testimony 107–8, 119–20
family homes in Derry and Cappanacreha 23–4
John: xvi, 23, 120, 129, 161–2, 185; language xix; statement 14–15, 61; testimony 107
Margaret (wife of Anthony) 26, 64
Mary 15, 108, 113, 161–2, 192
Pat: xvi, 4, 23, 185; language xix; testimony 107

Joyce family (Kilbride; relatives of the Joyces of Maamtrasna)
Bridget 189

Thomas 187–9
Joyce family (murder victims; the 'Máirtíns') *see also* Maamtrasna murders
Bridget (Breege, née Casey and formerly O'Brien): xv, 4, 8, 13, 22, 25, 27
family home in Maamtrasna 12–13, 21, 24, 76
funerals 13, 61
Catherine (ancestor of John): 25
John: xv, 3–4, 8, 22, 69, 72–3, 120, 136–7, 166; landholdings 25; suspected of informing 10–11
Margaret Jr (Peggy) xvi, 4, 8, 22, 73, 105, 119
Margaret Sr xvi, 4, 22, 105, 158
Martin: xvi, 81, 185–90; wife and family 189–90 (Johnny 190, 193)
Michael: xv–xvi, 4–6, 8, 22, 105–6, 121, 165, 216
Patsy: xvi, 4–6, 13–14, 22, 61, 100, 105–6; evidence 111–12, 158, 163–4, 216 (dismissal of 81, 106, 112, 132–3, 166); language 14; later life 185–90
Joyce family (of Shanvalleycahill)
Mary Ann (Patrick's wife) 69, 103
Patrick: xvi, 14–15, 24, 65, 77–8, 80, 101, 139, 159, 174, 216, *XIV*; arrest 61–2; execution xvii, 140, *XIV*; inquest 142–3, 145; language xix, 30, 64–5, 161; statement 136–7; trial 78, 101, 103, 105–17; verdict 115–17

Kane, John 91
Kaye, William 145, 147, 189
Kavanagh, Constable 82–3
Kee, Robert 173
Keenan, Patrick 187
Kelly, Sub-Constable Patrick 62, 79–81, 112

Kelly, Pat (alias for member of murder party) 78, 110–11, 120, 157
Kerrigan, Martin 132
Kerrigan, Matthias 132
Kilfeather, Siobhán 35
Kilkenny Independent 36
Kinkead, Richard 145, 181–2
Kirn, Maria 198–9

Land League 72, 155, 161, 171
land reform agitation xviii, 72
landlords 17–18, 20
language shift xviii–xx, xxii, 28–58, 199
reasons 55–8
Larcom, Thomas 40
Lee, Joe 56
Leerssen, Joep 93
Lefroy, Chief Justice 84
Leitrim, Lord 17, 25
Lenihan, Sub-Constable 4–5, 7, 64, 158, 163
Lenihan, Maurice 87–8
Letterfrack murders 66
trials 81–2
Levinge, Edward Parkyns 85
Leyden, Pat 159, 193
Limerick Reporter 87
Lloyd, Clifford 10
Loftus, Luke 91
Londonderry, Lord 167
Lough Mask trials *see* Huddy trials
Lubbock, Eric (Baron Avebury) xxi
Lydon, John 66, 81, 177
Lydon, Martin 66, 81
Lydon, Peter: 61, 70, 121; testimony 71
Lyster, George 81

Maamtrasna 9–10, 19, 24, 217–19, *VI, VIII*
language in xx, 19–20, 33, 52, 160, 218–19
place name xx, 3
region, map 23–4

'Maamtrasna alliance' 152, 167
Maamtrasna murders
aftermath, political 151–74; parliamentary debate 164–8
apocrypha 168–70, 202, *XIII*
coroner's inquest: 3–4, 6; Irish-language testimony 6–7
executions: xvii, xxiv, 134–48; inquests 142–4; inquiry 144–8
initial report of xvi, 3–4
inquiry: 61–2, 64–6; cross-examination 64–5; interpreter 64
interpreters, pre-trial 62; during trial xix, 79–80, 99, 105–9, 111–31, 153–4 (method 105–8)
petitions 167–8, 177–9
post-mortem examination 7–8
press coverage: 10–16, 72–6, *IX, X*
reprieves 134–5
RIC investigation 67–71, *VII*
suspects: xvi–xvii; arraignment 79; arrests 61, imprisonment 61, 76–7; language of xix
symbolism xxi
trials xvii, xxiv, 100–33; court reporter 124; crown brief 158; evidence 103; guilty pleas 130–1; juries 104–5, 117, 121; press coverage 101–3, 151–2, *X*; transcript 102, 129
verdicts 115–17, 124–8, 131, 133
violence of xvi
MacAdam, Robert 40–1, 46
M'Ardle, Sub-Inspector 10
McCarthy, Justin 166
McCausland, Richard 13
McCourt, John 198, 200
McDermot, W. 95
McDonnell, Fr J. 160–1
McDonnell, Robert 13
MacEvilly, Archbishop John 27, 155–7, 178

McHugh, Fr Michael 75, 130–1, 178–9
MacLochlainn, Brian 8
McMahon, Richard 86
Mac Mathúna, Liam 33, 52–3
McPartland, Constable J. 70
Mac Suibhne, Breandán 218
Maddox, Brenda 197
Maguire, Conor 45
Malcolm, Janet 74, 111
Malley, George Orme 83, 103–4, 107–8,
   110, 113–14, 117–18, 121–3
Manchester Martyrs 168
manor courts 86
Martin, Violet 95 *see also* Somerville
   and Ross
Marwood, William 134, 140–6
Maryborough Prison 176, 182, 184
Mason, Ellsworth 200
Mason, George 136, 140, 143, 170
Melchiori, Giorgio 200
Mellet, Fr Martin 178
Mellett, Thomas 86
Mertz, Elizabeth 98, 102
middle classes 35, 86
migration xx, xxii–xxiii, 220–2 *see also*
   emigration, immigration
Mill, John Stuart 138
monolingualism, ix–x, xx, xxii–xxiii,
   28–55, 221–2
   Derrida 205
   English 58, 95
   Irish xix–xxii, 29, 48–9, 109, 218–9
   paradigm (Yildiz) 208, 221–2
Montserrat 36
Moravia 57
Morley, John 88, 167, 199
Morley, Vincent 35
Morris, Ruth 98
Moycullen barony, language in 52
Murphy, James 104, 107, 114, 120, 122–3
Murphy, James H (literary critic) xviii,
   173

Nation 102, 159
Nee, Michael (alias for member of
   murder party) 78, 110–11, 120, 157
Nelligan, Nance 87
Neville, Grace 53–4
New Zealand Herald 144
Ng, Kwai Hang 97–9
Ní Mhungaile, Lesa 35, 87–8
Nun, Richard 85

O'Brien, Bridget (Breege, née Casey),
   see Joyce, Bridget
O'Brien, Daniel (first husband of
   Bridget) 24–5
O'Brien, James 83
O'Brien, John 5
O'Brien, Margaret 3–4
O'Brien, Mary 3–4
O'Brien, Patrick ('Pat') 184–5
O'Brien, Peter (prosecutor) 104–6, 115,
   119, 158
   language 44
O'Brien, Siobhán (Judy), *see* Joyce,
   Siobhán (Judy)
O'Brien, William 170–1
O'Connell, Daniel 30, 56
O'Connor, Arthur 165
O'Connor, T. P. xviii, 166, 171–2
Ó Ciosáin, Niall 30
Ó Cuirreáin, Seán xviii, 215, 217
Ó Cuív, Brian 28
O'Donovan, John 40–1
Ó Drisceoil, Proinseas 35
Ó Duithche, Máirtín 8–9
O'Loghlen, Johnny 95
O'Malley, Fr 156
O'Mara, Mr (juror) 142–3
Ó Néill, Pádraig 87, 218
O'Shea, William 154
Ó Súilleabháin, Amhlaoibh 33, 34–7

Palmer, Patricia 79, 89
Parnell, Charles Stewart 166–7, 171
Parnell Commission 16
Partry district 18–19
Pavlenko, Anita 54
Pearse, Patrick 196
petty sessions 15, 17–18, 64, 82, 86–9, 91, 95–6 *see also* Clonbur petty sessions
Phelan, Fr 181
Philbin, Anthony (Cappaduff) xvi, 14, 23, 135–6, 177, 192, *III*
    alibi 68
    approver xvii, 30, 77–8, *XIV*
    arrest 61, 64–5
    interviews 155–6
    language xix, 30, 33, 64, 110
    testimony 110
Philbin, Mary xvi, 64, 68
Philbin, Sarah 68
Phillips, District Inspector 67
Phoenix Park murders xviii, 10
Piccolo della Sera see Joyce, James
Pim, William 121, 165
Potts, Willard 198
poverty, rural 16, 19, 20, 41, 172
Prevention of Crime (Ireland) Act (1882) 76
Prezioso, Roberto 200
prison, 'secret' 137–9
prison chaplains, Irish-speaking 181–3
prison warders, Irish-speaking 181–2
prisoners, Irish-speaking 181–2, 218

Quinn, Mary 68

Rabadán-Gómez, Marina 220
Ravenstein, E. G. 47–8
Redmond, John 165
Redmond, William 184–5
Reeves, Bishop William 40
Reg. v. Burke 82–4, 104, 113
Ribbon Society 162, 166

Rice, Patrick 142, 145–6
Romaine, Suzanne 55
Roman Catholic Church 41
Ronayne, Edmund 33–4
Ross
    barony 17, 24, 29; language in 49–52
    district: 24; social conditions 16–22
    parish 24
Royal Irish Constabulary (RIC) *see also* Maamstrasna murders
    police huts xvi, 3, 14, 61, 67
    stations 67
Rudden, Constable Matthew 62
Russell, Charles 166
Rutledge, J. F. 91
Ruttledge-Fair, Major 18–21
Rwandan languages 220
Ryan, John Henry 21, 23–4, 105, 129, 132

Salisbury, Lord 166
Schmitz, Ettore 200
Schneider, Erik 198
schools, national 30, 43
Seoighe, Seán (Tomáis) 8, *IV*, *V*
Shanvalleycahill 23–4
Sheffield Telegraph 144
Sheridan, Margaret 82
Sigerson, George 181
Singleton, Edward 40
Skibbereen Eagle 90
Smyth, Sub-Inspector 62–3
Society for the Preservation of the Irish Language 47–8
Somerville, Edith 95
Somerville and Ross 95–8
South Munster Antiquarian Society 42
Special Commission Court 76, 99
Spectator 112, 151
Spencer, Lord Lieutenant (John, 'Red Earl') xviii, 21, 76, 134–5, 144–5, 147, 153–4, 157, 159, 163, 167, 169–70, 172–3, 179–80, 186–7, 191

Stoker, Bram 217
Stokes, Whitley 31–2
Stritch, John R. 79, 103, 111, 120–1
Svevo, Italo 200
Swanton, Thomas 40
Swartzlander, Susan 211

tenants 11, 16–17, 20
Thornton, Martin 83
Trevelyan, George 153, 165
Trieste 198–200
Triestino 198, 200
Trollope, Anthony 217

United Ireland 102, 165, 171–2
'Urabi, Ahmed 154

Valente, Joseph 211–12
Vaughan, W. E. 115
Victoria, Queen 186–7

Wadensjö, Cynthia 98

Waldron, Jarlath xviii, 26, 66, 82, 172–3,
    189–90, 192, 217
Waldron, Fr Kieran 215
Walker, Samuel 165
Walsh, John 81
Walsh, John Edward 86
Walsh, Michael 171
Walsh, Patrick 66, 81, 117, 171
Waterhouse, Kate 221
Weekly Freeman 102, 109, 117, *XVI*
Weekly Irish Times 72, 75, 102
Whelan, Máire 215
Wilde, Sir William 29–30, 40, 45–6,
    48, 53
Williams, Kenneth 219
Windele, John 30, 40, 42, 47
Wodehouse, Edmond 181
Wolf, Nicholas 32, 57–8, 86, 95

Yildiz, Yasemin 221–2

Zetland, Lord 167